From
to WOMAN
WOMAN

REVISED EDITION

From to WOMAN WOMAN

A Gynecologist Answers Questions
About You and Your Body

Lucienne Lanson, M.D., F.A.C.O.G.

1981
ALFRED A. KNOPF
New York

THIS IS A BORZOI BOOK
PUBLISHED BY ALFRED A. KNOPF, INC.

Copyright © 1974, 1975, 1981 by Lucienne Lanson
Illustrations Copyright © 1975, 1981 by Alfred A. Knopf, Inc.
All rights reserved under International and Pan-American Copyright‘Conventions.
Published in the United States by Alfred A. Knopf, Inc., New York, and
simultaneously in Canada by Random House of Canada Limited, Toronto.
Distributed by Random House, Inc., New York.

Library of Congress Cataloging in Publication Data
Lanson, Lucienne. From woman to woman.
Includes index. 1. Gynecology—Popular works. I. Title.
DNLM: 1. Gynecology—Popular works. WP120 L295f]
RG121.L28 1981   618.1   80-11226
ISBN 0-394-51293-6
IBSN 0-394-73996-5 pbk.

Illustrations by Anita Karl

Manufactured in the United States of America

First hardcover edition published May 8, 1975
First paperback edition published March 1977
Revised edition published January 1981

To my sister Jackie with love

Contents

Part VII. WHAT'S IN STORE FOR TOMORROW'S WOMAN?

Acknowledgments

Behind every nonfiction work, which by necessity relies heavily on the accumulation of facts and research data from multiple sources, there are many unseen and unsung contributors. And yet for me, there have been a handful of individuals without whose help and encouragement this work would surely have faltered.

I am particularly indebted to Jacqueline Idiart, who with persistence and patience devoted long hours and countless evenings in helping revise and polish the entire manuscript word by word. Moreover, the fact that by profession she is an educator and not medically oriented made her eminently suited to the task. For until every phrase and sentence rang with clarity to her nonmedical ears, it had to be revised, and then revised again.

Several friends also were of inestimable value. Peggy Emrey, a nurse-midwife, Dr. Marie B. Webster, Dr. Martha Biemuller, Dr. Anne Pike, and my associate in Obstetrics and Gynecology, Dr. Beth L. Reimer, were each gracious enough to review the manuscript and offer constructive ideas and objective appraisal regarding the handling of material. But to Dr. Beth L. Reimer I owe a special note of gratitude for cheerfully managing our entire practice single-handedly during the many long months it took me to complete the book.

My special thanks also go to Nancy Nicholas, my editor at Knopf, for her astute and invaluable suggestions which helped me over some difficult hurdles. I also want to thank Robert J. Donohue, who helped proofread the manuscript, and Darlene Choy for her assistance with the illustrations.

And lastly, a special tribute to Anna Lanson, the grand lady of the former San Francisco French newspaper *Le Californien,* whose spirited support and continuing encouragement made it all possible.

Introduction

From current articles and books, it is apparent that some women are disenchanted with modern medical practices and with gynecologists in particular. Condescending and judgmental attitudes by physicians and a reluctance to explain, discuss, or present possible alternate treatments in plain language are but a few complaints voiced by these women. I can appreciate some of these sentiments, for I too, prior to attending medical school, felt the same frustration in being unable to communicate properly with my doctor. Questions that I posed were not always answered to my satisfaction. Attempts to supplement my meager knowledge regarding female problems met with little success, for in those days there were no books available for the laywoman.

Moreover, during my thirteen years of college, medical school, and specialty training in obstetrics and gynecology, the situation had remained essentially unchanged. All in-depth information concerning female problems was still securely encased in ponderous volumes of multisyllabic medical texts and gynecological journals generally unavailable to the public. Oh yes, there were books for laywomen on pregnancy, childbirth, and breast feeding, some of them quite excellent, but what about all the other problems that related specifically to women?

As a practicing gynecologist, it became increasingly clear to me that women wanted and needed just this type of information. They also deserved more than a superficial explanation in the office or some mollifying mumbo-jumbo. And the more I thought about it, the more

I reasoned that among the five hundred or so active women physicians certified by the American Board of Obstetrics and Gynecology, one of us should write an honest and factual book for our sisters—a book that would not consider women or their problems solely from the standpoint of their ability to procreate, but rather a book that would encompass the multiple other physical concerns of women.

This book is written for all women regardless of age, social position, educational level, or sexual inclination. It is not a substitute for the advice of a trusted physician, nor is it a do-it-yourself text in diagnosis and treatment. Rather, it is a foundation toward a better understanding of yourself and your physical problems as a woman. Although virtually all the information that was in the first edition has been retained in some form, this new version of *From Woman to Woman* has been broadly expanded by the addition of much new material, new chapters, and considerably more in-depth discussion of vital health issues. You will become aware of what's really "normal," how and why certain things happen, and when to seek help. Many of the questions are taken directly from those asked by patients during the privacy of the gynecological examination. They are important questions that need frank answers. For example, what can be done about an unaccommodating vaginal opening, or the opposite problem —just too much room? Does estrogen therapy during the menopausal years really increase a woman's risk of uterine cancer? How can crash diets or being overweight affect your menstrual cycle? If you think that your problem is unique, you will undoubtedly be consoled to know that it is shared by many other women.

Other sections will bring to focus new methods in the diagnosis and treatment of female problems you may have thought insoluble. In our own lifetime we are witnessing the development of sperm banks, ovarian transplants, and the fertilization of human eggs in test tubes. In the field of cancer of the female organs, new drugs, techniques, and superrefined radiation therapy are giving back to many women their rightfully allotted time in which to live full, productive lives.

In addition to basic information, I have also tried to include the latest developments in the field of gynecology as reported in current medical journals and gleaned from specialty meetings. In fact, it may well be years before some of this information finds its way into standard medical texts. The greatest challenge to me, however, was attempting to cover various topics with sufficient depth and clarity so that they would be meaningful to all women irrespective of any previous medical knowledge. Some of you may object to my not including obstetrical care or problems specifically related to childbirth, but there are authoritative, readable works in these areas. Furthermore, to have included these topics with any degree of thoroughness and without immeasurably expanding the book would have been at the expense of other vital issues hitherto overlooked and ignored.

By virtue of the subject matter presented here, certain chapters dealing with relatively minor and benign problems will be written in a lighter vein; others will require more serious contemplation because they include problems that may threaten our very lives. This book is not written to offend or shock any of you. It is written from the heart, for I too am a woman and heir to all the problems of women.

November 1980

PART I

The Workings of the Inner Woman

1. All Is Not Vanity

We know more about sex, sensuality, and orgasm than any previous generation; yet, despite this vast array of available information, it is the exceptional woman who is well informed about keeping her female organs functioning with "all systems go." Whether she is a high school drop-out or has a degree in bio-chemistry, the average woman consulting her gynecologist is as enlightened about the workings of her own body as she is about the intricacies of the second-stage rocket blast-off. But is she really to blame for this lack of knowledge when there are almost no readable, authoritative, and readily understandable sources to which she can turn for help?

It is little wonder, therefore, that to the average woman the pelvic examination remains a mysterious ritual, her hormones and menstrual irregularities an enigma, and a negative Pap smear obvious proof that she's free of pelvic cancer.

Each year women spend millions of dollars on cosmetics, fad diets, and weekly appointments with their favorite hairdresser—all for their external beautification. The media are crammed with advice that could be lumped under one big heading, "How to Succeed in the Sex Game by Making the Most of the Natural You." But just how sensuous can you be with an irritated vulva or a distracting vaginal discharge?

And how romantic can an older woman feel if she is constantly seized with devastating hot flashes that send her scurrying for the nearest window?

It is the rare woman who will never need counsel regarding some female problem. Whether she be heterosexual, homosexual, bisexual, or asexual, no woman can escape or deny the existence of her female organs. No matter what her sexual preference, it is imperative that this unique portion of her body be kept in optimal health if she is to function effectively as a woman and as an individual.

Psychology has demonstrated the power of the mind over our physical well-being, and the converse is also true. How much peace of mind can a woman have if she suddenly discovers a breast lump and chooses to ignore it? Is it possible for an unmarried teenager to have mental equanimity if her period is two weeks late and she fears a possible pregnancy? What about the estrogen-deprived woman who, because of vaginal atrophy and increasingly painful intercourse, begins to avoid all intimacies with her husband? Can she really rationalize the fact that her behavior will not adversely affect their marital relationship? At best, it would be difficult for any of these women to continue functioning effectively when a portion of their mind is consumed with fear, uncertainty, and worry.

There are those of you who make solemn pilgrimages every year to your doctor for a routine checkup. You are to be commended. Others of you assiduously avoid all medical attention as long as you are feeling well. And still others immediately phone for an emergency appointment for the most fleeting twinge of physical discomfort. But there is another group, and one far larger than I care to contemplate. It is you who wait and watch, hoping that time will solve your problem. Surely, if that irregular bleeding or that breast lump is nothing serious, there's no reason to be examined. And as long as you don't know for sure, you needn't worry—but alas, you do worry.

Being a gynecologist as well as a woman, I can readily empathize and understand. I have seen some of my closest friends go through mental agonies with problems that could have been resolved easily and quickly. Other problems require longer treatment and management. But there are few afflictions, diseases, or abnormalities of the female organs that do not have satisfactory solutions provided you seek help.

And so this book is written for all of you, whether you are now in perfect or less than perfect health. But regardless of the problem you may now have, or the problems that may arise in the future, there is an answer, there is a solution.

2. The Woman's Department— What You Have and What It's There For

If you are like many women, your pubic area is a mysterious region exposed to your gynecologist with understandable reluctance. For lack of a better name, it has been tagged any number of things, but the term "privates" is by far the most descriptive. In fact, the pubic area is so private that few women really know what's there. Detailed and easily understood descriptions are still not readily available. And probably, if you are now over thirty, sex and genitals were not topics for dinner conversation or even part of the school curriculum during your formative years.

So here we are, mature women, still referring to our pubic area and genital organs as though we were talking about some uncharted southern land mass. But all that is going to change—at least, I hope so. No, you are not going to become a specialist in female anatomy, but as long as that 5 percent of your body is so vitally important (and who can deny that?), why not find out something about it? And that's what this chapter is all about.

Are you ready for the bold look?

If you have never really examined yourself "down below," get a large mirror, preferably one that magnifies, and a manageable lamp with a 100-watt bulb. Make sure you are all alone and lock the door.

Ready? For a warm-up exercise, strip from the waist down and stand facing a full-length mirror. You will immediately notice a triangular area covered with hair—the mons veneris (mountain of Venus), or just plain mons for short. Mons means little hill and refers to the pad of fatty tissue covering the pubic bone in women. By pressing against that fat pad you can easily verify the presence of the underlying pubic bone. Since in the mature female the mons is always covered with hair, let us zero in for a closer look.

What even your hairdresser doesn't know for sure—or does he?

Through casual observation you may also have noticed that your pubic hair tends to be crisp, coarse, and curly. Just how thick and how curly depends not only on your hormones but on your racial and genetic background. Even if you have hair marching up to the navel and creeping around the inside of the thighs, that too can be perfectly normal. In this case, your ancestors may have roamed the shores of the Mediterranean. In contrast, Oriental women tend to have less curly and sparser pubic hair. And that also is normal.

Does pubic hair serve any function?

Yes. During sexual excitement, the secretions of certain scent (apocrine) glands located in the pubic as well as axillary (armpit) areas emit a characteristic odor erotically stimulating to the male. Thus, these tufts of hair act as scent traps, thereby permitting the aroma to linger by delaying the evaporation of these glandular secretions.

How do hormones affect pubic hair?

The appearance of pubic hair at the time of puberty depends upon the increased output of two hormones. Estrogen from the ovaries and androgens from the adrenals are responsible for that almost overnight transformation.

After the menopausal years, as estrogen levels gradually decrease, there will be other changes, albeit more gradual. In women past the age of sixty, for example, pubic hair frequently thins out and becomes straighter.

Does pubic hair turn gray?

Yes, but unlike scalp hair, pubic hair will usually retain its original color well past the menopause.

But let's move on to more important matters.

What exactly are the privates?

In order to proceed, get a nice soft rug or mat and sit down. Bend your knees and spread them apart so that you now have an unobstructed view of the pubic area. Plug in the 100-watt bulb and focus the mirror.

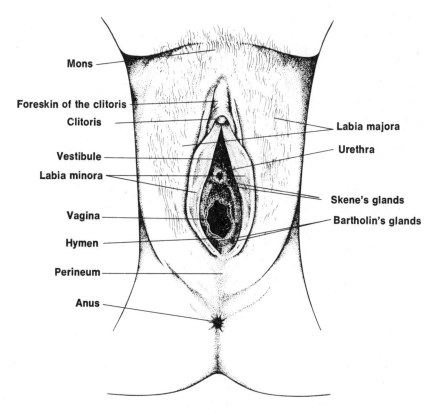

Fig. 1. Vulva
External genitalia of the female

For practical purposes, the entire area between the legs with the exception of the anus is called the vulva. (See Fig. 1.) In other words, the vulva represents your "privates" or external genitalia, and like your face, the vulva contains certain structures that you are about to identify. By the end of this section you should be able to recognize each part as easily as you can point to your nose, eyes, and mouth.

Did you know that your vulva has lips?

As you track the mons downward toward the anus, you will notice that the area covered with pubic hair divides and continues on either side for three to four inches. That hairy area on either side is called the labia majora, or the outer lips, or sometimes the big lips. In addition to being somewhat pigmented and well endowed with fatty tissue, sweat glands, and hair, the labia majora are also rich in sebaceous (oil) glands. Thus, such common problems as infected hair follicles, sebaceous cysts, and other skin troubles can occur there just as easily as they can anywhere else.

What is the function of the labia majora (outer lips)?

Protection—in the form of two plushy pillows cushioning the vital structures and keeping the inner area moist. If you have never had children, your labia majora may actually meet in the middle, forming a soft covering for the area lying underneath. On the other hand, some of you may notice that everything is, indeed, exposed. Whichever the case, spread the outer lips apart and observe that the area in between is hairless, including the inner edges of the labia majora. Why? Because the tissues in this area are highly specialized and do not contain hair follicles.

What about the inner lips?

Running along the inner edge of the labia majora are two elongated ridges or folds of tissue called the labia minora, or the inner or small lips. Not uncommonly, though, the inner lips are not really that small. In fact in some women they can be quite outstanding—even protruding beyond the outer lips. Not only can they vary in size, but the labia minora can also vary widely in color and texture—from light pink to brownish black, from fairly smooth to downright wrinkled.

What makes the labia minora so different from the labia majora?

In addition to being obviously devoid of hair, the labia minora have no fatty tissue or sweat glands. On the plus side, they are rich in sebaceous (oil) glands, apocrine (scent) glands, blood vessels, and elastic tissue. The presence of this elastic tissue, together with their intimate association with the clitoris, make the labia minora a sexy part of your anatomy.

How sexy?

Very sexy. The labia minora not only fuse together just below the mons, but also surround the clitoris to form its foreskin (prepuce). An extensive network of sensory fibers makes the clitoris and labia minora exquisitely sensitive to stimulation.

To make certain that you have actually identified the labia

minora, trace them to the point where they join together and surround the clitoris just below the mons. Although most of the clitoris is actually hidden from view beneath muscle and fibrous tissue, its tip or glans can be seen as a small pink fleshy projection (about the size of an eraser on the end of a lead pencil).

You still can't find the clitoris? Hmm. Press gently where you think the clitoris might be and you will notice a pleasant sensation. Continue to gently prod this area and you may experience a mounting excitement. That is the clitoris.

Where to now?

Trace the labia minora downward toward the vaginal introitus (opening). Here you will notice that the labia minora disappear between the vagina and anus.

If you have successfully identified all the above structures, you are now ready to proceed to the inner inner area.

What is the inner inner area?

An area known as the vestibule, which is lined with mucous membrane and surrounded by the labia minora (inner lips). Within the vestibule are two openings, the vagina and the urethra (the opening through which you urinate).

Are you sure you know where the urethra is?

Easy you say? You may think so—yet how many times when asked to collect a urine specimen have your efforts ended with a wet hand, a puddle on the floor, or an empty bottle? Finding the urethra may at times be difficult, unless yours is the obvious pouting type. Just remember that although the urethra lies between the clitoris and the vagina, it is always much closer to the vagina.

To locate the urethra, start again from the clitoris and work your way down toward the vagina very slowly. If you stay dead center, the first dimpled area that appears is the urethra. But it is very important to stay exactly in the middle, otherwise you might mistake those little niches (Skene's ducts) on either side of the urethra for the real thing. If you still have any doubts about the exact location of the urethra, better run the "urine test."

What is the "urine test"?

This examination is best done in a slightly stooped position in either the bathtub or shower; be sure to take your mirror with you. Focus the mirror and, while holding it in one hand, spread the labia minora with the other hand and urinate. If you keep a sharp eye, you will learn three things: (1) the exact location of the urethra, (2) one of the functions of the labia is to help direct urine in a steady stream, for you may have noticed that with the lips apart you were spraying, and (3) urine does not harm mirrors.

Now that you have satisfactorily identified the urethral opening, let's examine the entrance to the vaginal canal, also known as the vaginal introitus.

What's at the vaginal introitus?

This may come as a surprise, but all of you, regardless of whether or not you are virgins, still have a hymen. The hymen is nothing more than a semicircular strip of mucous membrane tissue lying across the lower portion of the vaginal opening. It is either quite obvious or hardly apparent, and if you cannot identify it, don't worry. The presence of an intact hymen is *not* equated with virginity, nor is its absence definite proof that you have been sexually initiated. Some women, especially those who have had children, may notice delicate little irregular fringes of tissue across the lower portion of the vagina. These tattered remains of the hymenal ring are of no importance, but on occasion some women may mistake them for small growths.

Can the hymen ever interfere with intercourse?

Since the hymen usually stretches easily and normally covers only a small part of the vaginal opening, it seldom interferes with sexual intercourse even the first time. On very rare occasions, however, the hymen may block the entire vaginal opening; this is called an imperforate hymen. Under these circumstances, normal intercourse would not be possible. But because an imperforate hymen would also trap menstrual blood within the vaginal canal, the apparent lack of menstruation in an otherwise well-developed girl would invariably lead to early diagnosis and correction of this condition. (See Chapter 3.)

Are you ready for the vaginal plunge?

If you have never examined your vagina, now is the time to become familiar with this truly amazing structure. There is nothing perverted or dangerous about exploring the inner vaginal area.

Like the other genital organs, the vagina develops and ripens under the influence of estrogen hormones. From a small, thin-walled, fragile structure in childhood, the vagina becomes transformed into a succulent, stretchable passageway some three to five inches long and wide enough to accommodate three or more fingers. During sexual excitement, it can extend an additional two inches in length and measure up to two inches in diameter. And, at the time of delivery, it can dilate to a full five inches across to accommodate the passage of the baby.

As you can see, inserting two fingers into the vagina for this examination should not cause any discomfort. Nor is it necessary to wear gloves. If you are right-handed, the examination can be made easier by placing your left foot on a small stool or step; if you are left-handed, just reverse the position. If you need lubrication, almost anything will do—baby oil, petroleum jelly (Vaseline), cold cream, or even water.

So lubricate the index and middle fingers and gently insert them through the vaginal opening. Or if you prefer, just one finger will suffice.

How does the inside of the vagina feel?

If this is the first time you are exploring your vagina, your initial impression may well be that everything feels "squishy." Perfectly normal; carry on. Sweep your fingers around the walls and feel how pliant and stretchable they are. Continue to probe as far back into the vagina as you can. You will notice that for all practical purposes the far end seems to be closed. This means that it is impossible for such items as tampons, diaphragms, and the like to get lost "up inside." In other words, with no place to go, all such items will remain in the vagina until removed or expelled.

If you press upward against the roof of the vagina, you may feel the urge to urinate. Some of you may have already experienced this temporary sensation while inserting a fresh tampon.

Why does pressure against the roof of the vagina make you want to urinate?

Because you are also exerting pressure on the bladder. Think of the vagina as occupying the middle apartment in a three-story building, with the bladder occupying the top floor and the rectum occupying the ground floor. Thus, the floor of the bladder lies against the roof or ceiling of the vagina, and the floor of the vagina lies against the roof or ceiling of the rectum. (See Fig. 2.) Since the tissues separating the vagina and the bladder are only a fraction of an inch thick, any pressure exerted against the roof of the vagina will be automatically transmitted to the nearby bladder.

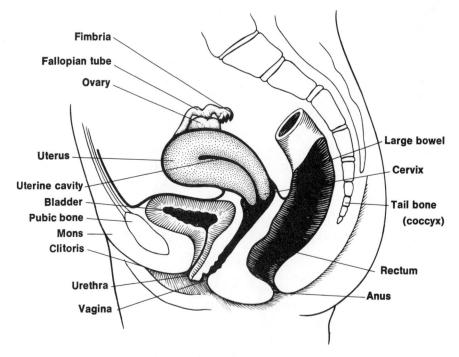

*Fig. 2. Side view of the female pelvis with organs in
their normal anatomical position*

What is located at the far end of the vagina?

The cervix. Projecting an inch or so into the far end of the vagina
is the lower portion of the uterus, which is called the cervix, or sometimes the mouth of the womb or the neck of the uterus. Those of you
who have had a complete hysterectomy (removal of the entire uterus)
will notice, of course, that the cervix is missing. In this case the upper
end of the vagina is simply sealed and closed.

Otherwise the easiest way to feel the cervix is to bend slightly
forward and insert your fingers as far back as possible. If your fingers
are somewhat short, straining or bearing down as during defecation
will make the cervix more readily accessible by displacing it slightly
downward.

What does the cervix feel like?

Somewhat similar to a rounded cabinet knob about one to two
inches across and about as firm as the end of your nose. If you have
located the cervix, push it around a bit. You will notice that instead
of being a rigid immovable object, the cervix actually has some give

pregnancy but new muscle fibers, elastic connective tissue, and blood vessels are also formed. Even the ligaments that partially support the uterus stretch and enlarge during pregnancy and snap back into place after delivery.

And, in nonpregnant women, those ligaments serve another useful function.

What function?

In addition to partially supporting the uterus in its normal position, the elastic ligaments also give the uterus a certain amount of flexibility. Thus, for example, the uterus will bend backward to accommodate a full bladder. But sometimes with advancing age and repeated childbearing, the uterine ligaments lose their elasticity the way worn-out rubber bands lose their snap, and occasionally the uterus may start to sag. (More about this in Chapter 14.)

Under normal conditions, however, where the ligaments and tissues are in good condition, the position of the uterus within the pelvis is fairly stable.

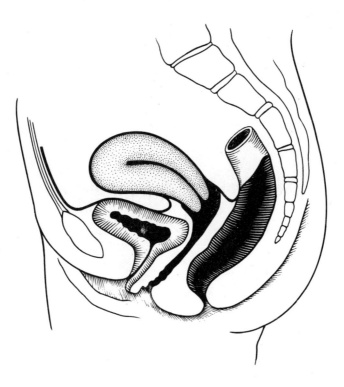

Fig. 5. Anteflexed uterus
Notice how the body of the uterus overlies the bladder.

What is the normal position of the uterus?

Most women have what is called an anteflexed uterus. This means that the uterus is tilted forward forming a right angle to the vagina. In this position the uterus normally rests on top of the bladder. (See Fig. 5.) To visualize this, imagine that the inside of your forearm is the vagina and the palm of your hand is the front of the uterus. Now flex your wrist forward ninety degrees. Your palm will be at a right angle to your forearm just the way the uterus is at right angles to the vagina.

In some women the reverse is true. The uterus is retroflexed, or tilted backward. (See Fig. 6.) Using the same example, extend your wrist back. There will still be an angle between the uterus and vagina, but now the uterus is bent in the opposite direction, or toward the rectum. That retroflexed position occurs in about one out of five women. Rarely does a normal retroflexed uterus cause backaches or decrease a woman's chances of becoming pregnant. Therefore, if you have been relying on that tipped uterus to keep you from getting pregnant, better read Chapter 18 immediately!

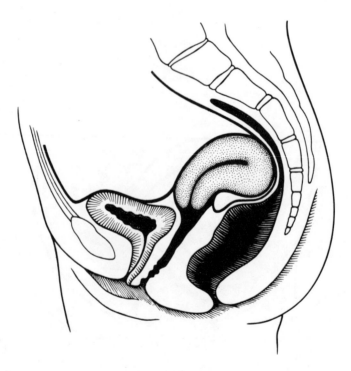

Fig. 6. Retroflexed uterus
Notice how the uterus is tilted back toward the rectum.

How large is the uterine cavity?

In the nonpregnant woman, the uterine cavity is hardly more than a triangular slit, with its widest point no bigger than a thumbnail. It is continuous with the cervical canal below and with the two minute

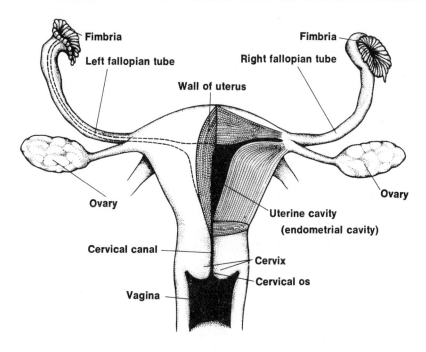

Fimbria
Left fallopian tube
Fimbria
Right fallopian tube
Wall of uterus
Ovary
Ovary
Uterine cavity
(endometrial cavity)
Cervical canal
Cervix
Cervical os
Vagina

Fig. 7. Back view of the uterus showing the uterine cavity
Notice how it is continuous with the cervical canal below and with the two minute openings of the Fallopian tubes above.

openings of the Fallopian tubes above. (See Fig. 7.) When you menstruate, it is the lining of this small cavity that is shed to produce the bloody discharge. During the intervening three to four weeks, the lining is rebuilt and the whole process repeats itself. The menstrual flow, which consists of blood, cellular debris, and mucus, comes entirely from the breakdown of the tissue lining the uterine cavity. Contrary to what some people think, no blood comes down from either the tubes or the ovaries.

What makes the uterus as big as a pear if the cavity is so small?

Muscles, thick heavily muscled walls, comprise almost 90 percent of the uterus. And attached to either side of the uterus near the top are the delicate Fallopian tubes.

What purpose do the Fallopian tubes serve?

It is the place where the egg and the sperm rendezvous.

How big are the Fallopian tubes?

Each of the inner tubal passageways is only slightly bigger than a bristle on a hairbrush. Outwardly, however, muscular elastic walls make each tube as thick around as a drinking straw. These relatively thick elastic walls are necessary to maintain the flexibility of the tubes, as well as to protect the delicate inner passageways. The length of each tube is about four to five inches.

What other function do the tubes serve?

In addition to being the meeting place for the sperm and the egg, the tubes are actually responsible for the survival and maintenance of the fertilized egg during the three days it takes it to reach the uterine cavity.

Why are the tubes so vital for the survival of the fertilized egg?

Would you be able to drive from New York to San Francisco without stopping for a bite to eat? Of course not, and neither can the fertilized egg travel the four inches of tube in three days without nourishment. This makes the highly specialized cells along the tubal passageway essential for the survival and growth of the fertilized egg. For when the fertilized egg arrives at its destination, it must be sufficiently mature and robust to dig a little niche and implant itself in the lining of the uterine cavity.

How does the egg get into the tube?

To answer this, we must follow the tubes from where they are attached to the uterus to their free ends, where they flare out into small, delicate fingerlike projections called fimbria. (See Fig. 7.) The fimbria, though less than an inch long, are absolutely vital to the safe transport of the egg from the ovary into the tube. Through some unknown mechanism, these little fingerlike projections have an uncanny way of knowing when the egg is about to be launched from the ovary (ovulation). At the moment of ovulation, the fimbria actually inch toward the nearby ovary and hover over it like a helicopter. With the help of specialized hair cells (located just inside the tubal fimbria) which beat in unison, a suction is created, and the egg is literally drawn into the tube.

In what part of the tube is the egg fertilized?

If conditions are favorable, as soon as the egg enters the tube, it finds itself surrounded by those long-distance swimmers, the sperm. It is here in the last two inches of one of the Fallopian tubes, near the fimbria, that fertilization most commonly occurs.

What if you have your tubes tied?

To put it simply, the tubal passageway is closed. The sperm can't swim up and the egg can't come down, and never the twain shall meet. No fertilization, no pregnancy. But you will still have your periods and your hormonal function just as before. (See Chapter 19.)

Women who may have had one tube surgically removed can still, of course, become pregnant as long as the remaining tube is normal.

For now, however, let's turn our attention to those stimulating and life-creating organs, the ovaries.

What about the ovaries?

As for their general size and shape, the ovaries resemble two large California stewed prunes. Their color is grayish white. They are attached to either side of the uterus by a special ligament one to two inches long, and actually nestle within the shadow of the tubal fimbria. The ovaries are further supported by other ligaments and surrounding tissues. Because they are suspended by these somewhat elastic ligaments, the ovaries also enjoy a certain freedom of movement. Thus at times they can shift position and lie behind rather than alongside the uterus.

What is the function of the ovaries?

Like two chemical factories they pour the ovarian hormones estrogen and progesterone into the bloodstream, letting the rest of your body and the world know that you are, indeed, a woman. Estrogen is the hormone responsible for giving your breasts that fullness, your hips those contours, and for changing your vagina from a fragile structure into that distensible, succulent, moist, throbbing receptacle of love. It accounts too for the growth and nourishment of the clitoris and labia.

Some investigators also believe that estrogen may be instrumental in the prevention or retardation of osteoporosis (softening of the bony skeleton) and hardening of the arteries. The fact that few women, compared to men of comparable age, are stricken with coronary artery disease supports the idea that estrogen may afford built-in protection in delaying some of these degenerative processes.

What else do ovaries do?

Ovaries also make eggs (ova). How does ovulation occur? Do the ovaries take turns making eggs? How well can you function with only part of an ovary? All this and more coming up.

3. Not All Women Are Born Equal—Congenital Problems of the Female Sexual Organs

In the last chapter we discussed the anatomy of the normal woman. We are now ready to see how genetic and developmental defects can affect the female sexual organs. Some of these conditions may be so minor that they never cause problems; others may exert a profound effect on the sexual development and reproductive capacity of the individual. Particularly stressful to parents are those congenital defects wherein the sex of the newborn may be uncertain because of the appearance of the external genitalia. Less obvious defects involving the internal female organs may remain undetected until puberty or even adulthood. A teenager, for example, with congenital absence of the ovaries may well wonder why she doesn't have breasts or periods like her friends. Or, a woman may habitually abort because of an undiagnosed maldevelopment of the uterus.

But before we can begin to understand some of these complex conditions and the factors which control them, it is important that we know something about the process of normal sexual differentiation.

What makes a female a female and a male a male?

Each cell in our body normally contains a total of forty-six chromosomes, twenty-two pairs of autosomes (non-sex chromosomes) and a pair of sex chromosomes. In the normal female the sex chromosomes are XX and in the normal male XY. In medical shorthand the symbols for a normal female and normal male with a full complement of chromosomes is 46XX and 46XY respectively. Genetic or chromosomal sex (XX for female and XY for male) is determined at the moment of fertilization as is the rest of our genetic makeup, which is inherited from both parents. If the ovum (which normally carries an X chromosome) is fertilized by an X-bearing sperm, the result is XX or a genetic female. Should the ovum be fertilized by a Y-bearing sperm, the result is XY or a genetic male. Since an ovum always carries an X chromosome, the genetic sex of an individual is determined solely by the type of sex chromosome (either X or Y) carried by the sperm. Thus, it is the male partner who determines the genetic sex of the offspring. But this is only the bare beginning of sexual differentiation.

During the first five or six weeks of pregnancy, the embryo is actually in an indifferent stage of sexual development. This means that although the sex of the embryo has already been programmed, there is as yet no ovarian or testicular tissue and no discernible development of internal or external sexual organs and ducts. Rather, there are two clusters of cells (the primitive gonads) which have the potential of developing into either ovaries or testes. Alongside of each primitive gonad is another mass of undifferentiated tissue which has the potential of developing into either the male internal duct system (epididymis, vas deferens, and seminal vesicles) or the female internal duct system (Fallopian tubes, uterus, and upper vagina).

How soon then do the ovaries and testes develop?

At about the sixth week of intrauterine life the differentiation of each primitive gonad into a testis will begin in genetic males. The development of the ovary in the female occurs somewhat later. Ultimately it is the sex chromosomes (X or Y) which control and direct the differentiation of the primitive gonad into ovary or testis. The development of a testis depends on the presence of a Y chromosome. The development of an ovary requires two normal X chromosomes. The differentiation of the sex glands is usually complete by the twelfth week with further maturity of these organs continuing throughout intrauterine existence.

What happens to the fetus after the sex glands (gonads) are formed?

The next stage is the differentiation of the internal sexual ducts. As previously mentioned, the mass of undifferentiated tissue lying alongside each primitive gonad has the potential to develop into male or female internal ducts. The female component of this tissue, the so-called müllerian duct system, forms the Fallopian tubes, uterus, and upper vagina. The male component, or the so-called wolffian duct system, develops into the epididymus, vas deferens, and seminal vesicles. If the fetus is a genetic male (XY), normal male sexual development depends entirely on the secretion of important "masculinizing substances" by the fetal testes. Among these masculinizing secretions are an "organizing substance" and various androgen hormones including testosterone. Beginning at about eight weeks in a genetic male embryo, the organizing substance causes the müllerian or female duct system to disappear while at the same time encouraging the development of the male or wolffian duct system. The androgen hormones secreted by the fetal testes are necessary for the further development of the male internal sexual ducts (epididymus, vas deferens, and seminal vesicles) and the full development of the male external genitalia (penis and scrotum).

What about the development of the uterus and other internal female structures?

If the fetus is a genetic female (XX), development of the müllerian duct system to form the uterus, tubes, and upper vagina begins around the second to third month of fetal life. In the normal process of events the middle and lower portions of the müllerian duct systems (one on either side) fuse to form a single uterus, cervix, and vagina. The uppermost portions do not join but remain separate and distinct as the Fallopian tubes. Any disturbance in the normal development and fusion of these structures can lead to a variety of anomalies including duplication of the uterus, cervix, and vagina. (More about this later.)

The potential for either sex is in every fetus. So it is at this time the undeveloped wolffian or male duct system in the female fetus begins to regress and gradually disappears. These changes do not depend on or require the presence of a fetal ovary. They occur because there is no fetal testis producing masculinizing substances. More specifically, without the testicular organizing substance, the development of the internal duct system is always along female lines. Similarly, the development of the external genitalia is always female in the absence of androgenic hormone stimulation. To further illustrate, individuals who through genetic error have neither ovary nor testis will still have the internal and external organs and ducts of a female. A fetus will invariably develop a uterus, Fallopian tubes, vagina, and the external genitalia of a female as long as there is no functioning testis to oppose that development. As you will soon see, this basic concept goes a long way toward explaining many complicated problems of sexual identity.

When are the external genitalia finally formed in the fetus?

The external genitalia can usually be identified as male or female by about the twelfth to fourteenth week of intrauterine life. Prior to that time there is an indifferent stage wherein each sex has similar-appearing structures. In the male, the development and growth of the penis (from the genital tubercle), the formation of the scrotum (from the fusion of the genital and labialscrotal folds), and the placement of the urethra so that it traverses the entire length of the penis all depend on androgenic stimulation from the testes.

In the absence of androgenic hormone stimulation in the female, the genital tubercle remains small and becomes the clitoris. The genital and labialscrotal folds do not fuse in the midline but instead develop into the labia minora and labia majora. And lastly, there is the formation of separate openings for the urethra and vagina.

In both sexes the formation of the urethra and urinary tract is intimately associated with the development of the internal and external sexual organs. Consequently defects in sexual organ and duct development may be associated with abnormalities of the urinary tract.

What are these abnormalities and maldevelopments of the sexual organs?

We are now ready to discuss some of the more important congenital maldevelopments which affect the female genital tract. Although it is true that males also have congenital defects of the sex organs, this chapter with few exceptions will be devoted exclusively to those problems involving the female. For purposes of convenience it might be well to divide these congenital defects into three groups: (1) those involving the external genitalia and usually detected in infancy and early childhood, (2) those affecting menstruation and/or sexual maturation and usually diagnosed during the adolescent years, and (3) those which can interfere with reproduction and are usually diagnosed during the adult years.

What about congenital defects of the external genitalia?

One of the most serious developmental problems is masculinization of the female newborn. Almost all such cases are the result of prenatal exposure to androgen (masculinizing) hormones either formed by the fetal adrenal glands or transmitted to the fetus from the mother. The most severe cases of masculinization are usually caused by congenital adrenal hyperplasia, a metabolic disorder that can affect both males and females.

Congenital adrenal hyperplasia—what's that?

This is a complex inherited genetic defect of the fetus in which one or several enzymes necessary for the manufacture or synthesis of cortisol (hydrocortisone) by the adrenal gland is deficient. As a consequence the fetal pituitary gland stimulates the adrenals to work harder and harder in an attempt to increase their output of this important hormone, vital in many metabolic processes. In many cases this pituitary overstimulation does ultimately achieve a more normal output of cortisol in the fetus, but at a terrible price—for the end result is enlargement and hyperactivity of the adrenal glands along with massive overproduction of various androgenic hormones from these glands. Exposure of the female fetus to this continuous high output of androgen hormones from its own adrenal glands causes the external genitalia to develop along male lines.

What do the external genitalia look like in these cases?

Although the appearance of the clitoris and labia can vary considerably from case to case there are some characteristic abnormalities. The most common deviation from normal is a marked and obvious enlargement and firmness of the clitoris. There can be complete fusion of the labia in the midline so as to give the appearance of a scrotum (albeit empty, no testes). In extreme cases the vaginal opening may be obliterated and the urethra may actually traverse the entire length of the clitoris, much as it does in a normal penis. Is it any wonder that in these instances there may be understandable confusion as to the sex of the newborn? Females with congenital adrenal hyperplasia, however, are normal genetic females with two X chromosomes, normal ovaries, and normal internal female structures—uterus, tubes, and upper vagina. As previously discussed, absence of a testis and the organizing substance will allow normal development of the internal female organs.

What else can happen to these infants with congenital adrenal hyperplasia?

In about one third of all infants with this disorder, the problem is further complicated by a "salt-losing" variety of congenital adrenal hyperplasia. These infants are unable to store and conserve sodium (salt) normally and can rapidly succumb to severe electrolyte imbalance and dehydration. Prompt diagnosis and treatment in the first few days following birth in these specific cases may be life-saving.

The diagnosis of congenital adrenal hyperplasia is verified by finding markedly elevated levels of androgenic hormones in the urine of these newborns. Since this disorder is a lifetime condition, treatment with cortisone or cortisol-like compounds to suppress adrenal hyperactivity is necessary throughout the life of the individual. In female infants surgical correction is usually necessary for genital appearance (more about this shortly).

Males with congenital adrenal hyperplasia are similarly exposed to high levels of androgen hormones but in these cases the problem is understandably not obvious at birth. Should the condition not be diagnosed and treated, there is progressive and rapid virilization in both male and female infants as a result of continuing excessive androgen stimulation.

How are these infants with congenital adrenal hyperplasia virilized?

By age two or three, pubic hair frequently appears, followed within months by underarm hair. The clitoris enlarges further and there may even be frequent erections. In male children the penis can assume adult proportions by the age of five. In both sexes there is rapid acceleration of long bone growth so that by the age of five or six these children may have the height of twelve-year-olds. As adults, however, they are shorter than normal because of the premature closure of the growing centers within the long bones. In untreated females there is no breast development and usually no menstrual periods. Excessive androgen production blocks the output of pituitary hormones (gonadotropins) necessary for ovarian function. Ultimately, most of these untreated females develop marked hirsutism (excessive facial and body hair), deepening of the voice, and a very muscular, stocky build.

Have newborn females with this disorder ever been mistaken for boys and raised as such?

Yes. On occasion extremely masculinized female newborns with congenital adrenal hyperplasia have been mistaken for newborn males with an underdeveloped penis and undescended testes. In some instances such females have even been circumcised prior to the diagnosis. Avoidance of errors in sexual identity makes it imperative that the genetic sex of the newborn be determined whenever any infant displays ambiguous genitalia or genitalia which do not completely conform to those of a normal male or normal female newborn. Further tests can then be performed to identify the particular disorder.

How can the genetic sex of an individual be determined?

Genetic or chromosomal sex (XX for females, XY for males) can be determined by the study of almost any body tissue, but the simplest screening test, particularly in infants, is the buccal smear test. The mucosa along the inside of the cheek is gently scraped with a tongue blade and the material spread onto a glass slide and stained with a special dye. The cells are then examined under a microscope for the presence or absence of the sex chromatin body, also called the Barr body after its discoverer. The Barr body is a minute particle of the female X chromosome and is seen under the microscope as a small dark mass within the nucleus of the cell. Twenty to 90 percent of all somatic or body cells of normal females contain a Barr body or sex chromatin body and as such are classified as chromatin positive. Normal males (XY) are classified as chromatin negative because their cells do not contain any Barr bodies. The number of Barr bodies found in a human cell always equals the number of X chromosomes minus one. Thus, normal females with the usual two X chromosomes will have only one Barr body per cell; normal males with the usual XY chromosomes will have no Barr body. Individuals with an excess number of X chromosomes as a result of genetic error (for example, XXX, the so-called super female) can have as many as two Barr bodies per cell but these cases are fortunately rare. That additional X chromosome, rather than creating a "Wonder Woman," frequently results in mental retardation and profound menstrual disturbances. Where more detailed information concerning genetic makeup is needed, the individual chromosomes can be studied by means of other tests.

Once the genetic sex of a newborn with ambiguous genitalia is determined the next important question to resolve is that of sex rearing or sex assignment. In other words, will this newborn ultimately function more successfully as a male or as a female? Since females with congenital adrenal hyperplasia have normal ovaries, Fallopian tubes, a uterus, and vagina and can with treatment develop as normal females with the capacity to have children, the sex rearing should be female. But being female also means looking female. This is why corrective surgery becomes an integral part of the total treatment.

What kind of corrective surgery is usually done in these cases?

The extent of the genital plastic surgery depends on the degree of masculinization but the intent is to have the female infant look and function as a normal female. In almost all cases this requires resection and reshaping of the clitoris to normal female dimensions. At the same time fused labia can be separated and refashioned into labia minora and labia majora. If the vaginal opening is covered by a thin bridge of skin, that too can be corrected. These surgical procedures are usually done as soon after birth as possible. Corrective surgery at this early date not only lessens parental anxiety about the appearance of their infant daughter but also helps promote healthy psychosexual development in the child. Since the need for vaginal plastic procedures to redirect or exteriorize the vaginal outlet is less immediate in terms of cosmetic appearance, these procedures, if necessary, can be postponed until just prior to puberty and the advent of menstruation. Results from very complicated vaginal reconstructive surgery are sometimes better if performed on an older child rather than on a small infant.

What else can cause masculinization of the female newborn?

Synthetic progestogens. Although progestogens are not androgens as such, some preparations do have androgenic (masculinizing) properties, notably Norlutin and Pranone. In years past these drugs were occasionally given to pregnant women with a history of habitual abortion. The rationale behind this treatment was the belief that some miscarriages were caused because of inadequate maternal progesterone levels. Nowadays, if there is a bona fide need for supplementing this hormone during pregnancy, doctors are careful to avoid prescribing any preparations which might cause masculinizing changes in the female fetus.

Masculinization from androgenic drugs is rarely as extreme as when the cause is congenital adrenal hyperplasia. Moreover, the condition is self-limiting, which means that once exposure to the androgen ceases there is no worsening of the problem. Hence, when these children are born they require no medical treatment as their own androgen metabolism is perfectly normal. But corrective surgery for restoration of normal-appearing female genitalia is usually required and performed as soon after birth as possible.

On rare occasion, masculinization of the female newborn can be traced to an androgen-producing tumor in the mother.

Are there other congenital problems specifically affecting the external genitalia?

Not really, but women sometimes voice concern about the size of the clitoris and labial lips.

Are protruding inner labial lips abnormal?

Inner lips, or labia minora, which hang, protrude, or extend well beyond the labia majora are neither abnormal nor unusual. They are merely a variant of normal with no clinical significance, although on occasion they can momentarily interfere with intercourse by draping across the vaginal opening. There is no truth to the myth that hypertrophied or large and flabby labia minora indicate a sensuous woman or one who climaxes easily. If a woman is concerned or perhaps even embarrassed about the cosmetic appearance, the labia can be surgically trimmed without compromising any of their important functions. (See Chapter 2.)

Can a woman be born without a clitoris?

There is no such thing as congenital absence of the clitoris but there can be underdevelopment. It is interesting to note that the clitoris in comparison to other genital structures undergoes the least amount of growth and change as a result of sexual maturation. Consequently its size in a mature woman is only moderately larger than that observed in a child. The clitoris is also unique in being the only structure whose sole function is to serve as a focus of sexual sensation.

In isolated instances where an underdeveloped clitoris can contribute to lack of sexual arousal, the local application of an androgenic ointment (testosterone propionate) has been helpful. Testosterone ointment when applied on a regular basis can enhance the sensitivity of the clitoris to tactile stimulation by increasing its size and vascularity. Oral testosterone preparations can achieve the same end result as well as enhance libido, but in these cases there is a significant risk of adverse masculinizing side effects. The treatment of sexual dysfunction with testosterone preparations is not routine but employed only in carefully selected cases.

What about congenital defects which affect menstruation and/or sexual maturation?

Not all congenital maldevelopments are obvious at birth. Many in fact are probably undetected until adolescence or even later when absence of menstruation or lack of sexual development causes the young woman to seek medical attention. Some of these problems include imperforate hymen, complete or partial absence of the vagina, and absence of the uterus.

What exactly is an imperforate hymen?

A hymen which completely blocks the vaginal outlet. The condition occurs in about one out of two thousand women and is usually not detected until after menarche when blockage and retention of the menstrual flow can cause problems. Initially, most of the menstrual discharge is confined to the vagina, which in turn stretches and distends to accommodate the growing volume of old blood. As each period occurs and more and more blood is trapped, the increasing pressure within the vagina causes the blood to back up through the cervix, uterus, and, in extreme cases, even spill out through the Fallopian tubes. The uterus itself can balloon out to the size of a two- to three-month pregnancy. If unrelieved, there is severe and recurring monthly pain. This cyclic pain plus the lack of menstruation in an otherwise normally developing adolescent are the clues which suggest the diagnosis.

How is an imperforate hymen treated?

If there has been considerable accumulation of menstrual blood within the vagina, the hymen can bulge outward. The condition is corrected by excising the hymen and making sure that all the retained material is drained out. It it is not, the retention of any old blood or menstrual debris can increase the risk of pelvic infection by providing the perfect medium for bacterial growth. The operation is best done in the hospital rather than as an office procedure. Recovery is usually rapid and with no aftereffects.

Other malformations of the hymenal opening may also require surgical correction. One such example is the cribiform hymen, which has several small perforations in place of a single opening. These small pin-size perforations are large enough to allow drainage of the menstrual flow but effectively prevent penile penetration, at least in most cases.

Can anything else block the vagina and prevent menstruation?

Yes—a complete vaginal transverse septa. This is simply a wall of tissue stretched across the vagina. It too prevents the discharge of menstrual blood, but unlike an imperforate hymen it is usually located further up the vaginal canal. Corrective surgery in these cases can be more complicated as the tissue can vary considerably in thickness.

What about developmental defects of the vagina?

The most serious is vaginal agenesis—complete or partial absence of the vagina, and most often involving the middle and upper vagina.

Oftentimes the uterus and cervix are also absent or else so poorly developed that menstruation and conception are never possible. Other female organs such as the external genitalia, Fallopian tubes, and ovaries are usually uninvolved and perfectly normal. Hence, breast development occurs as expected along with other secondary sexual characteristics.

Congenital vaginal defects occur in about one out of every three thousand women and are due to incomplete or faulty development of the müllerian duct system. The condition is sometimes diagnosed during infancy, but most cases are unrecognized until the early teen years. Here again, absence of menstruation in a normally developing girl is usually the symptom which prompts an examination, although there have been cases in which the problem was not discovered until after marriage. Cyclic monthly pain, however, is uncommon as there is rarely a functioning uterus and thus no retained menstrual flow.

On pelvic examination there may be a very tiny shallow vagina or else a dimpling of the skin over the area where the vaginal outlet should be. Since congenital absence of the vagina is frequently associated with anomalies of the urinary tract, an evaluation of the kidneys and ureters is a necessary part of the workup.

What can be done for the woman without a vagina?

The treatment is the creation of an artificial vaginal canal of sufficient depth for sexual intercourse. Should there be a functioning uterus, the new vagina would have to communicate with the cervix to allow external drainage of the menstrual flow. Ideally in such cases, the diagnosis should be made in infancy or early childhood and the operation performed prior to menarche. Even though surgery can be successful, these women rarely become pregnant. If the uterus is absent or rudimentary (as is usually the case), the creation of a vagina can be postponed until just prior to marriage or anticipated coitus.

How is an artificial vagina created?

There are basically two approaches—surgical and nonsurgical. The surgical approach consists of making a space between the bladder and rectum and then lining it with a skin graft usually taken from the thigh or buttock. The graft is held firmly in place by a polyacrylic mold, which also maintains the shape of the new vagina until healing is complete. Satisfactory results and avoidance of narrowing and scar tissue formation depend on keeping the vagina dilated through the long-term use of a vaginal mold (worn at night) or else through frequent intercourse. The surgical approach is used primarily where the vagina must communicate with the cervix because of a functioning, menstruating uterus.

In the absence of a uterus, the creation of a vagina by nonsurgical means is sometimes preferable and can in fact be done by the woman herself.

How can a woman make her own vagina?
Since the mucous membrane which overlies the area where the vagina should be is quite distensible, it is possible to indent this tissue by applying intermittent pressure. Starting with a small silicone rubber dilator plug (about one inch long and half an inch wide) and lubricated with K-Y jelly, the patient is instructed to apply rhythmic pressure against the area twice a day for fifteen minutes. As the tissue begins to "give," a larger dilator plug is substituted and the process continued. If the patient is really persistent and faithful about the exercises, she can usually have a very satisfactory vagina within three to six months—a vagina that will accommodate a dilator seven inches long and almost two inches in diameter.

This nonsurgical approach has been particularly successful in women who anticipate an active sex life because coitus will easily maintain the patency of the vagina. Being lined with mucous membrane rather than skin also makes this new vagina self-lubricating, which helps eliminate the need for lubricating jellies prior to intercourse.

Can there be other maldevelopments of the vagina?
There can be partial or complete duplication of the vagina or the so-called double vagina, but these conditions are usually associated with a double cervix and double uterus. Duplications of the genital structures are the result of improper fusion of the müllerian ducts as previously mentioned. More about these specific problems shortly.

What other congenital defects can account for lack of menstruation?
We have already seen how blockage of the vagina (imperforate hymen), absence of the vagina, and absence of the uterus can account for lack of menstruation (primary amenorrhea) in an otherwise normally developing female. Let us now consider two other congenital problems which also prevent menstruation but on the basis of entirely different reasons: testicular feminization and ovarian agenesis.

What is testicular feminization?

This unusual congenital problem is believed to be inherited as a sex-linked recessive condition and as such can and does occur in families. Individuals with testicular feminization are genetic males (XY) with testes and yet their appearance is totally female. During infancy and childhood their external genitalia so closely resemble that of a normal female that the problem is usually unsuspected. At puberty they become even more feminized with the development of large voluptuous breasts, rounded hips, and soft delicate smooth skin. On pelvic examination the vagina is usually quite shallow and internally there is no uterus, no Fallopian tubes, and no ovarian tissue. Sooner or later lack of menstruation brings these "girls" to the attention of a doctor.

What causes testicular feminization?

The problem is apparently caused by a lack of androgen sensitivity in target organs and tissues (hair follicles, genital structures, etc.). In other words, tissues and organs which normally respond to androgen stimulation remain unaffected. As a result there is no masculinization of the genital structures or other virilizing effects despite adequate output of testosterone and other androgen hormones by the testes. Absence of a uterus, tubes, and upper vagina is explained on the basis of the organizing substance secreted by the testes, which in effect prevents the development of these müllerian duct structures. (See earlier discussion.) Since these testes also produce estrogen much like normal testes, it is the estrogen stimulation (unopposed by androgens) which accounts for the breast development and other female secondary sexual characteristics.

How then is testicular feminization diagnosed?

In addition to lack of periods, there are certain physical findings which can help lead to the diagnosis. The breasts, although large, have comparatively small, underdeveloped nipples. Pubic and axillary hair is scant. This obvious lack of sexual hair is caused by hair follicle insensitivity to androgens. Even if these individuals were to receive massive doses of testosterone, they could not grow a single whisker to mar that soft velvety skin. But the biggest clue is the frequent presence of inguinal or groin hernias, on one or both sides. These hernias actually contain undescended testes. All these physical findings plus the confirmation that the genetic sex is male (chromatin negative buccal smear) help verify the diagnosis of testicular feminization.

Is there a treatment for this condition?

Since these individuals look completely female and have been raised as females, the sex assignment is always female. For despite their being genetic males with testes, these individuals will never function as males. No amount of testosterone will develop a penis nor will the most intricate surgery duplicate a normal and sexually functioning male organ. Furthermore, sperm formation in these testes is grossly deficient or totally lacking.

The best treatment is therefore to complete the transformation to female (as much as possible). This usually involves fashioning a more functional vagina, at least one of sufficient depth to permit intercourse. The testes are usually removed in the late teens or early twenties as they can become malignant if left in place. Interestingly enough, removal of the testes frequently causes severe hot flashes similar to those experienced by premenopausal women whose ovaries are removed. Following surgery, these individuals are placed on long-term estrogen therapy. This not only eliminates the flashes and maintains their female appearance, but also helps prevent premature aging and osteoporosis.

What about the female who is born without ovaries?

Lack of ovarian development (ovarian agenesis—sometimes called Turner's syndrome or gonadal dysgenesis) is a chromosomal defect. In this condition the sex chromosome from the sperm fails to be transferred at the moment of fertilization. Thus, these individuals are born with only a single sex chromosome, the X chromosome inherited from their mother. Since it takes two normal X chromosomes to develop ovaries and a Y chromosome to develop testes, they have no sex glands, but they do develop, for reasons previously discussed, a uterus, Fallopian tubes, vagina, and the external genitalia of a female.

How soon can Turner's syndrome be diagnosed?

Although many cases are not diagnosed until the teen years, the occasional presence of other associated congenital problems such as cardiac defects, various bony abnormalities, and webbing of the neck may call attention to the condition at an earlier age. Webbing of the neck when present can be a conspicuous feature. In extreme cases the neck is markedly short and wide with a fold of skin extending from the base of the ears to almost the tip of the shoulders. Among others with Turner's syndrome the only apparent abnormality in the preadolescent years is a retardation in growth resulting in a shorter than average height. Rarely will these individuals grow taller than four feet seven inches, but if the whole family tends to be short, this too may not arouse concern until later.

How much later?

Without estrogen hormone stimulation from the ovaries, there is no breast development, no feminine contours, and no menstruation. By the time this girl is twelve or even younger she may well wonder why she isn't developing like her friends. Eventually this total lack of sexual maturation both in terms of physical appearance and onset of menstruation will cause the girl and her mother to seek medical attention.

How then is the diagnosis of Turner's syndrome confirmed?

The short stature, absence of any sexual development, and no periods are the three big clues to the diagnosis. But verification by appropriate hormonal, laboratory, and chromosomal studies is necessary. A chromatin negative buccal smear test would also be confirmatory evidence that this girl has only one X chromosome. (See earlier discussion.)

At best it is difficult for any doctor to tell a young girl that she was born without ovarian tissue. For this means that she will never ovulate and never conceive a child of her own. It also means that she will need hormone therapy starting at age fourteen or fifteen for at least the next thirty to forty years.

Why the need for hormone therapy?

It is truly amazing what estrogen replacement therapy can accomplish. Almost overnight this girl will begin to develop breasts and other female secondary sexual characteristics. Estrogen will enlarge and mature the uterus thus making it possible to establish menstrual periods by the cyclic use of estrogen and progesterone. In addition, estrogen will prevent premature aging and degenerative changes which would otherwise occur earlier than normal. Equally important, hormone therapy by making this girl look like a female is a great psychological lift. For now, with the exception of being unable to have children, she can function like any other woman.

Will estrogen make her grow any taller?

In this case no amount of any hormone including the growth hormone given at any age will have any effect on height. Her adult height will remain essentially four feet seven inches.

But let's leave Turner's syndrome and move on to maldevelopments of the genital organs which are usually unsuspected until adulthood. Although these conditions are not nearly so complex as others already discussed, they can cause menstrual problems and complications during pregnancy.

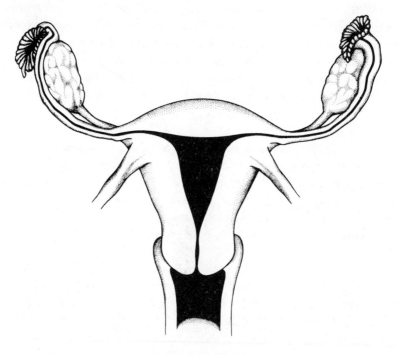

Fig. 1.　Normal uterus
Complete fusion of the two müllerian ducts so as to form
one uterus, one cervix, and one vagina

What kind of maldevelopments are these?

Specifically, maldevelopments of the uterus and cervix. As you will recall from our earlier discussion, the development of the müllerian duct structures in the female fetus to form the uterus, tubes, and vagina begins around the second to third month of fetal life. If conditions are normal, the middle and lower portions of the müllerian ducts (one on either side) fuse to form a single uterus, cervix, and upper vagina. (See Fig. 1.) The upper portions do not fuse but remain separate and distinct as the Fallopian tubes. The entire process takes approximately three months to complete. Any disturbance in the development of these tissues or

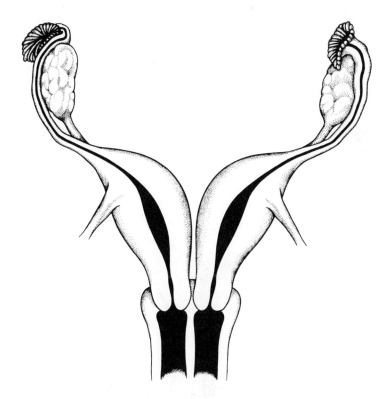

Fig. 2. Complete nonunion of the two müllerian ducts with subsequent duplication of all structures—double uterus, double cervix, double vagina

failure to fuse properly can result in all sorts of malformations.

At one extreme there can be complete nonunion, so that each müllerian duct develops independently. The end result is duplication of all the structures—hence, a double uterus, double cervix, and double vagina. (See Fig. 2.) At the other extreme is the so-called arcuate uterus with an indentation along its top giving it a heart-shaped appearance. This is perhaps the most common uterine malformation. (See Fig. 3.) Between these two extremes there can be any number of possible malformations, as you can appreciate from looking at Figs. 4–7.

How common are these maldevelopments?

They are probably present in about 1 out of every 1,500 women, but their exact incidence is unknown. Many uterine malformations are

never diagnosed for the simple reason that they never cause problems.
In fact they are sometimes inadvertently discovered during abdominal or pelvic surgery for non-related conditions.

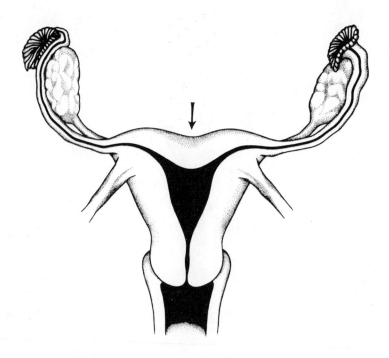

Fig. 3. Arcuate uterus
Notice slight indentation along the top giving it
somewhat a heart-shaped appearance.

What kinds of problems can they cause?

Pelvic pain, heavy menstrual bleeding, and irregular bleeding are
occasional problems which can occur in specific maldevelopments. A
woman with two uterine cavities, for example, may well have heavier
periods. And, if she also has cramps with her periods, imagine how
many more cramps she will have with two uteri. In rare cases there
may be a uterine horn which does not communicate or connect with
the vagina. This would of course result in menstrual blood being
trapped and ultimately require surgical removal of the uterine horn.
(See Fig. 6).

Can a malformed uterus cause infertility?

Not usually. As long as there is a functioning ovary and a uterine lining which responds to hormone stimulation, conception and implantation of the fertilized egg generally proceed normally.

Can such a uterus cause problems during pregnancy?

Yes, and the most common problem is spontaneous abortion, but not usually until the fourth to sixth month of gestation. The reason is probably insufficient growing room for the baby and/or poor placental growth because of a misshapen or smaller than normal uterine cavity. Surprisingly, such abortions are sometimes more likely to happen when a uterus has a comparatively minimal malformation. A woman with a double uterus, for example, may breeze through a pregnancy with no complications whatsoever. A woman with a septate uterus—one with a ridge of tissue partially dividing the cavity— may run into all sorts of problems. Look at Figs. 4 and 5. In the first

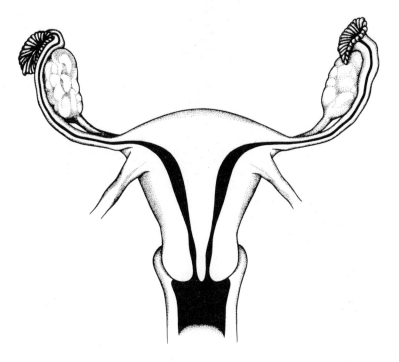

Fig. 4. Example of partial nonunion of müllerian ducts
Notice the two uterine cavities and the two cervical openings
but only a single vagina.

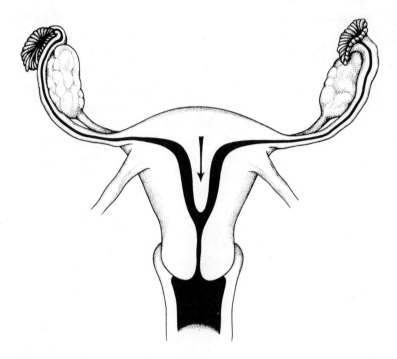

Fig. 5.   Septate uterus
Example of partial nonunion of müllerian ducts but less extreme than
example in Fig. 4. Notice, however, that the uterine cavity
is partially divided by a ridge of tissue.

example the uterine cavity is smooth and shaped fairly normally. In the second example the cavity is obviously irregular in outline.

If the pregnancy does proceed to term there are other increased risks: malposition of the baby (breech, transverse lie), long difficult labor, poor uterine contractions, and maternal hemorrhage. Developmental defects of the uterus can also cause premature birth, intrauterine fetal death, or even be a factor in fetal postmaturity with undue prolongation of the pregnancy. Approximately one third of all women pregnant with a malformed uterus will ultimately lose the baby.

Is corrective surgery the answer?

The presence of a malformed uterus is not necessarily a reason for corrective surgery. Many women have conceived and successfully delivered a healthy baby despite a uterine defect. Corrective surgery, if at all feasible, is therefore reserved for the woman who has had serious difficulties directly attributable to a uterine defect—repeated

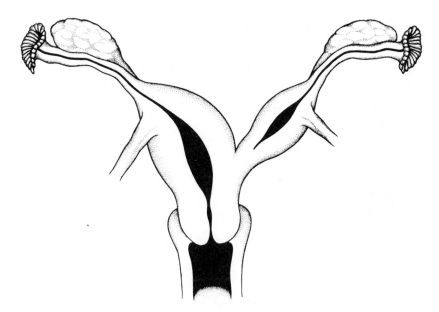

Fig. 6.   Example of a uterine horn which does not communicate or connect with the vagina. This would ultimately require surgical removal because of accumulation of menstrual blood.

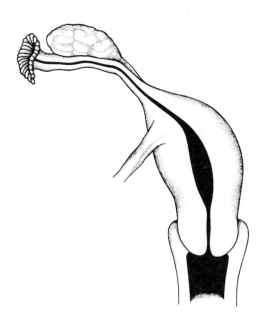

Fig. 7.   Complete lack of development involving the left müllerian duct Thus only the right Fallopian tube and right horn of the uterus are present.

abortions, late pregnancy complications, or else heavy, painful bleeding episodes unrelieved by more conservative measures.

If surgery cannot correct the problem and future pregnancies may endanger the woman's life, permanent sterilization is sometimes indicated. In the future, however, the ultimate solution for those women desirous of pregnancy may well be a uterine transplant.

4. Under the Seventh Veil— The Gynecological Examination

Running a close second in popularity to the dental appointment is the gynecological checkup. Even if you can stoically tolerate having your molars ground to a nub by your friendly dentist, it is only the pelvic that universally evokes the cry, "I hate this examination!" Rarely does a series of office hours pass without at least one woman verbalizing this sentiment. And regardless of whether she has had several pregnancies and innumerable pelvics, it is always with a deep sigh of resigned martyrdom that she slips her feet into the stirrups and inches her hips to the edge of the examining table.

What makes women dislike this examination?

Modesty for one thing. We don't usually mind exposing other parts of our anatomy for a physical examination, but when it comes to the external genitalia, that is a different story. And especially when that area is being scrutinized under a glaring 150-watt bulb—that is indeed dropping the seventh veil.

What makes some women so modest?

Conditioning during the early formative years. By virtue of our unique anatomy, we were not built to stand over public urinals and gawk at each other's genitalia, nor did we, as young girls, ever play the game "How big is yours?" Even in the most disreputable public facilities euphemistically called the powder room, there is usually the sanctuary of a toilet complete with door.

As a result many women are modest. But it is more than modesty that makes some women cringe when the term pelvic, internal, or female examination is mentioned.

What, for instance?

The possibility of offending. Regardless of how fastidious some of us are in our personal hygiene, many women would prefer taking time off from work to bathe or shower before a scheduled appointment. Although this is seldom necessary, the desire to be impeccable is as natural as brushing one's teeth or using an underarm deodorant in the morning. Just make it a point not to douche before a pelvic examination. More about this shortly.

Are there other disquieting things about a pelvic examination?

Yes, indeed. Whether or not we think we are in good health, there is always the concern that the doctor might find something wrong. But this somewhat uneasy feeling is a perfectly natural emotion associated with any physical checkup.

For those of you who have never had a pelvic examination, there is also the fear of the unknown. What is going to happen to me? Will it hurt? Will I bleed afterward? Will I still be a virgin? If you have listened to the stories of some of your well-meaning friends, you may have built up a solid wall of resistance. Allow me to allay your fears and uncertainties as to what really takes place and why.

Will knowing more about the pelvic examination make you like it more?

Of course not. But at least it might help you to relax. You may even react like one teenager after her first pelvic: "Gee, that wasn't so bad after all."

So who needs a pelvic?

We do, you and I. Since we were fortunate enough to have been born women, let us give ourselves every chance to live as vibrant, healthy women.

At what age should you have your first pelvic?

That, of course, depends on you and whether you have any problems. By the age of eighteen, however, all women should have had a routine checkup. This will reassure most of you that you are, indeed, perfectly normal. It may also be a good opportunity to air problems (sexual or otherwise) that you may have been reluctant to discuss.

For those of you contemplating marriage or just intercourse (regardless of your age) it would also be comforting to know that you are free of any physical problems, such as a hymenal ring just a little too snug to permit easy penetration.

Is a girl ever too young to be examined?

No. There is no age limit on a thorough gynecological examination provided that the symptoms warrant it. Although most gynecologists are competent in dealing with prepubertal problems, they may on occasion refer a case to a pediatric gynecologist who is a specialist adept at handling and examining young female children anywhere from infancy to early adolescence.

Specially adapted instruments make these examinations as easy as checking your child's ears or nose. So if you think that your daughter really does have a problem, do not hesitate. She is not too young.

Do you need to prepare yourself for a pelvic examination?

Not really, but knowing what to expect can certainly be helpful. For those of you making an appointment for your first gynecological checkup, a few preliminaries are in order.

When should you schedule your appointment?

If you feel your problem is not urgent, schedule your gynecological checkup for between periods. Although examination is possible during menstruation, certain smear tests are less accurate when mixed with menstrual blood. However, if your problem is one of constant bleeding or spotting, do not wait for it to stop. And, if you cannot remember or do not know when your period is due, make an appointment anyway. You can always cancel if necessary.

What about douching before a pelvic examination?

It is preferable not to douche for at least twenty-four hours before a pelvic examination. And if you have an unpleasant discharge, it is especially important *not* to douche. Douching in this case would be like wiping away the fingerprints at the scene of the crime. Flushing the offending organisms down the drain would make it more difficult for your doctor to identify the culprits responsible. Bathe or shower if you wish, but leave the inside vaginal area undisturbed.

How about intercourse before a pelvic exam?

Perfectly all right. Just make certain that you don't use any vaginal cream or lubricating jelly. These chemical substances can also interfere with certain smear tests.

How else should you prepare yourself?

If you are still having menstrual cycles, know the date of your last period. Invariably you will be asked this question. If you have trouble remembering, start now by keeping track of your periods. If your menses are completely irregular, or if you have had any unexpected spotting or bleeding, no matter how insignificant, make a note of it and bring this information with you. With regard to other health problems that may trouble you, making a list beforehand will help you to have all your questions answered.

If you are taking any medication prescribed by another doctor, your gynecologist will surely want to know. This will prevent any possible duplication and may even alter his choice of treatment for you. If you do not know the name of the drug, bring the medication with you. It can usually be readily identified. For those of you taking birth control pills, do not answer no, when asked if you are taking any medication. It is surprising how many women do not consider this a drug.

What is a thorough gynecological examination?

For many of you, your obstetrician-gynecologist may well be your primary physician. In other words, he or she may be the only doctor that you will ever consult under ordinary circumstances. Therefore, it is his responsibility to assure both you and himself that you are functioning as a total woman. The fact that the female organs influence other organ systems, and vice versa, makes it impossible to isolate them from the rest of the body. Whenever a problem exists in one area, it follows that other areas, as a consequence, may also be affected.

Don't be surprised if your appointment for a routine pelvic becomes a thorough physical, complete with a detailed medical history. So be prepared to answer some questions.

What kind of questions?

If you are just having a routine checkup, most of the questions will seem fairly genĕral. Really they are quite specific. In addition to the usual questions regarding menstrual cycles, pregnancies, the presence or absence of discharge, etc., your doctor may also ask for information about possible problems in other areas—bladder, bowels, heart, lungs, etc. You may wonder what all these questions have to do with a simple pelvic check, but be reassured; he is showing a real interest in your well-being.

Those of you with a specific complaint may be unaware that about 85 percent of the time, your doctor can make a fairly accurate diagnosis on history alone.

What about the physical examination?

Since you can anticipate a fairly thorough physical, you will usually be given an examining gown. You will have to remove all your clothes with the exception of your shoes, so dress simply. It is also best to empty your bladder just before a pelvic examination. But make it a point to ask the nurse beforehand whether a urine specimen will be wanted. This will help avoid the frustration of trying to coax urine out of an empty bladder. Just as in any complete physical, you will be weighed and your blood pressure will be taken. In addition, a good gynecological examination should include listening to your heart and lungs, peering down your throat, and even checking your neck for any enlarged or tender lymph nodes. If you wonder why your doctor is gently pushing against your windpipe, he is just examining your thyroid gland.

What does the thyroid do?

Think of the thyroid as your body's pace setter. If is is tuned up high, your motor will run fast; if it is sluggish, you may lack pep, energy, and may even gain weight. You are gaining weight? You think your thyroid is to blame? Probably not, but disturbances in the thyroid gland can occasionally be responsible for menstrual irregularities, which will be discussed later.

What about the breasts?

Since this is such a unique and important area of your anatomy, an entire chapter is devoted to breast problems. Suffice it to say for the moment, no physical is ever complete without a careful examination of both breasts.

Does your doctor examine your stomach?

Not specifically. But let us clarify the term stomach. Unless you have studied anatomy, what you commonly refer to as your stomach is in actuality your abdomen. The entire area lying between the lower ribs and the groin is known as the abdomen, of which the stomach constitutes only a very small part.

So what can your doctor tell by examining your abdomen?

Plenty. By just looking at the skin, for example, your doctor can usually tell if you have ever been pregnant. Most of you know about stretch marks, but even in their absence, there is frequently a faintly pigmented or darker line extending from just above the pubic hair to the navel. This darkening of the skin is caused by hormonal changes during pregnancy, and although this line will fade to a great extent, it will still be discernible to an astute observer.

More important than skin changes, however, is the presence of any enlarged organ, tumors, or areas of tenderness. All these findings may be valuable clues in helping to diagnose your particular problem, if you have one. In the normal nonpregnant woman, it is virtually impossible to feel either the uterus or ovaries on abdominal examination alone. That requires a pelvic.

What happens now?

We are finally ready to lower the seventh veil for the mysteries of the pelvic examination.

In addition to the examining gown you are wearing, you will usually be given a drape sheet to cover your lower abdomen and thighs. Its purpose is to preserve whatever modesty may still remain. It is not, as some of you may think, to hide what the doctor is doing.

What is the position for a pelvic?

Proper positioning and relaxation are vital for a good pelvic examination. Most examining tables will have metal stirrups for resting your heels while your hips hug the edge of the table. Help yourself as well as your doctor by relaxing as you lie on your back. Let those knees spread apart comfortably and focus your thoughts on something pleasant. If your mind is at ease, tension will drain from your body. And it will be over before you know it.

What is next?

Before examining the female internal organs, your doctor will visually inspect the external genitalia, or vulva. (See Chapter 2.) All the structures from the mons to the anus are scrutinized and a general evaluation of the vulva is made.

What is the doctor looking for?

Hormonal disturbances for one thing. Is the clitoris larger than normal? Are the labia majora (outer lips) plump, plush cushions or are they thin and flattened as a result of estrogen deficiency? And what about the pubic hair? Is it sparse and straggly or thick and luxuriant?

Anemia, too, can sometimes be detected. In some countries the color of the tongue is used as a rough barometer of anemia, but frequently the vulva can serve the same purpose. Are the tissues around the vaginal opening a nice healthy pink or are they somewhat pale?

What about signs of chronic and current infection? Are the labia red, swollen, and irritated? Has the skin become thick and leatherlike from persistent scratching as a result of chronic irritation?

Are there any warts, pimples, sores, or unusual swellings? Does the vaginal opening seem well supported, or does it appear large and relaxed?

From this partial list you can appreciate the importance of simple visual inspection.

Can your doctor tell if you have ever been pregnant?

If the only pregnancy you ever had terminated in an early abortion, either spontaneous or induced, it would be almost impossible to tell for sure. The nipples may have become slightly more pigmented, but in all probability an early pregnancy loss would have left neither the stretch marks nor the dark line between the pubic hair and the navel. In addition, there would be no evidence of an episiotomy (stitches), and even the cervical os, on further examination, would probably fail to show convincing proof of ever having been dilated.

Suppose you had a full-term pregnancy?

In about 95 percent of women, that fact can usually be verified by physical examination alone.

Can the doctor tell if you are really a virgin?

Sometimes. But the number of authentic virgins is definitely on the decrease. A girl whose vaginal opening will barely admit one slender finger is in all probability a virgin or, at least, successful penetration by a penis has not been accomplished. On the other hand, there are some women who can be examined easily but who are, indeed, virgins—at least they say they are.

The presence of an intact hymen does not prove or disprove virginity. With the increased use of tampons, a girl's hymen can easily be stretched and yet, by definition, she is still a virgin—in other words, she has never had sexual intercourse.

The presence of an intact hymen is also no guarantee that a girl is leading an austere or sheltered existence. Some girls have found themselves surprisingly pregnant in spite of a snug vaginal opening and an intact hymen. But more about these misadventures later.

Can the doctor tell if you masturbate?

If you are asking whether persistent erotic stimulation—autosexual, heterosexual, or homosexual—causes telltale signs in the form of a more prominent clitoris and labia minora, the answer is probably yes, at least with regard to the labia minora. However, if you want to know whether your doctor can tell if you masturbate, the answer is no.

Why is the answer no?

As was mentioned in Chapter 2 the labia minora normally come in a variety of colors and textures, not to mention sizes. Even if you have masturbated frequently over a long period of time, unless you are a participant in a research project in which minute, exact measurements of your labial dimensions are recorded over a period of years, you can breathe easily. In fact, you should breathe easily anyway, for there is nothing perverted or abnormal about masturbation.

Is masturbation really normal?

With few exceptions, almost every individual, both male and female, has masturbated at one time or another. Automanipulation will not harm you and at times may even be beneficial by allowing you to release pent-up sexual tension if the proper partner is not available. For some women, it has also been helpful in enabling them later to achieve orgasm more readily during sexual relations.

And since we are discussing sexual matters, let's bury another fairly common misconception.

Is your doctor thinking about sex because he is examining your sexual organs?

Emphatically no. And this information comes from those in the know. According to my male colleagues, the pelvic examination is as sexually exciting for them as clipping toenails is to a podiatrist. Ho hum. But let's get on with the examination.

What happens now?

After a thorough inspection of the vulva, your doctor will now focus on the vaginal entrance, or the vaginal introitus as it is frequently called. In women who have had children there may be some relaxation of the vagina as well as a shortening of the distance between the vagina and anus. This area, also known as the perineum or the perineal body, is where the episiotomy (see Chapter 14) is done just prior to delivery. Before proceeding to the inner vagina, the doctor will usually check your Bartholin's glands.

What are Bartholin's glands?

Two small mucus-producing glands located on either side of the vaginal introitus. No previous mention of them was made because under normal conditions they can neither be seen nor felt. However, by gently rolling this area between his fingers, the doctor can detect any swelling or tenderness. On occasion one of these glands can fill with mucus and form an obvious non-tender swelling known as a Bartholin's cyst. At other times a Bartholin's gland may become infected and form a painful abscess. Although they are not serious, recurrent cysts or abscesses of this type may require minor surgery to prevent future flare-ups.

What is the function of Bartholin's glands?

The mucus secretions from these glands help keep the vaginal entrance moist. It was once thought that they were solely responsible for the increased lubrication around the introitus at the time of sexual arousal. It has now been well documented that the vaginal walls are the main contributors of this lubrication. Nonfunction or removal of both Bartholin's glands, therefore, would not appreciably decrease the amount of moisture and secretion during sexual stimulation.

How is the inner vagina examined?

If this is indeed your first pelvic examination, you may well wonder at the array of cold, gleaming metal instruments. They are vaginal speculums—but don't be alarmed, they are not all intended for you. Before using a speculum to examine the inner vagina, your doctor will estimate the size of your vaginal introitus. Just as vaginal openings come in different sizes, so also do speculums—from the peanut size to the giant jumbo variety. With few exceptions there is one speculum just right for you. (See Fig. 1.) No competent doctor will insert a speculum that may be uncomfortably large, and, if he is also kind-

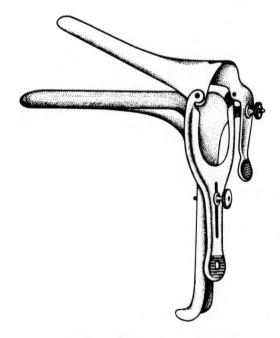

Fig. 1. Vaginal speculum

hearted, he will usually moisten that cold metal instrument with warm
water, thus making its insertion more comfortable.

What happens if your vagina is unusually small?

If there is no speculum that can be inserted without causing discomfort (a rare occurrence), then no speculum will be used. Any
necessary smears or cultures can usually be taken, if absolutely necessary, by inserting a cotton-tipped applicator (similar to a Q-tip)
through the vaginal opening.

Why is the speculum usually necessary?

Because the walls of the vagina normally rest against each other,
the speculum, by gently dilating the vaginal canal, allows your doctor
to examine not only the vaginal walls but also the cervix. (See Fig. 2.)
Thus, the presence of any discharge, cervical infection, or irritation
can be readily seen.

If there is an unusual discharge, your doctor may simply examine
the secretion under a microscope. If, however, you are concerned
about the possibility of a gonorrheal infection, a culture will probably
be taken. How this is done will be explained in Chapter 11.

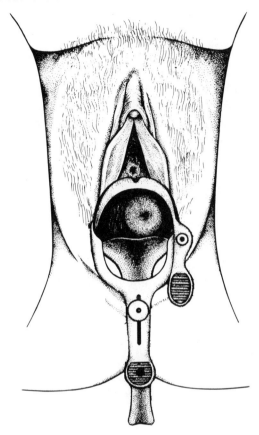

Fig. 2. Cervix and vaginal walls exposed by use of speculum

What other tests is he likely to do?

A Pap smear or cancer-screening test. (See Chapter 5 for complete details.) For the time being, be reassured that the Pap smear as well as the taking of any other vaginal smear or culture is a painless procedure.

A few gynecologists when examining the cervix may also use a colposcope, a telescopelike instrument which magnifies the surface of the cervix. Using the colposcope allows the doctor to see the cervix in greater detail and perhaps detect suspicious tissue changes. But this type of examination is neither routine nor generally done by most gynecologists. Screening for an early cancer of the cervix still relies primarily on a Pap smear.

What else can be seen besides the vaginal walls and the cervix?

If you explored your own vagina as described in Chapter 2, you know that nothing else can be seen. Not infrequently, however, a patient will ask, "How do my fibroids look?" or "How do my ovaries look?" It would be helpful if we could see the internal pelvic organs by means of the speculum, but unfortunately we have to rely on the bimanual examination for further information.

What is the bimanual examination?

After the necessary smears and cultures are taken, the speculum is removed and the doctor will gently insert one or two fingers into the vagina. For this purpose, he will usually apply lubricating jelly on the examining glove. With his other hand, he will then press along the lower portion of the abdomen.

Why are two hands necessary?

The vaginal hand (one or two fingers, that is) pushes up against the cervix and stabilizes it while the abdominal hand presses downward.

Fig. 3. Bimanual examination of the uterus

Thus, the uterus is literally being held and examined between your doctor's two hands. The same technique is applied in feeling the ovaries. (See Fig. 3.)

What can the doctor tell by this examination?

All about the uterus for one thing. Is it normal in size and shape? Is it as movable as it should be, or is it fixed in one position because of possible scar tissue from a previous pelvic infection or some other problems?

The more at ease you are, the easier the examination and the more informative. So give your doctor a fair chance by relaxing those abdominal muscles and let your knees spread apart comfortably. The proper evaluation of the uterus also depends on your having an empty bladder. Even if you are not reminded to empty your bladder, be sure to do so before the examination.

However, the interior of the uterus (the uterine cavity) cannot be examined bimanually.

Why not?

As discussed in Chapter 2, the entrance to the uterine cavity is through the cervical opening (os), which under normal conditions is not much bigger than the head of a kitchen match. Therefore, it is not humanly possible for anybody's fingers to explore the uterine cavity. Nonetheless, as you will learn later, there are ways of examining the inside of the uterus when necessary.

What else can be felt on bimanual examination?

Usually the ovaries. They are checked for any enlargement that might represent a cyst or tumor. In women who are well past the menopause, the ovaries will frequently be difficult to feel because of a natural decrease in size. And, if a woman is excessively overweight, feeling normal ovaries may be almost impossible—somewhat like feeling for a walnut through a mattress. Another good reason for staying slim!

What about the Fallopian tubes?

Because the tubes are such soft and pliable structures, it is rarely possible to feel them under ordinary circumstances. However, in the case of a tubal pregnancy (ectopic pregnancy) or in the presence of tubal infection, the tube or tubes may be sufficiently thickened and enlarged to be palpable (capable of being felt).

So what's that finger doing in your rectum?

Since the innovation of the rubber glove, the rectal exam has soared in popularity—at least for your doctor. Without a doubt, this part of the pelvic examination is the least understood and the least appreciated judging by such common remarks as "Is this really necessary?" or "What on earth can you tell from that?" Although not uncomfortable, a rectal examination may give you a temporary sense of anal sphincter insecurity. But no pelvic examination is really complete without a rectovaginal.

What is a rectovaginal?

As you learned in Chapter 2, the ovaries are fairly movable and at times may actually hide behind the uterus. When your doctor inserts his middle finger into the rectum and his index finger into the vagina, he is able to reach higher and further than by the vaginal route alone. Since the rectum is continuous with the large bowel, it is not limited in length as is the vagina. Ovaries, therefore, that may have escaped detection by the vaginal route may now be within easy reach.

Suppose the ovaries were already felt by the vaginal examination, is it still necessary to do a rectovaginal?

Yes. (You didn't really expect to get off that easily, did you?)

In all seriousness, doing a rectovaginal examination also enables your doctor to get a better feel of the back wall of the uterus. It is also important to check the space between the vagina and rectum for any tenderness, nodules, etc.

What about the rectum itself?

In addition to the obvious presence of hemorrhoids, other growths within the rectum, such as polyps, can be readily felt. In older women this examination is particularly important because a large number of early colon cancers first appear within five to six inches of the anus. Thus, your gynecologist may well be the first doctor to diagnose an early bowel lesion.

Is a rectovaginal examination always done?

No. In young girls or women whose vaginal opening is too small to accommodate even one finger, the digital vaginal exam would be bypassed in favor of a simple rectal and abdominal evaluation. Having a gynecological examination should not cause pain or hymenal injury.

How often should you have a gynecological examination?

That depends on you and what your gynecologist may advise. Otherwise, make it a point to get yourself checked at least once every twelve months. A physical examination on an annual basis will help you to stay in top-notch shape.

5. The Pap Smear or Cancer-Screening Test

Extensive publicity may have alerted you to the importance of routine Pap smears; other than that, little additional information has been made available to the average woman. For this reason it is not surprising that you, like so many others, know very little about the Pap smear beyond the fact that it has something to do with early cancer detection.

According to the Gallup poll taken in the early 1960's, only 12 percent of American women had ever had a Pap smear, and another 40 percent were completely unaware of the existence of such a test.

Have these statistics improved in the last twenty years?

Yes, to a great extent, but surprisingly little progress has been made in overcoming the general reluctance of even well-informed women to get themselves checked regularly.

It is currently estimated that only 50 to 55 percent of American women have routine Pap smears. This means that almost five out of ten women in the United States do not take advantage of this simple, potentially life-saving procedure.

What's so important about the Pap smear?

The Pap smear is by far the best method of detecting an early cervical malignancy. The fact that *there are absolutely no symptoms whatsoever in an early cancer of the cervix* makes this important procedure an integral part of a thorough gynecological checkup.

What exactly is the Pap smear?

The Pap smear is a method whereby cells that are normally shed from the cervix and the uterine cavity are collected, smeared onto a glass slide, and examined under a microscope. All of you know what dry, peeling skin or dandruff is. Well, essentially the same process of shedding and regeneration of cells occurs in the vagina, cervix, and lining of the uterine cavity.

What does the Pap smear really show?

Whether or not there are any abnormal or atypical changes within the cells themselves. In contrast to normal cells shed from the vaginal walls, cervix, and uterine lining, malignant or cancer cells have a totally different appearance. Their nucleus or central core is frequently larger and stains a much darker color when exposed to certain laboratory dyes. Then too, the tissue source of any suspicious cells can at times also be identified. In other words, a malignant cell shed from the cervix looks different from a malignant cell shed from the uterine lining. Needless to say, this valuable information can be of great help in pinpointing the possible location of an early cancer.

How did the Pap smear get its name?

The world owes a debt of gratitude to the late Dr. George N. Papanicolaou, who some forty years ago first demonstrated that cancer cells originating from the cervix and lining of the uterine cavity could be detected in vaginal secretions. Since his original research, much progress has been made in the processing and the interpretation of this cellular material, but in homage to him the term Papanicolaou smear, or Pap smear, has been popularly applied to the cancer-screening test.

Is the Pap smear ever used on men?

Yes, very definitely. In fact the Pap smear is also used for tracking down abnormal cells elsewhere in the body—for example, in the lungs and stomach. But by far its greatest clinical application is still the early detection of pelvic cancer in women.

How is the Pap smear actually taken?

Studies have shown that the most accurate method of detecting early pelvic cancer depends on the sampling of cells from three areas: the secretions normally found in the upper vagina, the surface of the cervix, and the area just inside the cervical os (endocervical canal). In collecting cells from the cervix proper, most doctors will scrape the surface of the cervix with a small wooden spatula or tongue blade. With respect to the collecting of samples from vaginal secretions and the endocervical canal, the technique may vary from doctor to doctor —a cotton-tipped applicator, a small pipette, or a wooden spatula may be used. All three samples thus collected are then separately smeared onto a glass slide. The slide is immediately sprayed with a fixative or else immersed in a solution containing a preservative. In other instances the slide is allowed to dry by simple exposure to room air.

Is it painful to have a Pap smear?

Emphatically no. Although your toes may curl at the thought of having your cervix scraped, the surface of the cervix is remarkably insensitive. Unless you are told that samples are being taken for a Pap smear, most of you will be completely unaware of any sensation. Discomfort, if any, is usually due to the insertion and placement of the speculum to expose the cervix properly for examination.

What happens to your Pap smear after you leave the doctor's office?

Few can appreciate the intricacies involved in the processing of a single Pap smear. Along every step of the way there must be rigid and specific handling of the slide to assure maximum accuracy in its interpretation. Its accuracy depends not only upon how well the smear was taken by your doctor, but also upon the proper fixation, staining, and interpretation of the material.

With rare exception your doctor will send your Pap smear to a cytology laboratory. Unlike most laboratories that analyze blood and urine specimens, the cytology laboratory is devoted exclusively to the processing and microscopic examination of cellular material.

All slides after proper staining with specific dyes will be assiduously scrutinized by specially trained medical personnel. In addition many cytology laboratories employ a second team to double-check randomly selected Pap smears that initially were labeled as normal. Any slide that is the least bit suspicious is always referred to a cytopathologist for final interpretation.

What is a cytopathologist?

A medical doctor who specializes in the microscopic interpretation of abnormalities in cellular material. Thus, any slide that is not completely normal is always checked by a cytopathologist. It is his responsibility to evaluate and classify all suspicious smears and to report his findings to your doctor. Not infrequently the cytopathologist may request a follow-up smear within three to six months for further evaluation. If for any reason a slide is technically poor and difficult to interpret, your doctor will be notified and a repeat Pap smear will be in order.

How reliable is a Pap smear in detecting early cancer of the cervix?

If you have an early cervical cancer, you have a 95 to 100 percent chance of having it detected by the Pap smear.

What about the 1 to 5 percent that may go undetected?

In almost all such cases, studies have shown that the subsequent Pap smear will reveal the abnormality. Equally important and far more comforting is the fact that even if there is a twelve-month interval between smears, the cancer, with rare exception, will still be early enough to be completely curable.

If there is an early cervical cancer, why can't your doctor see it?

Because at this stage there is nothing to see. In other words, your cervix may look completely normal and yet when those superficial cells are scraped off and examined under a microscope, they may show beginning malignant changes. That is the beauty of the Pap smear—it arouses suspicion where there is none.

How reliable is the Pap smear in detecting other female cancers?

Although the Pap smear is helpful in detecting cancer in other female organs, its accuracy in these instances is far less. With regard to cancer involving the lining of the uterine cavity (endometrial cancer), the accuracy of the Pap smear can range anywhere from 40 to 85 percent. Unlike cancer of the cervix, a malignancy involving the lining of the uterine cavity usually gives early symptoms that will alert your physician. In these cases, therefore, other procedures will be necessary to establish a diagnosis.

With regard to cancer of the Fallopian tubes, ovaries, or the early detection of a primary vaginal cancer, that is, a cancer which originates in the vagina, the Pap smear with rare exception is not reliable.

Can the Pap smear be used for anything else besides cancer detection?

Yes. As you may know, the cells of the vaginal walls undergo cyclic changes in response to hormone fluctuations. The examinations of smears taken from the vaginal walls may at times be helpful in assessing your estrogen hormone level.

Because of these cyclic cellular changes, it is also important that the doctor submit with each Pap smear such pertinent information as the woman's age, date of her last menstrual period, and current hormone therapy including the use of any birth control pill. All these factors must be considered to give a proper interpretation of the Pap smear.

If you have had a hysterectomy (removal of the uterus and cervix) is it still necessary to have a routine Pap smear?

That depends on several things. If the reason for the hysterectomy was a malignancy involving the cervix or the uterine cavity, then repeat Pap smears of the upper vagina are necessary because recurrent cancer from these sites can appear in this vaginal area. In these cases the Pap test should probably be repeated once every three months during the first year following treatment. This close follow-up with Pap smears and periodic pelvic examinations would insure early recognition of any recurrence. Thus, appropriate therapy could be promptly instituted, if necessary.

If the hysterectomy was done because of a benign condition (noncancerous)—for example, fibroid tumors—the taking of a Pap smear would not be essential unless your doctor were specifically interested in evaluating your estrogen level. As previously mentioned, primary vaginal cancers are seldom detected by routine Pap smears. More about this in Chapter 25.

For those of you who may have had a partial hysterectomy (removal of the upper portion of the uterus but not the cervix), a routine Pap smear is definitely called for at least once every twelve months.

How often should a woman have a Pap smear?

Under ordinary circumstances, most gynecologists would recommend routine Pap smears at least once a year. In the postmenopausal woman on hormone therapy, or in the woman who has a strong family history of malignancy, it may be advisable to repeat Pap smears more frequently. More recently there is evidence that women who have had at least three or four negative Pap smears in consecutive years are highly unlikely to develop cervical cancer in immediately succeeding years. On the basis of these findings some cancer experts feel that Pap smears in such women need only be taken every three years. But here again, there are no set rules. Each woman must be evaluated individually.

How is the Pap smear graded?

Before answering that question, it is important to understand that the *Pap smear, of and by itself, does not prove or disprove the presence of cancer.* For that diagnosis, other studies are necessary. The Pap smear, however, will alert your doctor to the fact that additional tests may be needed.

For practical purposes your Pap smear will usually be reported as belonging to one of five classes. By and large, most smears will be reported as Class I negative. This means that all the cells surveyed were normal in every respect.

Class II is also considered negative, but in this case some of the cells showed minimal or atypical changes probably as the result of a vaginal or cervical infection—rarely because of malignancy. A Class II Pap smear is not uncommon, and in the majority of cases it will revert to Class I on simple treatment of your particular vaginal or cervical infection. A Class II Pap smear is therefore no cause for alarm, but it does require a follow-up smear usually within three months after completion of local therapy.

A Class III Pap smear is questionable. It is frequently reported by the cytopathologist as being suspicious.

A Class IV Pap smear is interpreted as positive—possible malignancy; a Class V Pap smear is reported as positive—probable malignancy.

Pap smears reported as positive, that is, either Class IV or Class V, always demand further diagnostic studies.

What other studies are necessary for a diagnosis of pelvic cancer?

Because this is such a vital subject to all women, the discussion of how a cancer is diagnosed and treated is covered in Chapter 25.

With regard to Class III Pap smears, it is still best to proceed with the same diagnostic studies.

What percentage of women with a class III Pap smear do have an early cervical cancer?

In most surveys, less than 20 percent of women with a Class III Pap smear will actually have a malignancy. However, in those women whose studies prove negative for cancer, more frequent Pap smears would usually be advisable as an added precaution.

Is it ever possible to have a positive Pap smear and not have cancer?

It is possible, but in the presence of any positive Pap smear (Class IV or V) the burden of proof that you do not have cancer lies heavily on your doctor. He must be able to show beyond any doubt that you are indeed free of pelvic malignancy. All diagnostic studies would have to be completely normal and subsequent serial Pap smears would have to revert to Class I negative. Short of this, no competent doctor would dismiss the original positive smear as being incorrect.

What about do-it-yourself Pap smears?

They are not a new concept. Do-it-yourself Pap smears were originally devised to screen that vast multitude of women (five out of ten) who fail to get yearly Pap smears.

This self-administered test is essentially an irrigation method for collecting cells from the upper vagina. Most kits provide a plastic pipette filled with a mild alcoholic solution and fitted with a suction bulb—plus instructions. With the pipette inserted into the vagina, the bulb is then pressed and released. This in effect flushes the cervix and allows the solution (now containing vaginal and cervical cells) to be drawn back into the pipette. Everything is then mailed back in a special container to a designated cytology laboratory. If instructions are followed, the mailing time should not affect the accuracy of the test.

How reliable are do-it-yourself Pap smears?

Anywhere from 40 to 90 percent, depending on which statistics are quoted.

Why is their reliability sometimes so low?

One of the obvious disadvantages is that the sampling of cervical cells may well be insufficient. It is reasonable to assume that the mere flushing of the cervix (providing that the pipette is properly inserted and directed exactly at the cervix) cannot effectively replace the scraping of the cervix plus the sampling of the endocervical cells under direct vision.

In recent years, the greater availability of Pap smears in neighborhood health centers has contributed to the decreased popularity of this self-administered procedure. As of now, do-it-yourself Pap smears (although still used in mass screening programs elsewhere) are almost a thing of the past in this country. But in all fairness to enthusiastic proponents of this method, a mail-order Pap smear (if available) is better than no Pap smear at all.

6. Ebb and Flow— The Menstrual Cycle

Man has sounded the depths of the ocean floor and soared into outer space, and yet some of what we now accept as fact regarding the menstrual cycle is still woefully enigmatic. Even today certain aspects of the menstrual cycle are among the most controversial subjects in endocrinology. What you probably take for granted is in reality one of the most complex biochemical and psychophysiological processes in the human body, male or female. Part of the explanation lies in man's inability, as yet, to unscramble all the infinite and wondrous workings of the human brain and mind.

What does the brain have to do with the menstrual cycle?

Everything—or almost everything. Some twenty years ago, it was generally accepted that the pituitary gland was *the* brain center in control of ovarian function. More recent studies have shown that the pituitary gland is actually under the control of a higher brain center, the hypothalamus. But we can't stop there. For if the truth be known, the hypothalamus is also affected by and responsive to our mental and emotional state.

Women have been known to stop menstruating spontaneously

under great physical and emotional stress. Other women exposed to similar situations can run the opposite course. They can bleed continuously. And a stalwart few seem to carry on with regular menses in spite of all calamities. It is little wonder that in the whole realm of human physiology, probably no other bodily function has been the center of such passionate oratory, violent debates, and wild theories as our monthly flow.

What wild theories?

Incredible as it may seem, menstruation in the human female was equated with the estrus cycle of lower animals as recently as the turn of this century. In other words, most scientists at that time assumed that women, like the female dog, went into heat—except that women did it monthly instead of twice a year. There were other scientists who were equally confused. Were women like the domestic hen, capable of laying an egg every day? Or did they respond like the female rabbit, ovulating every time they had intercourse?

Fortunately for us, the work of Walter Heape early in the 1900's did much to advance the frontiers of science. Through his inspired research and liberal attitude, woman was at last elevated to the status of the monkey. It was Heape's contention that perhaps the human female, like the monkey, actually ovulated before the appearance of any menstrual discharge. Once this striking similarity between monkey and woman was confirmed, the poor rhesus monkey never knew another moment's peace. From that time on, the rhesus monkey has been one of the few mammals extensively used for studies involving the female reproductive system. Other animals also have contributed to our cause.

What other animals?

Would you believe sows and mice? In the early 1920's, while many of his less dedicated peers were dancing the Charleston, a young dynamic anatomist, Dr. Edgar Allen, in conjunction with a biochemist, Edward Doisey, was on the verge of making a momentous discovery —the hormone estrogen.

It was already a confirmed fact that each ovum (egg) within the ovary was enveloped in a small saclike structure called a follicle. However, the fluid within each follicle surrounding the ovum was not known to have any hormonal function. It was Dr. Allen's theory that the follicular fluid contained a specific substance that was somehow important to the reproductive cycle. As far as he was concerned, all he had to do was to prove it. But how? His monetary resources were pathetically meager and, besides, it was going to take hundreds of ovaries to extract even a measurable amount of this fluid. Fortunately, at long last the answer came. He would ask the Swift Packing Company to salvage ovaries from slaughtered sows. And as the story goes, on many a cold night Allen and Doisey, their arms straining from the weight of buckets brimming with pig ovaries, trudged home, grateful and triumphant.

Night after night with the help of their wives, they aspirated and collected the precious follicular fluid, later to be injected into female mice whose ovaries had previously been removed. After countless experiments, there was no longer any doubt in Allen's mind. The injection of this fluid caused specific cellular changes in the vaginal smear of the mice—changes that had previously been observed only in mature mice with two good ovaries.

But Allen's struggles were just beginning. Scientists scoffed when he presented his findings at the annual American Anatomists meeting. Skepticism rippled through that august body, and only the few who believed that this fluid could contain a hormonal substance nodded in admiration. Others violently challenged the idea that the studies done on mice could be applied to the human female.

There was only one recourse open to Allen; he had to prove his theory by successfully repeating his experiments on—the monkey. And thus, all doubt was forever removed. Now, everyone believed.

By virtue of the work done by Allen and Doisey, as well as notable experiments by such eminent pioneers as Corner, Bartelmez, Hartman, and Markee, many of the intricacies of the menstrual cycle have gradually been revealed and understood.

What follows in the next few pages is based on the contributions of these men and our friend, the rhesus monkey. But the final story of menstrual physiology is not yet written. It is for this reason that only the most basic concepts can be presented with any degree of reliability.

Are the basic concepts regarding the menstrual cycle important to you as a woman?

More than you may now realize. Many female bleeding problems (apart from tumors or other growths) are the result of disturbances in the menstrual cycle. Until you can appreciate the delicate balance of various hormones necessary for the maintenance of regular periods, many of these worrisome problems will not make sense to you. Only by knowing what is normal will you begin to understand the causes of such common disorders as irregular periods, skipped periods, premenstrual spotting, and the like.

Again, it must be stressed that you would be doing yourself a great injustice by using this chapter or any other chapter in the book as a guide to self-diagnosis. You as a woman are infinitely too complex to be bound between the covers of any book.

What is menstruation?

Ask any woman and you will probably get an inadequate answer. Chances are that you equate menstruation with your monthly periods, and in a sense you are right. But menstruation is more than a periodic bloody discharge from the uterine cavity. True menstruation implies the occurrence of two elaborate and precisely timed events prior to actual bleeding: (*a*) ovulation (release of an egg) by the ovary, and (*b*) specific changes in the tissue lining the uterine cavity as a result of that ovulation.

Where do the eggs come from?

Before a young girl matures sexually, the ovaries must be transformed from small nubs of inactive tissue into glorious plump organs capable of producing estrogen and forming eggs on a cyclic basis.

When a girl is born, each ovary already contains anywhere from 40,000 to 400,000 immature eggs (ova). By means of simple arithmetic, you can calculate that if a woman has regular, uninterrupted periods for some thirty years, she will have actually released only 360 of these eggs.

What happens to the rest of the eggs?

Many are called, few are chosen. For every egg that completely matures, untold numbers are lost in the attempt and become mere microscopic specks of scar tissue forever embedded in the substance of the ovary. But before even one egg can be released and even one drop of estrogen can be produced, certain profound changes must occur.

What kinds of changes and when do they start?

During the first seven to eight years of every woman's life, the immature ova (eggs) lie buried deep within the ovaries awaiting that magic touch from up above. What actually triggers certain cells in the pituitary gland to begin functioning remains obscure. It is known, however, that by the time most girls reach the age of seven or eight, the pituitary gland begins bombarding the ovaries with a special hormone, the follicle-stimulating hormone, better known as FSH.

What does FSH do?

As the name implies, the follicle-stimulating hormone stimulates the follicles. A follicle is a microscopic ovarian entity consisting of a small ring of cells forming a saclike structure within which an immature ovum, or egg, is contained. On a selective basis, certain follicles begin to enlarge and mature under the effect of this hormone.

After sufficient stimulation by FSH, specialized cells within each follicle begin to produce estrogen, which in turn is gradually released into the bloodstream. As more and more follicles ripen, greater amounts of estrogen are subsequently secreted and before too long, that marvelous estrogen makes its presence known.

What does estrogen do?

The very first sign of estrogen stimulation is the development of breast buds. Changes in both the nipple and breast tissue may begin as early as eight or nine years of age. Once the breasts start to develop, menstruation will usually begin within two or three years. Interestingly enough, the younger a girl is at the time of recognizable breast development, the shorter the waiting period until her first menses. Thus, a girl who has breast buds at nine may be menstruating by the time she reaches ten. On the other hand, some girls can remain as flat as ironing boards until much older. But regardless of how little or how much young girls have in the bosom department, *some breast development always precedes the onset of their first period.*

If vaginal bleeding should occur without any evidence of breast or nipple development, something other than normal menstruation is probably responsible. If this should happen, the girl should be seen by a physician.

What follows breast development?

Once the breasts have started to bloom, other changes both subtle and not so subtle begin to appear. Among the more obvious physical changes are those in body contour and a definite preadolescent growth spurt.

Estrogen with the help of androgen hormones (secreted by the adrenal glands) also stimulates the growth of pubic hair and axillary (underarm) hair. In the usual sequence of events, pubic hair appears several months before the onset of menstruation. Axillary hair, however, may be quite sparse or even absent until much later.

What about the less visible changes?

As the ovarian follicles continue to secrete estrogen, mass preparation for the first menstrual period is well under way. Unbeknownst to that young girl who may now be proudly sporting her first bra, size 32 AAA with padding, the uterus, cervix, vagina, and vulva are also being transformed.

How does estrogen affect the uterus?

Before the first menstrual period can ever take place, there is a marked increase in the size of the uterus, accompanied by dramatic changes in the endometrium. The word endometrium means within the womb. Therefore, endometrium, or endometrial tissue as it is sometimes called, refers to the tissue lining the uterine cavity. The term endometrial cavity is another way of saying the uterine cavity.

How does estrogen affect the endometrium?

As more and more estrogen stimulates the endometrium, it begins to thicken as new cells grow and develop. Because there is such a marked increase in cellular growth, the term proliferative endometrium is used to describe this normal thickening of the uterine lining. With sexual maturation, these same proliferative tissue changes normally occur on a monthly basis as a direct result of estrogen stimulation *prior to ovulation* in every mature menstruating female.

As long as the level of estrogen reaching the endometrium is maintained above a certain critical level, the tissue lining the uterine cavity will continue to grow and thicken. In other words, there will be no shedding and no bleeding. But when the estrogen level drops, the endometrium whose growth and support depended upon estrogen begins to disintegrate. Thus, the uterine lining sloughs and bleeding occurs.

What causes the estrogen level to drop?

Cyclic fluctuations of FSH and other pituitary hormones. As FSH increases, the estrogen level decreases and vice versa, as if they were on a seesaw. Like the pounding of the waves upon a shore or the beating of your heart—everything has a rhythm of its own. Nothing in nature is static. And so it is with estrogen production.

Thus, a young girl may have matured only sufficiently to experience the effects of estrogen, such as breast development, changes in body contour, uterine growth, and so on. She may also have experienced her first period as a result of a drop in the estrogen level on the endometrium. But without the final step in sexual maturity—*ovulation*—reproductive capacity is not possible.

What is ovulation?

It is the moment of truth: the rupture of a chosen follicle with the release of the egg it contained—the egg carrying half of the genetic inheritance of a potential human being.

How does ovulation come about?

A young girl may look physically developed, but before she can claim to be sexually mature, other hormones in addition to FSH and estrogen must come into being.

Once again it is the brain via the pituitary gland that brings forth yet another hormone, the luteinizing hormone, or LH for short.

What does LH do?

It springs the egg from the chosen follicle. FSH by itself stimulates the follicles to grow and secrete estrogen. FSH can also cause the chosen follicle to migrate toward the surface of the ovary, but something else is needed before the egg can break out of its follicular prison.

If you were actually able to observe an ovary just prior to ovulation, you would see the chosen follicle bulging on the surface of the ovary like a small blister, not much bigger than a quarter of an inch across—waiting. For what? For LH. It is that final surge of LH hormone released by the pituitary gland that ruptures the follicle and frees the egg from the ovary. As an aside, successful recovery of a ripe egg for in-vitro fertilization (test-tube fertilization) depends on timing the onset of this LH surge accurately. More about this in Chapter 17.

Has the moment of ovulation ever been observed?

Innumerable times in our friend the rhesus monkey, but seldom have scientists witnessed ovulation in the human female. The egg itself is just barely visible to the naked eye. Nonetheless, the residual evidence that ovulation has occurred can be seen in the remains of the ruptured follicle. In most cases there would probably be a trace of blood-tinged fluid oozing from the site of rupture on the surface of the ovary.

What happens to the ruptured follicle after the egg is released?

Everything in nature has a purpose—even the remnants of the ruptured follicle that stay behind in the ovary. Up to the time of ovulation, that follicle was primarily concerned with the production of estrogen. After ovulation the ruptured follicle continues to produce estrogen, but in addition it now secretes a second and exceedingly important hormone, *progesterone.*

Because of its new function—the production of progesterone—the ruptured follicle also acquires a new name, the *corpus luteum.* Corpus luteum literally means yellow body. Why yellow body? Because certain chemical changes associated with the production of progesterone cause the remnants of the ruptured follicle to turn a bright canary yellow.

What does progesterone do?

It prepares the tissue of the uterine lining (endometrium) to receive the fertilized egg. If you have ever had the wonderful experience of growing a prize flower from seed, you can appreciate the importance of careful preparation of the soil. The fertilized human egg is like an exalted seed. If it is to implant properly and continue to grow normally, progesterone must transform the proliferative endometrium into an even thicker, richer, more luxuriant tissue bed known as *secretory endometrium.* Thus, progesterone causes the growth of specialized cells that secrete certain nutrients (hence the name secretory endometrium) necessary for the support of the fertilized egg. Without these postovulatory changes in the endometrium, no respectable egg could survive. In fact, many early spontaneous abortions may be the result of poor preparation of the endometrium because of inadequate progesterone levels.

Regardless of whether or not the egg is fertilized, the transformation of the uterine lining into secretory endometrium invariably occurs after ovulation. Therefore, it is very easy for your doctor to determine whether or not you have ovulated.

How is that possible?

By simply taking a small shred of tissue from the uterine lining just before your period and examining it under a microscope (endometrial biopsy). Ovulation results in the production of progesterone, and progesterone is responsible for changing the uterine lining to secretory endometrium. Therefore the finding of secretory endometrium by means of an endometrial biopsy would be indirect proof that you had indeed ovulated.

Are there other indirect proofs of ovulation?

Many. Since progesterone is ultimately metabolized and excreted in the urine as pregnanediol, the finding of elevated levels of this substance is another, although more complicated method of determining ovulation. Unfortunately neither this test nor other hormone studies, temperature charts, and cyclic changes involving cervical mucus and vaginal cells can pinpoint the exact moment of ovulation. At best all these tests (including the endometrial biopsy) merely reflect hormonal and physiological changes associated with or occurring after the release of the egg from the ovary.

What would be direct proof of ovulation?

Short of actually recovering the egg, pregnancy would be irrefutable proof that ovulation had occurred.

What happens if the egg is not fertilized?

Through some mechanism, as yet not known, the corpus luteum gets the word that its offspring, the egg, did not make it. Without fertilization there is no further need for the elaborate preparation of the endometrium. As a consequence the corpus luteum begins to shrink, and the levels of estrogen and progesterone gradually decrease. The endometrium, whose support depended upon these two ovarian hormones, starts to disintegrate, resulting in menstruation. In time the corpus luteum becomes a residual speck of nonfunctioning gray scar tissue within the ovary.

Suppose the corpus luteum doesn't shrink?

Then you may have what is known as a persistent corpus luteum cyst of the ovary. (See Chapter 21.)

What else happens?

The drop in estrogen and progesterone levels signals the pituitary gland that the project was cancelled. The pituitary gland responds by increasing the output of FSH. Thus, another fresh crop of follicles is stimulated and the whole process repeats itself.

What happens if the egg is fertilized?

Then all systems are "go" for the corpus luteum. For the first two or three months following implantation of the fertilized egg, the continuing growth of the pregnancy depends upon a functioning corpus luteum. Rather than regressing, it continues to pour out those marvelous hormones, estrogen and progesterone, so vital for the growth of the fertilized egg now embedded within the uterine lining. By the end of this critical period (sixty to ninety days after conception) the placenta (afterbirth) is sufficiently mature to sustain all the needs of the growing fetus; the function of the corpus luteum then ceases.

What happens to the ovaries during pregnancy?

With the subsequent regression of the corpus luteum, there is no further activity within the ovaries for the duration of the pregnancy. They are literally in a state of suspended animation—no stimulation of follicles, no ovulation, and no hormone production. Estrogen and progesterone, as well as other hormones associated with pregnancy, are derived exclusively from fetal and placental sources.

How soon after the end of pregnancy does menstruation resume?

Approximately 85 to 90 percent of women will menstruate within the first three months following the termination of a pregnancy, whether the pregnancy ended as an abortion or a full-term baby.

For the remaining 10 to 15 percent, the first period may be delayed as long as four to six months.

What happens if you are breast feeding?

In this case the resumption of normal menstrual cycles may be even more delayed. Although some 30 percent of nursing mothers may have their first menses within twelve weeks of delivery, the majority of lactating women may not menstruate for several months.

Can you become pregnant even though you are breast feeding and have not had a period?

Yes, indeed. Breast feeding to a certain extent will inhibit ovulation, but it is a highly unreliable method of birth control. There have been many nursing mothers who were completely oblivious to a superimposed pregnancy until they felt it kicking. Therefore, if you do not want another pregnancy, take precautions. Otherwise, you may be like the woman who did not see a period for four years—but was blessed with three beautiful tax deductions.

7. Countdown—More About Menses and the Launching of Eggs

Dating back to the first clay tablets, historical records have been replete with misconceptions and myths regarding menstruation. Not only has the menstruating woman been ostracized, segregated, isolated, and labeled as unfit to touch, but she has also been reputed to have powers that would do credit to any nuclear detonation. To quote from a translation of Pliny's *Natural History,* written at the beginning of the Christian era, "The touch of a menstrous woman turned wine to vinegar, blighted crops, killed seedlings, blasted gardens, brought down the fruit from trees, dimmed mirrors, blunted razors, rusted iron and brass (especially at the waning of the moon), killed bees, or at least drove them from their hives, caused mares to miscarry," and so forth.

Fortunately for the thousands of girls who are about to experience their first period, some progress has been made in the dissemination of more accurate information. But there is still a long way to go.

Many parents today fail miserably in preparing their daughters for menstruation. What should be greeted as a perfectly natural and welcome event can become a traumatic experience. This is especially true for the girl ahead of her peers in sexual maturation. How emotionally prepared can a nine-year-old girl be for her first period unless she has been counseled by a wise mother?

It is no longer sufficient to expect that Susie will learn all about it in time. The time is now, because the average age at which menstruation first occurs is gradually getting lower.

At what age do most girls start menstruating?

Some girls will start menstruating at the same age their mothers did. According to statistics, however, the trend in the last several decades has been toward an earlier and earlier menarche, primarily because of better nutrition and improved living conditions. One hundred years ago in the United States the average age for the start of menses was fourteen. Today it is twelve and a half, and by the year two thousand it may be closer to twelve.

But statistics do not take into account the fact that each girl operates according to her own biological timetable. Anywhere from nine to sixteen is within the normal range. And the first menstruation of some 5 percent of all girls will occur between the ages of sixteen and eighteen.

How about the girl who menstruates before the age of nine: is there something wrong?

Not necessarily. There are many instances of true precocious puberty. These girls for some unknown reason experience a premature activation of hypothalamic, pituitary, and ovarian functions. In other words, sexual maturation starts much younger—but in all respects, these girls are completely normal.

On rare occasion such girls may menstruate at four, ovulate at five, and make the headlines at six by having a baby. And if you think that's young, there have been documented cases of true precocious puberty occurring before the age of two.

Is very early "menstruation" always a sign of precocious puberty?

Unfortunately no. Early breast development and cyclic vaginal bleeding in a very young girl may actually be a sign of organic disease. The differentiation between premature-normal development and premature-abnormal development can be at times difficult to establish. This is especially true if the girl is fairly close to what might be considered a normal age for her first menses. One is less likely to suspect an endocrine problem in a girl of eight than in a five-year-old.

Suffice it to say that if any question or doubt exists about whether bleeding is normal, the child should be seen by a physician.

What about the late bloomer?

Nothing causes more furrowing of maternal brows than a teenage daughter who is obviously lagging behind her contemporaries. By fourteen her mother is convinced that menstruation should have started. She may even wonder whether there is something physically wrong with her daughter.

In such cases, professional reassurance can do much for both daughter and mother. A thorough examination by a sympathetic doctor will, in the majority of cases, show that the girl is developing normally, albeit at a slower rate. By fourteen or fifteen there should be breast development and other signs of estrogen stimulation. A pelvic examination would also be important to rule out the presence of congenital defects or maldevelopments. As discussed in Chapter 3, an imperforate hymen, for example, as well as more serious defects could be responsible for lack of menstruation (amenorrhea). If all is normal the girl should be rechecked in six months. If, at that time, she has still not menstruated, a progesterone withdrawal bleeding test would be in order.

What is a progesterone withdrawal bleeding test?

This is a very simple and practical test to determine whether the elements necessary for menstruation are present. In other words, does this girl have a functioning and intact pituitary gland? Does this girl have ovaries which are secreting estrogen? Does this girl have a uterus which is capable of responding to hormone stimulation? If the answer is yes to all these questions, then the administration of progesterone (either by a single injection or by pills taken by mouth over a period of five to ten days) should provoke uterine bleeding within a few days. Such a positive test is further assurance that spontaneous periods are just around the corner. Lack of uterine bleeding following progesterone would imply some disturbance in the pituitary, ovaries, or uterus. Should this be the case, more extensive evaluation would be necessary.

What other factors can delay the onset of menstruation?

Any number of things. Nutrition, for example, is one of the most important factors in normal development. Girls who suffered from chronic malnutrition in Europe during World War II showed dramatic sexual retardation. In this country, emotional problems, nervous disorders, and various chronic illnesses have all been influential in delaying the onset of menstruation.

**Is there any relationship between the age at which you first
menstruate and the subsequent onset of the menopause?**

No. Here again you may follow your mother's pattern, but more
and more women are going through the menopause later and later.
At the present time, the average age at which all menstruation ceases
is about fifty.

How often should you menstruate?

Although most women menstruate every twenty-five to thirty
days, anywhere from twenty-one to thirty-five days is considered
within normal limits. But whether you have a period every twenty-
one days or tend to have longer cycles, the time interval between
periods is not as important as the establishment of a predictable pattern. For most women this pattern is usually determined by the third
year after the onset of the first menses. Thus, any consistent departure
from your regular cycle length, particularly if it falls outside the normal twenty-one- to thirty-five-day interval, may indicate a menstrual
disorder.

How do you calculate the length of your menstrual cycle?

This may seem like a simple matter to many of you—but oh, what
confusion exists!

The length of your cycle is calculated from the first day of one
period up to but not including the first day of the following period. For
example, if your period starts October 1 and your next period begins
October 28, your cycle length is twenty-seven days. Day one of your
menstrual cycle is the first day you see even the barest trace of blood.
In other words, any spotting or staining that may immediately precede the real flow must be taken into account when calculating the
length of your menstrual cycle.

Is it ever normal to have two periods in one month?

It can be. For those of you averaging twenty-eight-day cycles, it
stands to reason that if your period began March 2, then your next
period should begin March 30: two periods in one month—perfectly
normal in this case.

How long should your period last?

Anywhere from three days to five days, but there are many
women who consistently flow as long as eight days, while others stop
completely after only two days. And even from one month to the next
it can be normal for the length of your period to fluctuate slightly.

How much blood is actually lost?

Much less than you probably think. In one study, college women earned part of their tuition by assiduously salvaging every drop of menstrual blood over several months. After each period they submitted all of their used tampons and napkins to a gallant research team for chemical analysis of the iron content. The results? Most women lost between 50 and 175 cc. (approximately one-quarter to three-quarters of a cup) of blood per period and the average woman lost less than one-half cup. So if you are really convinced that your bleeding exceeds a cup per period, then maybe you had better schedule an appointment for a checkup. There can be many reasons for increased menstrual blood loss. (More about that later.)

Why are some periods heavier than others?

Contrary to what some women believe, the uterine cavity does not "store up" blood between periods. How much you do bleed, aside from such factors as emotional influences or organic disorders, is in part determined by the amount of endometrial tissue to be shed. As a general rule, the thicker the endometrial tissue, the heavier and longer the menstrual blood flow. Thus, just as the length of your cycle can occasionally vary, so too can the amount of bleeding. At the other extreme, women on birth control pills may experience very scanty periods. With this medication, the endometrial lining tends to be considerably thinner.

Why doesn't menstrual blood clot?

Because it has already clotted in the endometrial cavity, and the same blood can clot only once. However, before that clotted blood can pass through the cervical canal and into the vagina, certain enzymes within the uterine cavity dissolve the clots and reliquefy the blood. Therefore the blood that flows into the vagina and onto your tampon or napkin is in reality serum, the reliquefied portion of blood that can no longer clot.

Why, then, do you sometimes pass clots?

This is one of the areas currently under clinical and laboratory investigation. Part of the explanation may have to do with the amount of bleeding. The heavier the flow, the greater your chances of passing clots. It is reasonable to assume that if your flow is unusually profuse, some blood may escape so rapidly that it passes intact into the vagina where it can now clot. In other words, this blood does not linger in the uterine cavity long enough to go through the slower process of clotting and then being reliquefied.

The passage of clots therefore is not necessarily abnormal. Some of you may have experienced a sudden warm gush of blood and clots. Others may pass the biggest clots after a sudden change of position. This phenomenon can readily occur if you have been lying down and then suddenly stand. As you were lying down, the blood that failed to clot in the endometrial cavity subsequently pooled and clotted in the upper vagina. So what happens? You stand up—and out comes the clot!

What does the menstrual flow consist of?

Primarily a mixture of blood, degenerated cells, and mucus. The blood that you actually pass (with the exception of a few clots) is almost entirely serum. The degenerated cells are fragments of the sloughed (shed) lining of the endometrial cavity, and the mucus (the sticky stuff) is an outpouring from the glands of the cervical canal.

What causes the characteristic menstrual odor?

If you were able to reach inside the uterine cavity and remove the menstrual debris before it trickled down into the vagina, there would be no odor. That characteristic menstrual odor is caused by the action of normal vaginal bacteria on the blood elements. Therefore, regardless of how fastidious a woman is in her personal hygiene, it is impossible to eliminate this odor completely; at best it can only be minimized.

Just because your period comes every month, does that mean that you are ovulating?

Not necessarily. Even if you are perfectly normal it is not uncommon to have an anovulatory, or a no-egg, cycle. Your period may still come at the expected time, and yet you may not have ovulated. How often this happens is difficult to say, but once or even twice a year is not outside the realm of normality.

Are some women prone to anovulatory (no-egg) cycles?

Very definitely. In fact, anovulatory cycles are very common among young girls just starting to menstruate and among older women beginning the menopausal years. At one extreme the immaturity of both the ovary and the brain centers controlling ovarian function is responsible for the lack of ovulation. In older women the gradual waning of ovarian function results in the ovary's inability to eject an egg on a monthly schedule. In both instances the mechanisms are in a sense protective.

How is that?

Anovulatory cycles in a young girl protect her from conceiving until her body and bone structure are sufficiently mature to handle a pregnancy. The fact that anovulatory cycles are common in early adolescence has been documented by studies among ethnic groups where marriage at the time of puberty is a tribal custom. Rarely will these child brides conceive for at least two to three years despite extensive sexual activity. Fortunately for them, ovulation is initially sporadic. Thus, they are spared (and that goes for their midwives too) the hazards and complications commonly encountered in early adolescent pregnancies.

On the other hand, if you are approaching the menopause—how many of you in your late forties or early fifties would welcome a pregnancy? This does not mean, of course, that you cannot get pregnant, but your chances are considerably lessened.

Does ovulation ever cause abdominal pain?

Seldom. Although a few women will insist that they can pinpoint the exact moment of ovulation by the sudden onset of lower abdominal pain at midcycle, the majority of women are completely unaware of any physical sensation. Furthermore, any reliance placed on this pain phenomenon either as proof of ovulation or as a signal to abstain from intercourse for birth control demands a word of caution.

Pain arising from an ovary can easily be confused with pain from other abdominal organs and vice versa. Bowel spasms, for example, can readily mimic ovulatory pain. You can appreciate, therefore, how common practices such as overindulging in goodies or eating incompatible foods can easily confuse the issue. The pain you may interpret as ovulation might in reality be due to gas.

Is it ever possible to bleed at the time of ovulation?

Yes. Associated spotting or bleeding lasting anywhere from a few hours to two or three days may occur, but the presence of ovulatory bleeding is less common than ovulatory pain. The term *Mittelschmerz* (middle pain) has been used to describe this midcycle ovulatory pain with or without uterine bleeding.

Why does ovulation sometimes cause uterine bleeding?

At the time of ovulation, when the mature follicle ruptures and releases its contained egg, the ruptured follicle can literally be so shaken up that its estrogen output temporarily decreases. As you may recall from Chapter 6, the integrity of the endometrium (lining of the uterus) depends on the maintenance of a certain estrogen level: therefore, the temporary drop in estrogen may be sufficient to cause shedding of some endometrial cells with resultant bleeding in between regular periods.

It should be stressed that uterine bleeding during ovulation is relatively uncommon. Any and all bleeding between periods should be properly evaluated by your doctor.

How can you tell if you are really ovulating?

Short of becoming pregnant, there are more subtle ways you yourself can determine this event: by observing changes in the cervical mucus and by keeping a Basal Body Temperature Chart (BBT). Although these methods are not infallible, they can be useful in family planning. In fact one of the most popular methods of natural birth control is based on cervical mucus evaluation. (See Chapter 18.)

What about the Basal Body Temperature chart?

The only equipment needed is a thermometer, a pencil, a piece of paper, and perseverance. If you can read a thermometer and are faithful in recording your temperature every morning before getting out of bed, you will have indirect proof of whether or not you are ovulating. It is very important, however, that you take your temperature immediately upon awakening. No getting out of bed for a fast trip to the bathroom. No smoking, eating, drinking, talking, or brushing of teeth allowed. The term "basal body temperature" refers to the temperature of the body at complete rest.

What does your temperature have to do with ovulation?

At the time of ovulation there is a small but definite elevation of your basal body temperature. As you may recall, the ovum is launched from the mature follicle; the remnants of that follicle (corpus luteum) then begin producing a second hormone, progesterone, which in turn further prepares the uterine tissue bed to receive the fertilized egg. (See Chapter 6.) The hormone progesterone is responsible for the rise in basal body temperature, which is subsequently sustained until

shortly before the onset of menstruation. In other words, unless ovulation occurs there can be no production of progesterone, and hence no
elevation in basal body temperature. Although the rise in temperature
averages only 0.4 to 1.0 degrees Fahrenheit, it is nonetheless significant.

Under ordinary conditions your normal body temperature, taken
orally, is usually 98.6 degrees Fahrenheit. During sleep, however, your
temperature dips as a result of decreased muscular and metabolic
activity. How low it dips can depend upon both the length and the
depth of sleep. Not uncommonly, your basal body temperature may
register as low as 97.2. With subsequent activity as you wake up, it will
quickly return to its usual 98.6.

How exactly do you keep a Basal Body Temperature (BBT) chart?

If you do not have any graph paper, just take a sheet of ordinary
paper and number from one to thirty-five across the top of the page,
leaving a small margin above the numbers. These numbers represent
the days of your cycle. If your period comes every twenty-eight days,
then you will use only twenty-eight numbers. If your periods are
further apart than thirty-five days, make room for the additional days
needed.

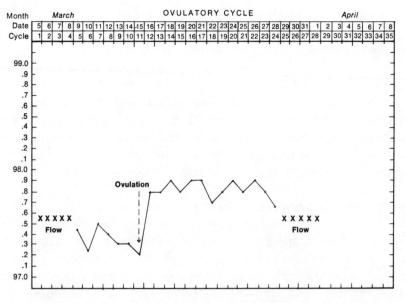

Fig. 1. Basal body temperature chart
Notice the drop and sharp rise in temperature at the time of ovulation.

On the left-hand side of the paper, starting at the top, write the degrees of temperature ranging from 99.0 down to 97.0. Make the first number appearing at the top left 99.0. Immediately below it write the number 98.9. Record the other numbers in the same manner, reducing each figure by 0.1 degree. In other words, directly below 98.9 would be 98.8, 98.7, 98.6, 98.5, and so on, all the way down to 97.0. (See Fig. 1.)

To avoid eye strain, as well as to ensure that you record each day's temperature in the right place, divide the paper in squares. Opposite each temperature figure draw a line across the paper. From the top of the paper to the bottom, draw a line separating each day of the cycle. You are now ready to start your chart—or almost.

What comes next?

Now you have to wait for your period to start. Day one is the first day of your menstrual flow. Above number one on your chart write down the date that your period begins. Above each subsequent day of your cycle write down the corresponding date.

It is not necessary to record your temperature during the menstrual flow, but it is important to begin *immediately* thereafter. For purposes of keeping a complete record, put an X under each day of your period.

As soon as your period is over, start your temperature record the next morning. Be sure to shake down the thermometer the night before and place it by your bedside. If you are taking your temperature orally, place the thermometer under your tongue for at least five and preferably six minutes—and keep your mouth closed.

For those of you who have trouble focusing in the early morning, you can purchase a special thermometer with big numbers just for this purpose. Most drugstores carry them. Otherwise, you can postpone reading your thermometer until later in the day. (Note: If left undisturbed, your thermometer will still register your temperature taken in the morning.)

Once your temperature is registered, locate that figure in the left-hand side of your chart, follow it across until it corresponds with the proper date above, and make an appropriate notation. A little dot will do. When your chart for one cycle is complete, draw a line connecting each of the dots.

It is equally important that you record your temperature for at least two consecutive cycles and preferably three.

What's wrong with keeping a BBT chart for just one month?

It is apt to be misleading. You may, for example, just hit the one cycle wherein you failed to ovulate. Then too, how many times have you felt a cold or sore throat coming on? Any slight infection, by elevating your temperature, will completely invalidate your basal body temperature for that month.

When are you most likely to ovulate?

That depends on the length of your cycle. Ovulation usually occurs fourteen days (plus or minus two days) before your next anticipated period. If you are running a twenty-eight-day cycle, then your most fertile time, the moment of ovulation, will occur around midcycle or just fourteen days before your next period. If you menstruate every twenty-five days, you are more apt to ovulate around the eleventh day of your cycle, or fourteen days prior to your next period. Similarly, if your periods come every thirty-five days, you may ovulate around day twenty-one, again fourteen days prior to your next period. As you can see, the time interval prior to ovulation (although there are many exceptions) tends to be the most variable portion of your menstrual cycle. Once ovulation has occurred, the subsequent menses will usually follow two weeks later.

For practical purposes, however, ovulation can occur either two days earlier or two days later than that fourteen-day time limit. For the woman who consistently runs twenty-eight-day cycles, ovulation can occur anywhere from day twelve to day sixteen. But even that can vary. (See Chapter 18.)

Is it important to keep a BBT chart?

Only if you are really interested in knowing whether or not you are ovulating. In fact, whenever a doctor is confronted with a woman who has failed to conceive, he will almost invariably request that she keep such a record for at least three months.

For those of you eager to avoid pregnancy, it might be advantageous to know whether you are ovulating—and if so, when. This application of the BBT chart is, however, more limited. In Chapter 18 you will find out why.

How can you tell by your BBT chart whether you are ovulating?

During the first few days following your period, you will notice that under normal circumstances your temperature is fairly stable, not varying more than 0.2 degree in most cases. At the time of ovulation, your temperature will drop to a point lower than the one recorded on the previous day. Following that low reading, there will be a steep rise in temperature the very next morning. If the difference between the low and the high reading in temperature on these two successive days registers between 0.4 and 1.0 degree, this would indicate that ovulation may have occurred. At other times this temperature rise, rather than occurring abruptly over a twenty-four hour period, will progress in a stair-step fashion over a span of three to four days. Additional evidence of ovulation would require that the temperature elevation be sustained (within the 0.2 degree of the high reading) until two or three days prior to your next period. At this time, as a result of a decrease in progesterone output, your temperature would return to preovulatory levels.

How about if you do not ovulate?

Without ovulation there is no corpus luteum (see Chapter 6) to produce progesterone, and without progesterone there is no change in basal body temperature. Your chart would therefore fail to show that characteristic temperature elevation associated with ovulation. For purposes of comparison between an ovulatory and no-egg (anovulatory) cycle, Figs. 1 and 2 may be helpful.

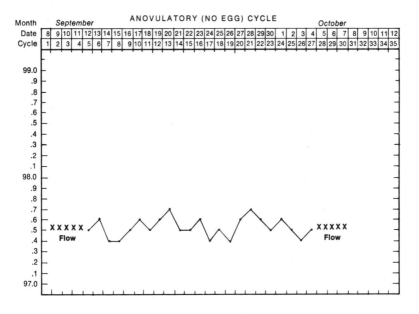

Fig. 2. Basal body temperature chart
Notice the flat curve.

What happens if the temperature does not return to preovulatory levels?

You might be pregnant. In fact, a sustained temperature level after ovulation which continues beyond the time when you would expect your period is probably one of the earliest methods of detecting a possible pregnancy. Remember, if the egg does get fertilized, the corpus luteum continues to pour forth estrogen and progesterone. And where there is progesterone, there is heat. (See Fig. 3.)

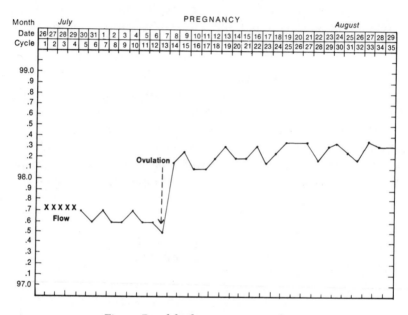

Fig. 3. Basal body temperature chart
Persistent elevation of temperature and no menstrual period
suggest pregnancy.

Can you ovulate more than one egg at a time?

Very definitely. All fraternal twins (nonidentical) are living proof that this does occur. They are the product of two separate eggs fertilized by two separate sperm. This double ovulation can occur either from one ovary or from both ovaries (one egg from each ovary). In either case, the tendency toward double ovulation seems to be an inherited trait.

On the other hand, identical twins seem to occur by chance only. They are the product of a single egg fertilized by a single sperm. The fertilized egg, after certain modifications, splits into two equal parts.

If two eggs can be released at about the same time, is it ever possible to have these eggs fertilized by two separate acts of intercourse?

Yes. But the only way to verify this phenomenon would be for a woman of one race to have intercourse (in fairly rapid succession) with two men of two other races—in short, three individuals of three different races. In addition, this woman would then have to give birth to fraternal twins, each twin showing the racial characteristics of its own father. Surprisingly enough, there have been documented cases of such twins! But they are mighty rare.

Can more than two or three eggs be released at any one time?

Yes, but more about that in the section on fertility drugs (Chapter 16).

How long does the average egg survive?

Within twenty-four hours most eggs will degenerate completely unless fertilized. However, the first twelve hours following ovulation are the most critical. If fertilization does not occur within this time span, the chances for proper impregnation and the subsequent development of a normal pregnancy are diminished. This may be another factor responsible for early spontaneous abortions—some eggs are just too old to make the grade.

Do the ovaries take turns making eggs?

According to studies on our friend the rhesus monkey, ovulation does seem to alternate on a monthly basis between the two ovaries. However, this ping-pong effect is by no means constant or absolute.

Women who have had one ovary surgically removed will usually continue to ovulate on a monthly basis provided that the remaining ovary is normal. In other words, losing one ovary will not necessarily make you any less fertile. Some women have even become pregnant with only a portion of one ovary remaining. In later chapters we'll see how ovarian transplants as well as donor-egg implants can bring the hope of pregnancy to women without ovaries.

PART II

The Unpredictability of Woman

8. Monthly Misadventure— Premenstrual Tension

Does your personality change for the worse seven to ten days before your period comes? Do you become tense, irritable, and nervous? Can you suddenly explode over the least irritation and then, in the next moment, dissolve into uncontrollable weeping? Or do you become sullen, withdrawn, and morose, defying anyone to make you smile? Then perhaps you are a victim of premenstrual tension.

The extent to which each woman reacts during this phase of her cycle depends in part upon her basic personality. For the average woman, these emotional upheavals tend to remain mild and well under control most of the time. But a few women have premenstrual tension of such serious proportions that they can be blasted right out of orbit.

How far out of orbit?

In extreme cases, way out. In court records, acts of aggression and hostility during the premenstrual phase abound. Four out of five major crimes committed by women in this country are perpetrated during that time. The very disturbed woman who directs her hostility inward stands a greater risk of committing suicide or having a fatal accident premenstrually than at any other time in her cycle.

Fortunately, such severely afflicted women are in the minority. Most women compensate remarkably well. However, even a stable, well-adjusted woman may on occasion suffer symptoms related to premenstrual tension.

What kind of symptoms?

That heavy, bloated, puffy feeling for one thing. And just about any part of your anatomy can be affected. In fact, during the week prior to menstruation, some women may carry as much as three to five pounds of extra fluid, and in extreme cases may tip the scales ten pounds heavier. Don't be too surprised, therefore, if you can't squeeze into your shoes or if your breasts feel as if they have been treated with silicone.

Extra fluid can also cause your stomach to stick out and your waist to expand overnight. Until fairly recently this premenstrual abdominal bloating was believed to be caused by gas, but studies have shown that the walls of the intestine temporarily store excess fluid and actually become waterlogged. Furthermore, there is also a shift of fluid from the bowel passageway to the walls of the intestine. As a result your stools may become somewhat harder. Thus, constipation can be another strain during the premenstrual phase. Fortunately this shift of fluid is only temporary, so don't reach too quickly for your favorite laxative. As soon as your period gets under way and the body fluid readjusts itself, you are likely to have the reverse situation for a day or two—loose bowel movements. That too can be normal.

So where does all this extra water come from?

Blame it on your hormones. Part of the explanation may have to do with estrogen. In addition to all those glorious effects on your body, estrogen also influences another physiological function—salt and water exchange. The more estrogen in your system, the less salt (sodium) and water pass through the kidneys. Thus, the higher the estrogen level the greater will be the salt and water retention. Therefore, just after ovulation, when the estrogen level is high, the kidneys will filter less water. Result? You will pass less urine. Consequently the water that bypassed the kidneys is redistributed back into your tissues.

What other symptoms can fluid retention cause?

Headaches, terrible pounding headaches that would be a challenge for any aspirin commercial on television. Only in this case, even aspirin with or without those extra ingredients would probably not help much. Surprisingly enough, the culprit responsible for true premenstrual headaches may well be water retention within the brain tissues. In fact, many of those emotional upheavals—irritability, nervous tension, insomnia, depression, and so on—have been attributed to "water on the brain." And you thought you were just hard to get along with.

How long can these symptoms sometimes last?

Until the estrogen level dips to its lowest point just prior to the onset of menstruation. When this happens, there is a subsequent decrease in salt and water retention. Consequently, you will pass more urine, and as your body rids itself of excess fluids, all those unpleasant premenstrual symptoms (bloating, constipation, headaches, and so on) will disappear.

Can all these premenstrual symptoms be blamed on estrogen and fluid retention?

To a certain extent, but there are still many unanswered questions. Even though estrogen can cause fluid retention, some investigators feel that the real basis for premenstrual tension is a hormonal imbalance, possibly too much estrogen and too little progesterone. There is even clinical evidence that certain women may be allergic to their own hormones—particularly progesterone. Such bizarre symptoms as giant hives, nasal congestion, and painful mouth sores experienced premenstrually by some women can certainly make one wonder.

Are there other theories to explain premenstrual tension?

The very latest theory revolves around the role of aldosterone, a salt-retaining hormone produced by the adrenal glands. Studies show that the blood level of this hormone undergoes cyclic changes; it rises at the time of ovulation and peaks just prior to menstruation. Moreover, an excess output of aldosterone can provoke all the premenstrual symptoms of fluid retention.

But regardless of what causes premenstrual tension, this phenomenon rarely occurs in the absence of ovulation. Women on birth control pills, for example, do not experience true premenstrual tension. They may be bothered with minor bloating or weight gain, but their symptoms tend to be mild and without cyclic regularity.

Can premenstrual fluid retention affect your sex drive?

Given the right partner, the proper setting, and the inclination, any woman can be sexually aroused regardless of what her ovaries are doing. For some women, however, there may be an increased sex drive during the week prior to menstruation. Some authorities relate the greater need for orgasmic release to a heightened physical awareness of the clitoris and labia minora as a result of premenstrual fluid retention within these tissues. But whether an increase in sex drive at this time is solely attributable to fluid retention is a debatable point.

Not uncommonly, these same women may be the ones who experience sudden surges of energy prior to menstruation. Windows get washed, furniture gets rearranged, and household projects abandoned the week before are completed in a flurry of activity. And in addition to doing all that plus playing a smashing set of tennis, presiding over the board meeting, and rewiring the stereo amplifier, they may still be eager for sex.

How about the woman who complains of being excessively tired?

Contrary to those old television commercials, all women do not drag around because of iron-poor blood. That listless, knocked-out, shaky feeling may well be related to premenstrual changes in carbohydrate metabolism, and more specifically to a lower blood sugar level. So if you find yourself irresistibly drawn to a candy bar or making tracks for the nearest bakery, that craving for sweets may actually be a physiological need to raise your blood sugar level.

Do all women suffer from premenstrual tension?

Of course not, but if you ovulate regularly and are between the ages of twenty and forty-five, you may be a candidate.

No one can predict how you as an individual woman will be affected during your premenstrual phase. On-the-job efficiency studies have shown that women during the premenstrual phase do function just as effectively as during any other time of their cycle. Tests measuring mental ability, muscular coordination, strength, and speed show that these activities are essentially unchanged when compared to previously established performance levels.

Needless to say, however, if you are among the 15 percent of women who really suffer, the time has come to seek relief. Gone are the days of putting up with unnecessary discomfort (not to mention making everyone else miserable) just because you think it is part of being a woman. Although your grandmother probably received a condescending pat on the shoulder from her doctor and was told, "Learn to live with it," the chances are that your own physician will be more attuned to your premenstrual blues.

So what can be done about it?

Even though some investigators deny the importance of water retention as a cause of premenstrual tension, many women do experience relief by eliminating some of that excess tissue fluid.

For those of you with only minor discomfort, the simple expedient of restricting your salt intake seven to ten days before your period can work a small miracle.

What does salt have to do with water retention?

Salt (sodium) plays an important role in proper water balance. Whenever you consume more salt than you need or excrete less salt than usual, your body responds by mobilizing the necessary fluid to dilute the excess salt in your system. To get an idea of how this works, think of what would happen if you drank only sea water. Your body, in an attempt to handle the excess salt, would respond by conserving fluid ordinarily lost through such channels as urine, feces, perspiration, saliva, etc. Result? With all that extra fluid ordinarily excreted now being retained and poured back to neutralize those salt-laden tissues, you would blow up like a balloon in short order.

To a much lesser extent, the same mechanisms operate when you excrete less sodium during the premenstrual phase of your cycle. If you remember, estrogen causes a decrease in the amount of sodium filtered through the kidneys. Therefore, during your premenstrual phase your body must handle more salt and water because of the estrogen effect. Reducing your own salt intake would certainly help that waterlogged feeling. But hiding the salt shaker is not enough. You must also be aware of what foods are normally high in sodium.

Like what for instance?

Such common items on your shopping list as ham, bacon, sausages, prepared lunch meats, including bologna, salami, and hot dogs, are particularly high in sodium. The same goes for baking soda, various food seasonings containing monosodium glutamate, packaged or canned soups, most salad dressings, sandwich spreads, and all those delectable goodies that in general crackle and crunch—potato chips, corn chips, pretzels, and nuts of all varieties. Cheeses too, with the possible exception of cottage cheese, are another big source of sodium. And oh, Mexican cuisine and Chinese cooking with a dash of soy sauce —delicious—but not for you, especially if you collect water like a rain barrel.

In addition to subsisting on low-salt meals that would ruin many a woman's reputation as a cook, the use of diuretics (water pills) may also be indicated.

What about water pills?

Although there are any number of diuretics your physician may prescribe for your particular fluid problem, two of the most common water pills used in the treatment of premenstrual tension belong to the thiazide group. These preparations are not only effective in flushing away excess fluid, but are also sufficiently mild so that side effects are seldom a problem.

However, you should follow the instructions of your doctor. One tablet or half a tablet per day taken in the morning for seven to ten days prior to your period is usually sufficient to give relief. In addition you will probably be instructed to take each tablet either with a glass of orange juice or a banana.

Why the fruit?

Not just any fruit, but specifically oranges, figs, or bananas that are naturally rich in potassium, one of the body's most important chemical elements. With increased salt and water loss as a direct result of the water pill, there may also be an increased excretion of potassium in the urine. And excessive loss of potassium could lead to muscle weakness, intestinal distention, constipation, and so on, just what you don't need. With the ordinary dosage schedule you would probably be following, this potassium loss is fortunately minimal. But women who require larger doses or more prolonged diuretic therapy (for conditions other than premenstrual fluid retention) may need a potassium supplement.

Will taking diuretics improve your premenstrual disposition?

Maybe—particularly if diuretics can help eliminate puffy eyelids, tight skin, a bloated stomach, and swollen hands, feet, and ankles. Diuretics can also help flush away some of that extra "water on the brain." This in itself can make you easier to get along with by decreasing some of your nervous tension and anxiety. But women whose main premenstrual problem is emotional instability find that diuretics are rarely the whole answer.

Are tranquilizers ever helpful?

A few women may need a mild tranquilizer to relieve some of the irritability and tension. Unlike a diuretic, which is usually taken only once a day, tranquilizers may be prescribed more frequently depending on the particular drug used and the severity of the symptoms. Here again, the medication would be started a week to ten days before the anticipated period.

Needless to say, tolerance for any tranquilizer varies from woman to woman. What would be just the right dose for one woman might make another feel like a zombie. Therefore, don't hesitate to decrease the dose prescribed if you feel overly sedated. But make it a point to inform your doctor.

A word of caution: tranquilizers, alcohol, sedatives (barbiturates), and pain killers such as codeine and Darvon are all central nervous system depressants. The cumulative effect of any two or three of these taken together could be potentially hazardous, if not fatal.

What besides tranquilizers can help?

On the theory that premenstrual tension may be caused by elevated levels of aldosterone (as previously discussed), one of the newer approaches to therapy is the use of the prescription drug Aldactone (spironolactone). This drug specifically antagonizes the effects of aldosterone. It increases sodium and water excretion while at the same time helping retain potassium. When taken as directed (usually 25 mg. four times a day for ten days before menstruation), the net result is relief from that water-logged feeling. Some experts consider it much more effective than other diuretics in alleviating the symptoms of premenstrual fluid retention.

Another therapeutic approach which is gaining support is the use of vitamins, particularly vitamin B_6.

What does vitamin B_6 do?

Vitamin B_6 or pyridoxine can help overcome premenstrual depression. Part of the explanation has to do with serotonin blood levels in the brain. Through various complicated biochemical pathways, elevated levels of estrogen indirectly deplete vitamin B_6. This in turn causes a reduction in brain serotonin blood levels which apparently triggers the symptoms of depression and insomnia. Although the Recommended Daily Allowance (RDA) of B_6 is 2 mg. per day, relief from this type of depression usually requires 20 to 50 mg. of B_6 taken twice daily for ten days before the period. Women on birth control pills (with relatively high estrogen levels) should probably increase their intake of B_6 for the very same reason. Foods that are rich in this vitamin include bananas, raw vegetables, liver, white chicken meat, walnuts, peanuts, sunflower seeds, and wheat germ.

**Suppose none of the above, including vitamin B$_6$, help—
then what?**

There is still hope. Hormone therapy may be the answer. As mentioned earlier, true premenstrual tension does not usually occur in the absence of ovulation. Since some authorities still believe that premenstrual tension is a result of the subnormal production of progesterone following ovulation, therapy is aimed at supplementing that sagging progesterone output with pure natural progesterone or with a synthetic progestin.

In the event that progesterone alone fails to bring the desired relief, complete suppression of ovulation by the appropriate combination of an estrogen-progestin may be the ultimate answer to premenstrual tension.

9. Periodic Overload—
More Menstrual Miseries and All About Cramps

If you have been blissfully spared from premenstrual tension, there may be other problems just prior to and during your period.

What problems?

Black-and-blues that seem to come from nowhere. Have you ever discovered an unsightly bruise on your leg or arm without any recollection of having tripped over the coffee table? That spontaneous bruising may be related to a decreased estrogen level just prior to menstruation.

What does a drop in estrogen have to do with bruises?

Ordinarily any blow severe enough to rupture capillary walls and allow blood to escape into the surrounding tissue will result in a bruise. Estrogen, in its own unique way, increases the strength and resilience of capillary walls so that a normal decrease of this hormone around the time of your period makes those delicate blood vessels more vulnerable. In a few women lower estrogen levels have even been implicated in those unusual instances of bleeding from the nose, rectum, or bladder during menstruation. A much more common complaint, however, is the annoying recurrence of premenstrual complexion problems.

Can a drop in estrogen also cause skin blemishes?

Teenagers aren't the only ones plagued with complexion problems. Prior to menstruation there is a normal increase in sebaceous, or oil, gland activity partially kept in check by estrogen. In women with oily skin especially, excessive production of sebum (oil) together with a cyclic drop in estrogen output can result in recurrent small outbreaks of premenstrual pimples.

What can be done about such pimples?

Aside from local cleansing and diet restrictions which usually don't help, more severe complexion problems are occasionally treated by suppressing sebaceous gland activity with estrogen. To be effective, this treatment usually requires high doses of estrogen, sufficient in many instances to inhibit ovulation. For this reason birth control pills are sometimes prescribed in selected cases. In other cases, decreasing the skin bacterial count by small daily doses of the antibiotic tetracycline or similar medication is sometimes equally effective in eliminating the pimple problem. Fortunately for all concerned, there is a new treatment for acne which is unparalleled in effectiveness, safety, and convenience. It is a synthetic derivative of vitamin A and should be released by the FDA within the next several months.

But let's switch gears and see how changing hormone levels can create other problems, namely dysmenorrhea.

What is dysmenorrhea?

Painful and difficult menstruation. Although some doctors dismiss painful periods as a normal physiological event or worse yet as a psychosomatic condition, dysmenorrhea is one of the most common gynecological complaints among teenagers and young women. When cramps occur in the absence of any organic disease or pelvic problem (as is the usual case in women under twenty-five), the condition is called *primary dysmenorrhea.* And, nausea, vomiting, diarrhea, and headaches can be superimposed physical distress. Yet, as incapacitating as severe dysmenorrhea can sometimes be, menstruating women are not the only victims.

Who else suffers from the cramps?

Employers. In this country alone over 20 million work hours are lost each year because of the cramps. Typewriters stand idle, drawing boards are deserted, manuscripts to be edited accumulate, and unpunched time cards gather dust.

In high school and college classes 10 percent of all female students are conspicuously absent from one to three days every month. Many of these girls may have already tried over-the-counter drugstore remedies with little success. For others, prior consultation with a physician may have been less than satisfactory.

Why unsatisfactory?

Women's menstrual cramps are not always given full consideration. Therapy is limited to aspirin, and if that proves unsuccessful the usual advice, "Wait until you have a baby," frequently serves as a substitute for proper evaluation and treatment.

Radical approaches in cases of severe dysmenorrhea are fortunately rare, but they do occur, as indicated by the following comment submitted by a reader and which appeared in a doctor's column in a West Coast newspaper. "When I try to talk to my family physician about it, his only answer is hysterectomy. At the age of nineteen, this seems to be a pretty drastic step."

While a hysterectomy would permanently cure this girl of her dysmenorrhea, the solution would be similar to treating a recurrent ache of the big toe by an above-the-knee amputation.

At the other extreme from those who would propose drastic surgical measures, we find a handful of psychiatrists who are equally radical in their own way. For them the universal solution to severe cramps is psychiatric help. Since most of these experts have never experienced the cramps, as far as they are concerned the majority of girls suffering from severe dysmenorrhea are undoubtedly maladjusted and neurotic. In short, these physicians feel that dysmenorrhea is all in a woman's head.

Are those cramps all in your head?

Some may be, but most menstrual cramps are located much further down. In fact a good case of dysmenorrhea installs itself in the middle of the lower abdomen and is frequently accompanied by a heavy aching sensation in the vulva, lower back, and down both legs. To quote one sufferer, "it feels like the uterus is being squeezed by a giant fist." Some of you may even notice that with a particularly severe cramp there is the distinct sensation that something has been discharged from the uterus. A sustained spasm of the uterine muscles can also aggravate existing pain by damming up menstrual debris within the uterine cavity.

Can using tampons aggravate cramps by blocking menstrual flow from the uterus?

Even if you should use two tampons (side by side for heavy flow), it is most improbable that they could block the cervical opening. Therefore, the use of tampons should not increase menstrual cramping by damming up drainage from the uterus.

When do the cramps usually start and how long can they last?

Menstrual cramps can start anytime around your period—either before or during the flow. Dysmenorrhea may even precede menstruation by two days, and although the cramps can persist for another three to four days, the most severe pain rarely lasts longer than four to twelve hours.

At times this pain can be of such intensity that nothing short of an examination by a physician can differentiate between severe dysmenorrhea and a serious abdominal problem. In such a case and especially if the girl is vomiting, she may well be whisked to a hospital emergency room in the middle of the night by distraught parents.

What causes menstrual cramps?

Nobody knows for sure but there is mounting evidence that dysmenorrhea may be triggered by prostaglandins, which stimulate uterine contractions. Prostaglandins are various hormonelike substances chemically classified as fatty acid derivatives and are normally present in many body tissues. To date, of the fourteen or more different prostaglandins known to occur in the human body, two in particular (prostaglandin E_2 and F_{2a}) have been found in both endometrial cells and menstrual fluid. These particular prostaglandins are apparently synthesized by the endometrial (uterine lining) cells and then released in large amounts during menstruation. And the higher the concentration of prostaglandins at the time of menstruation, the more intense, forceful, and frequent the uterine contractions. Furthermore, vigorous and prolonged uterine contractions can temporarily cut off the blood supply to the uterus by constricting and squeezing shut tiny arteries within the muscle. The resulting ischemia (decreased blood flow to the area) is probably what really causes the pain. If, however, the formation of these prostaglandins is inhibited or their levels decreased, dysmenorrhea can be relieved and even prevented. This is the rationale for the current use of antiprostaglandins in the treatment of menstrual cramps. More about this shortly.

What else can play a role in menstrual cramps?

Without ovulation and the subsequent formation of a lush thick secretory endometrium prior to menstruation, dysmenorrhea rarely occurs. The explanation in this case is again related to the formation of prostaglandins. As a general rule, the thicker the uterine lining and the heavier the menstrual flow, the greater the production of prostaglandins. Thus, women who ovulate regularly are more prone to dysmenorrhea. In contrast, women with scanty periods and relatively little endometrial tissue to shed may have little or no pain because of low prostaglandin production. This is why birth control pills are so effective in relieving dysmenorrhea—they drastically curtail prostaglandin synthesis by reducing the amount of endometrial tissue.

Why are initial periods in an adolescent girl usually painless?

Most probably lack of ovulation. With rare exception initial periods in a young girl are usually anovulatory (no egg or ovum released). Since ovulation is frequently associated with menstrual cramping, a girl can begin her periods at twelve and not experience cramps for perhaps one to two years—or until she ovulates on a regular basis.

Does absence of menstrual cramps mean that you did not ovulate?

Not necessarily. Periods can be painless even in women who ovulate monthly. The intermittent uterine contractions that normally occur during all menstrual bleeding may be so mild as to remain below the level of conscious awareness. Then too, some women definitely have higher pain thresholds.

What about the older woman whose periods become increasingly painful?

Painful periods after years of relative comfort, especially in women over twenty-five, are usually due to some organic disease or specific pelvic problem, for example, tubal infection, polyps, endometriosis, fibroids, adenomyosis, or even the presence an IUD. Since in these cases a specific cause for the cramps can be identified, the pain during menstruation is labeled as *secondary dysmenorrhea.*

Can your doctor always tell what is causing your cramps?

Despite the fact that dysmenorrhea in most young women is probably related to ovulation and increased prostaglandin production, an attempt should be made to exclude other possible causes. Here again there is no substitute for a detailed history and a thorough physical examination. Almost without exception the majority of young women who suffer from moderate or even severe cramps will have, upon examination, completely normal pelvic organs. This total lack of physical findings led old-time doctors to advance various theories to explain those awful cramps. Since some of these theories are still in circulation and may contain an element of truth, let's examine them briefly.

What were those theories about menstrual cramps?
One of the old favorites involved the so-called infantile uterus. In a few women the body of the uterus is somewhat small in relation to the size of the cervix. Doctors reasoned that such an underdeveloped uterus would probably have difficulty in expelling menstrual debris without cramping and significant pain. The theory, although reasonable, was largely discredited by the finding that women with an infantile uterus who suffered from cramps could be made comfortable by the suppression of ovulation.

Another popular concept put the blame on poor posture. Slouching teenage girls suffering from dysmenorrhea were instructed to throw back their shoulders, tuck in their hips, and flatten their tummy —a sure cure for the cramps. Those with more severe posture problems were fitted with shoulder straps; despite a possible improvement in general appearance, the cramps still won out.

But of all the theories, the most generally accepted explanation for cramps was the presence of a cervical stenosis, or a narrowing of the cervical canal. It was logical to assume that if the cervical canal were partially blocked, the uterus would respond by contracting harder in order to rid its cavity of menstrual debris and blood. Treatment was therefore directed toward relieving the obstruction. For years doctors assiduously dilated the cervical canal of dysmenorrheic girls. In the few bona fide cases of cervical stenosis, temporary relief was obtained.

Although cervical dilatation may still be necessary in the treatment of other conditions today, its use in relieving menstrual cramps has largely been supplanted by more effective therapy.

What can you do about relieving your menstrual cramps?
Giving birth to that first child can definitely relieve menstrual cramps, at least in some women. Why this should be is still speculative. Painless periods cannot be wholly attributed to the stretching and opening of the cervical canal during childbirth. Women who have had Caesarean sections without benefit of cervical dilatation can also simi-

larly experience cramp-free periods. The explanation of such pain relief may perhaps be related to permanent changes in the uterine blood supply as a result of pregnancy. A uterus that has supported a growing fetus probably has more blood vessels and a better vascular network than ever before. Thus, with more blood circulating through the uterine muscles, cramps are apt to be less painful.

Although that often repeated advice, "Wait until you have your first child," may be partly true, other home remedies short of pregnancy can give relief in not-too-severe cases of dysmenorrhea. Among the more popular do-it-yourself treatments are the following: heat, non-prescription analgesics, exercise routines, alcoholic beverages, and sex.

What about heat?

Ah, wonderful, soothing, relaxing, tension-releasing heat for the cramped pelvic and low back area and aching legs. Without a doubt heat is one of the oldest and most effective ways of decreasing pain. But whether you luxuriate in a warm tub or snuggle your lower abdomen against a toasty heating pad, thirty minutes at any one time will usually give you maximum benefit. Just make certain that the temperature is not too high. If you tend to fall asleep while using a heating pad, turn it to a medium setting. Prolonged exposure to heating pads at high temperatures can injure the skin. That temporary red-and-white splotchy look is a sure sign that you overdid it.

Since you can't take your bathtub or heating pad to work without being too conspicuous, most women need additional help.

What kind of help?

Non-prescription analgesics (pain killers) such as aspirin, APC, Bufferin, Excedrin, Vanquish, Cope, and so on. Although these compounds have been extensively advertised for other aches, pains, and tensions, they can also provide occasional relief from menstrual cramps. As far as dosage is concerned, follow the directions.

In order to gain the maximum benefit from any of these preparations, start the medication at the first twinge of discomfort. Pain is much easier to control if it is dealt with promptly. You will get faster relief and need less medication in the long run.

Other non-prescription drugs specifically marketed for menstrual cramps include Pamprin, Midol, Femicin, Easy-mens, and Trendar. Many of these compounds are primarily combinations of analgesics, diuretics, and caffeine with a few other things thrown in. For the woman who finds them effective, the additional cost may be worth it.

In any event, the same principle applies—take the medication promptly for maximum benefit.

How about the woman who has trouble swallowing pills?

Since this is not an uncommon problem, a small suggestion might be in order. For those of you who down three glasses of water in rapid succession and still find that pill or tablet obstinately clinging to the roof of your mouth or, worse yet, half dissolved and burning the back of your throat, there is a solution. Take the medication with food and everything will go down without a struggle. Apple sauce, a piece of banana, or soft bread will do. Put the food in your mouth and just before you are ready to swallow, slip the pill or capsule in, mix thoroughly, then swallow. It really works.

Can exercise help relieve menstrual cramps?

If you dislike taking medication and want to stay in shape, daily exercises may be the answer to your cramps. Among hundreds of dysmenorrheic teenagers who faithfully followed a prescribed exercise routine, almost 70 percent of them noted definite improvement in menstrual discomfort. If exercises are going to help, relief probably won't be noticed for at least three or four months. Just keep plugging away every day. Patience and perseverance may triumph in the end.

What are some of these exercises?

Although any daily exercise routine can minimize menstrual cramping, the following two exercises have proved effective in helping dysmenorrheic girls:

Exercise one. Stand with your feet together and the left side of your body eighteen to twenty-four inches away from the wall. Place your left forearm against the wall at shoulder height and your right hand against the hollow of your hip. Strongly contract the abdominal muscles and tighten the buttock muscles at the same time. If you do this properly your pelvis should be tilted forward—somewhat like doing the bumps. Keep those muscles contracted and move your pelvis sideways toward the wall. Hold this position for approximately three to four seconds and then relax. At no time should your heels leave the floor or your hips touch the wall. After doing this routine three times, change positions and repeat three times on the other side.

Exercise two. Standing with feet together, raise your arms out to the sides to shoulder height. Twist your trunk to one side and try to touch the outside of your left foot with your right hand. This should be repeated ten times on each side.

Remember, if you want results, these exercises should be done every day. Who knows, you may win a double bonus—no cramps and a better figure.

What about alcoholic beverages?

Liquor, taken either straight or mixed in a hot drink with boiling water, sugar, and lemon juice, stands high on the list of favorite home remedies for the cramps. The mechanism of pain relief, although not completely understood, may in part be due to the dilatation of pelvic blood vessels combined with an increased pain tolerance as a result of alcohol's numbing effect on the brain. Indeed, for many adult women, there is nothing quite so effective in relieving menstrual misery as two or three double shots of their favorite liquor followed by a nice warm tub bath.

Undoubtedly after that much therapy many of us would be ready for bed—if we could find it—but job and family responsibilities rarely allow us such abandon, especially on weekdays. Nevertheless, if the cramps should strike after hours and you are fresh out of your favorite anticramp medication, liquor may serve as a temporary soothing measure.

Can sex help those cramps?

Just plain sexual intercourse, no—but having an orgasm, yes. Since some of you may avoid intercourse during your period, automanipulation to the point of orgasm can be beneficial. In fact, many women say that orgasmic release can minimize menstrual cramping as well as associated low back or other pelvic discomfort.

Some of the relief obtained from cramping is again probably due to dilatation of pelvic blood vessels. However, you should be aware that following orgasm, there will usually be a temporary increase in the rate of menstrual flow, but the total amount of blood lost during your period will remain essentially the same. For those of you who prefer obtaining orgasmic relief with a partner, the use of a diaphragm during intercourse will help contain any excessive flow.

Suppose all those anticramp home remedies fail, then what?

If you've been through the heat and aspirin routine, have drunk yourself into a stupor, exercised for three months, and even masturbated—all for naught—the time has probably come for a gynecological consultation.

What can your gynecologist do for your cramps?

Besides offering a sympathetic ear, your gynecologist can also provide relief from those awful cramps. Any number of effective remedies are available, and one of them is bound to solve your problem.

Ideally, relief should be obtained with as little medication as possible. Although hormone therapy does alleviate pain in almost all cases of dysmenorrhea, 60 percent of women with moderately severe cramps can be made completely comfortable simply by the use of prescription analgesics. For this reason, many gynecologists initially prefer a therapeutic trial with non-hormonal drugs for two or three cycles.

What medications would initially be tried?

Pharmaceutical companies have not been lax in dealing with dysmenorrhea. Over a hundred prescription drugs variously listed as analgesics, antispasmodics, sedatives, tranquilizers, vasodilators, etc., are specifically listed as therapy for menstrual cramps. Among this vast array of medication, Daprisal and Edrisal were for many years two of the most effective preparations for dysmenorrhea until those medications were withdrawn from the market in 1972 because of their amphetamine content.

Other medications commonly prescribed for dysmenorrhea include Darvon, Darvon compound, and preparations containing codeine. However, the regular use of codeine even when combined with other ingredients has definite disadvantages.

What's wrong with taking codeine for menstrual cramps?

For some women it's like drinking three dry martinis on an empty stomach. Since the ideal treatment of your cramps should also allow you to stay mentally alert, codeine is rarely the answer. In spite of its ability to bring blessed relief from a variety of pains, some women find it surprisingly less effective in relieving cramps than other analgesics.

Because codeine is a narcotic, occasional dizziness and sedation (that heavy, drugged feeling) are common side effects. Narcotics also have a tendency to make you more sensitive to pain after their effect wears off. So without even mentioning possible gastrointestinal irritation or potential addiction, codeine for relief of recurring, severe dysmenorrhea leaves much to be desired.

Can anything else be done for the cramps?

Happily for all cramp sufferers, there has been a new therapeutic breakthrough in the past four years—the use of antiprostaglandins. As previously discussed, prostaglandins precipitate pain by causing uterine contractions. Well, antiprostaglandins interrupt this pain pathway by inhibiting the synthesis of prostaglandins and/or by blocking their action on uterine muscles.

What exactly are antiprostaglandins?

For the most part they are anti-inflammatory (non-steroidal) drugs used in the treatment of arthritis and related conditions. And included in this group are several analgesics, aspirin being the most notable. This may be one reason why aspirin can relieve moderate cramps, at least in some women.

As of this writing, Indocin (indomethacin) and Motrin (ibuprofen) are the antiprostaglandins most commonly used in the treatment of severe dysmenorrhea. They are taken by mouth and usually started one to two days before the anticipated period. According to various reports, pain relief has been dramatic in four out of five women so treated. In addition, nausea, vomiting, and diarrhea, which frequently accompany severe dysmenorrhea, are virtually eliminated. The explanation for the relief of these gastrointestinal symptoms may be the decreased production of other prostaglandins within the intestinal wall. Many women also report that subsequent periods require less medication. Side effects to date have been minor and tolerable. Headaches and mild mood changes occur in fewer than 10 percent of the women. Serious side effects such as peptic ulcer and anemia are exceedingly rare.

At the present time neither Motrin nor Indocin (although used to treat arthritis) has been approved by the FDA for the treatment of dysmenorrhea. This means that if your doctor does prescribe these drugs for your cramps, he or she needs your informed consent. Undoubtedly as more and more doctors report success with antiprostaglandins, their use in dysmenorrhea will finally be sanctioned by the powers that be.

What about the use of hormones?

If all else has failed including antiprostaglandins, proper hormone therapy can undoubtedly relieve even your cramps. At the moment, hormone therapy and specifically birth control pills are probably still the mainstay of therapy in severe and incapacitating dysmenorrhea.

For the woman also in need of contraceptive protection, the pill is the ideal solution. Ovulation is suppressed, pregnancy prevented, and the periods gloriously painless.

If, however, the pill is not for you, there is another form of hormone therapy—dydrogesterone.

What is dydrogesterone?

This is a synthetic steroid marketed under the trade names Duphaston and Gynorest and closely related to the naturally occurring hormone progesterone. Unlike birth control pills, it does not contain any estrogen nor does it suppress ovulation. Unfortunately it is also less effective in relieving cramps than the pill and considerably more expensive. Nonetheless, it can give pain relief by decreasing uterine contractions during menstruation. The usual dose is one tablet twice daily from day five to day twenty-five. Since it does not prevent ovulation, it has been used primarily in adolescent girls, in women who may not need a contraceptive, or in women hoping to conceive. Among women who have become pregnant while taking dydrogesterone, there have been to date no adverse effects on the fetus reported.

Are there any cases of primary dysmenorrhea beyond help?

Emphatically no. We've come a long way since your grandmother's day in alleviating menstrual cramps. No one is beyond help. So, if you are consistently losing time from work, school, or missing important social engagements, do check with your favorite gynecologist. You have nothing to lose but your cramps.

10. Issues and Answers—Irregular Periods and Common Bleeding Problems

> And a certain woman, which had an issue of blood twelve years, and had suffered many things of many physicians and had spent all that she had, and was nothing bettered, but rather grew worse. When she had heard of Jesus, came in the press behind, and touched his garment. For she said, if I may touch but his clothes, I shall be whole.
>
> And straightway the fountain of her blood was dried up . . .
>
> MARK 5:25–29

Two thousand years have passed since this woman of Biblical times was gloriously and instantly healed by the Great Physician, and yet we too live in an age of miracles. Today, as a result of tremendous advances in endocrinology, hormone therapy, and diagnostic and surgical techniques, bleeding problems previously considered insoluble can be treated and corrected.

Almost every woman at some time in her life will experience irregular bleeding. Rather than being a disease in itself, however, irregular bleeding is merely a symptom of some underlying disturbance. Hormonal imbalances, local tissue trauma, organic lesions (polyps, tumors, and so on), and even medical conditions not related to pelvic problems are some of the many reasons for menstrual irregularities and abnormal bleeding.

Hormonal disturbances resulting in lack of ovulation, for example, can be responsible for scanty and infrequent periods. By the same token, persistent lack of ovulation in an otherwise healthy woman can also mimic benign and malignant pelvic conditions by causing profuse, prolonged, and frequent bleeding. Curiously enough, lack of ovulation in some women will not interfere with their having regular periods. Needless to say, the diagnosis of female bleeding problems can be challenging at times.

Since irregular bleeding in women is a very complex subject, only the most frequently encountered problems will be reviewed. The first part of this chapter will discuss hormonal bleeding problems caused by lack of ovulation. Other causes of irregular bleeding, such as tissue trauma, infections, and organic lesions, will then be surveyed.

What is really meant by irregular periods?

By the time most girls reach seventeen or have been menstruating for at least three years, a fairly predictable menstrual pattern establishes itself. A significant menstrual irregularity persisting for at least three or more months would be an obvious departure from the established pattern. This irregularity could manifest itself in any number of ways: heavy bleeding, prolonged bleeding, more frequent bleeding, scanty bleeding, skipped periods, or even unexpected cessation of all bleeding.

Considering the complexities of hormonal interplay necessary for maintaining regular menstrual cycles, it is not surprising that this intricately balanced system gets out of whack from time to time.

Regular menstrual cycles depend on complete hormonal harmony and optimal physical health combined with mental and emotional equilibrium. Should you fall short in any of these rigorous requirements, you too might join the vast company of women intermittently plagued with bleeding problems. Nonetheless, there are times when even menstrual irregularities can be considered normal.

When is that?

At the two extremes of the reproductive years—in the young girl just beginning her periods and in the older woman approaching the menopause. In both instances lack of ovulation can result in menstrual irregularity.

How can lack of ovulation cause menstrual irregularity in the adolescent?

Until a girl matures sexually and ovulates regularly, menstruation may remain completely unpredictable. Periods of light to heavy bleeding may be followed by absence of menstruation for two or more months at a time, depending on the level of circulating estrogen. For many girls such menstrual irregularities may continue from one to three years. Bleeding in the sexually immature female is caused by a relative decrease in the output of estrogen, the only hormone produced by the ovaries until they are sufficiently mature to begin ovulating. With further sexual development, a second ovarian hormone, progesterone, comes into play as a direct result of ovulation. It is the production of progesterone that is largely responsible for the regulation of menstrual cycles. In other words, the gradual decrease of the progesterone level toward the end of the cycle (as the corpus luteum degenerates) is what causes the uterine lining to shed *on schedule.* (See Chapter 6.) Stated another way, once ovulation is established as a monthly event, the shedding of the uterine lining (endometrium) becomes controlled and predictable.

What about menstrual irregularity in the older woman?

In contrast to the adolescent girl whose periods become regular as the ovaries mature, the older woman approaching the menopause runs the opposite course: the ovaries begin slowing down, ovulation becomes more sporadic, periods become increasingly scanty and infrequent, until finally all menstruation ceases. For some menopausal women, however, persistent lack of ovulation for months at a time can lead to a different type of menstrual irregularity—heavy, flooding periods.

Why the heavy, flooding periods in some older women?

Even in the absence of ovulation, the ovaries of a menopausal woman continue to produce estrogen, which in turn stimulates the growth of the uterine lining. But, and this is an important *but,* without ovulation there is no progesterone to control and regulate the shedding of the uterine lining at predictable intervals. Since there may be a span of four to five years between the start of anovulatory (no-egg) cycles and the cessation of all menstruation, this means that the menopausal woman is particularly subject to small but continuous estrogen stimulation of the endometrium.

Since estrogen is responsible for the growth and support of endometrial tissue within the uterine cavity, the maintenance of the estrogen output above a certain critical level allows the growing endometrial tissue to remain intact—no bleeding. Thus, several weeks and even months may pass without any menstrual period.

However, this situation cannot go on indefinitely. Eventually there is an overgrowth or a superabundance of this tissue. Although estrogen production may continue essentially at the same rate, it is now unable to support the *surplus* of endometrial tissue. As a result the lining of the uterine cavity begins to disintegrate and shed, thereby producing a heavy and frequently prolonged bleeding episode. A woman who may not have menstruated for three or four months may suddenly find herself soaking four or five sanitary pads. Another woman may bleed intermittently for several days or even weeks. Although many menopausal women will have menstrual irregularities as their ovaries slow down (see Chapter 23), this particular type of heavy, flooding period may in some cases be the result of endometrial hyperplasia.

Endometrial hyperplasia—what's that?

Endometrial hyperplasia is an exuberant overgrowth of normal endometrial tissue (uterine lining) caused by long, continuous estrogen stimulation. Without ovulation and thus without progesterone to regulate the shedding of the uterine lining, continuous hormone stimulation of the endometrial tissue by estrogen *alone* can lead to endometrial hyperplasia. Moreover, this condition is so frequently responsible for abnormal bleeding in the menopausal woman as to be considered almost commonplace.

Endometrial hyperplasia is not malignant. It is a benign condition. Furthermore, it is not limited to older women. Any woman, even a teenager, who has long, persistent estrogen stimulation of the uterine lining without regular ovulation, can have grossly irregular periods as a result of endometrial hyperplasia.

As an aside, birth control pills (although they do suppress ovulation) do not cause endometrial hyperplasia even if taken continuously. On the contrary, the combination of estrogen and progesterone in the pill in most cases causes the uterine lining to become quite thin.

What can be done about endometrial hyperplasia?

Treatment will depend primarily upon age, the findings on pelvic examination, and duration and severity of the bleeding. In a young woman, cyclic hormonal therapy for three or four mouths may be all that is needed to correct the situation.

In older women, however, since organic lesions (both benign and malignant) occur more frequently in this age group, any abnormal or irregular bleeding must be approached more cautiously. In other words, when dealing with grossly irregular bleeding in older women, many doctors prefer to establish a definite diagnosis before proceeding with any specific therapy. This usually implies at the very least an endometrial biopsy or more likely a "D and C" (dilatation and curettage). The latter procedure essentially involves the scraping of the uterine lining under anesthesia. The endometrial tissue is thereby removed and microscopically examined for any abnormality or malignancy.

If the diagnosis of endometrial hyperplasia is verified, a D and C would effectively stop the bleeding as well as resolve the problem permanently for a number of women. In others, however, there could be a recurrence of the condition, particularly if the ovaries still produce a fair amount of estrogen. Under these circumstances, appropriate hormonal therapy could help to keep the condition in check.

Can endometrial hyperplasia ever lead to more serious problems?

In a few instances, it can ultimately develop into a premalignant or precancerous lesion necessitating a hysterectomy (removal of the uterus). For this reason it is important that women, and especially older women, with an initial diagnosis of endometrial hyperplasia be followed closely with regular pelvic examinations, as well as endometrial biopsies or similar studies when indicated.

What about the young woman whose periods never become regular?

Although most menstrual irregularities in teenage girls tend to correct themselves in time, a persistent lack of ovulation in younger women for months and even years is usually indicative of a definite hormonal disturbance. One such hormonal disorder, known as the polycystic ovarian syndrome (Stein Levinthal syndrome), can be responsible for irregular periods and ultimately cause cystic enlargement of both ovaries. During adolescence, girls thus affected may initially have heavy erratic bleeding interspersed with fairly regular periods. With continuous lack of ovulation, however, periods gradually become more scanty, less frequent, and in many cases cease altogether (amenorrhea). Under these circumstances, persistent lack of ovulation not only results in infertility but can also cause the ovaries to become enlarged as the result of being peppered with multiple small cysts (thus the name, polycystic ovarian syndrome). Since the polycystic ovarian syndrome is an important cause of infertility, as well as being responsible for gross menstrual irregularities in younger women, let's find out more about it.

How does the polycystic ovarian syndrome develop, and what are those cysts?

Normally, during each menstrual cycle many ovarian follicles begin to grow and develop under the influence of the pituitary hormone FSH. Ultimately only one of these follicles will fully mature, migrate to the surface of the ovary, and release the egg it contains. (See Chapter 6.)

In the polycystic ovarian syndrome, this orderly progression of events is disturbed. The chosen follicle does not rupture and release its egg, but instead continues to sit, just below the surface of the ovary —literally stuck. When this happens the pituitary continues to pour out its hormones in a frustrated attempt to trigger the release of the egg. As a consequence more and more follicles are stimulated but they too become entrapped in the ovary just below the surface.

Eventually, over a period of many months, both ovaries become studded with multiple follicular cysts, each cyst measuring only a fraction of an inch, but by virtue of their numbers, sufficient to cause an obvious enlargement of the ovaries—up to two or three times normal size.

Why does this ovarian disturbance happen?

Nobody knows for sure. There is evidence to implicate an internal biochemical disturbance in the ovaries themselves, or else a mix-up in central control, possibly at the hypothalamic level. More recent evidence seems to favor the latter possibility.

Why is amenorrhea so frequently associated with the polycystic ovarian syndrome?

Amenorrhea, or absence of menstruation for months at a time, may be the result of a relative decrease in estrogen output. Some women with this syndrome may initially go through a stage of endometrial hyperplasia because of persistent lack of ovulation and continuous estrogen stimulation. But in time it is also possible for the ovaries to become so disturbed that they are incapable of releasing enough estrogen to stimulate even a normal build-up of endometrial tissue. As a consequence, the endometrial lining becomes quite thin and, on rare occasions, even atrophic. Thus, all menstruation may cease for lack of sufficient tissue to shed. Interestingly enough, the polycystic ovarian syndrome is one of the major causes other than pregnancy of prolonged cessation of menstruation in younger women.

Are there any other problems associated with the polycystic ovarian syndrome?

Excessive weight gain may affect up to 40 percent of women with this condition. Moreover, 70 percent of women so afflicted are plagued with the growth of superfluous facial and body hair.

What accounts for the unwanted hair growth?

Hirsutism, or the abnormal appearance of dark, coarse facial and body hair, caused by this syndrome is definitely related to increased levels of testosterone in the blood. If you wonder how the male sex hormone, testosterone, got mixed up with this syndrome, you must realize that even *normal* female adrenal glands and ovaries produce small amounts of androgens that are ultimately converted into testosterone. In the polycystic ovarian condition, it is usually the affected ovaries that simply produce more than their normal share of testosterone. Fortunately, however, the extra testosterone manufactured by the deranged ovaries is not usually enough to produce other masculinizing effects, such as a decrease in breast size, temporal balding, or clitoral enlargement.

For those of you who want to rush right out and get your testosterone level checked because of a little fuzz on your upper lip, two additional comments are necessary. Unless the facial hair has just recently appeared, or the amount suddenly increased, chances are that it is the result of racial and genetic factors. Secondly, you probably won't be able to get the test done unless you are being extensively evaluated by a specialist in endocrinology for a specific problem. Laboratory determinations of blood testosterone levels are still too complicated, too tedious, and too expensive to be done routinely.

Can anything be done for women with the polycystic ovarian syndrome?

Very definitely. Even though the ultimate and ideal solution to this hormonal disorder lies in the establishment of regular ovulatory cycles, the selection of appropriate therapy depends in part on a woman's tentative family plans, as well as on clinical evaluation and the results of extensive hormonal studies.

In women who do want to become pregnant, ovulation can frequently be induced by the use of fertility drugs or, occasionally, by surgery on the ovaries. (See Chapter 16.) However, in the teenager or the woman not currently interested in becoming pregnant, attempts at induction of ovulation may be postponed in favor of temporary hormonal therapy.

In what way can hormonal therapy help?

Even without triggering ovulation, proper hormonal therapy can do much to straighten out the distressed ovaries. The use of an estrogen-progestin combination would halt continuous stimulation and growth of ovarian follicles by suppressing pituitary hormone output. Thus, further cystic enlargement of the ovaries would be held in check. And the cyclic use (three weeks on, one week off) of hormonal therapy would further assure the regular monthly shedding of the uterine lining.

As an extra bonus, testosterone output by the ovaries would also decrease, thus preventing further abnormal hair growth. In time this could mean the possible thinning and lightening of excess facial hair in a few cases. But in most women, superfluous facial and body hair present prior to therapy would not be affected.

Can emotional disturbances ever cause hormonal bleeding problems?

Absolutely. Adverse mental and emotional stresses can readily shake up the delicate hypothalamic-pituitary-ovarian system. Psychologically traumatic situations such as a blighted romance, marital separation, or the death of a loved one have all been implicated in upsetting previously normal periods.

However, all emotional upheavals affecting ovulation and menstruation need not be cataclysmic in intensity. A less dramatic but nonetheless common example is that of the young woman who leaves home for the first time. Her college dormitory may only be five miles down the road and yet the abrupt physical separation from her family is sufficiently distressing to disturb normal hormonal interplay. For many such women this could temporarily mean skipped or scanty periods. Less commonly, severe emotional or psychic stress can bring about the reverse problem—psychogenic bleeding.

What is psychogenic bleeding?

Few conditions so dramatically illustrate the power of the mind over the body as that typified by psychogenic or spontaneous bleeding under stress. One such case involved a young overwrought college freshman who virtually went to pieces at the thought of having to take an oral or written examination.

Invariably this girl would begin bleeding during every quiz, mid-term, or final examination. As the semester progressed, the bleeding became so increasingly predictable and heavy that it was necessary for her to put on a sanitary napkin prior to entering an examination hall. Needless to say, after weeks of frustration on the part of the campus physicians to diagnose and solve her problem, psychotherapy and the abandonment of college studies effected a solution.

Emotional factors aren't the only ones that can cause trouble. Any long-standing chronic illness or acute physical ailment, if serious enough, can disrupt hormonal balance. Medications, particularly tran-quilizers, have also been directly responsible for upsetting normal periods in some women. Along similar lines, crash diets when carried too far are notorious for creating general havoc in the hypothalamic-pituitary system.

How can crash diets affect your periods?

If you plan to limit your weight loss to a mere five or ten pounds, then the following need not concern you. But if you suddenly decide that those forty or fifty pounds of excess baggage must vanish instantly, you may be asking for trouble. Crash diets that transcend the bounda-ries of sanity can bring your menstrual periods to a screeching halt. Long before achieving your desired silhouette, a too rapid weight loss or continuous poor nutrition can adversely inhibit the hypothalamic and pituitary centers—and then, good-bye periods, hello amenorrhea.

Even with a return to sensible eating habits, it may be months before hormonal balance and menstruation are reestablished. If you have just changed your mind about going on a radical reducing diet, you should also know that being obese is another potential threat to regular menstruation.

How can being overweight affect your periods?

Lack of ovulation and irregular bleeding in some women have been linked to excess body fat. Since small amounts of estrogen are normally stored in body fat, the more fatty tissue you have, the more estrogen is likely to be removed from your bloodstream and retained in these areas. Being extremely overweight also means that the body needs an increased blood plasma volume to nourish the excess adipose tissue. A larger plasma volume further dilutes the concentration of circulating estrogen. In short, your ovaries may be perfectly normal and produce ample amounts of estrogen, but if too much estrogen is being stored in body fat, you may actually have too little estrogen circulating in your bloodstream. This can mean a relative estrogen deficiency, sufficiently severe to disrupt the normal hormonal balance necessary for ovulation and regular periods. For some women, just losing that extra weight can restore ovulation and normal menstruation.

As mentioned earlier, women with the polycystic ovarian syndrome may tend toward obesity. In this situation, however, a simple weight loss will unfortunately not restore ovulatory cycles because the hormonal disturbance is too profound.

Is your thyroid ever to blame for menstrual irregularities?

It can be, but less often than commonly supposed. An overactive thyroid can indirectly cause scanty and infrequent periods. At the other extreme, and in teenagers especially, a sluggish, underactive gland can be responsible for heavy and frequent periods. But unless there is a bona fide need substantiated by clinical evaluation and thyroid function studies, supplemental therapy with thyroid hormone is usually of little value in correcting menstrual irregularities.

If you ovulate regularly, can you still have hormonal bleeding problems?

Yes. Although the majority of hormonal bleeding problems are the result of anovulation (lack of ovulation), such is not always the case. Even in the absence of organic disease, irregular uterine bleeding can occur during ovulatory cycles.

Midcycle bleeding or spotting at the time of ovulation has already been described in Chapter 7. Slight imbalance in hormonal interplay during an ovulatory cycle can also account for other irregularities such as more frequent periods, prolonged periods, heavier periods, and one of the most common complaints, premenstrual staining.

What about premenstrual staining?

In order for your flow to start normally, the cyclic decrease of estrogen and progesterone levels just prior to menstruation must be perfectly synchronized. If your menstrual flow is invariably ushered in by a brown, gunky discharge or a continuous pink-tan staining lasting three to four days or even longer, your problem may be due to teetering levels of progesterone resulting in scanty premature shedding of the uterine lining. If the spotting becomes prolonged or a source of concern to the woman, supplemental hormonal therapy with progesterone during the last few days of the cycle will usually resolve the problem.

Besides hormonal disturbances, what else can cause irregular bleeding?

Even if your hormones have managed to stay in perfect balance despite all adversities, there are many other conditions that can cause irregular bleeding. To mention just a few in passing, iron deficiency anemia can provoke heavier periods, as can a deficiency in blood platelets, an important factor necessary for proper blood clotting. In fact, a decrease in blood platelets (thrombocytopenia) is occasionally the only explanation for profuse menses in a young woman.

Other causes of abnormal bleeding can be brought about by tissue trauma, polyps and adenomyosis (more about these shortly), certain fibroid tumors (see Chapter 21), endometriosis (see Chapter 22), and malignant changes (see Chapter 25).

Surprisingly enough, one of the most common causes of abnormal bleeding can occur during the first few weeks of pregnancy.

Abnormal bleeding in early pregnancy?

Whenever a woman of reproductive age complains of irregular bleeding or spotting, most doctors will automatically consider pregnancy as a possible diagnosis. Complications involving an early pregnancy constitute the number-one reason for abnormal bleeding in this age group.

Although missing a period is usually the first indication of pregnancy, not all women keep close track of their periods, nor do all women have consistently regular cycles. Therefore, it is not unusual for a woman to have bleeding as the result of a pregnancy of which she is unaware. A threatened loss in early pregnancy may cause intermittent spotting at the time of the expected period and can be easily mistaken for a scanty or unusual flow. Or a heavy, gushing later period may in reality be a miscarriage (spontaneous abortion).

Are bleeding and tissue trauma following first intercourse common?

Despite the popular use of tampons and the ease with which most hymens can be stretched, there are some women who at the time of first intercourse still have a relatively snug vaginal opening. If this is the case, persistent penile thrusts by an overly eager and generally inexperienced partner can cause pain and hymenal lacerations. Fortunately, most of these hymenal tears are not serious. Bleeding is minimal and healing occurs rapidly.

Aside from possible psychological trauma and making the area tender and off-limits for a few days, there are times when hymenal bleeding and tissue trauma can be sufficiently distressing to necessitate professional help.

Emergency-room doctors see their share of bruised and bleeding hymens. For young teenagers especially, this can be a particularly frightening and embarrassing predicament. Frightening because they don't know how to stop the bleeding and embarrassing because parents usually have to be notified before treatment is rendered.

Many of these emergency-room scenes could be avoided if the young couple involved were a little more knowledgeable.

Is there any way of avoiding hymenal injury during first intercourse?

Any woman contemplating sexual intercourse should have some awareness regarding the size of her vaginal opening. Being able to slip in a tampon is no assurance that penile penetration will be readily accomplished. Even super tampons do not approach the diameter of the average penis in full erection.

Perhaps the most practical method of determining the adequacy of the vaginal opening is the digital technique, or the two-finger estimate.

How can you be sure you have an accommodating vagina?

If you can insert the tips of your middle and index fingers into the vagina and then separate them at least one quarter of an inch or more, your vaginal opening is probably adequate. If your dimensions are such that this maneuver causes slight discomfort, the impetus of sexual excitement and increased vaginal lubrication may be sufficient to overcome any difficulty. However, if you do experience pain, gentle dilating exercises are probably in order.

What kind of dilating exercises can enlarge a small vaginal opening?

Lubricate the vaginal entrance with K-Y lubricating jelly (nonprescription), Vaseline, or a similar product and slip into a warm tub. Sometimes the added heat makes the tissues stretch more easily.

Insert the middle finger about halfway and gently press downward toward the rectum until you can feel the vaginal opening stretching. When you reach the point of mild discomfort, hold your finger there for a few moments and then relax. By alternately sustaining and releasing the pressure for three or four seconds at a time, the tissues will gradually give—but stop before it becomes painful.

If your vagina can initially accommodate the tips of both fingers, so such the better. In this case, just spreading the fingers apart intermittently will be sufficient. Exercising about five minutes a day should bring noticeable improvement in about two or three weeks.

If perchance you cannot even insert one finger into the vagina and are contemplating intercourse, the best advice is to check with a gynecologist. Under these circumstances you may need a minor surgical procedure (hymenectomy or hymenotomy) to enlarge the vaginal opening.

But since advice sometimes comes too late, let's go back to the first problem—bleeding after first intercourse.

What can you do if hymenal bleeding does not stop?

If you have just experienced first intercourse and there is hymenal bleeding that seems reluctant to stop, there may be a solution short of seeing a doctor.

But don't handle the problem by lying down and elevating your hips and legs. This method only serves to hide bleeding temporarily by allowing blood to pool in the upper vagina.

In many instances the source of the bleeding can readily be seen by simply examining yourself with a mirror. Therefore, unless the hymenal tear involves a fair-sized blood vessel or the injury lies further up the vagina, continuous firm pressure against the bleeding point will usually resolve the problem. A sanitary napkin rolled into a tight ball makes a handy, efficient pressure bandage. Place the rolled pad tightly against the vaginal opening and sit on a firm, flat surface for at least ten to fifteen minutes. This position should effectively compress the pad against the hymenal area. Avoid the temptation to check on the bleeding until the allotted time is over. If, however, bleeding still continues at a worrisome rate, you probably do need help. Better call your doctor or drop in at the nearest hospital emergency room.

Can bleeding ever occur after intercourse in a woman who has an accommodating vagina?

Yes. Postcoital bleeding, that is, spotting or bleeding after intercourse, can frequently be caused by benign cervical problems. The cervix, because of its location at the far end of the vagina, is particularly vulnerable to deep penile thrusts during intercourse. Thus, the impact of the penis against a raw, chronically irritated cervix (cervicitis) or a dangling cervical polyp can account for the unexpected and painless appearance of postcoital bleeding.

Cervical problems such as the above can also be responsible for intermenstrual bleeding (bleeding between periods) and bleeding after douching.

What causes these cervical problems in the first place?

Cervicitis and cervical polyps (which originate in the endocervical canal) are usually the result of a persistent, mild cervical infection. Since the vagina provides a warm, dark, moist environment, it is not surprising that the presence of organisms both normal and abnormal, menstrual blood, or tissue trauma resulting from childbirth can all contribute to making the cervix a frequent site of chronic irritation and infection.

What can be done about chronic cervicitis?

If the possibility of a malignancy has been eliminated as the source of the cervical bleeding (negative Pap smear), most cases of chronic cervicitis can be treated effectively in the gynecologist's office by simple cauterization—that is, destruction of the infected tissue by the application of heat, cold, or chemicals. (See Chapter 21.) Following cauterization and subsequent healing, a red, raw, and irritated cervix will revert to its normal pink and healthy state.

What about cervical polyps?

Since cervical polyps are small, fragile, tear-shaped growths that usually dangle on a stalk and protrude through the cervical os, they can sometimes be easily and painlessly removed in the gynecologist's office. On the other hand, the successful removal of polyps located well within the cervical canal may necessitate hospitalization. With rare exception, cervical polyps are always benign. Nevertheless, for diagnosis and verification, cervical polyps are routinely submitted to a pathologist for microscopic examination.

Not all polyps are cervical, however, nor are they all so easily dispensed with. Endometrial polyps are another common source of abnormal bleeding.

What's so different about endometrial polyps?

Unlike cervical polyps, endometrial polyps sprout from the uterine or endometrial lining. They are not the result of infection, but rather represent discrete and usually benign overgrowths of normal endometrial tissue in response to continuous estrogen stimulation. They are frequently multiple and can either spread out within the uterine cavity as broad, flat projections of tissue or dangle from small stalks. On rare occasion, if one of these stalks is long enough, an endometrial polyp can make an appearance through the cervical os just like a cervical polyp. Under ordinary circumstances, however, endometrial polyps can neither be felt nor seen on routine pelvic examination. Unless they cause symptoms—bleeding between periods, prolonged postmenstrual spotting or staining, or occasional heavy and prolonged periods—their presence may be completely unsuspected.

Diagnosis as well as the correction of the condition usually depends upon scraping the uterine lining under anesthesia (D and C, dilatation and curettage).

Can anything else cause prolonged, heavy periods?

Adenomyosis. In this unique situation, which most commonly affects women between the ages of thirty-five and fifty, misplaced fragments of endometrial tissue from the uterine lining actually become embedded within the muscular walls of the uterus. How or why this happens remains unclear, but the end result is an enlarged, soft, and boggy uterus. Periods can become increasingly long, profuse, and frequently associated with a sense of pelvic pressure and discomfort. Unfortunately, adenomyosis does not respond readily to hormonal therapy, nor can the symptoms be alleviated by a dilatation and curettage. Therefore, where pelvic discomfort does exist and bleeding is excessive, removal of the uterus (hysterectomy) is sometimes the best solution.

Similarly, the presence of misplaced fragments of endometrial tissue on the ovaries or elsewhere in the pelvic cavity (endometriosis) can also be a source of menstrual irregularity and pelvic distress. (See Chapter 22.)

Does cancer of the female pelvic organs usually cause irregular bleeding?

Not necessarily. Much depends upon the location of the malignancy and the extent of the disease. Although cancer of the female organs is reviewed in Chapter 25, a few pertinent comments are in order here.

Bleeding is never present with early cancer of the cervix. Detection of an early curable cervical cancer relies almost exclusively on routine Pap smears. In endometrial carcinoma, or cancer involving the lining of the uterine cavity, spotting may be the very first indication that all is not well. Fortunately, if these early symptoms are reported and properly investigated, chances are really excellent for a complete cure of endometrial cancer. As for a malignancy of the ovaries, irregular bleeding is rarely present as an early symptom.

Is it ever possible to bleed after straining or lifting a heavy object?

It is surprising how many women, particularly postmenopausal women, will attribute an unexpected episode of bleeding or spotting to some unusual physical exertion. Although abnormal uterine bleeding may on rare occasion coincide with strenuous physical activity, there is usually some other explanation for it.

What about postmenopausal bleeding?

Any bleeding or spotting that occurs twelve months or longer after the last period should be investigated. Estrogen supplemental therapy in the postmenopausal woman, for example, can and does cause uterine bleeding on occasion. But if there is any abnormal bleeding, the possibility that an early malignant or premalignant lesion may be the cause must always be considered. Moreover, staining that lasts only a day or so does not mean that the problem is of no consequence. Conversely, heavy or prolonged bleeding does not necessarily indicate a more serious condition. In other words, postmenopausal bleeding should be reported promptly regardless of whether it's profuse or nothing more than an occasional pink stain. The important fact is not the amount of bleeding but the presence of blood itself.

Why is it important to report any unusual bleeding promptly?

As you may appreciate from this brief survey of the more common bleeding problems, there are any number of reasons for irregular periods and abnormal bleeding, some quite simple and others profoundly complex. The proper management of abnormal or irregular bleeding, regardless of your age, begins with you. You may have the world's most competent doctor, but unless you make it a point to be seen and present your complaints without undue delay, you will be doing a disservice both to yourself and to your doctor. It goes without saying that any problem causing abnormal bleeding or menstrual irregularity has a good chance of being effectively resolved when treated promptly.

PART III

The Vulnerability of Woman

11. The Unwelcome Three— Infestations, Infections, and Irritations In and Around the Vagina

Living a celibate existence, steadfastly refusing to sit on a public toilet seat, and being fastidious in your personal hygiene are no assurance that you will be spared a visit from one of the "unwelcome three." If you are currently bothered with a vaginal discharge, a vulvar irritation, or itching of the external genitalia, you might find consolation in knowing that 25 percent of the women who go to a gynecologist seek help expressly for one or all of these problems.

Do you realize that crabs are staging a comeback?
Whether you call them cooties, pubic lice, or pediculosis pubis, crabs are back—and in epidemic proportions. Unlike body and scalp lice, this culprit is irresistibly drawn to pubic hair. With the apparent increase in sexual permissiveness, infestation of the hair-bearing area of the vulva by this six-legged louse is now a potential threat to many women.

How can you get crabs?
Easily. Although sexual intercourse with a person harboring the parasite is the simplest way, just an intimate hug *au naturel* will suffice. And close physical contact with contaminated articles such as

sheets, blankets, sleeping bags, clothing, toilet seats, etc. They too can invite an invasion.

What are the symptoms?

A maddening pubic itch, particularly devastating in the middle of the night. The itching is apparently caused by a noxious substance excreted into the skin by this mini-vampire. Since the crab louse requires human blood for survival, it latches on by piercing the skin and burying its head inside a pubic hair follicle. At times an inflammatory bluish gray area from a bite can be seen on the skin.

How can you be sure you have crabs?

By looking carefully. Even though an average infestation may have six or seven adult crabs, spotting one readily may not be that easy. Each crab louse measures only about 1.2 mm. in diameter and may require a magnifying glass for identification. Other telltale signs are the eggs or nits, small (0.5 mm.) oval white specks usually deposited near the junction of the hair and skin.

What should you do about those awful crabs?

First of all, don't panic. As loathsome as crabs may be, they don't carry any horrible disease.

Do not shave your pubic hair or use any questionable local medication. Injudicious self-treatment may add to your misery by superimposing a severe skin irritation while the crabs, undaunted, merrily carry on.

It is best to call your doctor or to visit a health center. For all you or anybody else knows, maybe you picked up the crabs while trying on that new bikini at one of the more fashionable shops. So don't let embarrassment delay your seeking help. Most doctors would probably be happy to phone in a prescription for you.

What is the best treatment?

Kwell, a prescription drug, which comes in a shampoo form and as a lotion or cream, is probably one of the most effective anti-crab remedies. A four-minute pubic hair shampoo with Kwell followed by a thorough drying will usually eradicate most infestations. The crabs will succumb and any remaining nits can be easily removed by a fine-tooth comb. Occasionally a repeat shampoo treatment in twenty-four hours may be necessary.

If Kwell cream or lotion is prescribed, it should be liberally applied over the infested area and left on for twenty-four hours. The cream and lotion have the added advantage of being able to kill the lice on clothing. If a repeat treatment is necessary, a delay of four days is recommended before reapplying.

In addition to getting rid of your personal culprits, you should also know how to avoid reinfestation.

How can you prevent a crab comeback?

All clothing, sheets, blankets, sleeping bags, mattresses, and anything with which you have been in close contact should be laundered (boiling water) or dry-cleaned. Moreover, remember to scrub the toilet seat and make sure that your partner, if any, gets his own Kwell.

If your budget can ill afford such a cleaning bill, or if your mattress can't squeeze into your washing machine, there is another solution. The crab louse once deprived of the blood of a human host will die within twenty-four hours. And since the tiny nits take about a week or ten days to hatch, all articles can actually be self-sterilized and made crab-free if left undisturbed and away from human contact for at least two weeks.

What about other vulvar afflictions?

Contact dermatitis of the vulva—an inflammatory reaction of the vulvar skin—is also definitely on the upswing. Slight reddening of the vulvar skin followed by an itching sensation may be the only symptoms. More severe reactions can progress to labial swelling and an eruption of clear, bubblelike blisters that eventually drain and crust over.

If you happen to have sensitive skin, or if you are allergic, any number of unsuspected agents may be responsible for a localized vulvar irritation. Just using a new bath soap or laundry detergent can cause trouble. Bubble bath products in particular have been blamed for acute vulvitis (inflammation of the vulva) in young girls. Sprucing up your bathroom with a flashy new colored toilet paper has been a source of allergic reactions in women sensitive to the dye. Condoms, douche ingredients, vaginal foams for contraception, sanitary napkins, new synthetic fabrics in undergarments, panty hose, girdles, and feminine spray deodorants have all been implicated in making sensitive women absolutely miserable.

Allergic reactions from drugs can also cause vulvar distress. Common medications such as aspirin, phenacitin, sulfa drugs, and phenolphthalein, an ingredient in many laxative preparations (for example, Ex-lax and Feen-a-mint), have on occasion been responsible for vulvar inflammation.

What can be done about contact or allergic vulvitis?

The cure depends on identifying and eliminating the offending agent. Brisk scrubs with soap and water should definitely be avoided. Calomine lotion applied three or four times daily is helpful in relieving moderate itching. For additional relief cool boric acid compresses (one tablespoon per quart of water) or else soaking in a tepid cornstarch sitz bath (two cups per half tub of water) twice a day may hold you over until you get help. It may even clear your problem. And be sure to pat yourself dry (no rubbing). Some women even use a hair dryer (cool setting) to facilitate complete vulvar drying. Since the object of the treatment is to keep the vulva cool, dry, and comfortable, don't wear nylon underwear, pantyhose (unless they have a cotton crotch), or tight-fitting jeans, slacks, or other garments which can aggravate the skin condition by trapping moisture. Instead, wear relatively loose outer garments and white cotton underwear. Cotton breathes and absorbs moisture.

If additional relief is necessary, your doctor would probably prescribe a soothing cortisone lotion to be applied locally. In severe cases, antihistamines as well as cortisone by mouth for a few days may be indicated to reduce the inflammation and allergic tissue response.

What if the itching is confined mainly to the anorectal area?

Then the possibility of hemorrhoids, anal fissures, or even pinworm infestation should be considered. Anal itching can also be triggered by traces of fecal material trapped within the tiny anal folds. If such is the case, simply washing the area with a cotton ball soaked with cool water or preferably witch hazel after each bowel movement will usually resolve the problem.

What about vulvar irritation in postmenopausal women?

Vulvitis in postmenopausal women and especially in elderly women deserves special attention. Lack of estrogen ultimately causes the vulvar and vaginal tissues to become thin, atrophic, and less resistant to trauma and infection. As a result, any irritation such as itching can become a chronic debilitating problem if not promptly treated. Itching leads to scratching and scratching, by causing breaks in the skin, can cause more inflammation and infection. Areas of scaling, leatherlike thickening of the skin, and the appearance of pale white patches on the vulva can all be signs of chronic vulvitis. The fact that cancer of the vulva is frequently preceded by a long history of vulvar itching and irritation makes it important that these symptoms not be ignored.

As in other cases of vulvitis, the cure depends on eliminating the cause and breaking the itch-scratch cycle with appropriate local care. Good nutrition with adequate protein intake and vitamin A and B supplements are especially important in the elderly in promoting healing. Skin lesions or sores that persist despite adequate local treatment should of course be biopsied.

What else can cause vulvar irritation?

Vaginal problems. Without a doubt vaginal infections and abnormal discharges are indirectly one of the most common causes of vulvitis.

Is it ever normal to have a vaginal discharge?

Yes, indeed. Vaginal secretions are both normal and necessary. Without secretions from the cervix, vaginal walls, and Bartholin's glands, the inside of the vagina would feel like a roll of dried parchment. Your vagina needs moisture and lubrication just as your mouth needs saliva.

Under normal and healthy conditions, the cervix produces a clear mucus secretion. As this mucus drains downward and mixes with discarded vaginal cells, normal bacteria, and Bartholin's gland secretions, it assumes a whitish color. Moreover, when this normal white vaginal secretion comes into contact with underwear, it gradually changes color to pale yellow as the result of oxidation (exposure to air). In young girls the appearance of this physiological discharge usually coincides with breast development and increased estrogen output by the ovaries. At the same time the vaginal mucosa thickens and the secretions become relatively acid due to the growth of acid-producing bacteria (lactobacilli). As long as the discharge is not excessive, does not cause itching, irritation, swelling, or an unpleasant odor, it is probably normal.

Under certain conditions, however, normal vaginal secretions can increase temporarily.

What changes can account for increased vaginal secretions?

Several factors—estrogen level, emotional stress, and sexual excitement.

As ovulation approaches, higher estrogen levels increase cervical secretions which may account for your noticing a clear mucus drainage at this time. In the same way, higher estrogen levels in women taking oral contraceptives can also cause a definite increase in vaginal secretions.

Emotional stress and sexual excitement in particular are commonly associated with a more obvious but temporary discharge. During sexual arousal, the profuse, clear secretion which bathes the entire vagina and introitus actually comes from the vaginal walls as an indirect result of dilatation and engorgement of vaginal blood vessels. Even women over sixty can still exude considerable vaginal lubrication when properly stimulated. Thus, factors such as age, relative lack of estrogen, or previous hysterectomy do not materially diminish the vaginal sweat phenomenon under conditions of sexual excitement.

Nonetheless, age alone can alter other normal vaginal secretions.

How does age influence vaginal secretions?

With gradual estrogen withdrawal in the postmenopausal woman, the thick, succulent, corrugated vaginal walls gradually become relatively thin, dry, and smooth. Cervical secretions diminish and normal bacteria indirectly responsible for maintaining normal vaginal acidity become scarce. As a result, vaginal secretions become scanty and relatively alkaline.

Why are normal vaginal secretions acid in the younger woman?

Protection. Maintenance of a relatively acid vaginal environment discourages the growth of some organisms responsible for distressing vaginal discharges.

In women during the reproductive years, for example, cyclic, normal decreases in vaginal acidity just before and after menstruation may be sufficient to give lurking culprits a foothold or even aggravate an existing abnormal discharge. Menstrual blood can also provide a delectable environment for the propagation of unwanted culprits.

What culprits?

Excluding gonorrhea (see Chapter 12), the top contenders currently responsible for plaguing many adult women with vaginal infections and abnormal discharges are *Trichomonas vaginalis* (protozoa), *Candida albicans* (fungus), and *Hemophilus vaginalis* (bacteria).

Although these impressive names will probably slip from your memory in short order, a personal encounter with any of these unwelcome culprits will undoubtedly leave a more lasting impression.

What about Trichomonas vaginalis?

Better known as trich or TV for short, this one-celled microscopic protozoan produces a copious, watery, malodorous, yellowish or greenish-white discharge. In severe infections this discharge can be so excessive as to cause marked vulvar irritation and chafing of the upper inner thighs and rectal area.

The associated itching, soreness, and inflammation of the vaginal opening and vulva can dampen any woman's enthusiasm for sex. Coitus if attempted during an acute trich infection can be painful.

Where does the TV culprit come from?

No one really knows. Although about one woman out of five harbors this protozoan without any telltale signs or symptoms, *Trichomonas vaginalis* is not a normal inhabitant of the vagina or anywhere else in the human body. Moreover, a TV vaginal infection is not acquired either by fecal contamination of the vagina or by oral genital sex (cunnilingus). Even if the trouble-causing TV protozoa are introduced into the mouth or transferred to the rectum in certain varieties of sexual play, they do not survive long enough in these two areas to ultimately become a source of vaginal reinfection.

How, then, do women become infected?

Since 60 to 80 percent of male partners of infected women do unknowingly harbor this organism in their urinary tract, the vast majority of TV vaginal infections are acquired through contact of sexual organs or coitus with an infected partner. Almost without exception this specifically implies either penis-to-vagina or close vulva-to-vulva contact. The fact that the organism does not survive in the mouth or the rectum makes the transmission of *Trichomonas vaginalis* among homosexual men virtually impossible. Men thus acquire the TV organism only through coitus with an infected woman. Furthermore, once contracted, TV can readily ping-pong back and forth between sexual partners.

Occasional cases of TV vaginitis have been attributed to interchanging moist washcloths, wet bathing suits, or to sitting on that infamous and perennially contaminated toilet seat, but these are unusual sources of infection. Similarly, sharing a swimming pool with a group of TV carriers is also a most unlikely mode of transmission. Most TV organisms will rapidly succumb when exposed to chlorinated water.

Do men ever suffer from TV?

Rarely. Even when TV organisms are present within the male urethra, only a few men will notice slight burning after ejaculation.

Thus, many men can be TV carriers and unknowingly infect and reinfect their female sexual partners.

Are there any special tests to detect a TV vaginal infection?

Other than the copious and malodorous discharge so characteristic of an acute TV vaginal infection, definite diagnosis depends on microscopic identification of the protozoa.

Nonetheless, since some women can harbor this organism without obvious signs of vaginal infection, many doctors routinely check vaginal secretions for TV. Interestingly enough, the presence of TV can also be detected by a Pap smear and is frequently reported as an incidental finding.

Can TV vaginitis ever cause other problems?

Acute vaginal or cervical infections can be a cause of atypical or slightly abnormal Pap smear reports. In this respect, the TV protozoan is the culprit most frequently responsible.

Appropriate treatment of the infection will allow the vaginal and cervical cells to return to normal and the Pap smear to revert to Class I negative. (See Chapter 5.)

What can be done about TV vaginitis?

Even if there are no symptoms, the presence of *Trichomonas vaginalis* still warrants treatment to prevent a possible flare-up of organism. Currently the most effective anti-TV medication is the prescription drug medronidazole (Flagyl). In about 95 percent of affected women, a single course of treatment with Flagyl by mouth will eradicate the infection if the sexual partner is treated simultaneously.

A decrease in discharge and vulvovaginal irritation will frequently be noticed within two to three days. However, improvement or disappearance of the symptoms is not an indication to stop therapy. Premature discontinuation of Flagyl or failure to treat the sexual partner has been responsible for therapy failures and recurrences necessitating repeat treatment. While on medication both partners should avoid drinking alcoholic beverages as the combination could cause abdominal cramps, nausea, flushing, and headaches. If a woman is pregnant, Flagyl should not be used during the first trimester. Although Flagyl has not been shown to cause birth defects (even among laboratory animals), its safety during early pregnancy has not been adequately studied. It is known, however, that Flagyl in exceedingly high doses can cause cancer in mice, but to date no such effects have occurred in humans.

Isn't local vaginal therapy for TV just as effective?

Not really. Because TV organisms can also set up headquarters in the female urinary tract (urethra or bladder), sometimes causing a burning sensation on urination, treatment limited to the vagina in the form of creams, suppositories, douches, etc., will rarely provide a complete cure. At best, local therapy only brings temporary relief by decreasing the vaginal TV population with no effect on possible urinary-tract culprits. Thus, TV organisms located outside the vagina would escape treatment and remain potential sources of self-reinfection.

On occasion, however, local vaginal therapy (medicated inserts, douches, etc.) in a few women may initially hasten comfort by reducing excessive discharge.

What about the fungus among us?

Whether your doctor calls it moniliasis, vaginal thrush, candidiasis, or just plain yeast, vulvovaginal infections caused by the fungus *Candida albicans* are currently the most prevalent and the most stubborn to treat.

Unlike TV, with its copious and offensive discharge, the *Candida* culprit excels in provoking intolerable vaginal and vulvar itching sufficient in many instances to drive the most placid woman frantic. Itching is invariably followed by scratching and, of course, the more persistent the itch-scratch cycle, the greater the irritation, inflammation, and swelling of the labial structures. Breaks in the skin from excessive scratching can also invite a secondary bacterial infection. Frequently, just voiding will cause a burning sensation as the urine comes into contact with the raw and irritated tissues.

The type of discharge produced by this fungus can vary from woman to woman. Some women may only notice a slight, watery, white drainage. Others might complain that the vagina actually feels dry. More commonly, thick curdlike chunks of a white cheesy substance mixed with a watery discharge may be seen at the vaginal opening. If it is profuse, the discharge can cause an intensely itchy rash on the entire vulva, from the mons to well beyond the rectum and along the upper inner thighs.

Where does this fungus come from?

Many places. In about 40 percent of women, *Candida albicans* is a normal vaginal inhabitant. It is also frequently harbored in the mouth and intestines of both sexes. Even in healthy individuals without any apparent signs or symptoms, this fungus has been recovered from urine, seminal fluid, and between folds of opposing skin surfaces (for example, under the foreskin, between the buttocks, etc.). All of these areas can be potential sources of vaginal infection or reinfection. But unless certain conditions favorable for its growth and propagation occur, the fungus when present ordinarily remains quietly unobtrusive.

In women who do not have *Candida* as a normal vaginal inhabitant, the fungus can readily be introduced by fecal contamination of the vagina or, less commonly, by cunnilingus or coitus with a partner who harbors the organism. On the other hand, the chance of developing a fungus (monilia) infection of the mouth is extremely remote. (See Chapter 15.)

But regardless of whether the fungus is a normal vaginal inhabitant or is introduced into the vagina, the same principle applies—as long as conditions remain unfavorable for its growth, nothing will happen.

What can cause a fungal flare-up?

Many things, including pregnancy, oral contraceptives, diabetes, increased blood sugar levels, antibiotics, and various unknown factors. Stress and tension have even been implicated as precipitating factors in recurrent infections.

How can pregnancy or birth control pills cause a fungal infection?

By creating just the right vaginal environment for the growth of this culprit. The explanation is indirectly related to the higher estrogen levels found both in pregnant women and in women taking oral contraceptives. Because estrogen normally causes glycogen (carbohydrate) to be deposited within the vaginal cells, a higher level of estrogen will therefore result in an increased amount of vaginal cellular glycogen and thus a "sweeter" vaginal environment.

What does glycogen have to do with this fungus?

This fungus grows, multiplies, and thrives in a glycogen-rich environment. Under these circumstances, a woman whose vagina was previously unreceptive to the growth of the fungus may experience her first real vaginal infection. Just starting on birth control pills, for example, can precipitate a sudden and acute vaginal fungus infection in some women, sufficiently distressing to discourage sexual intercourse. At times, a persistent vaginal fungus infection may even be aggravated by excessive intake of sweets and goodies and, less commonly, by an undiagnosed mild diabetic condition.

During pregnancy, vaginal fungus infections are exceedingly common and invariably affect 15 to 25 percent of all pregnant women. Until delivery and the reestablishment of a less "sugary" environment, treatment is seldom curative. Interestingly enough, many pregnant women will have a spontaneous disappearance of the infection following delivery, thereby requiring no additional treatment.

Can a vaginal fungus infection during pregnancy affect the baby?

Infrequently, and only during delivery, if then. As the infant passes through the vaginal canal, it may pick up the organism. Most fungus infections (thrush) in the newborn that are acquired this way are limited primarily to the mouth and throat. They are rarely serious and can be readily treated and cured.

Can anything else precipitate a vaginal fungus infection?

Antibiotics (particularly tetracycline—less commonly penicillin and others) prescribed for unrelated problems such as strep throat or urinary infections may also result in a vaginal fungus infection in susceptible women. Although the explanation for this phenomenon has been attributed to the suppression by the antibiotic of normal protective vaginal bacteria, which exert an antifungal effect, the exact mechanism is not completely understood.

How can a vaginal fungus infection be diagnosed?

Frequently by simple inspection or microscopic examination of vaginal secretions. Otherwise a culture can be taken.

What is a culture?

Whenever proper and definitive treatment of an infection depends on the accurate identification of the responsible organism (whether bacteria or fungus), the secretion, discharge, or material suspected of containing the offending organism is smeared onto a special medium capable of nourishing the culprit in question and causing it to proliferate. Within twenty-four to forty-eight hours, sufficient growth of the organism will have occurred to make a specific laboratory identification.

In regard to gonorrhea in women, for example, a culture is virtually indispensable in making the diagnosis. (See Chapter 12.)

What about treatment for vaginal fungus infections?

Since there is no magic pill that will effectively eliminate *Candida albicans,* treatment depends on local vaginal creams or suppositories.

To be really effective, therapy should be continued for at least two and, in stubborn cases, as long as five weeks. This usually means inserting a vaginal cream or suppository (for example, Mycostatin) twice a day for two weeks and then once a day thereafter, if necessary, for another one to three weeks. For some women, the gunky drainage from dissolving suppositories and creams frequently causes them to use the medication sporadically or even discontinue therapy at the first sign of improvement in symptoms. Needless to say, inadequate therapy invariably accounts for another flare-up. Newer preparations currently on the market include Gyne-Lotrimin (a vaginal tablet) and Monistat 7 (a vaginal cream). A single nightly application over a seven-day period of either medication is apparently able to clear the fungus, at least in some women.

In severe or persistent infections, the vagina can be treated with a gentian violet solution (a messy purple medication). This really does help, but watch out for stubborn stains on underwear that will challenge any enzyme detergent. Excessive use can also cause contact dermatitis of the vulva.

For the woman on birth control pills who is plagued with repeated vaginal fungus infections, sometimes nothing short of temporarily discontinuing oral contraceptives will effect a cure.

If the symptoms aren't too distressing, there is no reason to abstain from intercourse during treatment. But, under these circumstances it is advisable for the man to wear a condom to avoid possible penile irritation from the fungus.

Is there any other treatment for recurrent and stubborn vaginal fungus infections?

When vaginal reinfections have been persistent, many doctors recommend using a vaginal cream or suppository daily for at least four to five weeks plus the application of an antifungal ointment between the labial folds. The same treatment is then repeated just prior to and during menstruation for an additional three to four months. The use of Mycostatin oral medication can also be helpful. This suppresses the growth of bowel fungi that could cause repeated vaginal infections by fecal contamination. Eating unpasturized yogurt can similarly help reduce the number of intestinal *Candida* organisms. But neither oral Mycostatin nor yogurt will exert any effect on fungal organisms already present in the vagina or on the vulva. These can only be eliminated by local therapy.

According to some experts, deodorant soaps or soaps containing hexachlorophene that kill bacteria should be avoided. Their use may encourage fungus infections by destroying protective bacteria on the skin and mucous membranes. Substituting showers for tub baths may also cut down recurrences.

What about vaginal bacterial infections with Hemophilis Vaginalis (HV)?

Happily for all concerned, HV is probably one of the easiest vaginal infections to clear. Symptoms tend to be mild but the discharge, usually grayish-white, can have a most disagreeable and offensive odor.

For the affected woman, treatment with oral antibiotics such as Ampicillin or tetracycline for five or six days is usually curative. However, since transmission of this bacteria frequently occurs during sexual intercourse, the male partner should also be treated with oral antibiotics.

Other vaginal bacterial infections (*E. coli,* etc.) will usually respond to the same type of systemic medication. At times, local vaginal antibacterial creams can be used.

Is it ever possible to be infected with more than one culprit?

Not only possible but not that uncommon. TV and *Candida* in particular like to go steady, but any combination is possible—including all three together.

Is there any way to protect yourself against any of these vaginal infections?

Although avoiding oral contraceptives, pregnancy, or just giving up sex would certainly eliminate many potential problems, short of these drastic measures, there are a few precautions that might help in making you less vulnerable to vaginal infections.

Both bacterial and fungus infections can come from the rectal area. Thus, most fecal vaginal contamination may be avoided by always wiping away from the vagina toward the rectum. Sanitary napkins, because of their failure to stay securely in place, can also inadvertently spread unwanted bacteria from the rectal area to the vagina. Tampons, for this reason, are much more sanitary and have the added advantage of minimizing unpleasant menstrual odors. Then too, for added security, intimate contact with bare public toilet seats should be avoided.

If you have been plagued with repeated fungus infections, you should investigate your diet. Sometimes by cutting down your carbohydrate and sugar intake, and that includes cocktails and wine, fungus recurrences may be discouraged. If tetracycline or other broad spectrum antibiotics are prescribed for an unrelated problem and you are prone to fungus infections, the simultaneous use of an antifungal vaginal preparation may be advisable.

In order to avoid TV infections, no single measure is really effective unless you become celibate or have a TV-free partner. Otherwise, talking your partner into wearing a condom will prevent infection. Other measures that will afford partial protection are contraceptive creams, jellies, or foams if used prior to intercourse. Most of these preparations have some anti-TV ingredients.

12. Freud Runs Amok— Venereal Disease

In the recent past, only five diseases were traditionally classified as venereal: gonorrhea, syphilis, and the less commonly known lymphopathia venereum, chancroid, and granuloma inguinale. Today we know of at least twenty-five other diseases that can be sexually transmitted. To keep pace with this growing number of such infections, the term venereal disease or VD is gradually being replaced by the more inclusive and descriptive phrase, sexually transmitted diseases.

If you assume that these infections are reserved for the sexually promiscuous or limited to the socially disadvantaged, you are mistaken. Regardless of social background, education, or age, more and more women, including those who limit their sexual activity to one partner, run the risk of possible infection.

What is gonorrhea and what causes it?

Second only to the common cold, gonorrhea ranks as the most prevalent communicable disease in the United States with well over one million reported cases each year. Whether you are more familiar with the terms GC, clap, strain, drip, or dose, gonorrhea is an extremely contagious disease caused by the Gram-negative gonococcus bacteria *Neisseria gonorrhoeae*. The gonococcus requires a moist mucosal surface for survival. Loss of moisture or exposure to air will cause rapid death of the organism. In the majority of cases the gonococcus gains entrance to the body by way of the genital tract. The disease, therefore, is almost exclusively transmitted or acquired by sexual intercourse or other intimate contact with the genital organs of an infected person. Other sites of initial infection in the adult can include the rectum and pharynx (throat).

Can gonorrhea ever be acquired indirectly or by nonsexual means?

Gonorrhea can sometimes be spread by nonsexual contact. A gonoccocal eye infection of the newborn acquired by direct contact with a GC discharge in the birth canal of an infected mother is a well-known example. Since the gonococcus can survive for short periods of time outside the body if kept in a moist environment, a very young child can become infected by contacting contaminated objects. Moist washcloths with infected discharge, bedclothes, and freshly contaminated hands of an infected person are potential (albeit rare) avenues of indirect spread of gonorrhea. Among adults one sometimes hears the story of acquiring the infection by sitting on a toilet seat. This is by far the most improbable mode of transmission.

Can gonorrhea be acquired by oral genital sex?

Yes. Gonorrhea of the mouth and pharynx can be acquired by oral genital sex or oral copulation. Most cases in men and women result from fellatio, or mouth to penis copulation, with an infected partner. Cunilingus, or mouth to vulva stimulation, is a less frequent source of pharyngeal infections. Symptoms are usually absent but there can occasionally be a mild sore throat or tonsillitis. Usually the tongue, gums, and buccal mucosa are resistant to the gonococcus, but there have been cases of multiple ulcerations of these areas following oral copulation. Infection of the mouth and pharynx can also occur without genital involvement, although this is very rare. An individual with oral gonorrhea could theoretically transmit the infection to the mouth or genital organs of another person.

What is the incubation period for gonorrhea?

Usually two to seven days following sexual contact with an infected person. However, some men may harbor the GC organisms for as long as six weeks before symptoms appear. In women the incubation period may vary even more—from one week to twelve months. In other words, it is possible for a woman to be infected by the gonococcus for a year before any symptoms develop.

What usually happens when a person becomes infected with gonorrhea?

Once the gonococcus establishes itself, the infection can take one of several courses: (1) it can remain localized until treated or spontaneously cured by the body's own defense mechanisms, (2) it can spread to involve other organs of the genital tract, (3) it can gain entrance to the blood stream and set up disease elsewhere in the body, (4) it can remain hidden and unsuspected in the genital tissues and produce the so-called carrier state.

Does gonorrhea eventually produce symptoms in all infected women?

Emphatically no. Eighty percent of women with gonorrhea may never develop overt symptoms. Some of these women will overcome their infection without treatment. Others can become asymptomatic carriers and unknowingly be a source of gonorrheal infection to any sexual contacts. It is currently estimated that there may be as many as 800,000 women with undiagnosed and asymptomatic gonorrhea in the United States.

Do men always develop symptoms?

No. As many as 10 to 30 percent may remain free of or completely oblivious to all symptoms. For the others, burning on urination, pain on erection, and a urethral discharge drive them to seek prompt medical attention. The majority of gonorrheal infections are therefore probably transmitted by asymptomatic individuals, both male and female.

What are the early symptoms of gonorrhea in women?

For the 20 percent of women who do develop symptoms, an early gonorrheal infection initially tends to remain localized. Early symptoms are most commonly the result of gonorrheal involvement of the urethra, cervix, rectum, and, less frequently, a Bartholin's gland.

The urethra (urinary channel), because of its vulnerable position near the vaginal opening, is usually the first site attacked by the gonococcus. Inflammation of the urethral lining produces a purulent discharge associated with burning and frequent urination. Since these symptoms may be temporary and even mild, many women simply mistake them for a passing bladder irritation.

Subsequent involvement of the cervix and specifically the endocervical canal by the gonococcus usually provokes a purulent, copious, yellow discharge. However, distinguishing between a cervix infected by gonorrhea or by some other organism is not possible without specific tests. (More about this shortly.) In cases of more severe infections the gonococcus can invade the deep cervical glands, thereby making eradication of the infection more difficult. It is within these cervical glands that the organisms are frequently harbored by unsuspecting carriers.

Gonorrheal infection of one or both Bartholin's glands can cause painful swelling and abscess formation. But a Bartholin's cyst or abscess is not always the result of gonorrhea. Various other bacteria can cause similar problems.

Women can also have localized gonorrhea of the rectum.

How do women acquire rectal gonorrhea?

Women usually acquire rectal gonorrhea by anal intercourse with an infected partner or by contamination of the anal orifice by a copious vaginal gonorrheal discharge. A woman with gonorrhea of the cervix can also have her infection transferred to the rectum by engaging in anal coitus following vaginal intercourse. Rectal gonorrhea in men can usually be traced to anal intercourse with an infected male partner.

In rare instances there may be swelling of the rectal mucosa, pain, bleeding, and even pus formation, but in the vast majority of rectal gonorrheal infections there are no symptoms whatsoever. However, if gonorrhea is limited to the rectum (as it is in approximately 10 percent of women with GC), it means that the infection could ultimately find its way to the vagina and hence to the cervix. Equally important, a woman with such a condition could unknowingly continue to infect and reinfect her sexual partners.

How long can gonorrhea remain localized?

Nobody really knows. In some women invasion by the gonococcus may never extend beyond the cervix. Moreover, on occasion a localized gonorrheal infection has been known to clear without treatment.

In other women, a relatively silent invasion of the inner passageways of the Fallopian tubes can occur. But even here the body's natural defense mechanisms tend to destroy the GC organisms, leaving scarred and sealed tubes as mute testimony to a probable old and unsuspected gonorrheal infection.

However, 10 to 15 percent of all infected women ultimately develop obvious symptoms as the infection spreads beyond the cervix. Although the time interval is variable and often unpredictable, upward extension of the gonorrheal infection most frequently occurs during the first menstrual period following exposure to GC.

How does menstruation encourage the spread of GC in the pelvis?

Having a period is somewhat like rolling out the red carpet: the cervix softens, the canal dilates slightly, and the cervical mucus plug dissolves. Moreover, menstrual blood and cellular debris from the uterine cavity are the perfect media for the gonococcus to feed on and thrive.

From the cervix the GC organisms pass into the uterine cavity, but involvement of the uterine lining is transient and mild. The real trouble begins when the gonococci invade the Fallopian tubes, causing inflammation and the development of pus within the tubal passageways.

If earlier symptoms were minimal, ignored, or even absent, a GC infection of the upper genital organs usually produces pelvic distress. Postmenstrual lower abdominal tenderness, a more obvious discharge, fever, chills, and the aggravation of pelvic pain by sexual intercourse or physical exertion are among the common complaints.

What can be done about tubal infection (salpingitis)?

A GC involvement of the Fallopian tubes demands proper and immediate attention. A delay of as little as twenty-four to thirty-six hours from the onset of abdominal pain and other symptoms may well make the difference between complete recovery and permanent tubal damage. According to one report, 15 percent of women subsequently became sterile as the result of tubal scarring and blockage precipitated by a single episode of gonorrheal tubal infection.

Although hospitalization is frequently necessary, an early and mild tubal infection can occasionally be treated on an outpatient basis with adequate amounts of antibiotics, analgesics for pain relief, and bed rest—plus strict abstinence from all sexual intercourse for a minimum of at least six and preferably eight weeks.

Why no sex for so long?

Following prompt treatment of an early tubal infection, pain and discharge may be minimal within a week or ten days. Yet, despite a remarkable improvement in these obvious symptoms, much more time is needed before all inflammation subsides.

Premature resumption of sexual activity can be responsible for spreading other unwanted bacteria into the healing but still inflamed tissues. It is a well-known fact that recurrences or flare-ups of tubal infections are commonly caused by bacteria other than gonorrhea. GC may do the initial damage, but other bacteria (for example, *E. coli,* strep, etc.) can really finish the job in a devastating manner.

Women who foolishly resume sexual activity too soon, who delay seeking prompt treatment, or who otherwise have a history of repeat tubal infections run an increased risk of ectopic or tubal pregnancies and sterility. In one particular study, 13 percent of the women had blocked tubes after only one tubal infection. After two infections, 36 percent had blocked tubes and after three infections 75 percent of the women were sterile on that basis. In this country alone, close to 100,000 women each year become sterile because of tubal infections. And there can be other complications.

What other pelvic complications?

From the Fallopian tubes, the infection can spread to the nearby ovaries, forming massive tubo-ovarian abscesses that can literally fill the entire lower abdomen. More critical and life-threatening complications ensue when one of these abscesses ruptures, releasing pus into the pelvic and abdominal cavity (peritonitis). And in such cases, despite all our wonderful antibiotics, miracle drugs, and intensive-care units in the best hospitals, sometimes nothing short of complete removal of all the female pelvic organs—uterus, tubes, and ovaries—will save a woman's life.

Among women who recover without the intervention of major surgery, many frequently require repeat hospitalizations for recurrent pelvic inflammatory disease (PID): tubal and ovarian infections, intractable pelvic pain, abnormal bleeding, and incapacitating dysmenorrhea. Temporary relief can be obtained from appropriate medical treatment. But here again, permanent relief from pain and recurrent infections usually requires the ultimate removal of the female pelvic organs.

This aspect of gonorrhea, so conspicuously absent from most lay publications on venereal disease, is not included here to alarm you but rather to try to help overcome the apathetic and complacent attitude of some women who regard a gonorrheal infection as only a minor and temporary inconvenience.

Early and uncomplicated gonorrhea can be readily treated and cured, but the ravages of extensive gonorrheal infections with superimposed invasion by other bacteria on these already compromised tissues can make a woman a pelvic cripple, if not threaten her very life.

Can gonorrhea affect other body areas?

In 1 to 3 percent of individuals with gonorrhea the infection can spread through the blood stream to involve the skin, liver, joints, heart valves, and the brain. Women are more susceptible than men to these disseminated infections and are especially so when pregnant.

One such complication is gonococcal arthritis. It occurs in some 90 percent of blood-borne GC infections and can involve the knees, wrists, and ankles. Symptoms range from pain to acute arthritis with swelling and fluid formation within the joint. If the disease progresses there can be permanent joint damage and deformity. Prompt diagnosis and treatment with penicillin in non-allergic individuals readily clear the condition in most cases.

How does gonorrhea affect the pregnant woman?

If gonorrhea is acquired during the first few weeks of pregnancy, there is the possibility of a spontaneous abortion or direct extension of the infection to involve the Fallopian tubes.

Contraction of the disease after the third month of gestation tends to confine the gonococcus to the lower genital tract. The development during pregnancy of the cervical plug, a thick tenacious mucus blob within the endocervical canal, seems to afford protection against the upward extension of the organism. Symptoms, if present, are thereby restricted to the lower genital tract until the postpartum (after-delivery) period, when further spread of the infection can occur. If the gonorrheal infection is unrecognized and untreated, there is always the added danger that the infant may become infected during delivery.

How does gonorrhea affect the newborn?

The eyes of the newborn are particularly vulnerable to the ravages of the gonococcus. Contamination of the delicate ocular tissues by GC causes a violent inflammatory reaction that can rapidly progress to corneal ulceration and blindness. Although most of these neonatal eye infections are transmitted as the baby passes through the birth canal of an infected mother, they can be acquired before labor and delivery should the membranes rupture prematurely.

Because gonorrhea was once a common cause of blindness in the newborn, hospitals require that the eyes of every newborn be treated with a prophylactic instillation of a 1 percent silver nitrate solution immediately after delivery. On rare occasion gonococcal conjunctivitis can also affect adults whose eyes have come into contact with the discharge with similar devastating consequences unless promptly treated.

Do birth control pills have any effect on gonorrheal infections?

Apparently so. Oral contraceptives enhance a woman's chances of acquiring gonorrhea. Increased vaginal alkalinity, as well as increased moisture and secretions attributable to the hormonal content of birth control pills, makes for a perfect environment in which the gonococcus can flourish. According to some experts, a woman on the pill who experiences penile entry by an infected partner has almost a 100 percent chance of acquiring gonorrhea. The risk of acquiring GC decreases to 40 percent in women similarly exposed who are not on the pill.

How is gonorrhea diagnosed?

Since there are currently no reliable blood tests for gonorrhea, detection of a GC infection still depends on the identification of the organism by either a smear or a culture.

In the smear method, the discharge is spread onto a glass slide, stained with a special dye, and examined microscopically for the gonococcus. Smear tests in men can be highly accurate in diagnosing GC. In women, however, smear tests are notoriously unreliable in detecting gonorrheal infection. For this reason most doctors depend on the culture method. (See Chapter 11.)

An accuracy of almost 95 percent in diagnosing GC in women is obtained if cultures are taken from each of three areas: the endocervical canal, urethral opening, and anal orifice. Interestingly enough, in about 10 percent of infected women, cultures from the anal area were the only ones reported as positive for gonorrhea. Moreover, 60 percent of the women who have a positive cervical culture for GC will also have a positive rectal culture.

In both men and women, the diagnosis of pharyngeal and rectal gonorrhea is made by swabbing these areas with a cotton-tipped applicator and culturing the material. Nowadays with the prevalence of anal coitus and oral genital sex, many venereal disease clinics do take routine cultures from these extra-genital sites.

In women harboring the gonococcus without apparent symptoms, the external genitalia, vagina, and cervix may look completely normal. In these instances, tracking down gonorrhea may well depend on routine screening by culture methods or reliance on a history of a probable recent exposure.

What recent exposure?

If your partner suddenly admits that he has just been treated for a strain, get yourself checked immediately. Most doctors, if told, will not only take a culture but will probably treat you right then and there.

What is the treatment for gonorrhea?

Despite the increasing resistance to penicillin by many strains of gonococcus, penicillin is still the drug most favored for treating a gonorrheal infection.

When penicillin was first introduced in 1943, a single injection of 300,000 units completely eradicated an early GC infection. Today the recommended dose in uncomplicated gonorrhea (for both men and women) is 4.8 million units of aqueous procaine penicillin G, given at one time in two deep intramuscular injections (buttocks). At these dosage levels, penicillin, unlike other antibiotics, has the unique advantage of being able to abort incubating (that is, beginning) syphilis should it also be present. In addition, many doctors routinely give 1 gram of probenecid (Benemid) by mouth before the penicillin injection. This drug allows the penicillin to remain at higher and more effective concentrations in the body for a longer period of time.

Ampicillin (a form of penicillin) by mouth has been substituted for penicillin by injection, but treatment failures are more frequent. Ampicillin is also ineffective against pharyngeal gonorrhea and considerably less capable of aborting incubating syphilis. It is therefore not regarded as equivalent therapy.

For individuals who may be allergic to penicillin, the second drug of choice is tetracycline: 1.5 grams by mouth followed by 0.5 gram every six hours for four days. Total dose 9.0 grams. Premature interruption of therapy or the occasional practice of sharing the tetracycline capsules with sexual acquaintances accounts for frequent treatment failures. Of necessity, if the GC infection is to be eradicated, the entire prescribed dose must be taken by the individual patient. When instructions are followed treatment cures compare favorably with those obtained by penicillin injection.

In cases where a woman is pregnant and allergic to penicillin, Erythromycin by mouth could be substituted for tetracycline. Tetracycline during pregnancy may have toxic effects on fetal tissues as well as cause yellow discoloration and mottling of the child's permanent teeth. Failure rates, however, with Erythromycin can approach 25 percent.

What about treatment in resistant cases of gonorrhea?

In the past few years a drug-resistant form of gonorrhea has appeared in scattered areas throughout the United States. This so-called penicillinase strain of gonococcus produces an enzyme which protects it from penicillin, ampicillin, and tetracycline. When this gonococcus was first isolated in this country, public health officials feared an epidemic. Fortunately, all cases to date have responded to intramuscular injections of the drug spectinomycin HCL (Trobicin). At the moment this drug is strictly reserved for resistant cases of gonorrhea or treatment failures following other antibiotic therapy. Spectinomycin does not prevent incubating syphilis nor is it effective against pharyngeal gonorrhea. Safety of its use in pregnancy has not been established. Since it is also a very expensive antibiotic, other alternative drugs are currently being studied and tested for their potential usefulness against gonorrhea.

How can a woman know whether her GC infection is cured?

Proof of having been cured depends on two and preferably three negative cultures taken usually at one-week intervals following treatment. Needless to say, staying free of a recurrent gonorrheal infection implies adequate and prompt treatment of all sexual partners. Having had gonorrhea does not immunize a woman against subsequent infection.

Can a woman ever develop a natural immunity against gonorrhea?

Some researchers believe that the absence of symptoms in eight out of ten women may represent some form of an immune response. In other words, these women may be manufacturing specific antibodies in their genital tract that make them symptom-free carriers of GC.

If this antibody premise is proved true, two marvelous possibilities may be realized: the eventual development of a reliable and specific blood test to detect GC even in the absence of symptoms, and the perfection of a vaccine against gonorrhea.

Is there any way a woman can protect herself against getting gonorrhea?

It stands to reason that the more sexual contacts a woman and her partners have, the greater her chances of acquiring gonorrhea or syphilis. Although the condom (rubber, prophylactic) is the most effective protection against a potential GC invasion, its use of necessity depends on partner cooperation. Using contraceptive creams, jellies, or foams prior to coitus may discourage the growth of GC organisms, as can douching immediately after intercourse. Except for the condom, none of the other precautions is really dependable in protecting a woman against gonorrhea.

However, if you really think that you may have contracted GC, the best advice is to see your doctor promptly or visit a health clinic. A gonorrheal infection in many women is not clinically apparent. Therefore, unless you specifically go to a VD clinic, don't assume that your private doctor will detect or even check for GC unless you advise him of your concern.

What about syphilis?

Syphilis is by far the most awesome of the sexually transmitted infections. Early symptoms disappear spontaneously and yet, years later the disease can return with devastating consequences in 30 percent of all untreated cases. It is currently estimated that there are 500,000 individuals with untreated syphilis in this country.

What causes syphilis?

Syphilis is a highly infectious disease caused by the spirochete *Treponema pallidum.* This organism is shaped like a corkscrew and can twist and burrow its way through tiny breaks in the skin and mucous membranes. Even the slightest scratch on any skin surface or mucous membrane can provide a portal of entry for this spirochete. The disease is acquired by sexual intercourse or intimate contact with an individual having an open syphilitic sore. Should a woman have the disease while pregnant, the spirochetes can cross the placenta and infect the fetus. On rare occasion medical personnel have acquired the disease by careless handling of infected patients or contaminated laboratory material.

How long is the incubation period?

Anywhere from ten to ninety days following exposure, with three weeks being the average. The length of the incubation period depends on the total number of active spirochetes that enter the body at the time of contact with the infected partner: generally, the greater the number of spirochetes, the shorter the incubation period.

What is meant by the different stages of syphilis?

The disease progresses as follows: early syphilis (primary and secondary stages), latent syphilis (no obvious sign of the disease—detectable only by a blood test), and late syphilis, formerly called tertiary syphilis.

In the primary stage, the first detectable lesion is the chancre, a painless hard sore that heals by itself within six to ten weeks. Commonly associated with the primary lesion is a painless hard swelling of local lymph nodes that drain the area around the lesion (for example, inguinal or groin nodes in a genital chancre).

With the subsequent widespread dissemination of the spirochetes through the bloodstream, the disease moves into the secondary stage of early syphilis. The appearance of secondary skin lesions may occur during or shortly after the healing of the chancre or may be delayed for months. Most typically, the skin lesions appear as a generalized non-itchy rash or as multiple skin or mucous membrane eruptions— anywhere from the scalp down to and including the soles of the feet and the palms of the hands. Occasionally the rash is so transient and indistinct that it goes virtually unnoticed. Other times, an individual may develop flat wartlike growths involving the genital area. These syphilitic warts are called condyloma lata and are not to be confused with the common venereal wart or genital wart. Other symptoms of secondary syphilis may be nonspecific: sore throat with hoarseness, headaches, general malaise, aching muscles, and patchy loss of scalp hair. Some individuals may even pass through the secondary stage of syphilis with few if any of these symptoms.

Individuals with signs of early syphilis, that is, either the chancre or the generalized skin eruptions of the secondary stage, are highly infectious. Because all these skin lesions are teeming with spirochetes, it is during these stages of early syphilis that an infected individual can easily transmit the disease to a close contact.

If untreated, the skin lesions of secondary syphilis heal spontaneously within three to six weeks and the disease evolves into latent syphilis. During this stage there is no clinical evidence of the disease, nor can it be transmitted to another individual. The one exception is the pregnant woman with latent syphilis whose unborn child can readily be infected. The diagnosis of latent syphilis can only be made with a special blood test.

For the one out of three untreated individuals who will progress from latent syphilis to the final stage, late syphilis, symptoms may not appear for an additional ten to fifteen years. Because the spirochete can affect any organ, prediction of the final outcome in any individual is not possible. Destructive lesions of the heart, blood vessels, brain, spinal cord, bone, skin, etc., are all possibilities.

The fact that the incidence of this disease has been rising at an alarming rate since 1950 makes the recognition of early syphilis, as well as how to deal with a possible exposure, a matter of vital concern.

What does the chancre of early syphilis look like?

The very first sign of syphilis is the chancre, a painless red swelling about the size of a small pea. Within a week's time it usually enlarges to the size of a marble, ulcerates, and forms an open or crusted hard painless sore with firm raised edges and a central depression somewhat like a small crater. The chancre marks the place where the spirochetes originally entered the body and usually appears ten to ninety days after contact with an infected person. In most cases the chancre is located on the penis or vulva. At times it may be found on the lips, tongue, or breast. As a rule, there is only one chancre, but there can be more. Since a chancre is teeming with spirochetes, an individual is highly infectious at this time. Also, as previously mentioned, there is usually an associated painless swelling of the lymph nodes on one or both sides, typically the inguinal (groin) nodes. Whether treated or untreated, the chancre will heal and the lymph node swelling will subside within four to ten weeks.

Can a chancre sometimes go unnoticed?

Yes. In men, although the lesion is usually apparent, a chancre of the glans penis may initially go unnoticed in an uncircumcised male if it is under the foreskin. In women the chancre is most commonly present on the vulva or around the vaginal opening, but on occasion it may be located on the cervix or even along the inside vaginal wall. When the chancre appears in the latter locations its presence is frequently unsuspected by the woman.

How can early syphilis be accurately diagnosed?

There are two reliable methods of diagnosing early syphilis: identification of the spirochete in a skin lesion or serological testing (blood test). In primary syphilis the chancre is usually scraped and the material examined for the presence of spirochetes under a special dark-field microscope. Otherwise a blood test can be taken. In primary syphilis, however, the blood test is not usually reactive (positive) until one to four weeks *after* the appearance of the chancre. Since a chancre can sometimes go unobserved, any woman worried about having contracted syphilis should have an initial blood test. If negative, the test should be repeated in six weeks and again in three months (ninety days). A negative blood test for syphilis three months after possible exposure would be virtual assurance that there had been no contact with the disease. In secondary syphilis the blood test is *always* positive.

What kind of blood tests can detect syphilis?

A Wasserman, a VDRL, or just plain blood serology, as it is sometimes called, can detect syphilis. Currently, the most common blood test for syphilis is the serological screening test VDRL (Veneral Disease Research Laboratory). It is accurate in detecting syphilis but it can sometimes be positive in the presence of other diseases not related to syphilis. Such so-called biological false positive reactions can occur in a variety of illnesses. Patients, for example, with infectious mononucleosis, measles, chicken pox, hepatitis, and collagen diseases have at times turned up with false positive tests for syphilis. In fact any illness with fever or any immunization such as a small pox vaccination can result in a temporary (usually six months or less) false positive VDRL test for syphilis. For ths reason a positive VDRL test may require confirmation. Today, there is a specific and sensitive test for syphilis, the FTA-ABS (Fluorescent Treponemal Antibody Absorption Test). This test is not routinely used for the simple reason that it is complicated and expensive. At the present time routine testing for syphilis with the VDRL is almost standard procedure in all hospital admissions, during pregnancy, and for individuals applying for a marriage license (premarital blood test).

How about treatment for syphilis?

Once the diagnosis is confirmed the treatment of choice is penicillin. Unlike the gonococcus, the spirochete has not developed any resistance to penicillin. Consequently, control and cure of the disease in the early stages can be obtained with relatively low doses. In individuals allergic to penicillin, the second drug of choice is tetracycline, except, of course, during pregnancy, when Erythromycin may be substituted.

Following adequate treatment, repeat blood tests should revert to normal and register negative. This means that if an individual has been successfully treated for early syphilis, subsequent VDRL blood tests such as that required for a marriage license would show no evidence of previous contact with the disease. Should the infection be diagnosed and treated at a later stage (for example, during latent syphilis), the blood test in certain individuals may always remain weakly positive despite successful treatment and eradication of the infection.

If you have been treated for early syphilis, can you get reinfected?

Yes. Prompt and adequate treatment of early syphilis affords no protection against future reinfection.

What about congenital syphilis, or syphilis acquired before birth?

A disease that was almost extinct in this country is making a shocking comeback. Early diagnosis and treatment of syphilis in the pregnant woman is vital if the fetus is to be spared. Since maternal spirochetes do not pass the placental barrier until after the fourth month of pregnancy, treatment before the sixteenth week will completely prevent syphilitic infection of the unborn child. Once the fetus becomes infected, however, every month that passes without treatment increases the chances of serious involvement and possible death for the fetus. An undiagnosed, severe infection during pregnancy may end in spontaneous abortion, a still-born baby at term, or a term live infant with syphilis. Since the spirochetes invade the bloodstream of the fetus directly, there is no primary or chancre stage in congenital syphilis.

How does syphilis affect the newborn?

If the infant is born alive, it has a 40 percent chance of having multiple skin or mucous-membrane lesions in addition to bone, liver, and spleen involvement. Treatment at this stage may or may not save the child's life.

For the remaining 60 percent of affected infants, the disease may be latent and unsuspected for at least two years and frequently asymptomatic until just prior to puberty. Early diagnosis in these children depends on a blood test. Any delay in recognition of the disease can cause the child to develop corneal scarring with blindness, saddle nose deformity (destruction of nasal bones), notching of the permanent teeth (upper incisors), eight-nerve deafness, and/or brain, spinal cord, and bone damage. Treatment at this stage will halt further progression of the disease but will not reverse damage already done.

What are some of the other common veneral diseases?

Genital herpes and chlamydial infections. These two diseases are important not only because of the genital problems they create but because they can also be transmitted to the newborn at the time of delivery.

Genital herpes in particular is being seen with increasing frequency. Although this infection can be transmitted by a single act of coitus with one infected partner, it is more apt to occur in women with multiple partners and especially among those previously treated for other veneral diseases.

What about genital herpes infections?

Most of you are probably familiar with the common fever blister or cold sore caused by the herpes simplex virus type I, but a closely related virus, herpes simplex virus type II, can affect the vulva, cervix, and upper vagina. The fact that it may be a precursor to cancer of the cervix or in some way linked to its development has recently put herpesvirus type II in the medical spotlight.

Most genital herpes infections are caused by contact with the type II virus during sexual intercourse; however, recent studies indicate that individuals who harbor the type I herpes simplex virus around the lips and mouth can transmit the virus to their partner's genital organs during cunnilingus or fellatio. In fact, some 10 percent of all genital herpes infections may be caused by the type I virus because of an apparent increase in oral genital play. Since type I virus is not implicated in the possible development of cervical cancer, the infection is potentially less serious than exposure to type II, but the physical symptoms can be just as distressing.

What are the symptoms of a genital herpes infection?

Following a two- to seven-day incubation period, the very first sign may be a tingling sensation or vague discomfort of the vulva. This is quickly followed by the appearance of small vesicles or blisterlike eruptions usually along the labia minora and/or around the vaginal opening. These blisters, which are intensely painful, soon rupture and become small shallow ulcers. Other symptoms include fever, sometimes as high as 101, general malaise, and enlarged tender groin lymph nodes. Swelling and inflammation around the urethra may make urination very painful, if not impossible, thus necessitating catheterization until the edema subsides. In infections with herpesvirus type II, the cervix is apt to be red, irritated, and ulcerated, often leading to discharge and vaginal spotting.

As an aside, the lesions in the male are similar in appearance and occur predominantly on the glans and corona of the penis.

Symptoms may vary depending on whether it is a woman's initial exposure to the virus or a recurrent infection. If a woman has had no previous encounter with any of the other herpesviruses (for example, cold sores, shingles, etc.) and thus has no antibodies against this group of viruses, running into herpesvirus type II for the first time can be downright distressing. Fortunately, however, primary genital herpes infections will clear spontaneously within three to four weeks with no residual scarring from the vulvar ulcerations.

Are recurrent infections as distressing as initial exposure?

As a general rule, recurrent infections are considerably more mild. Itching and slight burning discomfort of the vulva may signal the onset of a flare-up, but unlike a primary attack, the blisters are smaller and frequently localized to a single area. In addition, recurrent infections are not associated with fever, aches, or flulike symptoms.

Repeat infections are usually reactivations of the virus rather than the result of reexposure. In other words, once infected, a woman continues to harbor the virus, which under certain circumstances can precipitate another active infection. But exactly what triggers viral reactivation remains unknown. Among some women, emotional stress, nonrelated illnesses with fever, menstruation, or even hormonal imbalances have been blamed for recurrences of genital herpes. Some experts contend that flare-ups can be caused by increased genital warmth through the wearing of nylon underwear and pantyhose. As the body builds up more antibodies against this viral disease, repeat attacks tend to be milder, less frequent, and of shorter duration. Most cases will clear within seven to ten days.

How common are repeat infections?

Some individuals, following a primary attack, are never again bothered. Why they should be so spared is one of the puzzling aspects of this disease. Others may have two, three, or more recurrences within the space of a year. Generally, there is an 80 percent recurrence rate within the first six months following a primary attack.

How is genital herpes usually diagnosed?

Primarily by symptoms and physical findings. Few diseases can cause such distressing vulvar pain in association with small, shallow, labial ulcerations. Laboratory diagnosis can be made by taking a special smear test of the ulcers. Although the virus would not be seen, the presence of certain multinucleated giant cells would be indirect proof that the herpesvirus was present and responsible for the lesions. Where facilities are available, the virus can be isolated and grown in special tissue cultures. This method of diagnosis, however, is expensive, time-consuming, and rarely necessary. Apart from these studies, special blood tests can detect past infection with herpesvirus by the presence of antibodies.

What are the dangers of genital herpes during pregnancy?

Genital herpes during pregnancy can cause miscarriages and premature labor, but the biggest risk to the baby is at the time of delivery. With few exceptions, babies acquire herpetic infections by being exposed to the virus as they pass through an infected birth canal. Women with no signs of active infection at the time of labor are probably not infectious. This means that a woman could deliver normally and without fear of infecting the baby if she were not having a flare-up at the time of labor. If, however, there was a repeat infection of genital herpes near term or obvious genital lesions (blisters, ulcers) at the time of labor, delivery would be by Caesarean section. This would help protect the baby from contacting the virus.

Since there is no known effective treatment for disseminated herpes of the newborn, prevention of this disease is of the utmost importance. Once infected (and there is a 40 percent risk if exposed) 50 percent of the newborns will die. Among those infants who do survive, 25 percent may have severe neurological damage and an additional 25 percent may have extensive skin lesions.

The severity of this disease in the newborn makes it imperative that any pregnant woman be alert to the possibility of genital herpes. Primary infections near term can be especially threatening to the newborn. A woman with a past history of genital herpes should be closely followed during pregnancy and particularly as she approaches her due date. She, herself, should be on the lookout for any suggestion of recurrence. Where the diagnosis may be uncertain the doctor may take serial smear tests of the cervix to check for the presence of herpesvirus.

Although most herpetic infections of the newborn are the result of exposure to herpesvirus type II at the time of delivery, any contact with herpesvirus during the first forty-eight hours of life is potentially dangerous to the newborn. Thus an individual with any herpetic lesion such as a fever blister or cold sore (herpesvirus type I) on the lips or anywhere on the body should not handle or touch any newborn during those critical first two days. For some inexplicable reason, contact with herpesvirus after the third day of life is rarely a serious problem. At this time most newborns can usually handle and successfully overcome a herpetic infection.

Does genital herpes increase a woman's risk of cervical cancer?

There has been growing concern that genital herpes may predispose a woman to cancer of the cervix. At the present time there is no conclusive evidence of a cause-and-effect relationship. Nevertheless, it is known that the same factors associated with a high risk of cervical cancer are also associated with a high risk of genital herpes—namely, first intercourse at an early age and a history of multiple sex partners. Studies have shown that women with antibodies to herpesvirus type II are up to ten times more likely to develop cervical cancer than women with no antibodies to this virus. Some experts suggest that the virus may make the cervical cells more susceptible to malignant change. Until the issue is clearly settled, women with a known history of genital herpes should probably have routine Pap smears every six months.

Is there any specific treatment for genital herpes?

There is currently no available treatment that will permanently eradicate the virus. Therapy for acute genital herpes is still limited to relief of symptoms and prevention of secondary infection. Applications of cold milk compresses four to six times a day for five to ten minutes as well as a local anesthetic ointment such as lidocaine may be helpful. Where pain during urination is extreme, spraying cold water onto the vulva while voiding can minimize discomfort. For this purpose a small plastic bottle filled with cold water and equipped with a spray top can be very helpful. In some instances the application of ether-soaked cotton balls directly onto the lesions has helped relieve pain and shorten the course of infection. In the recent past a technique using special dyes applied to the lesions in conjunction with fluorescent lighting was providing marked relief within twenty-four hours. This photodye technique has now been largely abandoned because animal studies have shown that virus particles so treated may become malignant.

Treatment aimed at reducing the frequency of repeat infections by building up antibodies against viral diseases has also been tried. Smallpox vaccinations, BCG vaccinations, and even polio vaccinations have been used, but to date, none of these treatments has been consistently effective.

There are, however, several new antiviral drugs that appear most promising. As of this writing their release in this country is being delayed pending the results of clinical trials.

Another new treatment currently under investigation is the use of vaginal tampons impregnated with zinc sulfate (changed daily) and worn for ten to twenty-one days during and immediately following a primary herpetic infection. Originally devised as a barrier contraceptive, these new vaginal tampons (at least in limited studies) can accelerate healing of the ulcers as well as reduce the incidence of recurrent infections. Undoubtedly as large-scale studies are conducted more definitive results and conclusions can be reached.

Is there any way a woman can protect herself from ever getting genital herpes?

Protecting yourself from genital herpes comes down to avoiding direct contact with active lesions. For practical purposes this means not having intercourse with someone who has obvious herpetic ulcers, or who otherwise is just beginning or getting over a herpes infection. Determining this, however, can be difficult as signs and symptoms of active herpes can be vague, especially in the initial stages. When in doubt, the use of a condom definitely gives protection. Contraceptive foams as well as thorough genital cleansing with soap and water after intercourse can also reduce the chance of infection. Since genital herpes has a short incubation period (two to seven days), lack of symptoms on your part after this time period following a possible exposure should be consoling.

What are chlamydial infections?

Recently, another organism has come to the attention of gynecologists, the bacterium *Chlamydial trachomatis*. Although already known to be a major cause of urethritis in men (NGU or nongonorrheal urethritis), it was not previously thought that this bacteria affected women. Now we know better. *Chlamydial trachomatis* can cause vaginal discharge, cervicitis, and tubal infection. Infants born to women infected with *C. trachomatis* can acquire the bacteria as they pass through the birth canal. This can result in eye inflammation (conjunctivitis) and possibly even respiratory infections and pneumonia during the first few months of life. Fortunately, most infections respond to the antibiotic tetracycline.

Can anything really be done about the problem of venereal disease?

Mass awareness of any public health menace begins with individual awareness. With the astronomical increase of venereal disease in this country, every sexually active person now runs a higher risk of infection.

If your sex life is not confined to a mutually faithful relationship with a single partner, you may well have reason to be concerned. Until researchers develop effective vaccines against gonorrhea, syphilis, genital herpes, and other venereal diseases, you must assume responsibility for yourself.

More and more women are making appointments for the specific purpose of being checked for venereal disease. So don't let possible feelings of guilt or embarrassment delay you. After all, only you can evaluate your own situation.

13. Odor Is a Four-Letter Word

No longer content with making the American public superconscious about halitosis, bromidrosis, armpitosis, and questionable household odors, Madison Avenue has also intimated for several years that if the truth be known, all women need a feminine hygiene spray deodorant.

From the climbing sales figures reported for feminine hygiene deodorants, now in excess of $58 million annually, there is no denying that many American women are seeking a gyno-cosmetic product comparable in effectiveness to underarm deodorants. Despite the biological differences between the sexes that make potential odors more of a problem for women, it is also true that American women as a group are the most aseptic, germ-free, scrupulously impeccable, and odor-conscious Homo sapiens ever to walk the earth.

It is therefore time to analyze this provocative and hush-hush subject of odors from a more objective viewpoint.

Is it normal to have a biological scent?

Yes. Since it was nature's intent to make the human female the more sexually attractive of the species, woman is endowed with 75 percent more apocrine (scent) glands than her male counterpart. These glands, which normally develop during puberty, are particularly concentrated in the labia minora, circumanal region, underarm area, and around the nipples and umbilicus. Unlike ordinary sweat (eccrine) glands that excrete primarily an odorless combination of water, salt, and lactic acid, the apocrine glands intermittently exude a somewhat milky, organic material that emits a characteristic but inoffensive odor.

Just as fingerprints are individually specific, each person has a distinct olfactory signature resulting from differences in glandular activity of the skin, hormone levels, and emotional tension. These individual differences account for the common observation that the same perfume does not have the same fragrance when worn by different women.

Yet, although each woman is unique, there are certain factors common to all women that can adversely alter the normal biological scent.

What factors?

Because of the vulva's anatomical configuration, perspiration, for example, is frequently combined with decreased absorption of moisture. In overweight women, further deepening of the normal vulvar folds along with close contact of the upper inner thighs tends to increase normally retained moisture. Similarly, panty hose or tight-fitting underwear, particularly nylon, also work to trap moisture and prevent its evaporation. Since body odors are caused by bacteria acting upon perspiration as well as upon other normal secretions from sebaceous and apocrine glands, the more bacteria interacting with normal or increased vulvar skin secretions the greater the possibility of an unpleasant odor.

What can decrease odor formation?

Nothing has yet challenged the effectiveness of plain soap and water in reducing the number of skin bacteria, in addition to eliminating any accumulated skin secretions. But unless one gently but thoroughly washes between the vulvar folds, bacteria and skin secretions may be untouched by even the soap and water routine. Plush, luxurious washclothes are usually too bulky to be effective. Much more efficient is the use of either a lightweight washcloth or a well-soaped finger, particularly between the inner and outer lips and junction of the labia minora and the clitoris. This latter area especially tends to accumulate bacteria and cellular debris (smegma) that might be a factor in the formation of clitoral adhesions. (See Chapter 15.)

If you are planning to travel or vacation where modern bathroom facilities are either at a premium or nonexistent, towelettes can provide a temporary solution.

What exactly are towelettes?

In case you are not familiar with this handy product, feminine hygiene towelettes are small premoistened cloths individually wrapped in aluminum foil packets. They can be used just like a washcloth for external vulvar cleansing.

One word of caution is needed. Do not confuse Wash 'n Dri towelettes, which have a 20 percent alcohol content, with feminine hygiene towelettes. Wash 'n Dris are marvelous for face and hand cleansing but will cause a severe burning sensation if used on delicate vulvar mucous membranes.

To douche or not to douche—is that the question?

Whether you do or don't douche is a personal matter. If douching makes you feel secure, confident, dainty, or whatever else you want to call it, your freedom of choice in this matter should be tempered by knowing what douching can and cannot accomplish.

Since normal vaginal secretions are odorless, and a healthy vagina maintains a certain acidity and cleanses itself through the action of normal bacteria and mucus drainage, douching is theoretically not necessary. However, there are times when douching may be indicated.

What times?

Primarily after menstruation and especially if tampons were used. The practice of using only one tampon during the entire last day of menstruation can on occasion encourage the growth of unwanted vaginal organisms by temporarily trapping mucus and blood. For this reason some doctors will suggest douching after a period.

Are there any other times when douching may be advisable?

As mentioned in earlier chapters, douching immediately after intercourse can afford some protection against possible infection with *Trichomonas vaginalis* (TV) and even against gonorrhea. But as for keeping you from getting pregnant, douching after intercourse (see Chapter 18) is doomed to failure. By the time you run to the bathroom (a real mood-breaker), many of the sperm will already have passed the point of no return. Moreover, if you are using a contraceptive cream or jelly, douching may well wash away your protection.

Aside from these practical considerations, most women douche purely for aesthetic reasons. The desire to be impeccable in intimate situations and especially in oral genital sex is only natural. For most women, however, such precautions are rarely necessary. Simple vulvar cleansing beforehand is usually sufficient to ensure one's being free of any unpleasant odor.

How often can one douche?

Although normal vaginal bacteria return within a few hours after douching, no one really knows how long a normal vagina can maintain its natural protective mechanisms when exposed to repeated irrigations over a long period of time. Some women admit to douching every day and have never experienced any particular problem. On the other hand, too frequent and improper douching (particularly with strong solutions) can, by altering the normal vaginal environment, create irritation and discharge.

Therefore, to be on the safe side, two or three times a week is a good limit if you must douche, unless specifically advised otherwise by your doctor.

Are prepackaged vaginal douche products safe to use regularly?

Yes, provided of course you aren't allergic or sensitive to one of the ingredients. With the advent of prepackaged and premeasured vaginal douche powders, most of which are properly buffered to maintain normal vaginal acidity, vulvovaginal irritations from improper douching now seem less common. For those of you who can resist such tempters as raspberry or orange sherbet flavored douches, the old-fashioned two tablespoons of plain white vinegar in a quart of warm water, although not as enticing, is just as good and a lot cheaper. Douching daily with plain tap water, however, can in a few women create problems by upsetting vaginal acidity.

When shouldn't you douche?

During pregnancy and for at least four weeks following delivery. Since the cervical os and canal may be slightly open especially during late pregnancy, douching may inadvertently cause either premature rupture of the membranes (bag of waters) or the introduction of fluid within the uterine cavity. In either case the development of an intrauterine infection could potentially jeopardize the fetus. Similarly, douching too soon after delivery, before the uterine lining has a chance to heal completely, could also lead to an intrauterine infection. In this case, bacteria from the vagina could be flushed against the cervix and thus work their way into the uterine cavity.

Is douching harmful during menstruation?

No. By the same token, douching during menstruation accomplishes very little other than momentarily flushing out the blood and cellular debris from the vagina. Nonetheless, some women who have intercourse during menstruation will douche at this time and insert a diaphragm before coitus solely for aesthetic reasons.

Is there a right and wrong way to douche?

In a personal survey, 80 percent of the women queried were found not to douche properly. Eight out of ten women douche while sitting on the toilet. At best, even with the douche bag sufficiently elevated, douching in the sitting or squatting position rarely accomplishes more than a token flush of the vagina. If you still prefer this method because it's faster, more convenient, and seems to do the job, that's fine. However, if you have been given a special douche prescription to treat a vaginal infection and can rely on being undisturbed in the bathroom, why not get the greatest benefit from the medication by douching properly?

What is the proper way to douche?

In the bathtub lying down. If you are using a bag and hose (preferable to a syringe), mix the douche ingredients with warm water as instructed and place the bag so that it will hang about two feet above your hips while you douche. In many bathtubs, attaching the bag to the faucet will be just about the right height. For added comfort, heat the tub by rinsing it with warm water before stepping in. You are now ready to proceed.

Gently insert the douche nozzle into the vagina as far as it will go and lie back. Allow the solution to begin flowing and at the same time (using both hands) close the vaginal opening against the nozzle so that the vagina literally becomes flooded. If this is done correctly, you will notice a slight pressure sensation as the vagina expands to accommodate the fluid. At this time clamp off the hose, release your hold, and allow the vagina to drain. If sufficient fluid was retained for proper douching, it will be rapidly expelled with a swoosh. Repeat the same process until the bag hangs empty.

What about the presence of an unpleasant odor despite frequent douching?

Normal vaginal secretions from a healthy vagina do not have any odor. If an unpleasant odor or obvious discharge persists or returns fairly promptly after douching, it may indicate a vaginal or cervical infection and should be checked out.

In the absence of any discharge or irritation of the vagina or vulva, the presence of a particularly fetid odor may be the result of a forgotten tampon.

How can a woman forget a tampon in the vagina?

Easily. Changing tampons is done so automatically by regular users that often one cannot remember having removed the used tampon before inserting a fresh replacement. Even checking for the telltale string can at times be deceptive. Occasionally that little string adheres so snugly to the vulva that unless you probe the vaginal entrance or examine yourself with a mirror, you too might inadvertently insert a fresh tampon without removing the old one.

What happens now?

Because a forgotten tampon encourages the growth of undesirable bacteria, you will invariably notice an increasingly unpleasant odor within a few days—usually after your period is over. Despite the odor, however, forgotten tampons do not cause vaginal problems. Equally consoling is the fact that a tampon lost in the vagina remains in the vagina until removed or spontaneously expelled. There's just no other place for it to go. Therefore, if you suspect that a lost or retained tampon might be the problem, don't be alarmed. Just check it out.

How can you remove a lost tampon?

If your vagina can accommodate two fingers, recovering a lost tampon can be quite easy. Either squat or bend forward from a standing position and insert the index and middle fingers into the vagina as far as you can reach. Prior lubrication of your fingers with cold cream or Vaseline also helps. Since the tampon is probably lying next to the cervix, you may have to strain or bear down as if you were having a bowel movement in order to bring it within reach. Once located, the tampon can usually be grasped and removed by your fingers, chopstick style. Douching afterwards in such a case would definitely be advisable.

What about feminine hygiene deodorants?

Presumably able to cover up odors and to inhibit the growth of bacteria, feminine hygiene deodorants come in either spray or spray powder form. All of them contain a propellant, but information about other substances that they might contain is not readily available. The fact that feminine hygiene deodorants are currently listed as cosmetics exempts the manufacturers from having to list the ingredients or to demonstrate the effectiveness or safety of these products.

Do feminine hygiene sprays really eliminate odors?

The answer is elusive. Further studies may clarify this point, but as of now, questions are being raised about whether the pretesting of these products adequately substantiates their deodorizing claims.

Be that as it may, feminine hygiene deodorants have found a ready market despite questionable pretesting and potential hazards to some women.

What potential hazards?

Acute and diffuse inflammation of the vulva for one thing. Other complaints attributable to the use of feminine hygiene deodorants range from itching and burning of the vulva to severe local allergic reactions requiring hospitalization.

Some women will be sensitive or allergic to any product even when properly used and proved safe. However, the point to be made is this: when a product is known to be so chemically irritating to the vaginal mucous membranes that even the manufacturers contraindicate its vaginal use, how really safe are feminine spray deodorants when by their very intent they must be sprayed near and around the area that is to be avoided? In women with relaxed vaginal openings, for example, even spraying at the recommended distance of six to twelve inches can in no way avoid contact with exposed vaginal mucous membranes.

The restrictions banning their use on tampons and prior to sexual intercourse because of potential vaginal and penile irritation raise another provocative question.

Of what real value are feminine hygiene deodorants?

Since odor-conscious women are probably most concerned with the possibility of offending during menstruation and at the time of sexual intercourse, limitations prohibiting the use of spray deodorants on tampons and prior to coitus seem to greatly detract from their value.

So although feminine hygiene deodorants presumably can be used after intercourse or for those in-between times, so can other and more effective products such as soap and water and even towelettes.

In all fairness to the cosmetic manufacturers of feminine hygiene deodorants, for some women they are no doubt on the right track. At the present time, however, the available products seem to fall short in both efficacy and safety.

Will a new and better deodorant spray be produced?

In view of the inherent sensitivity of vulvar mucous-membrane tissue, plus the occurrence of menstrual bleeding and sometimes abnormal vaginal discharges, it is very debatable whether even concerted research efforts will eventually produce a spray so magical that a single squirt or two will eradicate any or all objectionable odors for X number of hours.

So while the search goes on for the ideal product, the use of soap and water is still the best way to maintain an odor-free and hygienic external genital area.

14. Bladder Infections, Urinary Control Problems, and Sagging Pelvic Supports

If you have recurrent bladder infections, lose control of your urine, or have the sensation that your vagina is way too big for your husband, there is an answer—and the solution can begin with you. This does not mean that you can ignore your prescription for bladder medication or circumvent vaginal plastic surgery where truly indicated. But it does imply that distressing urinary disturbances and problems related to sagging pelvic supports can frequently be improved and at times even prevented by the knowledgeable and motivated woman.

Sexual intercourse, pregnancy, childbirth, and the law of gravity all work to stretch and strain the vaginal tissues and pelvic supports. Aging and gradual estrogen depletion also cause those supports to weaken, thin, and lose their snap. Moreover, the unique anatomy of the female genital urinary system further predisposes women to a variety of bladder disturbances. As you will soon see, this can sometimes mean intermittent loss of urinary control. For others, bladder irritations and bladder infections seem to recur with annoying regularity.

Are women really more susceptible to bladder infections than men?
Bladder infections (cystitis) are without a doubt one of the most common medical problems of women. They can occur as a single

acute infection or they can be chronic, recurrent, and linger into the postmenopausal years. Women under forty have three times more bladder infections than men in the same age group. And the precipitating factor for acute and recurrent bladder infections in the female can sometimes be sexual intercourse. In fact, for the young woman just beginning an active sex life, "honeymoon cystitis" may be her very first encounter with a urinary problem.

Are you a candidate for honeymoon cystitis?

Whether or not you are on your honeymoon, sexual intercourse can set the stage for a cystitis, that is, a bladder infection.

Why this should be is readily explained. A lot has to do with the female's shorter urethra. The male urethra averages seven to eight inches from the tip of the penis to the bladder, whereas the female urethra measures a scant 1.6 inches in length. Furthermore, the presence of bacteria around the vulvar mucosa and the closeness of the urethral opening to the vagina also help set the stage for a potential bacterial invasion of the bladder.

Now, if you add one more factor, penile vaginal intercourse, the curtain rises on act one of acute honeymoon cystitis. Although any woman is vulnerable, the young bride whose vaginal opening is relatively snug is most susceptible. Intercourse for her in the conventional male-on-top position will automatically direct the penis along the roof of the vagina—or, from another point of view, against the floor of the urethra and bladder. The pumping action of the penis in this position not only irritates those structures above the vaginal wall but also pushes bacteria from the outside vulvar area into the woman's urethra and bladder.

Since invading bacteria normally take a day or so to establish themselves, acute cystitis usually strikes about thirty-six hours following the initial precipitating intercourse. Don't blame last night's love making for this morning's problem. Symptoms initiated *last* night wouldn't show up until tomorrow.

Honeymoon cystitis is no joke. It is a real bladder infection that requires treatment and supportive care.

Are all sexually active women more vulnerable to cystitis?

They may all be more vulnerable, but interestingly enough, many women seem strangely resistant to any bladder infection. Just why this should be is currently being investigated.

Some experts attribute the lack of infection in some women to a highly developed local immune mechanism in the bladder wall. Other evidence indicates that women with recurrent cystitis have substantially more bacteria around the urethral and vaginal areas than women who remain uninfected. The fact that personal hygiene plays no significant role in this phenomenon has lent support to the idea that perhaps there may be a subtle biological difference among women in regard to the prevalence of vulvar mucosal bacteria.

In a few isolated instances, uncircumcised males harboring bacteria beneath the foreskin have been a source of recurrent urinary infections in their sexual partners. Even less common, but nonetheless a potent method of introducing bacteria, is the practice of having anal intercourse and then reinserting the penis into the vagina without taking the precaution of washing or cleansing the male organ.

What else can increase a woman's risk of bladder infections?

Pregnancy. Pregnant women are definitely more vulnerable to bladder infections because of hormonal and physiological changes. Bladder tone, for example, is normally reduced during pregnancy. This allows the bladder to fill and retain more urine before a woman feels the need to void. As a consequence, less frequent voiding can lead to urinary stasis with the increased chance of infection. As many as 10 percent of pregnant women do have an asymptomatic and unsuspected bladder infection. Since these silent bladder infections during pregnancy can lead to pyelonephritis, kidney damage, and even precipitate premature labor, it is important that they be detected and promptly treated. This is one of the reasons for routine urinalysis during pregnancy.

Other factors that predispose a woman to urinary tract infections include diabetes, obstructions to the flow of urine (stones, strictures, tumors, etc.), bladder disturbances because of nerve damage (for example, spinal cord injuries), and frequent catheterizations or instrumentations of the urethra and bladder.

How can you tell if you have a bladder infection?

In contrast to some acute kidney infections with resultant shaking chills, high fever, flank pain, and general malaise, the symptoms of most bladder infections are tame. Most women with cystitis complain primarily of frequent urination, a burning, stinging pain along the urethra during and immediately after voiding, and occasional mild cramping discomfort over the pubic area. Fever, if any, rarely causes the temperature to exceed 99 degrees Fahrenheit. When the cystitis is particularly severe with marked irritation and inflammation of the bladder lining, there may even be the passage of bloody urine in an otherwise healthy woman.

Symptoms, however, can be misleading. Not all painful urination can be blamed on an actual bladder infection. Any irritation or inflammation of the tissues around the urethra or bladder can produce similar complaints. Vaginal infections, vulvar irritations, and gonorrheal involvement of the urethra in particular (see Chapter 12) can readily mimic acute cystitis.

What else can cause pain on urination in the absence of infection?

Painful urination occurring *shortly after intercourse* is most commonly the result of trauma to the urethra during coitus. Penile friction against the floor of the urethra and bladder in a woman with insufficient vaginal lubrication and/or a snug vaginal opening can be contributing factors.

In the postmenopausal woman, for example, the relative thinness of the vaginal walls and their diminished capacity to expand and dilate during coitus make the overlying urinary structures even more vulnerable to injury and inflammation.

But sexual intercourse is not always the precipitating factor. Urethral pain, burning on urination, and at times slight urethral bleeding noticed after voiding in postmenopausal women can be the result of an estrogen deficiency. An estrogen deficiency by itself can cause chronic low-grade inflammation of the urethral mucosa as well as vaginal and vulvar atrophy. Fortunately, most of these urological complaints in older women can be markedly improved by either oral estrogen or local estrogen therapy in the form of vaginal creams or suppositories. (See Chapter 23.)

How, then, is a bladder infection diagnosed?

Most commonly by the microscopic examination of urine for the presence of bacteria and white blood cells (pus cells). Since the majority of bladder infections are caused by Gram-negative bacteria (bacteria that will stain pink when subjected to certain dyes for identification purposes—specifically, *E. coli*) that respond to most bladder medications, your doctor will probably order a routine urinalysis simply to confirm the presence of bacteria and pus cells.

If, however, following treatment, your urine still shows a significant number of bacteria and pus cells, or if you have had recurrent flare-ups of cystitis, a urine culture and sensitivity test may be necessary. As explained in Chapter 11, a culture has the advantage of identifying the bacteria responsible for the infection. A urine culture can also gauge the severity of the infection by specifying the number of bacteria present per cc. (cubic centimeter) of urine.

A urine sensitivity test goes one step further by actually testing the bacteria's resistance or sensitivity to the more commonly used antibiotics and bladder medications (urinary chemotherapeutic agents). In other words, a urine culture and sensitivity test will tell your doctor what bacteria are causing your infection, how severe the infection is, and what medicine will work best against it.

Needless to say, if the diagnosis and treatment of your case of acute cystitis depends upon an examination of your urine, you should know how to collect a specimen properly.

What is the best way to collect a urine specimen?

Under normal and healthy conditions, urine is sterile (no bacteria). It is therefore important that you not confuse the diagnosis or your doctor by allowing your urine specimen to be contaminated with bacteria from the outside of your urethral or vaginal area. Short of catheterization, the only reliable way of collecting a clean, uncontaminated urine specimen is with the midstream clean-catch method, which is summarized as follows:

(1) Gently but thoroughly cleanse the outside of the urethral and vaginal area. If you happen to be menstruating at the time, plug the vaginal opening with a tissue or tampon to avoid contaminating the urine with blood. (2) Since proper collection of the specimen is best done while standing, either step into a tub or shower or, if you prefer, straddle a toilet facing the tank. (3) While holding the urine receptacle in one hand, spread the inner lips apart with the other hand and begin voiding. If you are having just a routine urinalysis, a clean, dry jar with a screw top is adequate. Specimens for urine cultures require special sterile containers that either your doctor or the laboratory will provide. (4) As soon as you are certain that your urine stream is not deflecting off any vulvar surface, simply catch the urine in the container. Just make sure that the container does not come into contact with your vulva.

If there is going to be any delay in submitting the specimen to the laboratory, better refrigerate it. Urine culture results require at least forty-eight hours. A routine urinalysis takes only a few minutes. In any event, most doctors will start treatment while awaiting laboratory confirmation.

What is the usual treatment for acute cystitis?

Other than drinking six to eight glasses of water a day to keep the urine diluted and the bacteria flushed out, treatment can never be generalized. Currently there are any number of effective antibiotics and urinary chemotherapeutic agents that can be used. The sulfonamides are an old and reliable group (Gantrisan, Gantanol, etc.). Antibiotics such as Furadantin, Macrodantin, ampicillin, and tetracycline are also highly effective. And there are many others.

Regardless of what medication your doctor prescribes, *follow the instructions*. Symptoms may disappear within one to three days, but continue taking the medication as prescribed. This is particularly important in dealing with urinary infections. Depending upon the drug used, most bladder infections require a minimum of ten to fourteen days and sometimes as long as three to five weeks to eradicate. Some infections may even need months of continuous therapy.

The all too common practice of stopping the medication as soon as the symptoms subside should be avoided. You may be comfortable, but the infection is still there. Premature interruption of therapy only invites another flare-up, and in short order. Worse yet, you also run the risk of having the infection ascend into the kidneys. Kidney infections can be very serious, and a serious kidney infection can also be silent —no symptoms. It is therefore important that your urine be rechecked following treatment. Only then can you and your doctor be sure that the infection has been eradicated.

If symptoms should recur, another course of therapy will be needed. This may mean changing to a different antibacterial drug depending upon the results of the urine culture. At times the examination of the urethra, interior of the bladder (cystoscopy), as well as an IVP (intravenous pyelogram) to outline the kidney may be indicated. These studies can give important information as to whether there is an obstruction or abnormality present that could contribute to continuing urinary problems.

But regardless of the possible causes, for those of you who suffer from recurrent bladder infections, or for those of you taking off on your honeymoon, a few helpful suggestions, if followed, may well prevent a bout with cystitis.

Can you really avoid an acute cystitis?

Often, yes, providing you know a few basic facts and are willing to take precautions.

To begin with, an empty bladder is not so readily infected. Despite the fact that bacteria may be "milked" into the bladder during sexual intercourse, an infection is unlikely to occur unless sufficient urine is present to stimulate the growth of the bacteria. Secondly, should urine be present in the bladder at the time of intercourse, the more dilute it is the better your chances of avoiding a possible infection. Dilute urine definitely lowers the bacterial count. This means making sure that your intake of water and fluids is more than adequate. For you June honeymooners or others exposed to hot weather, excessive loss of body fluids through perspiration will normally result in the excretion of a more concentrated urine. To maintain a dilute urine under these circumstances it is especially important to increase your intake of fluids to the point where your urine may actually be colorless.

Thus, to avoid cystitis: (1) Make sure you empty your bladder before intercourse. (2) Empty your bladder after intercourse. (3) In addition—and this is extremely important for women who have recurrent flare-ups of cystitis—drink two to four glasses of water after intercourse. This will ensure an adequate bladder volume to effect proper voiding, as well as the presence of a dilute urine. You will undoubtedly have to get up during the night to urinate, but that's what it's all about—flushing out the bacteria before they can cause trouble.

Women who follow this regimen have enthusiastically endorsed it as being very effective. Some urologists suggest that as an extra precaution showers be substituted for tub bathing to further reduce the incidence of bladder infections among susceptible women.

Where recurrences of cystitis are frequent despite conscientious efforts, a small dose of an antibiotic taken on a regular basis prior to intercourse has helped some women remain symptom-free.

What about disturbances in urinary control?

As adults, most of us take urinary control for granted. And yet, it is one of the body's most complicated functions. Urinary continence or the ability to control one's urine requires a normal nervous system (brain and spinal cord), an intact urinary system, and well-toned pelvic muscles and tissues, which in turn support the bladder and urethra in their proper anatomical position. Disturbances in any one of these areas can result in temporary or permanent loss of urinary control. Here again, women because of their anatomy and childbearing capacity are particularly susceptible to such disturbances. Although lack of urinary control can take many forms, some of the more common examples worth discussing are urinary retention, complete urinary incontinence, and stress and urge incontinence.

What is urge incontinence?

Urge incontinence is a small involuntary loss of urine when the urge to urinate strikes suddenly. Unless a bathroom is immediately available, a woman with this problem may inadvertently wet her underwear. This condition can stem from inflammation and irritation of the urethra or bladder. Sometimes the problem is linked to an obvious urinary infection. In postmenopausal women an estrogen deficiency can aggravate and even cause urge incontinence.

Correcting the condition depends on finding and treating the cause. Since this type of incontinence frequently occurs with a full bladder, taking the time to void at regular intervals throughout the day can greatly minimize the problem.

In contrast, stress incontinence is more serious and totally different.

Ever laugh so hard that you actually wet yourself?

At times this can be perfectly normal if you happen to be sitting on a full bladder. For some women, however, incontinence can be a real problem and they don't laugh about it.

So-called *stress incontinence,* or the sudden and involuntary expulsion of a few drops of urine as the result of increased intra-abdominal pressure, is probably (other than bladder infections) one of the most prevalent and distressing urological complaints among women. For women with this problem any strain, bearing-down effort, or even a sneeze, cough, or laugh can cause a sudden, small loss of urine. And although urinary control is immediately resumed, the problem is embarrassing and unpleasant.

Is there a basic cause for stress incontinence?

Yes. Most cases can be traced to a weakness of pelvic muscles and connective fibrous tissue. As previously mentioned, these structures support the bladder and urethra in their normal anatomical position. (See Fig. 2, Chapter 2.) Furthermore, the angle at which the urethra joins the bladder is of critical importance in urinary control. Therefore, any weakness in these vital pelvic supports that allows the urethra to sag, thus changing its normal position in relation to the bladder, can set the stage for stress incontinence. The fact that women with this problem rarely have incontinence while lying down (even if they sneeze) is further evidence that stress incontinence is primarily a problem of inadequate pelvic support.

What can be done about stress incontinence?

The problem can be corrected. Since marked stress incontinence is most commonly associated with inadequate urethral support (see urethrocele, Fig. 2), the solution depends upon getting the urethra back up where it belongs. There are basically two approaches depending upon the severity of the problem: (1) surgical correction, or (2) retraining and strengthening the pelvic muscles.

Surgical correction for stress incontinence?

In long-standing and severe cases of stress incontinence vaginal plastic surgery can successfully reposition the urethra and return normal urinary control in a good percentage of women. The operation, which is performed entirely within the vaginal canal, repairs the defect in the muscles and connective tissue supports. The procedure can also include (if necessary) a snugging-up of an overly stretched vagina. Another fairly common surgical approach to resuspending the urethra is the Marshall-Marchetti operation. Unlike the vaginal operation, this procedure is performed through a lower abdominal incision. The selection of either operation is of course individualized. Prior to any surgery, it is important that there be a thorough evaluation of the urinary problem.

In cases of mild stress incontinence, some women can be relieved of symptoms by the simple expedient of exercising and strengthening the pubococcygeus muscle.

What exactly is the pubococcygeus?

One of the most important muscles you have as a woman—a broad band of muscular tissue that stretches like a taut hammock from the pubic bone in front to the coccyx, or tail bone, behind. Try visualizing this muscle as an internal sling or G-string stretching between the legs from front to back. The pubococcygeus (pronounced pu-bo-cocks-uh-gee-us) forms the floor of the pelvic cavity and supports the pelvic organs. In a normal and healthy state, this muscle encircles the urethra close to where it joins the bladder, surrounds and supports the middle third of the vagina, and encompasses the rectum just above the anal opening. (See Fig. 1.) A good toned-up pubococcygeus is also necessary for normal bladder and bowel control.

Exercising this muscle regularly can definitely minimize and even overcome any tendency toward sagging organs and vaginal relaxation,

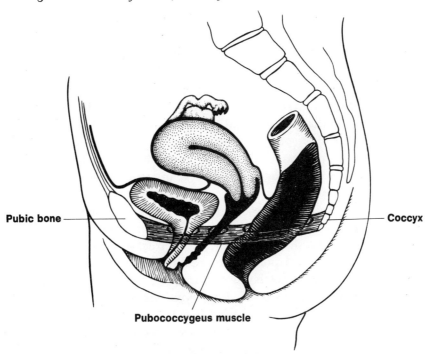

Pubic bone ———————————————————— **Coccyx**

Pubococcygeus muscle

Fig. 1. Pubococcygeus muscle
Muscular sling between the pubic bone and the coccyx (tail bone) which
helps support the female pelvic organs in their normal anatomical
position

whether the result of childbirth or aging. On the other hand, a flabby
or overstretched pubococcygeus can ultimately result in stress incontinence, widening and shortening of the vagina, and sagging of the
urethra, bladder, uterus, and rectum. Since the pubococcygeus at the
time of birth is weak and underdeveloped, observing the vulva of a
newborn female infant may further convince you of the importance
of this muscular support.

What does the vulva of a newborn female infant look like?
    Much like the vulva of a woman with marked inadequate pelvic
support. The entire external genitalia sags and protrudes to such an
extent that all orifices gap open—the urethra, vagina, and rectum.
    Not until the infant begins to assume an upright position does the
pubococcygeus begin to strengthen, tighten, and gradually draw up
the pelvic organs into their proper anatomical positions. As the muscle
further strengthens, all that previously bagged and sagged becomes
tucked up inside. And lo and behold, the toned-up pubococcygeus
muscle now makes urine and feces control possible.

How can you exercise the pubococcygeus muscle?

If you have never consciously used or contracted this muscle, doing these exercises may initially be difficult—but stay with it, you will soon learn.

First and most important, you must know beyond any doubt that you are indeed contracting the pubococcygeus. Since this muscle surrounds the urethra, vagina, and rectum and extends from the pubic bone to the tail bone, contracting this muscle will produce a tightening sensation from the urethra to the rectum. Some women describe the sensation as a "pulling up" or a "drawing together" of the external genitalia.

Contracting the pubococcygeus muscle can be done in any position—lying down, sitting, standing, walking, or even while standing on your head. You should not have to contract any other muscle. All too often women will hold their breath, make terrible facial grimaces, tighten their stomach muscles, squeeze their buttocks together, or worse yet, push down. *Pushing down as if you were having a bowel movement is to be avoided.* Contraction of this muscle does just the opposite. It draws the anus closer to the urethra, tightens up the rectal sphincter, and prevents the inadvertent passage of flatus (gas).

If you are still not sure whether you are contracting the correct muscle, the next time you go to the bathroom check yourself by alternately stopping and starting your urine stream until your bladder is empty. Being able to stop voiding on command involves contraction of this muscle. Relaxing it will allow you to resume voiding. For additional confirmation, you might try inserting one finger into your vagina. As you contract the muscle your vagina will tighten and squeeze your finger.

Now that you have identified the muscle and know how to contract it, let's proceed with the exercise program.

What exercise program will strengthen the pubococcygeus muscle?

If you expect results, you are going to have to be conscientious. Muscles don't increase in bulk and strength overnight. But those of you with mild stress incontinence should start to notice definite improvement within two months.

An effective exercise program should include at least two hundred or more contractions every day. Each contraction should be as forceful as possible and held for a full three seconds. Relax in between for the same amount of time. Some experts suggest spacing the exercises over several hours, or perhaps doing eight to ten per half hour.

Since you can do them anywhere, in any position, and without anybody being the wiser, there are really no excuses. It's up to you.

How else can you benefit from exercising this muscle?

Regular exercise of this muscle will also promote healthier and firmer tissues by increasing the blood flow through the pelvis. With better circulation your female organs will look better, feel better, and function better. Even hemorrhoid problems may become a thing of the past.

Last but not least, exercising the pubococcygeus can help to keep the vagina the way it was meant to be—snug, sensuous, and responsive.

Will exercising the pubococcygeus improve your love life?

Perhaps not your love life, but surely your sex life.

If you will recall, the pubococcygeus normally encircles and supports the middle third of the vagina. Slackness or loss of tone in this middle area, whether the result of childbirth, aging, or lack of exercise, will gradually cause the vagina to become shorter and wider. In effect, such a vagina is no longer able to contract or expand properly, nor to ensheath the penis effectively during coitus.

Women with this problem frequently complain of a lack of vaginal sensation during sexual intercourse. Men complain that their organ seems literally lost inside the woman. When sensation decreases for both partners, sexual satisfaction is obviously lessened.

Proper exercises done conscientiously not only maintain a normal, functioning vagina in optimal condition but also help restore any loss of shape and tone to the important middle third of the vaginal canal. Instead of being loose and flabby, the vagina can once again become snug and cylindrical. Keep working and within a couple of months both you and your mate will begin to notice a difference. In fact, try contracting the pubococcygeus while having intercourse. Your partner will enjoy being nipped, and your own sexual pleasure will also be enhanced.

What is complete urinary incontinence?

Continuous and uncontrollable leakage of urine. Assuming that there are no disorders of the nervous system, the most common cause of this condition is usually a fistula. This is an abnormal opening, passageway, tract, or connection between two organs or structures. In women, such fistulas can occur between the urethra and vagina, between the ureter and vagina, and between the bladder and vagina.

The most common is the so-called vesico-vaginal fistula, an abnormal passageway between the bladder and vagina. If the fistula is very small, urine loss through the vagina from the bladder may be slight and even intermittent. If the fistula is large, however, urine drainage is constant. In these cases the vulva and upper thighs are red, inflamed, and frequently covered with pustules or caked with deposits of urinary salts. A large vesico-vaginal fistula is one of the most intolerable and miserable urinary problems of women. Although such fistulas are relatively rare in this country, they are not uncommon in other parts of the world. Most vesico-vaginal fistulas are caused by prolonged obstructed labor and injuries during childbirth. They can also result from operative accidents during difficult pelvic surgery. Less commonly, they may appear following extensive radiation for cancer of the cervix or uterus.

Treatment is of course surgical closure of the defect. Results are predictably better when the tissues are in good condition and the area free of scar tissue.

Other causes of urinary incontinence (common to both men and women) are spinal cord injuries, anatomical defects such as spina bifida, and neurological diseases that can affect bladder control (for example, multiple sclerosis, brain or spinal cord tumors, and diabetes). A form of incontinence can also occur in severely disturbed mental and emotional states.

What about urinary retention?

This is just the opposite of complete urinary incontinence.

Acute urinary retention is the inability to urinate despite a full bladder. Although this problem occurs most commonly in men because of an enlarged prostate, women too are sometimes susceptible. Acute inflammation and swelling of the urethra from a genital herpes infection is certainly one of the most common causes of urinary retention. Voiding may also be impossible in cases where the bladder has become overly stretched and distended with urine. This type of urinary retention is sometimes seen in the postpartum (after-delivery) period and particularly among women who have had regional anesthesia (epidural, caudal, spinal) and intravenous fluids for childbirth. Under these circumstances, temporary lack of bladder sensation for the need to void because of the anesthesia coupled with increased fluid intake all add up to a full bladder and urinary retention. These problems are fortunately short-lived and promptly respond to catheterization, usually over a one- to two-day period. Where urinary retention is caused by a tumor or cyst blocking the urethra or bladder outlet, surgical intervention may be necessary to correct the situation permanently.

But apart from all these urinary disturbances, women are uniquely vulnerable to other pelvic support problems.

What kind of pelvic support problems?

Conditions such as a sagging urethra, sagging bladder, and a dropped uterus can all be explained on the basis of inadequate pelvic support. Although some women seem naturally predisposed to weakness of the pelvic muscles and ligaments, most prolapse problems result from unavoidable trauma and injury to these tissues during childbirth. Being overweight places additional strain on these supports as can coughing excessively because of a lung condition. Chronic constipation with bearing down efforts during defecation can further weaken these supports. But a common cause that none of us can avoid is aging. As previously mentioned, aging and estrogen depletion can really aggravate the situation.

We have already seen how a woman with mild stress incontinence and perhaps a bit of urethral sag can be materially helped by strengthening the pubococcygeus muscle. Thus, in some cases surgery can be avoided. In other women, however, pelvic organ relaxation from inadequate pelvic support can present a more serious problem.

How serious?

What originally may have started as a weakness in the pubococcygeus muscle and connective tissue support can become an actual defect. In essence, the weakened muscle may have become so stretched and thin that its fibers literally begin to separate and tear. With more and more separation between muscle fibers, a hole or defect is eventually created—somewhat like wearing a hole through the heel of a sock.

So what happens?

Without proper support maintaining the pelvic organs in their normal anatomical position, they gradually prolapse or herniate through the defect and in time bulge down and into the vaginal canal. The urethra, instead of being nicely tucked against the pubic bone, visibly sags downward; this condition is called a urethrocele. (See Fig. 2.) In a similar manner the bladder or the rectum can herniate through the muscle and connective tissue defect and bulge into the vaginal canal. (See cystocele, Fig. 3; rectocele, Fig. 4.) In women with marked loss of pelvic support, the uterus may also start to prolapse and inch

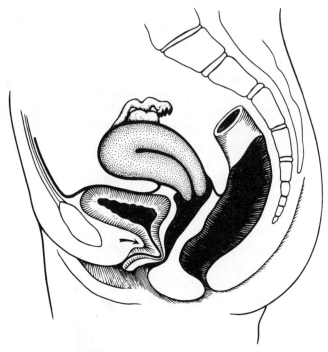

Fig. 2. Urethrocele
Notice how the urethra bulges into the vaginal canal.

its way down the vaginal canal. Exercises under these circumstances will obviously not repair the defects or tuck those organs back in place.

Does that mean that surgery is necessary?

Not always. The need for corrective surgery really depends on how much trouble this causes. Surprisingly enough, some women with marked pelvic organ relaxation have very few complaints. Others may have minimal relaxation and yet experience great distress.

What kind of problems can you expect with pelvic organ relaxation?

Everything is relative. Symptoms will vary depending on the extent of the defect, the degree of relaxation, and the particular organ involved. Thus, for example, a woman may complain primarily of stress incontinence because of a sagging urethra, whereas her bladder and rectum may still be fairly well supported. Another woman with good urethral and bladder support may only be bothered by increasing constipation attributable to an enlarging rectocele. Any combination of symptoms is possible. Symptoms, when present, are primarily related to the organ involved.

What about a prolapsed bladder (cystocele)?

Most women with a large cystocele complain of a lump or bulge just inside the vaginal introitus. Other women, particularly after prolonged standing, will be bothered with a heavy, dragging sensation in the pelvic area. On occasion the bladder may be sufficiently prolapsed to appear at the vaginal opening as a ball or swelling. Not uncommonly a woman will mistake this swelling for a dropped uterus or even a tumor.

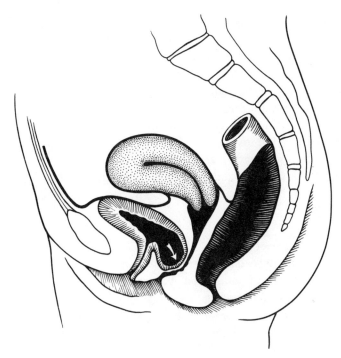

Fig. 3. Cystocele
Notice how the bladder wall bulges into the vaginal canal.

In any event the woman with a large cystocele may have difficulty emptying her bladder completely. As you can see from Fig. 3, marked prolapse of the bladder can actually cause a large portion of the bladder to sag below the level of the urethral outlet. Therefore, trying to empty the bladder completely when this has happened would be somewhat like trying to urinate uphill. For this reason a woman with a large cystocele will still have the sensation of "having to go" after she has just been, or the feeling that her bladder is not quite empty, which of course it isn't. This sort of distress may become particularly severe at bedtime. Although the woman may just have been to the bathroom, as soon as she lies down, she feels the need to go again.

One solution, of course, is corrective surgery to eliminate the problem. Some women have discovered that simply by inserting a finger into the vagina and elevating the "bulge," they can empty their bladder.

As expedient as this maneuver may be for the moment, it does not resolve the problem for long.

Why not?

The tendency for some urine to be retained in the bladder at all times (residual urine) makes the stagnant urine a perfect breeding place for any lurking bacteria. Thus, women with cystoceles are much more susceptible to chronic and recurrent bladder infections with all the attendant distressing symptoms, such as frequent and painful urination. Chronic irritation of the bladder floor almost invariably leads to urinary incontinence—not stress incontinence but *urge incontinence,* or the sudden loss of a few drops of urine whenever the all too frequent, strong desire to urinate hits unexpectedly.

It should be emphasized, however, that not all cystoceles provoke such problems. Many women function surprisingly well despite an obvious bladder prolapse.

What about a rectocele?

Even when quite large, rectoceles, unlike urethroceles or cystoceles, do not usually cause too many problems. (See Fig. 4.) The possible exception may be the woman who has always been troubled with constipation. Occasionally a woman with a large rectocele may suffer with intermittent fecal impaction unless bowel movements are regular and the stool kept reasonably soft. What can happen is that material may collect and subsequently harden in the pouched-out rectal wall just above the anus. As more and more stool accumulates in the rectal passage, it becomes increasingly difficult to have a bowel movement. Here again, some women have resorted to using a finger to exert vaginal pressure against the bulging rectal wall, thereby facilitating evacuation.

What kind of symptoms does a prolapsed uterus cause?

Although special ligaments help maintain the normal position of the uterus, its support also depends on the integrity of the pubococ-

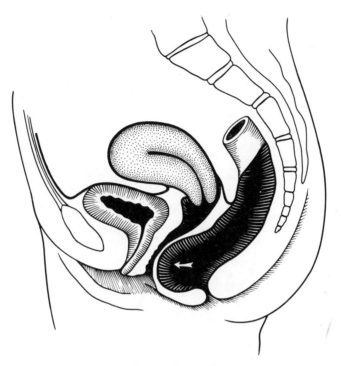

Fig. 4. Rectocele
Notice how the rectal wall bulges into the vaginal canal.

cygeus and pelvic connective tissue. Any subsequent weakening of these supports can result in a prolapse, or descent, of the uterus into the vaginal canal (dropped uterus).

With minimal sagging, there may be few or no symptoms. With a more perceptible uterine prolapse, the sexual partner may be the first to notice the problem. As the uterus gradually descends into the vaginal canal, with the cervix leading the way, the cervix in effect becomes an obstruction to complete penile penetration during coitus. (See Fig. 5.)

More marked loss of uterine support will materially interfere with the proper flow of blood through the uterus. Thus, with engorgement of blood vessels and pelvic congestion, a heavy, dragging sensation in the pelvis plus occasional low backaches are common complaints.

Is childbirth responsible for all these problems?

There is no doubt that the problems of inadequate pelvic support and subsequent vaginal relaxation most frequently begin with the

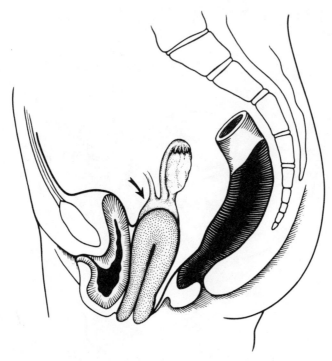

Fig. 5. Marked prolapse of the uterus (dropped uterus)
In this particular example, the cervix has descended all the way
to the vaginal opening.

unavoidable stress of childbirth. In countries where obstetrical care is minimal, it is not surprising that loss of pelvic support is fairly prevalent even among young women.

For those of you currently pregnant, a conscientious pubococcygeus exercise program may well minimize tissue trauma during labor and delivery. As the baby's head descends through the vaginal canal, a pubococcygeus with good tone and elasticity will give to allow the baby's head to pass and, following delivery, will contract back to its normal position around the middle third of the vagina. Exercising during the postpartum (after-delivery) period will further help the inner vagina resume its original shape and tone much sooner and perhaps even improve on what was there before.

On the other hand, a flabby pubococcygeus muscle can easily be overstretched, and some of its fibers can actually be torn and pushed downward by the pressure of the baby's head. In such a case the muscle may never recover completely.

Even with a good pubococcygeus muscle, other unrecognized tissue damage can also occur during childbirth.

Tissue damage—where?

To the lower vagina and introitus when, just prior to delivery, the baby's head begins to appear at the vulva (crowning). Unnecessary prolongation of this stage of labor, with repeated bearing-down efforts, invariably causes thinning and disruption of the underlying muscle and fibrous supports of the vaginal introitus.

It is the rare woman who can go through an unaided delivery (particularly her first) and give birth to a full-term baby without suffering tissue trauma. *Even in the absence of any tear or laceration during childbirth, there can be significant injury to the lower vaginal supports.*

Obstetricians have long recognized that shortening the end stage of labor by means of an episiotomy and the use of forceps when necessary can minimize tissue trauma, thus making delivery easier.

What is an episiotomy and how does it help?

An episiotomy is an incision through the lower vaginal wall and underlying tissues in order to temporarily enlarge the vaginal outlet. The purpose of this minor procedure is to maintain the integrity of the vaginal introitus by preventing the tissue from overstretching, thinning, and tearing to let the baby out. Following delivery, it is a simple matter for the doctor to close the incision, thereby returning the tissues to their normal position. Without an episiotomy the vaginal introitus would be permanently widened and relaxed.

What can be done about inadequate pelvic support?

Unless you are having pelvic problems, most gynecologists would prefer to postpone any definitive surgical procedure. If symptoms should be present, treatment and/or the selection of a surgical procedure will vary depending on your age, your desire to have more children, your physical condition, the presence of any other associated pelvic problem, and the extent of your discomfort.

For the younger woman whose pelvic muscles have relaxed but who desires another pregnancy, surgery will usually be delayed until completion of her family. Plastic repair can be rapidly undone by another vaginal delivery.

What kind of surgery is usually done?

With the exception of true stress incontinence, which can be corrected by either vaginal or special low abdominal surgery in selected women, problems attributable to poor pelvic support can be handled most effectively by vaginal plastic surgery.

In contrast to a face lift, which erases wrinkles and sagging skin by removing excess tissue, a vaginal plastic procedure actually repairs the defect in the underlying muscles and connective tissue supports. Thus, the pelvic organs are resuspended in their normal anatomical position and can once again function properly. In addition, a slack or a too wide vagina can be snuggled up to your specifications—honeymoon size if you want.

Will a prolapsed uterus always be removed?

Not necessarily. Much will depend on the age of the woman and the degree of prolapse. Most gynecologists, however, will remove the prolapsed uterus of an older woman when they do a vaginal plastic repair. This will help to ensure a good, permanent surgical repair and also eliminate potential uterine problems that might develop in later years.

There are no hard and fast rules, however. Treatment must always be individualized.

Can anything else be done for those sagging supports besides surgery?

If symptoms are present and sufficiently distressing, corrective surgery is by far the best answer. Nevertheless, there are instances in which an associated disabling medical problem may increase the risk of any surgical procedure. Elderly women with severe cardiac conditions or respiratory insufficiency generally make poor candidates for surgery. Thus, symptomatic relief in a few women may necessitate their being fitted with a vaginal pessary to keep those sagging organs tucked up.

A vaginal pessary—what's that?

A simple appliance usually made of hard rubber or plastic. In contrast to contraceptive diaphragms worn solely for birth control purposes, vaginal pessaries are not designed to cover the cervical opening. Their sole purpose is to help support the uterus and vaginal walls in their normal position. Since pessaries come in various shapes and sizes (see Fig. 6), the selection of the most appropriate device

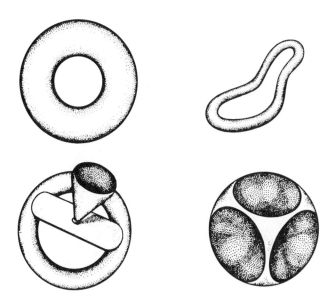

Fig. 6. Vaginal pessaries

depends on the extent of vaginal relaxation and the degree of uterine prolapse.

Vaginal pessaries are no panacea. They have many inherent drawbacks.

What's wrong with vaginal pessaries?

For the woman who does obtain symptomatic relief, a vaginal pessary is undoubtedly a real blessing. However, any device left in the vagina tends to create an irritating and malodorous discharge. Regular douching and the use of vaginal creams are necessary to decrease discharge and odor formation. Moreover, the pessary must be removed, cleaned, and replaced periodically. Since this must be done professionally, it requires a visit to the doctor at least every six to eight weeks.

Even when properly fitted (see Fig. 7), a vaginal pessary can abrade vaginal tissues with subsequent discomfort and spotting. This is especially so among elderly women, whose thin vaginal mucosa is very susceptible to any irritation. On the other hand, a pessary that fits too loosely may be readily expelled during defecation or straining down.

But the biggest disadvantage of the pessary for women who are sexually active is its interference with normal intercourse. Although

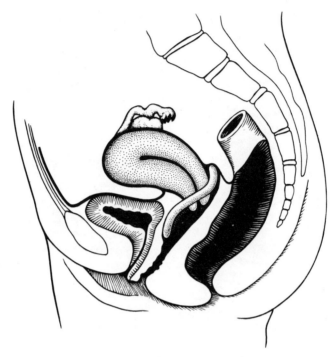

Fig. 7. Vaginal pessary in place

the extent of interference during coitus will vary depending on the type of pessary used, any such device will tend to limit the depth of penile penetration.

To say the least, vaginal pessaries are rarely the first-choice, ideal solution even for the elderly. Fortunately, with improved anesthesia, women who were previously resigned to a pessary are now safely undergoing surgery. Every day more and more women in their seventies and even in their eighties are having their prolapse problems surgically corrected. In fact, many of these women bounce back faster and are in better physical shape than many younger women.

Is there any real answer to the problem of sagging pelvic supports?

Since nature endowed us with a vulnerable anatomy in exchange for our unique ability to bear children, we must cope with the situation as best we can. Factors such as proper nutrition, good general health, competent obstetrical care, in addition to those pubococcygeus exercises, can certainly help minimize vaginal relaxation and loss of pelvic support. Yet at times, in spite of good medical and personal care, a few women will still face some of these unpleasant problems.

Today, the notion that nothing can be done or that it's all part of being a woman is completely unwarranted. You may be beyond the aid of preventive measures, but regardless of your age or the severity of your condition, you are never beyond help.

PART IV

The Sexuality of Woman

15. A Look at Intercourse and Other Sexual Activities from a Woman's Viewpoint

If visitors from outer space suddenly popped into one of our bookstores, they would soon be convinced that earth people, unlike other creatures of the universe, are equipped with only two bodily functions —eating and sex. Next to cookbooks with recipes that titillate the taste buds and diet guides that take the joy out of cooking, sex books have continued to be one of the hottest-selling items in print for the past twenty-five years. Ever since Kinsey, with pen and paper poised, dared to ask intimate, probing questions, and then had the audacity to publish his results, the world hasn't been the same. Before that time, sex was strictly a private matter, for better or for worse. Today, because of Kinsey and the myriad publications on sex that followed in the wake of his original work in 1948, topics previously considered by some as taboo are now discussed with disarming candor. As a result, women have become increasingly aware of their own sexuality and what it means in terms of their total expression as individuals. Women are expecting more from sex and are willing to give more. They are also exploring new dimensions in sensuality and physical gratification.

This chapter does not pretend to have the answer on how to make every sexual encounter a memorable moment of rapturous ecstasy. Rather, its purpose is to provide the individual woman with an insight into seldom discussed factors that can affect her total sexual response. Attention is also focused on changes, both temporary and permanent, involving the female organs which can influence sexual gratification. Furthermore, this chapter is about the act of sex and how other expressions of physical intimacy can work to the good or to the detriment of a woman's mental and physical well-being.

Ideally, what happens to a woman's body during the act of sex?

All women vary in their sensory awareness and response to love making, depending upon a number of factors—age, general health, estrogen level, mood, type and intensity of stimulation, etc. And yet there are basic physiological and anatomical changes common to all women who do reach climax during the act of sex. For practical purposes, the physiology of the female sexual response is divided into four phases: the excitement phase, the plateau phase, the orgasmic phase, and the phase of resolution. Failure to reach orgasm implies that the woman's sexual response was arrested either at the excitement or the plateau phase.

What about the excitement phase?

The first response to sexual stimulation is vaginal lubrication, whether it be psychologically induced (for example, by reading a sexy story) or initiated by direct physical contact. Within ten to thirty seconds of effective erotic stimulation, the vaginal walls and introitus become moistened and bathed with lubricating fluid. Vaginal lubrication, the female equivalent of penile erection, is not a secretion from any gland or organ. Rather, it is a thin, mucuslike fluid that seeps through the vaginal walls when there is vascular engorgement of vaginal blood vessels. The production of vaginal lubrication does not therefore depend upon the presence of an intact cervix, uterus, ovaries, or even functioning Bartholin's glands. In women past sixty, for example, atrophic vaginal tissue changes resulting from age and estrogen deficiency do not materially interfere with the production of this lubricating material. And although two or three minutes of effective sexual stimulation may be required to achieve an adequately lubricated vagina, the older woman nonetheless still reacts in the same basic manner as does a woman forty years younger.

As sexual stimulation continues and more and more blood is pumped into the pelvic region, there is a gradual venous congestion of all the sexual organs; the labia minora (inner lips) thicken and enlarge noticeably and the diameter and length of the clitoris increase. The labia majora (outer lips) of women who have never had children tend to thin out, flatten, and elevate outward and upward, thus exposing the vaginal opening. In multiparas (women who have given birth at least twice), the labia majora also flare away from the vaginal opening in preparation for penile penetration, but in this instance there is marked enlargement of the lips, sometimes to as much as two or three times normal size. At the same time, and common to all women, the inner two-thirds of the vagina (the area closest to the cervix) begins to widen and lengthen. As the plateau phase approaches, the cervix and the body of the uterus, now markedly engorged, are gradually elevated and pulled higher into the pelvic cavity, thus further ballooning and expanding the innermost third of the vagina.

But sexual response is not limited to the pelvic organs. It is a total body response as evidenced by a rise in blood pressure, an elevated pulse rate, more rapid breathing, and an increase in muscular tension throughout the body. The nipples become erect and the breasts may noticeably increase in size by as much as 25 percent during the latter stages of the excitement phase. Seventy-five percent of women on occasion also develop a fine rash or skin flush involving the chest, back, and abdomen.

How does the plateau phase differ from the excitement phase?

The plateau phase is essentially a continuation and an accentuation of all the changes that occurred during the excitement phase. However, there are three notable differences involving the outer third of the vagina, the clitoris, and the labia minora.

As tension mounts, the outermost third of the vagina (the area closest to the outside) actually decreases in diameter as a result of marked vasocongestion of the lower vaginal tissues. This constriction of the lower vagina allows the vaginal walls to grip the shaft of the penis more firmly. The clitoris, which previously had been relatively enlarged, retracts and disappears beneath its hood or foreskin, and decreases some 50 percent in length. And the labia minora (sometimes referred to as sex skin) change color from light pink to bright red to a deep burgundy hue. Interestingly enough, once these marked color changes of the labia minora occur, orgasm invariably follows. Pupils dilate, breathing accelerates, nostrils flare, and the cords of the neck stand out.

And then comes orgasm?

Yes—an almost seizurelike, tension-releasing, exquisitely pleasurable response which is the acme of physical gratification in sexual activity. The lower vagina and surrounding tissues, as well as the uterus and at times even the rectal sphincter, contract rhythmically. A few women at the time of orgasm may have a compelling urge to urinate, which can be accompanied by a small involuntary loss of urine. The more intense the orgasm, the more intense the total body reaction and the more numerous the contractions. Most orgasms rarely last longer than ten to fifteen seconds, and yet a really good strong orgasm can have as many as twelve to fifteen distinct pelvic contractions that gradually become weaker and spaced further apart as the climax ebbs.

What about the phase of resolution?

The phase of resolution begins when the last vaginal contraction fades, and continues until all the pelvic organs have returned to their preexcitement state. The involuntary muscular contractions that are experienced primarily as vaginal contractions allow the pooled and stagnant blood in the pelvic organs to dissipate rapidly. Thus, within thirty minutes, the uterus, vagina, labia, and clitoris return to their normal state. In fact, the clitoris resumes its usual size and position within ten to twenty seconds after orgasm. In contrast, the uterus, which can enlarge as much as twice normal size, may take anywhere from ten to thirty minutes to become decongested following orgasm. Needless to say, without orgasm there can be no rapid decongestion of the pelvic organs such as that experienced during the phase of resolution. (More about this shortly.)

What percentage of women actually experience orgasm during coitus?

That depends on whose statistics are quoted. According to various surveys conducted on married women, anywhere from 22 to 75 percent usually or almost always experience orgasm during coitus; 30 to 45 percent experience it sometimes or occasionally; and 5 to 22 percent have never once achieved orgasm during intercourse.

Orgasm during coitus for women as contrasted to orgasm for the vast majority of men is not a one, two, three push-button affair. It is a complex process that can be affected by a multitude of factors, some obvious and some obscure.

Does coital position or length of foreplay affect a woman's ability to achieve orgasm?

Coital position is apparently not a crucial factor in a woman's ability to experience orgasm. And yet many women do find that the superior position (face to face and on top of the male partner) may succeed where other positions have failed. In the superior position, a woman is essentially in control: she can change the angle, depth, and tempo of penile thrusting, and she can maneuver her body so as to provide close clitoral contact depending on her erotic needs. Because the male partner experiences less physical strain while reclining on his back, this position may allow him to delay his orgasm more easily.

On the other hand, the length of time devoted to foreplay and the actual duration of penile vaginal intercourse seem to play a greater role in enhancing a woman's ability to reach orgasm. According to some experts, foreplay prolonged for at least twenty minutes and penile vaginal intercourse sustained for fifteen minutes (quite a feat for many men) allow nearly 98 percent of women ultimately to reach orgasm.

In addition to the above factors, however, it is even more important to be spontaneous and to experience each moment for its own pleasure. Assessing or monitoring one's sexual performance or lack of it on the basis of achieving the one big goal—orgasm—can be distracting. When orgasm becomes the sole objective, sometimes the harder one tries the more difficult and elusive it becomes. Sexual arousal and desire are emotions. A mere act of will will not induce vaginal lubrication or achieve orgasm.

Can the size of the penis play a role in a woman's sexual satisfaction?

Some women are sexually aroused at the sight of a well-endowed man. But in actuality the size of the erect penis bears very little relationship to a man's ability to satisfy a woman sexually. There is also no truth to the prevalent belief that the bigger the penis, the greater the man's virility or prowess as a sexual partner. Therefore, unless a woman is psychologically conditioned to believe differently, penile size as such should have no effect on her ability to respond sexually or to obtain satisfaction from intercourse. However, two rare exceptions should be noted: when the penis is so large as to cause actual physical discomfort despite adequate lubrication and a normally accommodating vagina; and when the penis is so abnormally small that effective coital contact cannot be maintained.

Can vaginal size affect a woman's enjoyment of intercourse?

Although there are a few women who do have an exceptionally small or large vagina, they are just that—exceptions. Since the vaginal walls normally lie against each other, most healthy average vaginas effectively ensheath the penis during intercourse. This close contact between the penis and the vaginal walls enhances physical enjoyment for both partners. With continued stimulation and arousal, the normal vagina will dilate and expand to accommodate deep thrusting by almost any size penis.

However, difficulties during first intercourse can be encountered if the woman has too snug a vaginal opening. This is occasionally seen in women who have never used tampons or have never engaged in sexual play wherein the vaginal opening was dilated manually. For such women, pain at the vaginal opening during penetration or, less commonly, complete inability to permit penile entry can definitely be a detriment to sexual enjoyment. Fortunately, however, a hymen rarely offers much resistance to firm but gentle stretching. In fact, if the woman is sufficiently aroused and lubricated, penile penetration even the first time can frequently be accomplished with little difficulty. The idea that all first intercourse must be accompanied by pain and obvious hymenal bleeding just isn't so. Nonetheless, if you are concerned about the adequacy of your vaginal opening, see Chapter 10 for details on how to determine its size and what you can do if it doesn't seem to measure up.

The opposite problem, a too relaxed vagina, is not only a common complaint of many women but may also be a source of sexual dissatisfaction for some. Most women who express concern about a too relaxed or overly stretched vagina are usually in their late thirties or forties and have had at least two children. Even with the best obstetrical care, the unavoidable strain and stress of childbearing can weaken and disrupt the normally firm muscle and connective tissue supports of the vaginal walls and introitus. The vaginas of these women tend to become wider, shorter, and less capable of making tight contact with the penetrating penis. Women who have this problem will notice that the penis no longer seems to fill the vagina. And their partners will complain that their organ feels lost inside. For some couples, this relative disproportion between penis and vagina, although a source of decreased sensory awareness, does not detract from their enjoyment of the sexual act.

For other women, a too relaxed *vaginal opening* may also interfere with clitoral stimulation during coitus. In these instances effective *indirect* clitoral stimulation, which normally occurs when downward traction is exerted on the labia and clitoral hood during active penile thrusting, is greatly impaired.

Can anything be done for the vagina and introitus that seem too large?

Very definitely. Where an overly stretched vagina seems to be interfering with the full enjoyment of sexual intercourse, a change in coital position may be helpful. Since the object is to tighten the vaginal canal as well as the vaginal opening, some women find that bringing their legs together once the penis has been introduced allows for closer contact. This maneuver is easily accomplished if the woman lies on her back while the male partner, on top, places his legs outside of hers.

If a too relaxed vaginal opening prevents adequate indirect clitoral stimulation during coitus, the woman-on-top position or the side-by-side position can help resolve the problem. In either of these positions, direct clitoral stimulation can occur during deep penile penetration.

For women, however, whose main concern is a too wide or relaxed vaginal canal, a more satisfactory solution (other than changing coital position) would be the firming and strengthening of certain pelvic muscles essential for the maintenance of normal vaginal tone. Exercising the pubococcygeus muscle (Kegel's exercises) can significantly improve a too relaxed vagina. (In Chapter 14 these exercises as well as the benefits derived therefrom are extensively discussed.)

If vaginal relaxation or stretching has progressed beyond the help of corrective exercises, vaginal plastic surgery is an effective procedure for restoring the vagina to more normal dimensions. Although most vaginal plastic procedures are done to alleviate the symptoms associated with the prolapse of pelvic organs, such as the bladder (see Chapter 14), more and more gynecologists are accepting the idea that tightening the vaginal canal and introitus when specifically requested to enhance sexual enjoyment is a warranted procedure.

If a woman has never had children, can an active sex life lead to pelvic relaxation and an overly stretched vagina?

Not really. Even if a woman has frequent intercourse with multiple and physically well-endowed partners, the vagina will maintain its tone and elasticity to a remarkable extent. Pelvic organ relaxation or a vagina that lacks tone and firmness is primarily the result of childbearing. Advancing age, however, can further aggravate or even initiate such a condition.

Can a hysterectomy (removal of the uterus) shorten the vagina and thus interfere with deep penile penetration?

No. A carefully performed abdominal hysterectomy (through an abdominal incision) should not shorten the vagina in any way. According to a recent report, 66.7 percent of the women who underwent this procedure showed an average increase in vaginal depth of 1 cm. (0.39 inch). Of the remaining one-third, 21.2 percent showed no change in vaginal depth and only 12.1 percent showed any shortening. Even in these instances, the decrease in vaginal canal length was less than 0.5 cm., or approximately 0.18 inch. Perhaps of greater interest is the fact that although a hysterectomy seals and closes the vaginal canal at the top (where the cervix used to be), there is no impairment to the vagina's ability to dilate and expand during sexual intercourse.

What about the woman who has a vaginal hysterectomy?

Most vaginal hysterectomies (removal of the uterus through the vagina), unless done for the express purpose of sterilization, are frequently combined with vaginal plastic surgery. Since this type of surgery, as opposed to what is done in an abdominal hysterectomy, does involve resuspending sagging pelvic organs, there is a slightly increased chance of shortening the vaginal canal. But here again the shortening, if any, is minimal and occurs in only a minority of women. Even when vaginal plastic surgery is performed on women past seventy, most doctors make it a point to preserve a sexually functional vagina.

Does removal of the uterus lessen a woman's ability to enjoy sex?

There is no denying that a few women will attribute their lack of sexual interest or ability to be aroused to their hysterectomy. These women almost without exception have a history of some sexual maladjustment, often the result of preexisting psychological factors. Apart from mental and emotional variables that can adversely affect sensuality, there is no scientific basis to support the idea that the removal of the uterus has an effect on sexual response.

Meticulously documented studies have repeatedly shown that vaginal lubrication during sexual excitement can be just as copious without as with a uterus. Also, the inner vagina can expand and dilate whether or not the uterus is present. And equally important, orgasm as a physical and emotional experience can be of the same intensity as before a hysterectomy. In fact, women who have had a hysterectomy still report feeling pleasurable *uterine* contractions along with the vaginal contractions and other pelvic throbbing at the time of orgasm. The explanation for this interesting phenomenon, although not completely understood, may be the result of a conditioned response. In other words, if a woman was previously aware of uterine contractions during orgasm, the same physical sensation may occur even in the absence of the uterus.

What about sexual enjoyment for the woman whose ovaries are removed?

If a woman's ovaries are removed prior to the menopause, her sexual response will ultimately resemble that of a postmenopausal woman. (See Chapter 23.) Without normal estrogen stimulation to help maintain the tone and vascularity of pelvic tissues, there is a gradual thinning of the vaginal and vulvar tissues. As described elsewhere, this usually means a delay in the onset of vaginal lubrication and a decreased ability of the vaginal walls to expand and dilate. And although orgasm can be just as emotionally and psychologically gratifying, its physical intensity is apt to be diminished.

Wouldn't estrogen replacement therapy in such a woman prevent these physical changes?

To a remarkable extent, yes, and for several years. But advancing age does eventually slow and decrease sexual response with or without estrogen therapy. And yet, if regular and effective sexual stimulation is maintained throughout the years, there is no reason why the older woman can't continue to enjoy sex all the days of her life. Interestingly enough, 60 percent of all women over sixty are still sexually active.

Can other physical problems contribute to a woman's inability to reach orgasm?

According to some experts, clitoral adhesions may be a possible cause for lack of orgasm and even painful coitus. During infancy the prepuce or foreskin of the clitoris normally adheres tightly to the glans, thus acting as a sheath encasing the clitoris. With maturity the clitoris becomes free, but on rare occasions, the prepuce of an adult woman may still adhere firmly to the glans. Moreover, the accumulation of smegma between the glans and the prepuce may also contribute to the formation of clitoral adhesions. In a few women, such adhesions, by preventing adequate exposure of the clitoris during the excitement phase of sexual stimulation, might be a factor in their being nonorgasmic. In a limited study involving nonorgasmic women where clitoral adhesions did exist and were removed, a small percentage subsequently did become orgasmic.

And yet, there can be so many reasons for lack of orgasm as well as painful intercourse in women, that to attribute clitoral adhesions (even if they should be present) as a possible cause demands further evaluation.

Does pain during coitus usually interfere with a woman's ability to experience orgasm?

Not necessarily. It all depends on where the pain is located, its intensity, and how sexually aroused the woman may be. Moreover, if a woman has previously enjoyed coitus on a regular basis, the excitement as well as the anticipation of the moment may, to a great extent, allow her to disregard any subjective discomfort. On the other hand, pain during intercourse can be a real detriment to a satisfying sexual encounter for some women.

What are some of the physical reasons for pain during intercourse?

The location of the pain during intercourse and the type of discomfort experienced are frequently important clues to the possible cause. For example, pain that is localized around the vaginal opening or lower vagina can usually be attributed to one of three causes: a too snug vaginal opening, insufficient vaginal lubrication, and irritation or inflammation from a vaginal or vulvar infection.

Pain from a too snug vaginal opening is not necessarily limited to the woman with no previous sexual experience. It can also occur in the postmenopausal woman because of vaginal atrophic changes and particularly if sexual intercourse is infrequent. If a woman has recently been delivered, the overly enthusiastic repair of an episiotomy can temporarily tighten the vaginal opening just a little too much. Fortunately, however, all of these causes of pain related to a snug vaginal opening can usually be remedied by appropriate measures which, of necessity, must be individualized.

Insufficient vaginal lubrication at the time of penile penetration is perhaps one of the most common causes of dyspareunia, or painful intercourse. Friction of the penis against relatively dry vaginal walls can irritate and traumatize the nearby urethra and bladder. As mentioned in Chapter 14, intercourse without sufficient lubrication can result in bladder spasm and painful urination immediately following coitus. Without adequate lubrication to bathe the vaginal opening and labia minora, even clitoral stimulation can be unpleasant. Although the use of lubricating jellies applied around the introitus prior to intercourse can be helpful, a persistent lack of effective lubrication does reflect inadequate sexual arousal.

In contrast to the above, the sudden development of a stinging, burning discomfort around the introitus (vaginal opening) and lower vagina during intercourse can usually be traced to tissue irritation. Acute inflammation of the vulva resulting from contact with an irritating substance or perhaps an individual allergy is being seen with increasing frequency. (See Chapter 11.) Similarly, any of the vaginal infections can also be a source of acute discomfort in an otherwise sexually well-adjusted woman.

Curiously enough, a few women (even in the absence of infection) have complained of a vaginal burning sensation immediately following ejaculation by their partner. But if a condom was worn, or the penis withdrawn prior to the release of semen, the distress was completely avoided. In these unusual instances, the problem was eventually traced either to a prostatic infection in the male or to a rare allergic reaction of the woman to her partner's semen.

What about pain on deep penile penetration?

Pain that is felt deep inside the vagina during active penile thrusting can be caused by a variety of factors. Endometriosis, or the condition wherein fragments of displaced endometrial tissue become implanted and grow along pelvic structures, is one of the most notable examples. As discussed in Chapter 22, endometriosis is notorious for creating a sharp, stabbing pain during deep penile penetration. Then too, the impact of the penis against a tipped (retroverted or retroflexed) uterus and especially if the uterus tends to be somewhat enlarged, boggy, and congested can be another source of pain. Actually, penile impact against any inflamed pelvic tissue, such as that which develops during an acute tubal infection (see Chapter 12), can also be a source of distress. Less commonly, excessive scar tissue formation along the upper vagina as a result of extensive surgery or radiation therapy for malignant disease can be a cause of recurring pain on deep penile penetration.

When the pain is persistent and unamenable to corrective therapy (as in the case of the scar tissue), changing coital position so as to limit the depth of penile penetration can bring relief. Employing the rear entry position, that is, with the woman lying on her stomach with her buttocks facing her partner's abdomen, can help. Or if the woman prefers lying on her back with her partner on top, she can still limit the depth of penile penetration by bringing her legs together after the introduction of the penis.

Is forcible sexual intercourse, or rape, invariably painful?

Rape or forcible sexual intercourse without consent is a subject that is receiving increasing publicity. Moreover, the incidence of this crime of violence continues to increase in many of the larger cities. Since rape is a potential threat to all women and especially those living in urban communities, let's discuss it more fully.

For the woman who is sexually assaulted, there is no question that such an experience is emotionally and physically devastating. Even the sexually active woman who otherwise is not physically abused during an attack can experience vaginal tissue trauma and pain.

Yet, three out of four women who are sexually assaulted never report the incident or seek medical attention. The necessity of having to relive the experience by giving minute details to investigating police officers, and the need to be further questioned and examined by a doctor who may or may not be sympathetic, are among the reasons why women are reluctant to report sexual attack. But the trauma doesn't end there. If the rapist can be identified and apprehended, legal proceedings are frequently weighed in favor of the accused. To obtain a rape conviction, a woman must be able to prove that she was sexually assaulted and that the act occurred without provocation on her part. All too often this puts the woman's character on trial. In addition, it must be proved that there was penile entry and that the victim in all probability resisted the attack. Is it any wonder, then, that only one out of seven reported rapes ever ends with a conviction?

Today, interested groups are trying to amend the laws to protect the rights of women. But apart from legal matters and the need for emotional support, any woman who is sexually assaulted should receive medical attention. For even if she was fortunate enough to have escaped obvious physical injury, the possibility of venereal disease and pregnancy should also be considered.

What exactly is the medical procedure in cases of alleged rape?

Since rape is not a medical diagnosis but rather a decision to be reached by a court of law, examining doctors are not permitted to draw conclusions regardless of the physical findings. All medical reports on an alleged rape should include only objective findings. This means that the general appearance of the woman as well as any obvious physical injury and, more specifically, evidence of trauma to the genitalia must be noted in detail and recorded in writing. If a woman is planning to prosecute the offender, it is especially important that she not bathe or change her clothing prior to the medical examination. The fact that even in bona fide rape cases a careful medical examination cannot always corroborate *forcible* penile entry makes it imperative that evidence such as torn or bloody clothing that could substantiate a woman's testimony be presented for proper inspection.

In addition to a careful physical examination, it is also necessary that certain laboratory tests be performed.

What kinds of laboratory tests?

Although ejaculation at the time of penile penetration is not a necessary requisite to obtain a conviction of rape, the finding of semen in or around the vagina can be extremely helpful. For this reason swabs from the vagina and vulva are taken and examined for the presence of acid phosphatase, an enzyme found in semen. Moreover, it is also possible by subjecting the semen to certain tests to establish the blood group of the attacker. Material taken from the upper vagina and vulva is also examined immediately for the presence of motile sperm. And equally important, smears as well as cultures from the vagina, cervix, and rectum for gonorrhea are also an integral part of any examination in a case of suspected rape.

What is done to protect the rape victim from venereal disease?

First, any sexually assaulted woman should receive prophylactic antibiotic therapy for protection against venereal disease. An injection of 2.4 million units of benzathine penicillin G (Bicillin) given intramuscularly will usually protect the woman against the development of gonorrhea and probably syphilis. Where there is a history of an allergic reaction to penicillin, other appropriate antibiotics would be substituted. (See Chapter 12.) If the smears and/or cultures taken for gonorrhea prove to be positive, follow-up visits for repeat cultures are in order. It would also be advisable to do a blood test for syphilis. A positive blood test for syphilis immediately following the attack would mean that the woman already harbored the disease, as the incubation period of the spirochetes runs anywhere from ten to ninety days. A positive blood test would, of course, require immediate treatment. A negative blood test would call for repeat testing at six and twelve weeks following the attack. If the blood test for syphilis was still negative after ninety days subsequent to the assault, a woman could be virtually certain that she had not contracted the disease.

**What precautions are taken against pregnancy in a woman
who has been raped?**

Currently most doctors are recommending the use of the synthetic estrogen diethylstilbestrol, or DES (25 mg. twice daily for five days) as a precaution against pregnancy. (See Chapter 18.) If started within seventy-two hours of the assault, such high doses of estrogen make the lining of the uterus unreceptive to the implantation of a fertilized egg. It is important that a woman also be advised against having sexual intercourse without contraception during the remainder of that particular menstrual cycle. Should a period fail to come within three to four weeks following treatment, menstrual extraction (see Chapter 20), or a dilatation and curettage of the uterine cavity, is recommended. Where pregnancy does occur as a direct result of rape, most doctors advise therapeutic abortion. However, because DES has been linked with vaginal cancer in female offspring, the drug should not be used in rape victims who may, if pregnant, not consent to abortion. In these situations other estrogens, although not currently approved by the FDA for this purpose, may be substituted: Estinyl (2 mg. twice a day for five days) or Premarin (25 mg. twice a day for five days).

Other than the precautions against pregnancy just mentioned, resumption of normal intercourse in a sexually assaulted woman will of course depend upon the extent of her physical injuries, if any, and how emotionally traumatized the incident has left her.

Can there be psychological reasons for pain during normal intercourse?

Pain during intercourse in a physically normal and healthy woman is more common than generally supposed. Even today, despite changing moral values and greater permissiveness about sexual activity, with or without the sanction of marriage, many women still feel guilty, fearful, and apprehensive about their own sexual needs and drives. Many of these psychosexual maladjustments can be traced to early childhood influences stemming from overly rigid parents with condemning attitudes toward all sexual expression. More often than not, the problem is further compounded by gross ignorance and misinformation about sex. It is therefore not surprising that intercourse for some women, rather than being a pleasurable experience, is frequently a painful ordeal to which they reluctantly submit.

Of all the possible mechanisms that can account for painful intercourse because of deep-seated psychosexual conflicts, the most outstanding example is vaginismus.

What exactly is vaginismus?

An involuntary and usually painful contraction of the muscles surrounding the lower vagina. If a woman anticipates pain or subconsciously resists the entire idea of intercourse, this muscular tightening can be so extreme as to prevent penetration of the penis. In such instances, consummation of the sexual act is virtually impossible despite a normal vagina and pelvic organs.

These same women frequently make it impossible for themselves to be examined pelvically. For as soon as they are approached (and prior to any physical contact), they automatically clamp their knees together, arch their back off the examining table, and effectively squeeze their vagina shut, making the insertion of an examining finger an exercise in futility. Needless to say, for a doctor to persist under these circumstances would not only aggravate the patient's pain but could also adversely affect any future attempts at corrective therapy.

Where vaginismus is extreme, successful resolution of the problem may necessitate long sessions of psychotherapy. In addition, a good sexual counselor should be able to help a woman decondition the reflex vaginal spasm.

How can a woman overcome vaginismus?

One of the most successful deconditioning methods consists of using graduated vaginal dilators. The woman herself inserts each vaginal dilator, beginning with one as thin as a lead pencil and working up to one as large as an erect penis. She does not progress to the next larger dilator until she can easily and painlessly insert the smaller one. These sessions are done in the privacy of her home and at her own pace. Involvement of the partner with this "homework," which can extend over a period of several weeks, is definitely advantageous, but attempts at intercourse should be avoided until the woman can comfortably, easily, and confidently insert the largest dilator.

Among couples who truly want to correct the situation and save their relationship, the outlook for resolving the problem is considerably more favorable. Sometimes a patient, gentle, yet firm and knowledgeable partner is ultimately the determining factor in success. All too often, however, even if such women eventually overcome their fear of and reluctance to vaginal penetration, they are unable really to enjoy sex.

For them as well as for other women who rarely or never experience orgasm for a variety of reasons, lack of sexual gratification despite regular intercourse may lead to other problems.

What sort of problems can persistent lack of orgasm during sexual intercourse cause?

Regular sexual stimulation up to but not including orgasm can, over a period of weeks and months, ultimately be detrimental to a woman's sense of well-being. During sexual arousal the pelvic organs become flooded with arterial blood. Objectively, this can be noted in the woman's initial response to stimulation by the production of vaginal lubrication. Along with this vaginal sweating phenomenon, further stimulation causes the cervix, uterus, vulva, and clitoris to become congested, swollen, and enlarged as more blood is shunted to the genital area. If, however, the stimulation is only transient or quickly withdrawn, the pelvic tissues become rapidly decongested as the blood vessels promptly return to their normal (nonengorged) state. But if the stimulation is prolonged, more intense, and carried up to but short of orgasm, upon cessation of stimulation the pelvic blood vessels do not empty rapidly. Instead, the genital tissues remain congested and engorged with stagnant blood for varying amounts of time. The uterus itself, which can frequently enlarge in size by two or three times during prolonged sexual excitation, may take hours to return to its former size.

Therefore, in women who are consistently aroused sexually and yet fail to reach orgasm, persistent engorgement of the pelvic blood vessels (chronic pelvic congestion) can ultimately cause a variety of symptoms.

How does consistent lack of orgasm affect these women?

In many ways. Vague abdominal discomfort, backaches, and a sense of pelvic fullness are among the most common complaints. If congestion of the cervix and vaginal walls is particularly marked, a constant vaginal discharge in the absence of any infection may be the most notable symptom. For other women, chronic pelvic congestion (because of consistent lack of orgasm) may ultimately make them tense and irritable and interfere with normal sleep.

Can anything relieve the symptoms of chronic pelvic congestion?

The answer is simple—orgasm by whatever means are available. But for some women, that answer isn't so simple.

Why isn't orgasm a simple solution to chronic pelvic congestion?

A few women are truly their own worst enemies. Although consistently ungratified sexually, they are still reluctant to express this fact to their partners. Some women even compound the problem by feigning orgasm regularly. For others, if orgasm isn't achieved during intercourse, the idea of obtaining sexual release by masturbation (whether by their partners or by themselves) is totally unacceptable and an obvious sign of their own sexual inadequacy—at least to their way of thinking.

The fact that the sex drive, in contrast to other bodily functions, can be suppressed indefinitely by sheer will power makes the entire realm of sexuality and, particularly, the desire to be sexually gratified an area frequently loaded with guilt feelings and self-deprecation. Sex is a natural bodily function. Being sexually stimulated up to but not including orgasm is not the way nature intended it to be. Eating is also a natural function, but how much nourishment and satisfaction could we derive from food if we simply chewed and never swallowed?

This does not mean that for the woman every act of sexual intercourse must be accompanied by orgasm in order to be emotionally and physically satisfying. Sometimes just being held closely or knowing that you are giving pleasure to someone you love can be intensely gratifying. Rather, what it does imply is that regular sexual stimulation without orgasm over weeks and months can be an important factor in many seemingly unrelated pelvic and other physical complaints.

For when it comes to avoiding or even relieving chronic pelvic congestion, a small orgasm is better than no orgasm.

How does orgasm or reaching a climax solve pelvic congestion?

During orgasm, involuntary muscular contractions (involving the vagina, uterus, and other pelvic structures) not only block further arterial blood from entering the pelvis but also rapidly drain off all the pooled and stagnant blood. Thus, within minutes, all the congested and swollen tissues are back to normal. Subjectively, this rapid emptying of pelvic blood vessels after orgasm is experienced as a warm, pleasant, flushing, glowing sensation in the pelvis.

Although orgasms do differ in intensity depending on a variety of factors—mood, length and type of stimulation, etc.—even having a less intense or a less physically satisfying orgasm can still resolve the problem of pelvic congestion. Under these circumstances, it just may take a little longer for the pelvic organs to return to their normal preexcitement state.

But penile vaginal intercourse or manual masturbation aren't the only ways to experience orgasm and thus avoid chronic pelvic congestion. Oral genital sex is another variety of sexual activity that can lead to the same pleasurable end result.

What is meant by oral genital sex?

Stimulation of the penis or vulva by the mouth, lips, or tongue for purposes of sexual gratification. Fellatio is oral stimulation of the penis; cunnilingus is oral stimulation of the vulva. There is nothing new or different about oral genital sex. Records of this type of sexual activity date back to the first clay tablets. Nor is oral genital sex practiced exclusively by homosexuals. According to various surveys 60 percent of all college-educated heterosexual couples admit to engaging in both fellatio and cunnilingus. The higher the educational level and economic status, the more likely these couples are to include oral genital sex as a regular part of their normal sexual activity.

There is nothing perverted or abnormal about this type of sexual play. Moreover, the idea that oral genital sex is dirty because it involves mouth contact with organs associated with excretory functions is really without foundation. There is no reason why the genitals can't be as clean as any other part of the anatomy. All it takes is the simple hygienic expedient of a little soap and water. Needless to say, without proper cleansing of the body, oral genital sex can be less than exciting. By the same token, having regular intercourse with a partner who never bathes, changes his underwear, or who doesn't bother to brush his teeth can also be a turn-off.

Whether you do or don't engage in oral genital sex is a matter of personal choice and preference. But for many couples this type of love making remains one of the most pleasurable and exciting forms of sexual activity. So whether fellatio and cunnilingus are performed simultaneously or alternately as a preliminary to intercourse, or whether mouth to genital stimulation is carried all the way to orgasm, oral genital sex is here to stay.

Can infections of the mouth or throat ever be acquired by oral genital sex?

Yes, indeed. Avoiding infection during love making really boils down to choosing your partner with care. Nonetheless, when it comes to transmitting or acquiring infections, oral genital sex is much less hazardous than penile vaginal intercourse. *Trichomonas vaginalis,* for example, a protozoan that commonly inhabits the male urethra as well as the female vagina, can never be transmitted to the mouth. This organism is unable to survive outside the confines of the genital urinary tract.

Fungus or yeast infections of the mouth acquired by oral genital sex with an infected partner are exceedingly rare. In the first place, the partner in question would have to have a roaring fungus infection of the vagina or penis. Moreover, the partner performing either cunnilingus or fellatio would have to be physically debilitated and suffering from chronic malnutrition. Fungus infections of the mouth are virtually never seen in relatively healthy and sexually active adults.

Venereal diseases, on the other hand, can be transmitted during oral genital sex. Women can acquire gonorrhea of the mouth and pharynx (throat) during fellatio with an infected partner; men can acquire gonorrhea of the mouth and pharynx during cunnilingus with a woman who has the infection. Similarly, a syphilitic chancre of the lips, tongue, palate, or tonsils can develop if the sexual partner has a syphilitic lesion of the genital organs.

With regard to the transmission of viral infections from the genital organs to the mouth (such as genital warts and herpes simplex virus type II), there have been a few reported cases. Virus infections of the mouth or lips and specifically herpesvirus type I (responsible for the common cold sore or fever blister) can be transmitted to the genital organs of the sexual partner during cunnilingus or fellatio. (See Chapter 12.)

What other infections can be transferred from the mouth to the genital organs during oral genital sex?

The three principal organisms that could be transferred from the mouth and ultimately be a source of genital infection are the gonococcus (gonorrhea), the spirochete (syphilis), and *Candida albicans* (a fungus). Although remote, it is possible that an individual with either a syphilitic chancre or gonorrhea of the mouth and pharynx could infect the genital organs of his or her partner during oral genital sex.

Similarly, a few cases of vaginal fungus infection may originally have been acquired during cunnilingus. But the fact that the fungus *Candida albicans* is frequently a harmless inhabitant of the mouth and intestinal tract of both sexes, as well as the vagina of many healthy women, makes its possible transmission during oral genital sex a matter of little concern. In other words, unless conditions are favorable for its growth, the fungus, even when introduced into the vagina, will remain quietly unobtrusive. (See Chapter 11.)

Other than infection, can oral genital sex ever be hazardous to a woman?

Only if air is blown into the vagina of a pregnant woman. As mentioned in Chapter 19, this type of sexual activity could lead to a fatal air embolism of the *mother's* brain by forcing air into the blood vessels lining the pregnant uterine cavity. As an aside, douching with a *bulb syringe* during pregnancy could also inadvertently force air into the uterine cavity and thus result in a similar maternal catastrophe.

Don't some couples also engage in anal sex?

Anal intercourse is in a class by itself. Although some couples will experiment with this form of intercourse just to satisfy their curiosity, the incorporation of anal intercourse as a regular part of sexual activity can lead to problems. To begin with, the anus was not biologically or anatomically designed to accommodate the erect penis. Therefore, if anal intercourse is to be tried at all, it is essential that the woman be receptive to the idea; that the introduction of the penis be done extremely gently; and that the organ be well lubricated with Vaseline, K-Y lubricating jelly, or a similar product. Saliva just won't do. Moreover, once the penis is introduced into the rectum, it should never be reinserted into the vagina or permitted to contact the vulva without careful cleansing of the organ. Failure to take this simple precaution allows the contaminated penis to introduce unwanted rectal bacteria and other organisms into a woman's urethra and vagina, thus leading to urinary and/or genital tract infections. (See Chapter 14.)

What about the possibility of acquiring other infections through anal intercourse?

Some men have acquired penile urethral infections from rectal organisms during anal intercourse. But here again, gonorrhea is by far the most common infection acquired through such sexual play. In men, gonorrhea of the rectum can usually be traced to anal coitus with a homosexual contact. In women, rectal gonorrhea is probably acquired through anal intercourse with an infected partner or through contamination of the anus from a copious gonorrheal discharge emanating from the cervix. Or, a woman with gonorrhea of the cervix can have her infection transferred to the rectum by engaging in anal coitus following vaginal intercourse. (See Chapter 12.)

Besides possible infection, anal intercourse, even when performed gently and with the necessary precautions, can be injurious and a cause of local anal and rectal problems.

What kind of rectal problems can anal intercourse provoke?

The most common injury, and one that can occur the very first time, is a crack or split in the mucous membrane of the anal canal due to the disproportion in size between the penis and the anus. Such injuries can cause pain and bleeding that can be further aggravated during normal bowel evacuation. Subsequent attempts at anal intercourse under these circumstances can compound the problem by deepening and widening the split (anal fissure). Anal fissures are notoriously slow to heal and frequently become infected. Needless to say, preexisting problems such as hemorrhoids can also flare up as a result of this type of sexual activity.

But anal intercourse, if practiced regularly and over a long period of time, can result in an even more serious problem—relaxation and dilatation of the anal sphincter. This means that excessive stretching of the important muscle fibers surrounding the anal opening could eventually make it difficult for an individual to control the passage of flatus (gas). In extreme cases (and a few have been reported), control of fecal material, especially if the stools were loose, could be further impaired.

Why, then, do a few couples include anal intercourse as part of their sexual activity?

The anus can be exquisitely sensitive to sexual stimulation. Furthermore, anal intercourse can evoke the same erotic sensations as those experienced during vaginal intercourse. In women who perhaps have a relaxed or overly stretched vagina, the tightness of the anal sphincter may create for both her and her partner an added dimension in sexual excitement. Since anal intercourse is also done most commonly in the rear entry position, this further frees the male partner to simultaneously stimulate the breasts, clitoris, or labia minora. For some women, orgasm under these circumstances can be more intense than that experienced otherwise.

Can orgasm per se ever be detrimental to a woman?

Orgasm in a pregnant woman with a ripe cervix (a cervix that is already partially thinned and dilated), particularly if she is several weeks from term, can bring about the onset of premature labor. Orgasm causes rhythmic contractions of the uterus. Therefore, orgasm in women with a ripe cervix could, by precipitating uterine contractions, provoke the onset of labor. Although of no consequence to the woman already close to term and with a mature baby, there have been reported cases of premature labor and delivery apparently precipitated by orgasm. For this reason, any woman whose cervix begins to dilate and thin, eight or more weeks before term, should be cautioned against any type of sexual activity that could induce orgasm.

What type of sexual activity produces the most intense orgasm?

According to carefully documented studies, masturbation in women not only induces the most physically intense orgasm but also evokes the greatest number of pelvic contractions. Automanipulation can also bring the average woman to orgasm faster than any other type of sexual stimulation. Why this should be can probably be explained by an old French saying, "on n'est jamais aussi bien servi que par soi-même,"—which means, one is never so well served as by one's self. Despite the fact that masturbation, at least for women, can elicit a really great orgasm, there's nothing like sharing sex with a compatible partner to make the experience emotionally rewarding.

What, then, is really good sex?

Good sex is more than technique, timing, position, or even experiencing orgasm. It is also more than an accelerated heart rate, increased blood pressure, and vascular engorgement of the genital organs. Really good sex involves total physical, emotional, and psychological satisfaction. But it can seldom attain that peak unless there is a strong, continuing relationship between two sensitive and responsible individuals who mutually love and respect each other.

Sex, like any other form of human expression and interaction, cannot remain static. A good sexual relationship needs to grow and to be nurtured if it is to become the physical expression of love between two people. It means feeling good about your body and having an open attitude toward the needs of both you and your partner. Equally important, spontaneity and feeling free to communicate are essential.

No individual responds exactly the same way every time to the same sexual stimulation. Moods change from day to day and from moment to moment. What might have been terribly exciting last night may be undesired this morning. So why not open up to your mate about what really pleases you and when. You may happily discover that what you secretly dreamed in your fantasy world coincides with what your loved one has also wanted to share with you, but never dared.

PART V

The Prerogatives of Being a Woman

16. To Have—How to Become Pregnant

With the current emphasis on family planning and birth control, the subject of how to become pregnant might seem irrelevant or of minor concern. Yet 10 to 12 percent of the marriages today are involuntarily barren.

For the couple unable to conceive and anxious to have children, the decreasing availability of babies for adoption has made their infertility problem even more of a concern and challenge. It is, therefore, important that all factors in the barren couple that could contribute to infertility be investigated and evaluated.

The last decade has seen remarkable advances in the field of reproductive medicine. Today 60 to 70 percent of infertile couples can eventually achieve their desired goal of conception. More recent work in the field of immunology, antigens, sperm antibodies, and in-vitro fertilization may in the near future offer hope for others.

How can you become pregnant?

A sperm must get together with an egg. Exactly how this happens may seem obvious, but misconceptions still abound.

How does a sperm get together with an egg?

With the exception of artificial insemination, there is only one way. The male partner must have an erection and deposit sperm in or around the vagina. Penile penetration into the vagina is not absolutely necessary. Sperm deposited around the outside of the vaginal opening can result in pregnancy. On occasion sperm can also be present at the tip of an erect penis *prior to ejaculation.* The practice of coitus interruptus, or the withdrawal of the penis from the vagina before ejaculation, has at times been responsible for impregnating an unwary woman.

Once deposited, those speedy sperm move at an incredibly fast rate. From the vagina they swarm into the cervical canal, swim across the uterine cavity, and ascend into the Fallopian tubes. If all conditions are favorable, total travel time from the cervix to the rendezvous with the egg in the outer third of the Fallopian tube has been clocked at less than five minutes.

Can you become pregnant the first time you have intercourse?

Yes, the very first time can do it. However, for the young couple having sexual intercourse at least every other day, 25 percent of the women will be pregnant within one month. At the end of six months 60 percent will have conceived, by the end of one year 80 percent, and after eighteen months 90 percent. If after trying for eighteen months you still haven't conceived, then regardless of your age or the frequency of intercourse, your chances of becoming pregnant rapidly decline.

At what age are women most fertile?

Between twenty and twenty-four, with age twenty-four probably being the time of maximum fertility. From age twenty-five to thirty there is a slight decline followed by a steady drop-off during the thirties. After forty there is a marked drop, and after forty-five your chances of becoming pregnant are rather slim.

What about fertility in men?

Here again, age twenty-four seems to be a very good year. Unlike women, men maintain a fairly high rate of fertility throughout a longer period of their life. The ability to have an erection, ejaculate, and discharge healthy sperm may continue into the sixties, seventies, and beyond. Nevertheless, by age forty-five there tends to be a slight decline in male fertility.

How old is too old?

For some men no age is too old. In women, however, the ovaries do retire eventually. But even if you are over forty-five, as long as your periods are regular, don't despair. Ovulation and conception can occur up to age fifty and beyond. You might just beat the world's record—pregnant at fifty-seven.

However, there are disadvantages to starting your family after age thirty or thirty-five.

What's wrong with having that first baby after thirty or thirty-five?

By age thirty a woman's fertility is already slowly declining. This means that if you are waiting to be financially secure or to have just the right home and surroundings in which to raise children, you might find that becoming pregnant may not be that easy. Furthermore, since such common female problems as endometriosis, fibroid tumors, and other pelvic conditions manifest themselves in the late twenties and thirties, here again you may have passed the optimal reproductive years in which to start your family.

Statistics have also shown that women past thirty-five in particular tend to have a higher rate of complications during pregnancy and delivery. There is also a small but decided risk of giving birth to a congenitally abnormal infant. Mongolism, for example, among the general population occurs in about one out of seven hundred live births. Interestingly enough, there is a marked variability of its incidence depending upon maternal age. For women under thirty the incidence of mongolism runs about one out of two thousand live births, whereas in women over forty, their chances of giving birth to a mongoloid child can be as high as one to two percent.

But for those of you who are anxious to conceive regardless of your age . . .

How often should you have intercourse if you want to become pregnant?

More often than you probably think. Most sperm quickly lose their ability to impregnate after forty-eight hours, while the ovum is most receptive to fertilization during the first twelve hours of its twenty-four-hour existence. Possible conception, therefore, in any one menstrual cycle is primarily limited to a scant forty-eight- to sixty-hour period. This means having sexual intercourse at least four times a week, or at least every other day. Less frequent intercourse decreases your chances for speedy conception.

Does having more sex improve your chances of becoming pregnant?

If four times a week is ideal, then five times or more should be even better. Not necessarily so. Too much sex can actually work against you especially if your partner is somewhat subfertile. On an average most men discharge anywhere from 3.5 cc. to 5 cc. (one-half to one teaspoon) of semen at any one time. Ejaculations in excess of four times weekly decrease the volume of semen. And less semen means less sperm being deposited. So unless your partner is superfertile, taper off.

Can position during sexual intercourse influence conception?

Yes, indeed. Varying your position may add zest to your sex life, but if your aim is pregnancy, let's be practical. Nothing is quite so successful in keeping the sperm in close contact with the cervix than the conventional position of male on top and woman on her back with hips flexed and buttocks elevated on a small pillow.

Following ejaculation the man should not withdraw his penis from the vagina until it has resumed its normal flaccid state. Pulling out too soon will allow some of the semen to fall away.

And by all means don't jump out of bed immediately afterward. Gravity can be your enemy. It is better to lie on your back for at least half an hour or longer.

Does having a tipped uterus make any difference?

Despite the fact that there may be less contact between the cervix and pool of semen, a tipped or retroverted uterus (contrary to what many believe) does not decrease your chances for conception. All other things being equal, if the sperm are anywhere near the cervix, they'll make it.

What about the use of lubricating jellies or Vaseline before intercourse?

Not if you want to get pregnant. In exchange for allowing the penis to penetrate more easily in the woman with a snug vaginal opening or insufficient lubrication, Vaseline or lubricating jellies will inhibit effective sperm movement. The same applies to any of the hygienic suppositories such as Norforms. On the other hand, saliva will not interfere with sperm movement. In fact many women resort to using good healthy spit around the vaginal opening when natural lubrication may be less than adequate. Douching before intercourse will also not interfere with sperm motility.

Will having an orgasm improve your chances of becoming pregnant?

If orgasm in a woman was necessary for conception, there would be a prompt and precipitous drop in world population. Nevertheless, having an orgasm may aid migration of the sperm through the cervical canal by causing a slight protrusion of the alkaline cervical mucus. (More about this soon.) Aside from this minor factor, orgasm in the woman is not a prerequisite to conception.

When are you most fertile?

During the ovulatory phase of your cycle, or approximately two weeks before your next period. If your periods tend to be irregular, keeping track of your basal body temperature as described in Chapter 6 may help pinpoint the moment of ovulation. But don't despair if your chart doesn't look like the example. Temperature charts sometimes need professional interpretation.

If you can pinpoint the moment of ovulation, when's the best time to have intercourse?

Usually twenty-four to thirty-six hours before the actual moment of ovulation as evidenced by the rise in your basal body temperature. If you hit it just right, impregnation is much more likely to occur if the sperm are eagerly assembled on the tubal runway and awaiting the arrival of the freshly launched egg.

However, if you want to try to influence the sex of your child, you might want to change your timing somewhat.

How can timing intercourse influence the sex of the unborn child?

The closer you can time intercourse with the moment of ovulation, the better your chances of having a male child. On the other hand, having intercourse after ovulation or two to three days before anticipated ovulation will much more likely result in a female.

Other factors can also play a role in sex determination.

What factors?

Since the sex of the child is predetermined by the sperm (X sperm for female, Y sperm for male), factors such as vaginal acidity, depth of penile penetration at the time of ejaculation, and orgasm in the woman can favor impregnation by either an X sperm or a Y sperm. However, *results cannot be guaranteed.*

According to several clinical studies, by manipulating these various factors your chances of achieving the desired sex of the child may run close to 80 or 85 percent.

How can you increase your chances of having a boy?

To speed the Y sperm on their way, the following routine is suggested: (1) The most important factor is, of course, timing. Plan intercourse at the time of ovulation or just a few hours before you ovulate. Be sure that you abstain three or four days beforehand. (2) Prior to intercourse take an alkaline vaginal douche by dissolving two to three tablespoons of baking soda per quart of warm water. The increased vaginal alkalinity will further enhance the passage of Y sperm. (3) There should be deep penile penetration at the moment of ejaculation to assure the deposition of Y sperm close to the cervix. (4) Plan to have an orgasm yourself. The protrusion of the alkaline cervical mucus at the time of climax will also aid Y sperm migration.

In essence, the easier it is to conceive (fresh Y sperm meeting fresh egg) and the more you enjoy it, the greater the chances of having a boy baby.

Suppose you want a baby girl?

Then you must give the X sperm the edge by making it more difficult for the Y sperm to get through: (1) Have your *last* intercourse about two to three days before your anticipated ovulation. (2) Prior to intercourse take a vinegar douche (two tablespoons of white vinegar per quart of warm water). (3) At the moment of emission, penile penetration should be fairly shallow. (4) Bypass the orgasm this time.

As you might guess, conception under these circumstances will certainly be more difficult. Should impregnation occur, however, the chances of having a female offspring are definitely increased. In this instance the winning combination is the result of an old X sperm meeting a fresh, young egg.

To what extent should you rely on a BBT chart?

For those of you anxious to conceive regardless of the baby's sex, don't get carried away or compulsive about this type of record keeping. Three or four months of temperature taking is plenty. If at the end of three cycles you have a fairly good indication of when you ovulate, the time of subsequent ovulation can be projected with some degree of accuracy. Obsessive timing of intercourse around the exact day of ovulation is both unnecessary and a potential source of marital friction. The best advice is to just go ahead and enjoy intercourse every other day or so during your most fertile week. At that frequency of coitus, your chances of conception are probably just as good as adhering to a meticulous time schedule.

If you haven't been able to conceive, when should you consult a doctor?

Many gynecologists will advise trying for at least a full year. However, for the older childless couple, it might be foolish to postpone evaluation for that length of time. Age, general health, and specific medical problems, past or present, may make an earlier evaluation desirable.

Is the female partner usually to blame?

The female partner is accountable for only slightly more than half of the infertility problems. In approximately 35 percent of all barren marriages, the husband is solely responsible for lack of conception, and in an additional 10 percent, the husband is partly responsible. For this reason, many doctors prefer to evaluate the male partner first before proceeding with the more involved studies necessary to determine any female infertility factor.

If the man can perform sexually, does that mean he's fertile?

Not at all. Being able to have an erection and ejaculate semen inside the vaginal canal is no guarantee of fertility. You may be sleeping with the world's greatest lover, but unless he can deliver vigorous sperm, he'll never make you a mother.

Fertility in the male or the ability to impregnate an egg requires the following: (1) The testicles must produce normal sperm; (2) the sperm must then pass through the male genital tract (vas deferens) and mix with secretions (seminal fluid) from the prostate and seminal vesicles; and (3) the semen (seminal fluid plus sperm) must be ejaculated from the penile urethra and delivered preferably against the cervix.

How is fertility in the male evaluated?

By the simple expedient of examining the semen—if your doctor can get a specimen. Unfortunately few men will willingly accept the inference that they may be subfertile. Many infertility investigations have ground to a halt because of a recalcitrant male with a sensitive ego. Nevertheless, if your partner does cooperate, part of the battle is won. Should he pass the test with a high score, he will be more inclined to discuss "your" infertility problem with the doctor.

How is semen collected?

Usually by masturbation or coitus interruptus following four or five days of sexual abstinence. Best results are obtained if the entire ejaculate is deposited in a clean glass jar (not necessarily sterile), tightly capped, and submitted to a designated laboratory within one hour.

When it comes to semen specimens, how fertile is fertile?

According to recent studies it takes at least 20 million sperm per cc. for the fertilization of a single ovum. Thus, with the average ejaculate measuring 3 to 4 cc., this means that a *minimally* fertile man should release at least 60–80 million sperm during a single act of coitus to effect conception. But, apart from the total number of sperm ejaculated, the most important factor affecting male fertility is sperm motility; at least 60 percent of all sperm must be motile and normal in shape if impregnation is to occur.

What happens if your partner flunks the semen test?

He should be given another chance. The quality and number of sperm can be adversely affected by emotions, physical stress, febrile illnesses, as well as too frequent intercourse and even prolonged sexual abstinence. Don't give up hope yet. His second or third performance may dazzle everyone.

What about the man who never measures up?

He needs to see his doctor. Even assuming that your partner is hormonally and genetically normal, other conditions can readily account for a poor sperm count. Having had mumps complicated by orchitis (inflammation of the testes) as a child is frequently a cause of zero sperm production (azoospermia). Similarly, any past infection (gonorrhea, for example), scrotal injury, or obstruction to the proper blood supply of the testicles can contribute to a decreased sperm count.

Interestingly enough, subfertility may also stem from less obvious and unsuspected reasons.

Is your partner's job too hot for his own good?

Have you ever wondered why those priceless testicles dangle in such a precarious location? The reason is literally a matter of degrees. To be functional, the testicles must hang in the cool of the scrotum. An undescended testicle or one retained within the warmth of the abdominal cavity just can't manufacture sperm. Too much body heat eventually destroys the special cells that produce sperm.

Similarly, men exposed to excessive heat around the genital area, such as truck drivers who spend long hours in hot engine cabs or men employed as stokers on blast furnaces, have notoriously low sperm counts.

On the less dramatic side is the low-sperm man who further compromises his fertility by being a hot bath devotee. A fast shower would be preferable if he is really eager to get you pregnant.

Men's shorts can also be a detriment in cases of borderline infertility.

Does your partner need to change his underwear?

As improbable as this may seem, many a subfertile husband has finally impregnated his wife by the simple expedient of changing his underwear. Jockey shorts, athletic supports, and trousers with snug crotches can raise the testicular temperature by hugging the scrotum closer to the body.

Switching to breezy boxer shorts has made more than one man a father.

Can anything else help a low sperm count?

No specific treatment, including vitamin and hormone therapy, has been universally effective. However, since sperm counts can be adversely affected by physical and emotional factors, general health measures such as proper diet, regular exercise, adequate rest, and cutting back on alcohol and tobacco consumption along with avoidance of unnecessary tension may be beneficial.

In addition to these measures, men with low sperm counts can occasionally impregnate their wives by employing the split ejaculate technique.

The split ejaculate technique?

This technique involves withdrawing the penis from the vagina as soon as the first spurt of ejaculation occurs. The remainder of the ejaculate is then deposited outside and away from the vagina. Studies have shown that sperm in the first part of the ejaculate are consistently more concentrated, more motile, and more vigorous. In contrast the remainder of the ejaculate tends to contain sluggish, relatively non-motile sperm with a decreased survival rate. Thus, by depositing only the "better half" of the semen specimen, chances for conception can be increased.

In the event that this maneuver also fails to produce the desired results, perhaps your partner should consider having his sperm frozen.

How would freezing his sperm help?

If one ejaculation doesn't have enough sperm to impregnate you, pooling several emissions might do the trick. With more and more frozen sperm banks being established and available to the general public, semen specimens from low-sperm husbands can be frozen, stored, and subsequently used to artificially inseminate their wives.

With the technique of three to four repeated inseminations during the ovulatory phase, approximately half the women will become pregnant within two to four months. In unusual cases where the husband has no sperm, the couple may elect artificial insemination with a donor's sperm. Under these circumstances, the pregnancy success rate can be as high as 60 to 80 percent.

If your partner is fertile, what's your trouble?

Most young and apparently healthy women fail to conceive for one of the following reasons: their cervix is working against them, the tubal passageways are blocked, or they simply do not ovulate regularly.

Do you have a friendly cervix?

You will never get pregnant unless the sperm can squirm through the cervical canal and reach the tubes in time to meet the incoming egg. A friendly cervix implies both a healthy cervix free from chronic infection and an unobstructed cervical canal whose glands secrete the right kind of mucus at the proper time.

What's so important about cervical mucus?

Without a certain quality of cervical mucus, most sperm will be entrapped and die before they can pass through the cervical canal.

Under normal conditions, both the quality and the quantity of the cervical mucus changes during the menstrual cycle. Right after your period, the cervical canal normally contains a thick plug of tenacious mucus—a sure trap to ensnare those sperm, thus keeping them from swimming up through the canal. As estrogen levels increase and ovulation approaches, miraculous things happen. The small cervical os gaps slightly and the mucus now becomes profuse, watery, and stringy. You may notice an increased amount of clear discharge during the ovulatory, or fertile, phase of your cycle. Interestingly enough, it is only during these few days at midcycle that sperm can successfully penetrate the cervical mucus in any great number.

Following ovulation the cervical os narrows and the mucus returns to its preovulatory thick, unreceptive state.

How can your doctor tell if that mucus is receptive?

By checking the cervical mucus within two to fifteen hours after intercourse just prior to the time of expected ovulation. This postcoital test (Sims-Huhner test) is simple, painless, and consists of aspirating some mucus from the cervical canal and examining it under a microscope.

If your cervix is friendly, a certain number of living, moving sperm should still be squirming around in the cervical mucus. In contrast, an unreceptive mucus will show no sperm or only dead ones in spite of the presence of motile sperm in the upper vagina.

For women whose mucus obstinately defies any sperm to sneak through, very small doses of estrogen prior to ovulation may stimulate a greater output of normal cervical mucus. When an obvious cervical infection and discharge may be interfering, treating and clearing the infection may well solve the problem.

Are those tubes keeping you from buying a maternity outfit?

Since fertilization of the ovum normally occurs in the Fallopian tubes, any blockage or obstruction involving the tubal passageways can make you infertile. For pregnancy to occur, at least one tube must be open and functioning normally.

There can be many reasons for blocked tubes. A gonorrheal tubal infection is certainly a common cause, but other pelvic infections as well as congenital tubal anomalies have been known to take their toll. In some parts of the world, notably Scotland and Israel, tuberculosis of the tubes accounts for 5 to 10 percent of infertility problems.

Blockage of a perfectly normal tube can also occur if the tube is kinked by surrounding scar tissue or old adhesions from previous pelvic problems or surgery, for example, a ruptured appendix.

How can the Fallopian tubes be checked?

Several ways. Most commonly, either by a special X-ray of the uterus and tubes (hysterosalpingogram) or the so-called Rubin test (carbon dioxide insufflation test).

What exactly is the Rubin test?

A simple office procedure that checks for the passage of gas (carbon dioxide) through the tubes. With a small rubber-tipped adapter inserted just inside the cervical opening, a stream of pure carbon dioxide gas is slowly released into the uterine cavity. If either or both tubes are open, the carbon dioxide gas will gradually pass through the tubal passageway and escape into the abdominal cavity. If both tubes are blocked, there will obviously be no passage of gas.

How does the doctor know whether the gas has escaped through the tubes?

He can frequently tell by the way the pressure rises and falls on the special gauge. Imagine for a moment that the tubes are drinking straws through which you blow air. If the straw is not plugged, the air will flow easily and smoothly. If the straw is bent or obstructed, no matter how hard you blow, no air will pass through it. The Rubin test works on almost the same principle.

Verification that at least one tube is open will depend upon your experiencing a mild, temporary shoulder pain after the test.

Why the shoulder pain?

Sitting up or standing up after the examination will cause the small amount of carbon dioxide in the abdominal cavity to ascend automatically and lodge against the diaphragm (the muscle that separates the chest and abdomen). Irritation of the diaphragm from the gas will result in reflex shoulder pain. If you should lie down again, the gas will automatically shift away from the diaphragm and the pain will be relieved. But don't worry. Nature quickly absorbs that harmless small amount of carbon dioxide and you will be completely comfortable very shortly.

If you don't experience any shoulder pain, your doctor may either repeat the test at another time or else take an X-ray of the tubes. Sometimes a simple muscle spasm in the wall of the tubes can prevent any gas from escaping. A negative Rubin test is not absolute proof that those tubes are blocked.

What about an X-ray of the tubes?

A hysterosalpingogram involves taking X-ray pictures during the injection of a small amount of radiopaque dye through the cervical canal. This has the advantage of outlining the contours of the entire uterine cavity as well as the tubal passageways.

If there should be a blockage in either tube, its location can be accurately pinpointed. If both tubes are open, the dye will simply spill out the ends and into the abdominal cavity.

You might have some temporary, mild uterine cramping during the test, but no shoulder pain afterward. The dye, which is heavier than carbon dioxide, will simply gravitate to the pelvic area and undergo rapid absorption.

If your tubes are blocked, can anything be done?

Since anywhere from 15 to 35 percent of infertility problems are the result of blocked tubes (depending on whose statistics you quote), the possibility of surgically unblocking the tubes assumes prime importance.

Tuboplasty, or plastic reconstructive surgery of damaged tubes, is painstaking, meticulous, and delicate surgery. When you consider that the tubal passageway isn't much bigger than the bristle on a hairbrush, you can appreciate why results, even in the hands of competent and experienced gynecologists, are less than perfect.

Reestablishing the continuity of the tube is also no permanent guarantee of success. A tube successfully opened by surgery may subsequently reseal because of scar tissue formation or in some instances may even cause a tubal or ectopic pregnancy.

But even an open tube is not necessarily a functional and healthy tube. As you might remember from Chapter 2, the Fallopian tubes are more than just passageways. Specialized cells within their lining must also nourish the fertilized egg during its three- to four-day trip to the uterine lining.

For these reasons, success in terms of conception and full-term pregnancies cannot always be guaranteed following tubal plastic surgery.

What are your chances of getting pregnant after tuboplasty?

Pregnancy rates among women following tubal surgery vary from 7 to 40 percent. Much depends on where the tube is blocked, how much of the total tube is affected, and the severity of the involvement. Needless to say, all these factors are vitally important in evaluating the potential success of any procedure.

As might be expected, surgery on tubes severely compromised by extensive disease can easily fail. If there is only minimal tubal damage, results predictably are better. Your chances for success are further enhanced if the surgery is performed by a gynecologist who is specialized in tubal surgery. Tuboplasty is not a routine procedure.

What about the woman who just does not ovulate?

No young and respectable ovary will ever release a single egg unless the pituitary is in perfect working order. Lack of ovulation in women of reproductive age resulting from inadequate or poorly timed ovarian stimulation by the pituitary accounts for another 10 to 25 percent of infertility problems.

As you may remember from Chapter 5, it takes two pituitary hormones (FSH and LH) working in absolute harmony to mature and launch an egg. Too much or too little of either hormone at the wrong time equals zero egg output.

Until fairly recently, most women who did not ovulate because of this problem were just out of luck. Adoption was the only answer. There was no magic elixir that could straighten out pituitary function or coax an egg out of those ovaries. Today, with the advent of the new fertility drugs, ovulation can be induced in about 80 percent of such women.

Are you a candidate for one of the fertility drugs?

Being a candidate depends upon eliminating all other possible causes of infertility. This implies that everything else should be working for you: cervix, tubes, and a fertile partner. In addition to basic blood and urine studies, a complete hormonal evaluation is also necessary to determine how well the pituitary and other endocrine glands are functioning. If lack of ovulation owing to a pituitary hormonal dysfunction is established as the only apparent reason for your failure to conceive, a fertility drug just might be the answer.

How do fertility drugs induce ovulation?

There are basically two different kinds of fertility drugs: the first induces ovulation by simply prodding the pituitary to release its hormones more effectively; the second induces ovulation by actually replacing the needed hormones.

The results of your pituitary hormonal evaluation will determine which fertility drug, if any, is the possible answer to your particular problem. If your pituitary is essentially normal but just slightly off-balance in relation to complete hormonal harmony between FSH and LH, it might need just a little nudge to function properly. Less commonly a woman may fail to ovulate because of an inadequate pituitary output of FSH and LH. Prodding the pituitary in this situation would do no good. As the old saying goes, "You can't get blood out of a turnip." Under these circumstances, nothing short of actual replacement of both FSH and LH will work.

What fertility drugs are available?

Currently only three: Clomid (clomiphene citrate); Pergonal, also known as HMG (human menopausal gonadotropin); and HCG (human chorionic gonadotropin).

What is Clomid?

Clomid, or clomiphene citrate, is a synthetic drug preparation that induces ovulation by stimulating the pituitary to work more effectively. If your pituitary and ovaries are functionally intact but your problem is one of hormonal imbalance, Clomid may be the drug of choice.

Prior to its release by the FDA, Clomid underwent six years of intensive clinical evaluation. Four thousand anovulatory women were given this drug for a variety of menstrual and hormonal disorders, and ovulation was induced in some 80 percent of the women so treated.

How is Clomid taken?

By mouth, usually for five days during the menstrual cycle. However, since no two women will respond in the same manner, dose and length of treatment will vary.

If ovulation is going to occur, it will frequently be triggered within five to nine days following the last tablet. For best results, make sure your partner is around. Some women will ovulate the very first month. Others will require repeat treatment for several months. For others, Clomid just doesn't work—no egg.

Should pregnancy occur, there may or may not be resumption of normal ovulation following delivery. In some instances, therefore, repeat treatment with Clomid may be necessary should a subsequent pregnancy be desired.

What about side effects while on Clomid therapy?

Hot flashes sometimes occur because of increased pituitary FSH activity. In a small proportion of women, overstimulation by the pituitary may cause an ovarian cyst. Clomid-induced ovarian cysts, however, tend to be small and readily disappear within one to four weeks following discontinuation of therapy.

When properly used, Clomid is a safe drug, but your chances of having a multiple pregnancy are slightly increased. Twins can be expected in about one out of sixteen Clomid-induced pregnancies.

What about other fertility drugs?

Pergonal in combination with HCG triggers ovulation by literally substituting for the two pituitary hormones, FSH and LH.

Pergonal, or HMG (human menopausal gonadotropin), is essentially a hormonal extract of FSH from the urine of menopausal women. HCG (human chorionic gonadotropin), on the other hand, is a hormonal extract of an LH-like substance from the urine of pregnant women.

The combined use of these two extracts in a sequential fashion is primarily limited to that small group of women who are anxious to conceive but who fail to ovulate because of an inadequate pituitary output of FSH and LH.

Among women treated with these preparations, up to 90 percent ovulate and 65 percent subsequently conceive. As impressive as these figures may seem, only about 30 percent of the women who do conceive actually give birth to living, healthy babies. The remaining women unfortunately either abort spontaneously or give birth to grossly immature infants incapable of surviving. Furthermore, because of the somewhat unpredictable nature of these two drugs (Pergonal in particular), their use is further restricted to sophisticated hospital centers where facilities are available for close hormonal monitoring and constant supervision during treatment. This means that being on this medication necessitates frequent pelvic examinations plus numerous and elaborate urine and blood hormonal studies to evaluate progress during treatment. Needless to say, the cost of a single month's treatment to effect ovulation can at times be exceedingly high, running as much as four hundred dollars and up. Since Pergonal and HCG are human hormonal extracts and not synthesized commercially, most of the expense stems from the price of the drugs, in addition to the necessary hormonal studies.

Why is such close supervision necessary?

Even with close supervision and carefully regulated dosages of Pergonal and HCG, there is a substantial chance of overstimulating the ovaries. As a result, large ovarian cysts can develop virtually overnight. Withdrawal of medication will usually result in cyst regression, but compared to Clomid-induced cysts, ovarian enlargements with Pergonal and HCG occur with greater frequency and are potentially more serious.

What about multiple pregnancies with Pergonal and HCG therapy?

Your chances are good. Overstimulation of the ovaries can also cause superovulation with the simultaneous release of several eggs. In fact, many of the famous multiple births so highly publicized in the past few years are Pergonal and HCG babies. Among women successfully treated with these preparations, about 30 percent of all pregnancies will result in multiple births—twins, triplets, etc.

Undoubtedly with continuing research there will be better and more effective ways of controlling the problem of ovarian overstimulation.

Is there any other way to induce ovulation besides fertility drugs?

For some women with the polycystic ovarian syndrome (see Chapter 10), wedge resection or the surgical removal of a portion of each enlarged ovary may correct the basic hormonal disturbance. Exactly how ovarian wedge resection works is still open to debate. More recently, Clomid therapy has largely supplanted this surgical approach in women who want to become pregnant. Nonetheless, for some women with polycystic ovaries, surgery may still be the best answer in bringing about resumption of normal periods and monthly ovulation.

What else can make you infertile?

Endometriosis indirectly accounts for many infertility problems by interfering with the egg's passage from the ovary into the tube. (See Chapter 22 for details.)

What about the couple who seems perfectly normal but just can't conceive?

Since 1964 there has been mounting evidence to suggest that many obscure and previously unexplained infertility problems among normal, healthy couples may have an immunological basis. Stated simply, you may be producing antibodies against your partner's sperm.

Are you immune to your partner's sperm?

As farfetched as this may seem, you and your partner may be incompatible on a cellular level.

In the same manner, for example, that a smallpox vaccination stimulates the production of antibodies against that disease, sperm acting as a foreign protein substance (antigen) may provoke the formation of sperm antibodies in some women. Since sperm remaining in the female genital tract following intercourse are probably engulfed and removed by special scavenger cells, it is possible that those absorbed sperm protein fragments may subsequently stimulate antibody formation. Under these circumstances, repeated coitus with deposition of sperm in the vagina gradually allows the woman to build up more and more circulating and tissue-fixed antibodies against that foreign protein sperm material. In time, therefore, it is possible that antibodies present in the blood and in various body tissues (vagina, cervix, uterus) may rapidly inactivate any new sperm invaders long before they can ever reach the egg.

To further complicate the situation, there may be different types of sperm antigens and therefore different types of sperm antibodies. Thus, a woman exposed to repeated intercourse with different partners might possibly have a greater variety, as well as a higher level, of sperm antibodies.

Does this mean that promiscuity may be an obscure cause of infertility?

Not necessarily. Some women never develop sperm antibodies regardless of how many sexual partners they have or how frequently they engage in coitus. On the other hand, a woman with relatively little sexual exposure may have difficulty conceiving because of a significantly high level of sperm antibodies. Exactly what triggers the development of these antibodies in some women and not in others remains to be discovered. Since the immunological aspect of infertility is a very new field, much of the work is still limited and experimental. Moreover, tests for sperm antibodies are neither generally available nor perfected.

How can you know whether your infertility has an immunological basis?

Here again the answer is elusive. However, if you are tested and found to have a high level of sperm antibodies, your situation may be more hopeful than you think. There may still be a way to get pregnant even if you are producing antibodies against your partner's sperm.

How can you possibly get pregnant if you have sperm antibodies?

By temporarily preventing further exposure to sperm. It stands to reason that if you can build and maintain a high antibody level against sperm by repeated intercourse, then it follows that by avoiding further contact with sperm your antibody level should drop. In brief, there are only two possible methods whereby this can be accomplished: stay away from all sex or have your partner wear a condom during intercourse for at least nine to twelve months.

Among couples apparently unable to conceive because of a sperm antibody problem and who subsequently elected to try the condom method, 100 percent of the women showed marked reduction in their sperm antibody level after one year of protected coitus. Even more exciting, approximately 60 percent of these women subsequently became pregnant after their partners discarded the condom.

Therefore, if there doesn't seem to be any apparent reason for your infertility, this method of protective coitus may be worth a try.

Suppose it doesn't work—then what?

In regard to other couples who may have other obscure reasons for their infertility, medical science may soon provide an answer even for them. With so many rapid advances being reported in the field of human reproduction, the couple who today has an infertility problem may in a few short years be the couple most in need of contraceptive advice.

17. Bypassing the Tubes—In-vitro Fertilization

On July 25, 1978, the birth of a five-pound-twelve-ounce healthy baby girl in a small English hospital made medical history. For on that day, Louise Brown was delivered by Caesarian section, the first baby ever to be born as a result of in-vitro fertilization. Gynecologist Patrick C. Steptoe and physiologist Robert Edwards had achieved what had never been done before. They had fertilized a single human ovum in the laboratory and then successfully implanted the growing embryo into the mother's uterus. In so doing, they showed that conception outside the human body was not only possible, but could result in the birth of a normal, healthy child. In January, 1979, the birth of Alastair James Lauchen Montgomery, the second child and first male resulting from this revolutionary technique, gave additional proof that a new era in medicine had indeed been launched.

What is meant by in-vitro fertilization?
    The term "in-vitro" literally means "in glass." In-vitro fertilization therefore refers to the fertilization of an ovum by a sperm outside of the body or in an artificial environment. Since impregnation or fertilization normally occurs within a Fallopian tube, in-vitro fertiliza-

tion is a technique to bypass the tubes. The phrase "test-tube fertilization" is sometimes applied to describe this procedure.

Is test-tube fertilization the same thing as a test-tube baby?

No. A test-tube baby would imply both conception and complete development of the infant wholly apart from its mother's body. Such a feat to date has never been accomplished, nor is medical technology sufficiently advanced to envision such an event in the foreseeable future.

Which women are candidates for in-vitro fertilization?

At the moment, the procedure is exclusively limited to women who are infertile on the basis of absent, blocked, or non-functioning Fallopian tubes. Such non-functioning tubes may be the result of infections, previous ectopic pregnancies (with partial or complete removal of one or both tubes), or tubal sterilization procedures unamenable to corrective surgery. Other criteria for selection require that a woman have an intact and healthy uterus, at least one normal, functioning, and accessible ovary, and preferably be younger than 36. In addition, the husband's semen must be free of infection and contain healthy, vigorous sperm in adequate number. To date, in-vitro fertilization has been limited to married couples who contribute egg and sperm.

What further diagnostic and screening tests are required?

Once a woman is selected as a potential candidate, the next step is a complete physical, medical, and endocrinological evaluation. Extensive laboratory tests to rule out the presence of genital tract infection are also an integral part of the workup. These include testing for pathogenic bacteria, viruses, protozoa, and other organisms in either partner which could affect fertility or even be a factor in causing a birth defect. A diagnostic laparoscopy is another important part of the initial workup.

What is a diagnostic laparoscopy?

This operation involves the inspection of the female pelvic organs through the use of a telescopelike instrument (laparoscope) inserted through a small abdominal puncture wound. The procedure allows a more critical evaluation of the tubes. More importantly, laparoscopy determines the feasibility of extracting an ovum from the ovary: there must be at least one ovary which is free and accessible before any attempts to recover an ovum can be made. A pelvic infection, for example, may have left the ovaries so deeply buried and obscured in scar tissue that even extensive surgical attempts to free an ovary of adhesions may be fruitless. Among women with less extensive scarring, removal of ovarian adhesions discovered via laparoscopy is sometimes possible.

Assuming that a woman does "pass" the diagnostic laparoscopy, the next step in this complicated process of in-vitro fertilization is a thorough study of her menstrual cycles with emphasis on pinpointing the moment of ovulation.

Are fertility drugs used to control ovulation?

Fertility drugs including various combinations of clomiphene, HMG (Human Menopausal Gonadotropin), and HCG (Human Chorionic Gonadotropin) were initially used during the early years of in-vitro fertilization research. These drugs evoked the ripening of multiple healthy ova as well as regulating the moment of ovulation. This made scheduling laparoscopy for ova recovery prior to ovulation considerably more accurate. But despite the great convenience of fertility drugs, it was later discovered that their use somehow interfered with the normal mechanisms of implantation. These drugs (for reasons still unknown) seem to render the uterine environment hostile to the reception of an artificially (in-vitro) fertilized embryo. As a consequence, superovulation resulting from fertility drugs was ultimately abandoned. Today, the technique of in-vitro fertilization depends on the recovery of a single ovum just prior to normal and natural ovulation uninfluenced by any drug, chemical, or exogenous hormone.

The decision to follow a woman's natural ovulatory cycle, however, created a whole new set of problems.

What kind of problems?

It now became necessary to ascertain the precise moment of natural ovulation. In fact, accurate timing to recover an ovum is of critical importance. If laparoscopy for ovum recovery is performed too early, the egg may be insufficiently mature to permit normal fertilization. If one delays too long, ovulation with release of the ovum from the ovary may already have occurred. If success is to be achieved, it is necessary that laparoscopy coincide with the imminent release of the egg.

But how? All current tests to detect ovulation (including BBT charts, vaginal and endometrial cellular changes, serum progesterone levels, and so forth) are retrospective and even presumptive. At best these tests only reflect the fact that ovulation has already occurred.

How then is the moment of ovulation determined?

By the use of a special urine test to detect the surge of LH. If you will recall (see Chapter 6), ovulation is always preceded by a rapid and sudden rise of luteinizing hormone (LH) from the pituitary gland. It is this surge of LH which triggers the release of the ovum from the ovary. As Drs. Steptoe and Edwards discovered, the peak in LH production could be spotted in the majority of women by running this urine test every three hours beginning about the ninth day of the menstrual cycle. It was later verified after considerable trial and error that under optimal conditions, ovulation in the human female occurs about twenty-one hours following the LH surge. With this information, laparoscopy for recovery of a properly mature ovum could now be scheduled with some assurance of success.

How is the ovum extracted from the ovary?

Under general anesthesia, laparoscopy for recovery of the ovum is performed approximately twenty to twenty-one hours after the LH surge. Although the ovum itself is microscopic, it is surrounded by a ring of specialized cells and contained within a fluid-filled sac known as a follicle. It is the follicle which is visible and appears to the naked eye as a tiny blisterlike projection on the surface of the ovary. Once the follicle is identified, its contents are aspirated into a small bottle by means of a fine needle and gentle suction. The aspirated material is then taken to an adjoining laboratory and placed under a microscope. The egg is identified and rapidly separated from the other material. While all this is going on, a freshly collected semen specimen from the husband is being processed in the laboratory. Thus, in only a matter of minutes, the ovum is transferred into a dish containing a solution of sperm and special nutrients necessary for normal fertilization and cellular growth.

How soon does fertilization occur?

Usually within seven to ten hours. The fertilized egg is then carefully observed over the next several hours to days. Under normal conditions the fertilized egg divides into two cells during the first twenty-four hours; within thirty-six hours it becomes four cells; by two and a half days, eight cells; and after about five days, sixteen cells. Implantation is usually done during the eight-cell stage.

How is the embryo implanted?

The embryo is loaded onto the tip of a tiny narrow tube (cannula), which is then inserted through the cervical canal and into the uterine cavity. Although this may sound simple, it is in fact regarded by Dr. Steptoe as the most difficult of the procedures associated with in-vitro fertilization. To appreciate the enormous difficulty of this step it must be realized that the embryo at the eight-cell stage is still invisible to the naked eye. It must therefore be maneuvered onto the cannula tip under a microscope and then "blindly" and trustingly deposited into the uterine cavity. The cannula is then withdrawn and again inspected under a microscope to make certain that the egg is indeed gone. It is also important that not more than a droplet of culture medium accompany the embryo during this transfer, as too much fluid could precipitate uterine contractions with subsequent expulsion of the embryo. Since no anesthesia is used, the procedure must be done gently and without causing the woman any discomfort. Pain in itself could similarly precipitate uterine contractions with loss of the embryo. The actual attachment of the embryo to the uterine lining apparently occurs two to three days later. Interestingly enough, embryo transfers performed between 10 P.M. and midnight have (at least to date) been the only ones to be successful. Although the reason for this remains unclear, it may be related to nocturnal variations in hormone levels and decreased uterine irritability and contractility during those hours.

Should implantation fail to occur, the entire procedure of ovum recovery, in-vitro fertilization, and embryo transfer can be repeated in two months.

How soon can pregnancy be detected if the embryo does implant successfully?

There is now a very sensitive and accurate blood test which can detect pregnancy as early as seven days following fertilization. The test is a specific assay for chorionic gonadotropin hormone produced by the tissue immediately surrounding the embryo. This tissue (better known as synctial trophoblast) is actually responsible for attaching the embryo to the uterine lining and in time ultimately becomes the placenta.

Once pregnancy is confirmed, other tests are conducted to determine whether the fetus is growing and developing normally.

How is the pregnancy monitored?

In addition to close prenatal supervision, one of the very first tests is an amniocentesis performed at about sixteen weeks' gestation. This test involves the withdrawal of a small amount of amniotic fluid by means of a needle puncture through the abdominal and uterine walls. Cellular and biochemical analysis of this fluid can give important information regarding genetic disorders, chromosomal abnormalities, and metabolic disturbances. As an aside, it is not as yet known whether in-vitro fertilization and embryo transfer are associated with an increased risk of congenital defects. The sex of the fetus is also determined at this time by checking for the presence of the chromatin sex mass (Barr body) in discarded fetal cells. (See Chapter 3.) During the remainder of the pregnancy, ultrasonic scanning as well as placental function tests are done periodically as a further check of progress.

Can an in-vitro baby be delivered normally?

Absolutely. In-vitro fertilization does not prevent or preclude a woman from having a normal vaginal delivery. A Caesarian section, which could happen with any pregnancy, would only be performed because of a specific obstetrical indication—not because of in-vitro fertilization or embryo transfer.

What is the success rate of in-vitro fertilization?

As of this writing the success rate for achieving pregnancy by this technique is running approximately 12 percent. Out of a total of thirty-two women who underwent in-vitro fertilization and embryo implantation between November 1977 and early 1979, only four became pregnant. Two subsequently gave birth to healthy children and two spontaneously aborted, at eight and twenty weeks gestation.

The success rate is expected to increase substantially as more of the problems and difficulties of this technique are resolved.

Will in-vitro fertilization soon be available to American women?

Since this procedure requires specialized knowledge, training, and laboratory facilities apart from a general hospital setting, it will probably be a matter of several years before in-vitro fertilization becomes a viable option for even a modest number of American women. It is currently estimated that well over a million women in this country could be potential candidates for this procedure on the basis of tubal disease.

There are presently two centers in the United States which are beginning investigative work in this field. One clinic is at the University of North Carolina Medical School at Chapel Hill and the other at the Eastern Virginia Medical School of Norfolk. Both these facilities hope to offer in-vitro fertilization to selected women within the next few years.

Could other infertility problems be helped by in-vitro fertilization?

Although at present the procedure is being geared to women infertile on the basis of tubal disease, far-sighted experts predict that in-vitro fertilization might be a possible answer to other previously insoluble infertility problems. It might, for example, be useful in cases of low sperm counts in men. Under laboratory conditions, ova have been successfully fertilized with sperm from men with counts as low as five million spermatozoa per cubic centimeter. In-vitro fertilization could also help overcome infertility in women with genital tract antibodies which destroy sperm prior to impregnation. There is even the possibility that this procedure using a donor ovum (from another woman) may one day be a method of achieving pregnancy in the woman without ovaries or in women whose ovaries are inaccessible to ovum recovery.

As of now, however, in-vitro fertilization is a new, exotic, and exceedingly complex and difficult procedure. It is not a panacea for infertility problems, nor is it likely ever to become so. At best it will take years of slow, steady progress to make this innovative approach to infertility practical and reasonably accessible to those in need.

18. To Have Not—How to Avoid Pregnancy

Ever since man and woman discovered that one plus one makes three, they have been searching for the ideal contraceptive. According to recent statistics, it has taken five thousand years to achieve the present world population of 4.32 billion. At the current rate of human fertility this figure will be almost double in another thirty years.

If you already have that hemmed-in feeling, be thankful that you won't live to celebrate the year of the big squeeze, 2772. With a predicted one square foot of terra firma per person, human beings will be forced either to copulate in the vertical position or to find more breeding room. And so, while the search goes on for the ideal contraceptive . . .

Can a fertile couple find sexual fulfillment and still avoid pregnancy?

All contraceptive methods can and have failed on the basis of human error, product failure, or a combination of both, so there is really no absolutely foolproof way to avoid pregnancy. But don't give up hope yet. There are many ways to thwart the meeting between egg and sperm. All it takes is a little motivation, some basic information, and the selection of the contraceptive method best suited to your individual needs.

What methods are available to prevent the sperm from meeting the egg?

Currently all known methods of contraception prevent pregnancy in one of seven ways: (1) suppressing ovulation through various hormonal medications; (2) making the lining of the uterine cavity unreceptive to egg or sperm; (3) imposing a physical barrier to prevent migration of sperm; (4) destroying or inactivating sperm by the use of various chemical substances; (5) withdrawing the penis from the vaginal canal prior to ejaculation; (6) flushing the vaginal canal with various solutions immediately after intercourse; and (7) abstaining from sexual intercourse during the woman's fertile period.

How can you select the best method of birth control for yourself?

Begin by evaluating your personal requirements. Do you need constant protection or is intercourse an infrequent event? Is pregnancy to be avoided at all costs or will you accept some risk by using a less effective contraceptive method? Can you depend on partner cooperation or is it all up to you? And equally important, are you sufficiently motivated to be bothered with creams, foams, or perhaps a diaphragm?

Selecting the best method for your needs also depends on knowing what contraceptive methods are available and the advantages and disadvantages of each.

Are you as safe as you would like to be?

All birth control methods are evaluated on their ability to prevent pregnancy based on 100 women years. For example, the table below states that an intrauterine device has a 3 percent average pregnancy rate per 100 women years; this means that if 100 fertile and sexually active women use an IUD for one year, three of them will probably become pregnant. Stated another way, if you use an IUD for one year, you have about three chances out of 100 of becoming pregnant.

The range of possible risk (right-hand column) is much more variable. This is where human error really gets into the picture. Take the diaphragm, for example. How you use it may well make a difference between a 5 percent risk or a 28 percent risk of pregnancy.

As you will soon see, regardless of the method of birth control you choose, there are ways of decreasing your potential risk of pregnancy. In short, being safe depends not only on what you use but how you use it.

Contraceptive Methods and Pregnancy Risk

Method	Average Pregnancy Rate per 100 Women Years	Range of Possible Risk per 100 Women Years
Oral contraceptives (birth control pills)	Less than 1%	(combined) 0.2%
Minipills	3	?
Intrauterine device (IUD) (Loop, coil, shield, etc.)	3	2–7
Diaphragm	12	5–28
Condom (rubber, prophylactic)	15	8–15
Coitus interruptus (withdrawal)	16	?
Rhythm	16	15–34
Foams, jellies, suppositories	variable	4–40
Douching (after intercourse)	over 40	
Taking your chances (no method)	80	

What exactly are birth control pills?

They are various combinations of the two female hormones estrogen and progesterone in synthetic form. Although these synthetic preparations mimic the actions of the natural ovarian hormones, they should not be considered identical. They are chemically and physiologically different in many respects. Their metabolic or breakdown products are different and as a consequence their effect on various organs and tissues can be dissimilar. At the present time there are over twenty-five different preparations of birth control pills. These pills differ from one another both in dosage and in type of synthetic estrogen and progestin used. (As an aside, the terms progestin, progestogen, and synthetic progesterone are synonymous and are used interchangeably.) Moreover, all of the birth control pills currently available are now in a combined preparation, which simply means that all the pills contain both an estrogen and progestin.

As late as 1976, birth control pills were also available in a sequential form. In these preparations (Oracon, C-Quens) the first six-teen tablets contained only estrogen whereas the remaining five tab-lets contained both an estrogen and a progestin. These sequential preparations ultimately proved to be less effective as contraceptive agents; they were also more likely to cause thromboembolic prob-lems and in isolated cases were linked with a potentially increased risk of premalignant and malignant changes in the uterine lining. For all these reasons sequentials were removed from the market by the FDA.

Why are the pills so effective in preventing pregnancy?

They keep you from ovulating. No egg, no pregnancy. The hor-mone content of the pill (estrogen and progestin) prevents the pitui-tary from stimulating the ovary by suppressing the output of pituitary hormones (FSH and LH) necessary to mature and launch an egg. (See Chapter 6.)

How should the pills be taken?

Regularly and as prescribed. Most of the newer preparations now contain either twenty-one or twenty-eight pills per package.

For those of you on a twenty-one-day package, begin the very first month's supply on the fifth day of your menstrual cycle, count-ing day one as the first day your period begins. Take one pill every day until the package is finished (twenty-one days). Wait a full seven days, then start your next month's supply. Once you start taking the pills, your schedule will be three weeks on the pill and one week off the pill regardless of when your period comes. Therefore, each new twenty-one-day package will always start on the same day of the week. In other words, if you started your first month's supply on a Saturday, the following month's supply will also start on a Satur-day.

During the seven days off the pill, you should have your period. In time, your flow may become more scanty but this is perfectly normal when you are taking most oral contraceptives. If you should miss a period, be sure to resume the pills anyway. If, perchance, you should miss two periods in a row, better check with your doctor. You probably aren't pregnant, but perhaps a different preparation would suit you better.

If you are on a twenty-eight-day package, your schedule is even simpler. Once you start the pills, continue to take one pill every day without interruption. Just make certain that you take the pills in their proper sequence. The last seven pills (for days twenty-two through twenty-eight) have no hormonal content, only iron in some instances. Twenty-eight-day pill packages were devised for the woman who finds it easier to remember to take a pill every day. Regardless of whether you are on the twenty-one or twenty-eight-day package, your periods will usually come every twenty-eight days because they are now being artificially regulated.

How soon do the pills protect you?

The very first month, providing you begin on time and don't forget or skip any pills. However, if you normally (without medication) have short cycles averaging less than twenty-five days, it would be advisable to use some additional birth control protection during the first month on oral contraceptives. Since ovulation normally occurs two weeks before the anticipated next period, women having relatively short cycles may ovulate on day eight to nine; therefore, if the pill is started on day five as prescribed, the amount of hormonal medication (only four days) may be insufficient to suppress ovulation for the first month. Starting with the second month, however, you should be completely protected by the pill.

Are you still safe from pregnancy if you forget a pill?

Since the pill prevents you from ovulating at midcycle, the most crucial pills *not* to forget are the first ten or twelve. Missing a pill during this time is definitely more risky than forgetting a pill toward the end of your month's supply.

Should you inadvertently skip a pill, be sure to take two pills the following day. If you miss more, check with your doctor and plan to use some additional protection. Missing a pill or two may also cause some spotting or bleeding.

Therefore, to help you remember, make it a habit to take the pill at a certain time every day, either in the morning at breakfast or at bedtime. Some women find it helpful to post a big reminder in some conspicuous place.

How long can you stay on birth control pills?

At the present time, there is no set limit. Although some doctors advise going off the pill every eighteen months or so for two or three cycles, there are no known harmful effects from continuous and prolonged use of oral contraceptives. Many women have been on the pill for years without apparent problems.

However, if you have completed your family and perhaps still need contraceptive protection for another five to ten years or so, it might make sense to consider a more permanent solution, such as tubal ligation or even a vasectomy for your partner. Birth control pills are potent hormones that affect other body systems. So why take the pill for years and years if there is an alternate and satisfactory answer for your contraceptive needs?

For maximum interval protection between pregnancies, birth control pills are the ideal contraceptive. Once the pill is stopped there is usually a prompt return of normal ovarian and pituitary function.

How soon can you get pregnant after stopping the pill?

Almost immediately. About 60 to 70 percent of fertile women will become pregnant within three months after stopping the pill. Contrary to what many believe, however, your fertility will not be increased as a result of having been on the pill. If you had prior difficulty conceiving, you may again experience the same problem.

It is suggested, however, that a woman postpone pregnancy for at least three months after stopping the pill. Although statistically unconfirmed, there may be a slightly greater chance of spontaneous abortions in pregnancies conceived soon after stopping the pill. Other than that, prior oral contraceptive use does not adversely affect subsequent pregnancies.

Do your periods return to normal once you stop the pill?

If your periods were previously regular, they will probably return to normal. If your periods were previously irregular and unpredictable, they may resume their old pattern. Nonetheless, the first period off the pill may be delayed one or two weeks. On occasion, resumption of menstruation may be further postponed because the suppression of pituitary function by the pill may continue for a time despite cessation of medication. Although this is fairly uncommon, it tends to occur more frequently among women whose periods were never really regular. For this reason many doctors are reluctant to prescribe the pill in women with grossly irregular periods. In fact, women with irregular periods should probably avoid birth control pills if other methods of contraception can be substituted. Lack of menstruation for six months or longer following discontinuation of the pill in a non-pregnant and/or non-nursing woman merits special attention. This is particularly true if there is an associated milky discharge (galactorrhea) from the nipples. The combination of amenorrhea (no periods) and galactorrhea can be an early sign of a pituitary tumor. (See Chapter 24.)

Will taking the pill postpone the menopause?

Fortunately no. If saving those eggs or resting the ovaries for years at a time could delay the menopause, you would have to worry about pregnancy in your fifties and sixties. Can you imagine collecting your old-age pension and still having to use birth control—or worse yet, having your delivery covered by Medicare?

What about common side effects from the pill?

There is no doubt that birth control pills have become the chemical scapegoat for a variety of physical and even emotional problems. But just how often is the pill really to blame? Surely not all aches, pains, headaches, feelings of fatigue, nervousness, depression, dizziness, excess weight gain, constipation, stomach upsets, rashes, falling hair, or insomnia can be directly attributed to the pill. Nor can apparent changes in sex drive be blamed solely on the pill. In one clinical study involving 100 women taking the identical oral contraceptive for the same duration, approximately eighty-five did not notice any change in libido. Interestingly enough, of the remaining fifteen, eight complained of a decreased interest in sex and seven hailed the pill as a new aphrodisiac.

Actually, most bona fide side effects from oral contraceptives are definitely related to the total hormone content per pill and to the relative proportion between the estrogen and progestin. When birth control pills first became available in 1960, many women initially became disenchanted because of undesirable side effects. Prominent among their complaints were symptoms suggestive of early pregnancy —extra weight gain, nausea, bloating, fluid retention, and at times even an increased pigmentation of the skin, especially around the face (chloasma). To keep millions of American women happy while advancing the cause of family planning, research scientists soon discovered that a lower total hormone content could minimize unpleasant side effects without jeopardizing contraceptive effectiveness.

Today, with the new low-dose preparations, less than 5 percent discontinue the pill because of annoying side effects. Most disturbances, including breakthrough bleeding or irregular spotting, tend to be mild and short-lived. However, women who persistently tend to gain weight or find their particular preparation generally unsatisfactory might find it helpful to change to another oral contraceptive.

Is there a pill just right for you?

With so many different pills among which your doctor can choose, prescribing the right pill may well make all the difference in your comfort. As with any medication, no two women will respond exactly the same way.

In general most women do well on a preparation in which the estrogen and progestin content are fairly well balanced. A few women may need a pill containing either more estrogen or more progestin. Take, for example, the woman with a slightly higher than normal premenstrual estrogen level. For her, fluid retention, tender breasts, and heavy periods may always have been a problem. With such a history she would probably do better with a pill containing more progestin and less estrogen. In contrast, the woman with premenstrual pimples, normally scanty periods, and small breasts might benefit from a pill having more estrogen and less progestin. Under any of these special circumstances, your doctor should be able to prescribe a pill almost tailor-made to your needs.

Can birth control pills cause any serious problems?

There is no denying that serious problems and even fatal catastrophes have befallen women while on the pill. Thrombosis (blood-clot formation) with pulmonary embolism (clot to lung) and strokes have been the cause of death in a few instances.

If you are one of the 8 million American women currently taking oral contraceptives, or among those contemplating starting the pill, it is time you considered some facts and rationally evaluated the potential risk you may or may not be running.

Are birth control pills associated with an increased risk of blood clots and strokes?

In 1968, as the result of British reports, the first real pill scare caused thousands of women to abandon oral contraceptives. According to the British study, pill users were seven times more apt to have a fatal embolic episode and nine times more apt to be hospitalized for blood-clotting problems than women not on the pill.

During the past several years, intensive research as well as innumerable surveys involving thousands of women have continued both here and abroad for the express purpose of determining whether there is an association between the pill and blood-clotting problems. There is now little doubt that the use of oral contraceptives and specifically those with a high estrogen content do increase the risk of vascular disorders. These would include superficial and deep vein thrombosis of the legs and pelvis, pulmonary embolism, cerebral thrombosis, cerebral hemorrhage, and possibly coronary occlusion (heart attack). Aggravating factors which can further predispose women to these vascular problems include diabetes, obesity, and a past history of preeclampsia-eclampsia during pregnancy. Hypertension and recurrent migraine headaches have in particular been linked to an increased incidence of strokes in women of reproductive age. Smoking (fifteen or more cigarettes per day) among pill users has also been associated with an increased risk of cerebral hemorrhage.

How great a risk are you taking by being on the pill?

According to statistics, a woman on the pill has about one chance out of 2,000 of being hospitalized for some vascular or blood-clotting problems. Among nonusers only one out of 20,000 will probably require hospitalization for a similar problem. However, the overall mortality rate or risk of dying from a stroke or pulmonary embolism is fortunately low and varies with age. If you are between twenty and thirty-four you have approximately 1.5 chances out of 100,000 of dying from such a complication. If you are over thirty-five your risk is assessed at 3.9 chances out of 100,000.

What is seldom mentioned is the relative risk of pregnancy itself. In the United States, out of 100,000 pregnant women approximately twenty-nine die as a direct result of the pregnancy or the delivery. Among women legally aborted the mortality rate is currently running close to five deaths per 100,000. From these figures it would seem that staying on the pill may be safer than being pregnant or having a therapeutic abortion.

Nonetheless, the pill should not be taken by women with a past history of thrombophlebitis or thromboembolic problems. It should also be remembered that rarely if ever do serious complications strike without warning. There are premonitory signs and symptoms—sometimes days in advance—of any such vascular catastrophe. Women on the pill should be particularly alert and promptly report any of the following: persistent and unusually severe headaches, numbness or tingling of the face, arm, or leg, blurring of vision, unexplained calf, abdominal, or chest pain, shortness of breath, or painful breathing. Just because you have been on the pill for X number of years without adverse effects does not necessarily mean that you are immune from developing blood-clot problems. Interestingly enough, women belonging to blood groups A, B, and AB seem to run a slightly greater risk of developing these problems as compared to women with blood type O. Why this should be has not been clarified.

More recently, heart attacks have been linked to birth control pills.

What about the risk of a heart attack while on the pill?

Although the chances of having a fatal heart attack increase with age and the presence of risk factors previously mentioned (high blood pressure, diabetes, obesity, etc.), women who smoke and use contraceptive pills are especially vulnerable. In fact, cigarette smoking, especially among women over thirty, may be the most important factor in increasing the likelihood of myocardial infarction (heart attack) among pill users. According to studies, if you are between thirty and thirty-nine, smoke, and use birth control pills, you have about one in 10,000 chances of having a fatal heart attack. If you are forty, smoke, and use the pill you have one in 1,700 chances of succumbing to a myocardial infarction. And the more you smoke the greater your risk. For heavy smokers over forty (fifteen or more cigarettes per day) the risk can be as high as one chance in 1,250. In contrast, fatal heart attacks in nonsmoking pill users aged thirty to thirty-nine is one chance in 50,000 and for those over forty, one chance in 10,000. The association between myocardial infarction and the synergistic effect of smoking and the pill is now so firmly established that women over thirty who smoke and use the pill are strongly advised either to give up cigarettes or use an alternate method of birth control. In fact, most doctors now regard smoking as a relative contraindication to prescribing the pill.

Can there be other serious problems associated with the pill?

Certain exceedingly rare liver tumors (hepatic adenomas) as well as focal nodular hyperplasia of the liver have been reported in women using birth control pills. Although these tumors are benign and do not spread they are highly vascular. Thus, in isolated cases they have been the cause of intra-abdominal bleeding. Stopping the pill will usually cause gradual regression of these liver tumors.

Is there any association between birth control pills and cancer?

There is absolutely no evidence that birth control pills will cause or initiate cancer of any organ in the human body. However, in women who already have a known malignancy of either the breast or endometrium (uterine lining), estrogenic substances may in certain cases stimulate the growth of dormant cancer cells. In such cases, birth control pills should, of course, be avoided.

With regard to benign breast disease and specifically certain types of fibrocystic disease, the pill may in fact be protective. Women who have used the pill for two or more years have statistically less fibrocystic disease than nonusers. Some studies even indicate a decreased incidence of breast fibroadenomas among pill users, but these findings require further confirmation.

Are periodic physical examinations necessary while taking the pill?
Yes, indeed. No conscientious doctor will prescribe the pill or refill birth control medication for any extended period without a thorough gynecological checkup including a breast examination and a Pap smear.

At times, migraine headaches, diabetes, and a tendency toward high blood pressure can be aggravated by oral contraceptives. Similarly, fibroid tumors of the uterus, if present, may enlarge more rapidly as a result of estrogen stimulation.

For these and other reasons, periodic physical examinations should be scheduled at least every six to twelve months. Should you have any problems or complaints between visits, inform your doctor promptly. If you plan to stay on the pill, be sure to schedule your return appointment before your prescription runs out.

In the final analysis, birth control pills continue to be for millions of women not only safe but also the most effective contraceptive method available.

What are the minipills and how are they different?
In contrast to other oral contraceptives, the minipills (of which there are three currently available) contain progestin only and are taken on a continuous daily basis. Moreover, their contraceptive effectiveness (97 percent) does not depend primarily on suppression of ovulation. In fact, most women taking the minipills continue to ovulate.

How, then, do the minipills prevent pregnancy?
Primarily in one of two ways: sperm penetration through the cervical canal is inhibited by alterations in the property of the cervical mucus (see Chapter 16), and tissue changes involving the uterine lining make implantation unlikely.

Are there any advantages or disadvantages to taking the minipill?
Since the minipill does not contain any estrogen, some of the side effects associated with combined and sequential oral contraceptives may be minimized. Whether this also means a decreased risk of thromboembolic problems currently attributed to the synthetic estrogen content of these other preparations is not yet known. Only time and more extensive studies will furnish that answer.

On the minus side of the ledger, the minipill has two disadvantages: annoying breakthrough bleeding and, at times, irregular menstrual cycles. Researchers are trying to overcome these problems, but here too, much work remains before the perfect minipill becomes a reality.

What exactly is an intrauterine device (IUD)?

A device of soft, flexible plastic material that comes in a variety of fanciful shapes. (See Fig. 1.) When properly fitted and retained within the uterine cavity, an IUD is second only to the pill in contraceptive effectiveness, or just about 97 percent foolproof.

How does an IUD prevent pregnancy?

In a most devious and indirect manner. Studies have shown that shortly after the IUD comes into physical contact with the uterine lining, a local tissue reaction within the uterus creates an environment hostile to both egg implantation and sperm. In effect, the IUD, which acts as a giant foreign body, stimulates an outpouring of intrauterine scavenger cells (macrophages). Alien intruders such as sperm or even an egg, should it be fertilized, are quickly engulfed and dispatched by these scavenger cells.

Can any woman be fitted with an IUD?

Until fairly recently, fitting nulliparous (never pregnant) women with an IUD posed some problems. Insertion was frequently difficult and subsequent distortion of the uterine cavity by the IUD almost invariably caused painful cramping and heavy bleeding.

Today, with new and improved IUDs in various shapes and sizes, almost any woman can be properly fitted.

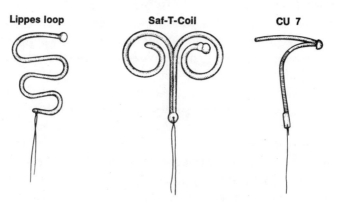

Fig. 1. Intrauterine devices

What kind of IUDs are available?

The most popular devices currently in use are the Lippes loop, Saf-T-Coil, and CU 7. The Lippes loop and Saf-T-Coil are simple inert plastic devices which come in different sizes. The CU 7 is a small plastic device shaped like the number 7 and wound with a fine copper wire. The copper apparently reduces uterine muscle irritability (cramping) in addition to exerting a marked antifertility effect. The device has a low expulsion (fall-out) rate—4 to 6 percent—high contraceptive effectiveness—close to 99 percent—and minimal side effects.

Because of the copper content, the Food and Drug Administration reclassified this device as a drug. For this reason it was necessary that the CU 7 be subjected to stringent testing to prove that the presence of copper in the uterine cavity would not produce harmful systemic effects. Other such devices containing copper are now available.

How long can you wear an IUD?

IUDs containing copper should be replaced every two years. On the other hand, if you have been fitted with one of the simple plastic devices such as a Lippes loop or Saf-T-Coil and are having no problems, there is no specific time limit.

What are the advantages of using an IUD?

Convenience. Once an IUD is inserted, your contraceptive worries are over—or just about. If you can't take birth control pills or find other contraceptive methods messy, unaesthetic, and generally unsatisfactory, an IUD may be your answer.

When's the best time to have an IUD inserted?

Although IUDs have been inserted immediately following full-term deliveries and even after therapeutic abortions, the expulsion rate (IUD falling out) may be slightly increased. Therefore, the best time in which to insert an IUD is during menstruation. Because the cervix is softer and more pliable at that time, insertion is somewhat easier. In addition, the presence of menstrual bleeding will further assure your doctor that you probably aren't early pregnant.

If you are early pregnant, can inserting an IUD cause an abortion?

No reliable figures are available. Inadvertent abortion might be possible. Then again, a healthy and well-implanted egg may continue to grow even when nudged by an IUD.

How is an IUD inserted?

Carefully and with sterile precautions. Although the technique will vary among doctors, the procedure is quite simple.

Once the cervix is exposed and cleansed with an antiseptic solution, the depth of the uterine cavity is checked by passing a small probe through the cervical canal. This maneuver tells your doctor how deep to insert the device and also which size IUD will fit best.

Most IUDs now come in sealed, sterilized packs with a disposable introducer not much thicker than the head of a kitchen match. The introducer with the preloaded IUD is simply inserted through the cervical canal and gently advanced into the uterine cavity. When the proper depth is reached, the introducer is detached and presto, the IUD is in place. The whole procedure rarely takes longer than three minutes.

Will it hurt much?

Women who have had a full-term vaginal delivery usually find the procedure relatively painless. Others may notice definite cramping pains for a few minutes immediately following insertion. Most of the discomfort actually results from a slight stretching of the cervical canal as the device is advanced inward. For this reason women who have never been pregnant or who otherwise have a tight cervical canal usually find the procedure temporarily more uncomfortable. About 10 percent of nulliparous women may even feel faint, become nauseated, and break out into a cold sweat because of a transient drop in blood pressure. This involuntary nervous-system reaction, although short-lived and not serious, can be disconcerting.

What kind of problems can you expect initially with an IUD?

You might never have any problems. Otherwise, intermittent spotting between periods and occasionally heavier and longer periods during the first two or three months are not unusual. Thereafter, the bleeding should taper off and your monthly flow resume a more normal pattern. In about 10 percent of the women using an IUD, persistent and annoying bleeding with or without uterine cramping may necessitate removal of the device.

You should also be alert to the possibility of losing your IUD. IUDs have a greater tendency to fall out or be expelled during the first few months following insertion and particularly during menstruation. Needless to say, the expulsion of some devices may go completely unnoticed.

To be on the safe side, you should periodically check to see if your intrauterine device is where it belongs.

How can you tell whether your IUD is still in place?

Find the nylon thread. All IUDs are attached to a small, stiff thread that protrudes into the upper vagina for about one to two inches. To locate the thread, sweep your finger deep inside the vagina as far as you can reach or else simply feel around the cervical opening. (See Fig. 2.) Some women appoint their partners as guardian and keeper of the thread. Regardless of who assumes the responsibility, check at least after every period and preferably more frequently during the first few months.

If nobody can find the thread, better see your doctor. In the meantime, be sure to use some other birth control protection just in case.

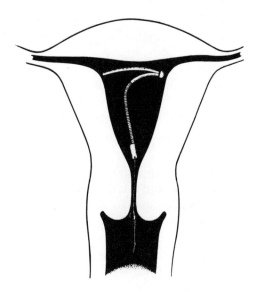

Fig. 2. Intrauterine device in place

Can that IUD thread ever bother your partner?

Surprisingly enough, a few men do complain of being pricked by the thread during coitus. In this situation humoring your partner won't help but seeing your doctor will. The problem can usually be remedied by shortening the thread.

Can you still use tampons if you have an IUD?

Absolutely. You will not inadvertently pull out the IUD. There is no way that the nylon thread can wrap itself around the tampon. It's been tested scientifically and found to be impossible.

What happens if you become pregnant with the IUD in place?

Although more than one IUD has been delivered with a normal full-term baby, the incidence of spontaneous abortion is significantly higher if the device is left in place. It has also been reported that if pregnancy does occur, there is a greater risk of its being an ectopic or tubal pregnancy. Moreover, devices left in place during pregnancy can be a cause of potentially serious and even life-threatening infections. Therefore, if you think you might be pregnant and do have an IUD, check with your doctor promptly. All such devices should be removed during early pregnancy whether or not a woman elects to maintain the pregnancy. If retrieval is not possible, some doctors advise termination of the pregnancy. On the brighter side, IUDs have not been known to cause congenital abnormalities or defects in the newborn.

Can there be serious complications from an IUD?

Performation of the uterus at the time of insertion or the subsequent migration of the IUD through the uterine wall and into the pelvic cavity continue to be the more serious, albeit unusual complications. IUD users also run a greater risk of pelvic infections and tubo-ovarian abscesses. Although the incidence of these infections is not known, women with IUDs should not ignore possible warning signs of beginning pelvic inflammation such as lower abdominal pain, tenderness, and fever.

Is there any association between an IUD and the subsequent development of pelvic cancer?

According to all reports, IUD users are at no greater risk for uterine and cervical cancer than nonusers.

What about the Progestasert IUD?

Although inserted into the uterine cavity and classified as an IUD, the Progestasert system (also known as the IPCS or intrauterine progesterone contraceptive system) works on an entirely different principle. Unlike the conventional IUD, this T-shaped plastic device is filled with tiny progesterone crystals. The progesterone is slowly released in small daily doses and exerts local changes on the cervical mucus and uterine lining. As a result the cervical mucus becomes unreceptive to sperm penetration and the uterine lining is sufficiently altered so as to prevent implantation of a fertilized egg.

When compared with other IUDs, the Progestasert system does seem to reduce menstrual blood loss and cramping. It may also be easier to insert because of its relatively small size. Its contraceptive effectiveness (97 to 99 percent) and its expulsion rate (3 to 8 percent) are on a par with the more conventional IUDs. On the minus side of the ledger, it is more expensive than other devices. But its biggest drawback is its loss of efficacy after four hundred days or approximately thirteen months; thus, yearly replacement of the device is necessary.

What did the liberated woman do in grandmother's day to avoid pregnancy?

Long before the pill and the IUD made the scene, avant-garde women interposed some mechanical barrier between the cervix and semen. Back in the 1700's, a resourceful woman could always rely on her lemon recipe. Half a squeezed lemon inserted over the cervix at bedtime was marvelously effective. It blocked the cervical canal, and the citric acid probably acted as a spermicidal agent.

With the vulcanization of rubber, however, not only did the world start spinning on tires, but sexuality too was given a new snap. Today, condoms and diaphragms made of pliable and durable latex rubber have become an acceptable contraceptive method for many couples.

What is a diaphragm?

A dome-shaped latex rubber device mounted on a circular base containing a metal spring. (See Fig. 3.) A diaphragm must be professionally fitted and requires a prescription for purchase. A properly fitting diaphragm when correctly inserted should cover the entire cervix and upper vagina. It should also remain in place despite straining on your part or vigorous penile thrusts. Equally important, it should be so comfortable that you are completely unaware of its presence.

How do diaphragms differ?

On two counts: size, which in most women averages between 70 and 85 mm. in diameter, and the type of metal spring used in the base. The metal spring (either a flat or a coiled type) serves to decrease or increase the flexibility of the diaphragm so as to conform more precisely to the contours of the vagina. To be effective, a diaphragm must be specifically fitted to the size and shape of your vagina.

Can all women be properly fitted?

Not always. Some women just make poor diaphragm candidates because of a too relaxed vagina with poor muscular tone. If this is the case, a diaphragm is apt to slip out of place at the wrong time, or even be difficult to insert properly. A tipped (retroverted or retroflexed) uterus may also at times make proper insertion difficult.

At the other extreme is the young woman with a fairly snug vaginal opening. Initial attempts at both squeezing in and removing the diaphragm can be an exercise in patience and perseverance. Then, of course, there is a third group of women who can be properly fitted but who instinctively dislike inserting any object into the vagina. They too would do better with some other type of contraceptive control.

How reliable is a diaphragm against pregnancy?

Close to 95 percent if you use it properly at all times. Most diaphragm failures probably result from improper use of spermicidal jelly, careless insertion of the diaphragm, premature removal, or just plain neglecting to use it.

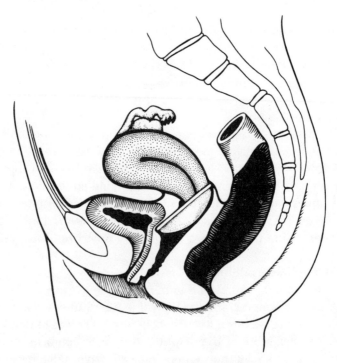

Fig. 3. Diaphragm in place

How can you be 95 percent safe with a diaphragm?

If you are being fitted for your very first diaphragm, make sure you understand how to insert it properly (cervix covered) and remove it easily *before* leaving the doctor's office. Most women find that handling a diaphragm is awkward at first.

To make your diaphragm as effective as possible, you will also need a tube of spermicidal cream or jelly, which can be purchased at any drugstore without prescription. Although it makes no difference which side of the rubber dome will be in direct contact with the cervix (dome up or dome down), it is important to use an adequate amount of spermicidal cream or jelly. Before every insertion squeeze about one teaspoon of jelly onto the side of the diaphragm that will be against the cervix and smear some around the entire rim. For best results smear a little jelly on the other side of the diaphragm too. The spermicidal jelly will effectively kill sperm as well as form a protective seal around the rim of the diaphragm.

The diaphragm must be in place before every act of intercourse. If, following insertion, there is a delay of six or more hours before coitus, or if you have repeated intercourse, it is advisable as an added precaution to insert additional spermicidal cream with an applicator —but without removing the diaphragm.

If yours is an active sex life, you may find it easier to slip in your diaphragm before going to bed every night. With a little practice, it will take you less than fifteen seconds.

When should you remove the diaphragm?

The following morning—or not for at least six to eight hours after the *last* intercourse. Douching is not necessary. However, if you prefer to douche, wait at least six hours following intercourse. Otherwise you might flush away the contraceptive protection afforded by the vaginal jelly or cream. After removing your diaphragm, you should wash it in warm water, dry it thoroughly, dust it with corn starch, and put it back in its compact.

Prolonged wearing of the diaphragm is not harmful, but it is a good idea to remove and wash it at least once every twenty-four hours for hygienic purposes.

How often should you have your diaphragm checked or changed?

Even with good care, your diaphragm should probably be replaced at least every eighteen months. It is also advisable to examine it periodically for any tiny defects or holes that may appear along the rim.

Any change in your vaginal dimensions will also necessitate a refitting. If you have recently had a baby, have gained or lost ten or more pounds, are newly married, or otherwise have begun an active sex life, you may need a diaphragm of a different size.

What are the disadvantages of using a diaphragm?

Success with a diaphragm requires motivation. You must be willing to take the time and accept the minor inconvenience of using your diaphragm properly.

Are there any advantages to using a diaphragm?

Certainly. Although less effective than either the pill or the IUD, the diaphragm can compete favorably as a reliable method of contraception when properly used. Equally important, there are no contraindications to its use or any side effects. A diaphragm cannot get "lost inside," create infection, or interfere with intercourse.

The initial diaphragm expense is minimal and the purchase of spermicidal jelly as needed will not strain most budgets.

What exactly is a condom?

A fine, delicate sheath made from latex rubber or animal membrane (sheep cecum) that completely covers the penis during intercourse. Thus, the condom by serving as a reservoir to receive the entire ejaculate acts as a mechanical barrier to pregnancy.

The use of the condom (rubber or prophylactic) places the responsibility for avoiding pregnancy squarely on the man. For every one hundred fertile couples who use this method exclusively for one year, approximately sixteen of the women will become pregnant. Here again, a few extra precautions can reduce the risk of pregnancy.

What precautions?

Following ejaculation your partner must take care in withdrawing the penis from the vagina. Pulling out too abruptly may cause the condom to slip off or allow the semen to escape. To be on the safe side, he should grasp the condom firmly as he withdraws.

For additional security at midcycle, many women combine the use of a condom with a vaginal spermicidal cream. With this kind of double protection, your chances of becoming pregnant should be minimal.

What are the disadvantages of using a condom?

It might tear at the wrong moment. In addition, since a condom must be rolled onto an erect penis, the biggest disadvantage by far is an interruption of sexual play. For the highly aroused woman in particular, this can be an annoying intermission. In men who may have difficulty in obtaining and maintaining an erection, the need to fiddle with a condom may be their undoing. Then too, good-quality lubricated condoms are not inexpensive. Considering the fact that condoms are throw-away items used only once, having an active sex life and relying exclusively on condoms can be a drain on a young couple's budget.

The condom also tends to lessen sexual sensation. Men especially complain of decreased penile sensitivity. For some couples, however, the use of a condom for this very reason is a distinct advantage.

Why would decreased penile sensitivity be an advantage?

According to some sexologists, 98 percent of women would achieve orgasm if their partners could sustain an erection intravaginally for at least fifteen minutes. This may be like putting sexual enjoyment on a computer basis, but nonetheless, a condom, by decreasing penile sensitivity, may allow some men to sustain an erection longer. Aside from perhaps improving sexual performance, using a condom as a method of contraception has other advantages.

What other advantages?

No prescription is needed, and condoms can be purchased at most drugstores and even from vending machines. Furthermore, condoms are also a woman's best protection against contracting venereal disease. In fact, word has it that condoms will soon be available in women's rest rooms right alongside the sanitary napkin dispenser.

What about coitus interruptus?

This requires masterful self-control by your partner. Withdrawing from the vagina before ejaculation also demands experience and know-how. As mentioned earlier, penile urethral secretions prior to ejaculation may contain sperm (as many as 50,000), but chance impregnation under these circumstances is less likely to occur than from other unintentional slip-ups. Most failures—and this method does have a 16 percent risk of pregnancy—are primarily the result of withdrawing too late. Lack of precision timing can also cause inadvertent ejaculation of semen against the outside vaginal opening rather than directing it well away from the vulva.

Yet, despite all its drawbacks, many couples consider coitus interruptus an effective and satisfactory form of birth control.

Anyone for the rhythm method?

The prevention of pregnancy by the avoidance of sexual intercourse during your fertile days is a great theory. However, the big question remains, how can you know with certainty the moment of ovulation? With a pregnancy risk ranging from 15 to 34 percent among users of this method, it is apparent that the answer is elusive.

Is there another way to calculate your fertile period?

Since you already know that ovulation tends to occur fourteen days (plus or minus two days) before your next period and that a sperm can survive at least forty-eight hours and the egg twenty-four hours, impregnation is theoretically possible from day ten through day seventeen of an ideal twenty-eight-day cycle. But, and this is an important consideration, how many of you are so regular that you can unerringly predict the date of your next period? Mighty few. This is where the magic formula comes in!

Are you ready for the magic formula?

To make the rhythm method work most efficiently, you should keep a record of the length of your menstrual cycles for at least eight months and preferably longer. In other words, by recording the first day of every period for eight consecutive months, you can calculate the length of each menstrual cycle. For example, if your period starts April 2 and your next period comes April 27, your cycle length is twenty-five days.

Once you have gathered this valuable information, you are now ready to apply the formula. Pick out your longest cycle and subtract the number 11. Pick out your shortest cycle and subtract the number 18. The days in between are your unsafe days or your fertile days—no intercourse. If, for example, your longest cycle ran thirty-four days and your shortest cycle ran twenty-seven days—34 minus 11 equals 23, and 27 minus 18 equals 9. You should therefore avoid intercourse from day nine through day twenty-three of every cycle. If your cycles varied from twenty-three to twenty-eight days, you'd have to abstain from day five through day seventeen—23 minus 18 equals 5, and 28 minus 11 equals 17. Under these circumstances conception could occur in some women during their period even though the risk of impregnation during the first five days of menstruation is exceedingly remote—less than one chance out of 1,000. However, if you consistently have short cycles or if your periods are completely irregular, having intercourse after the fifth day from the start of menstruation (whether or not you are still bleeding) definitely increases the risk of pregnancy.

By now, you can understand how any fluctuation in cycle length can greatly prolong the duration of your unsafe time—up to a full two weeks or longer. Under these circumstances, the rhythm method becomes an exercise in sexual abstinence.

Nevertheless, if your cycle lengths are completely irregular and you depend on the rhythm method because of personal preference or religious convictions, there is a way to avoid pregnancy without prolonged sexual abstinence.

How is that possible?

By controlling the moment of ovulation. Knowing when you ovulate can certainly help limit the days of sexual abstinence.

Recent studies have shown that in women given a very small dose of estrogen from day nine through day sixteen of the menstrual cycle, ovulation consistently occurred within a five-day period (days thirteen to seventeen). Previously, ovulation in these women had been completely unpredictable. In addition, the small repeated dose of estrogen proved safe and without side effects. This method, however, is not a routine procedure. As yet, it has been used only in selected cases by a few doctors.

Are there any hazards in using the rhythm method?

There is a small but potential risk of having an abnormal pregnancy. Since ovulation is physiologically geared to occur around mid-cycle, any egg that is released either before or after its expected and optimal time interval has a somewhat greater chance of being abnormal. This is particularly true in the egg that is "overripe" and released after its expected time. Inadvertent fertilization of such an egg does increase a woman's chances of having either a spontaneous abortion or a congenitally abnormal child.

No couple is immune to this possible tragedy. However, in couples who use the rhythm method exclusively and who therefore consistently have intercourse either before or after the calculated fertile period, their chances of running into an abnormal egg are somewhat greater than average.

On the more positive side, women who want to conceive and who previously have had spontaneous abortions or fetal abnormalities of unexplained origin can increase their chances of having a normal pregnancy by limiting intercourse strictly to the fertile period or by using some birth control method at all times except during their most fertile days. Thus, by avoiding the inadvertent impregnation of an abnormal egg, they have a better chance of having a normal baby.

Are there other methods of natural birth control?

Certainly. These include the BBT method, the vaginal mucus method, and the sympto-thermal method. With regards to the astrological concept of calculating your fertile period by the sun-moon angle at the time of your birth, this will have to be further investigated.

What is the BBT method?

The BBT or basal body temperature method involves taking one's temperature in the morning before arising and then recording the result on a special graph. This method is based on the fact that following ovulation there is a slight but definite elevation in temperature. (See Chapter 16.) Although BBT charts are primarily used to determine ovulation in women anxious to conceive, they can occasionally be used to prevent conception. By knowing approximately when ovulation does occur, intercourse can be avoided during the most fertile days. Unfortunately, BBT charts can be inaccurate, difficult to interpret, and a source of conjugal friction because of the required periods of extended sexual abstinence.

What about the vaginal mucus method?

This method, also known as the Billing's method of birth control, is based on the fact that as ovulation approaches, there is a distinct change in the mucus secreted by the cervical glands. The cervical mucus associated with ovulation is thin, clear, slippery, profuse and stringy much like the white of a raw egg. This mucus may be present for from one to several days in succession until it builds to a "peak of wetness" that is subjectively felt as increased lubrication around the vaginal opening. It is this sensation of increased lubrication that indicates the imminent release of an egg, usually within twenty-four to thirty-six hours. Women who have learned to observe and interpret their mucus patterns correctly can avoid pregnancy by abstaining from intercourse during those "wet days" and for an additional three days after the day of "peak" lubrication. As mentioned earlier, it is only during the ovulatory or fertile phase of a woman's cycle that sperm can easily penetrate the cervical mucus and thus reach the Fallopian tubes in time to greet the incoming egg. During non-fertile days the cervical mucus reverts to a thick, cloudy, and scanty secretion which effectively blocks the passage of sperm through the cervical canal.

Success with this method depends on motivation and great patience in learning one's own vaginal mucus pattern. At times, however, changes in vaginal lubrication as a reliable sign of approaching ovulation can be limited. Vaginal infections, for example, can completely obscure or change the normal amount and appearance of mucus secretions. Women approaching the menopause may have a greater difficulty in interpreting mucus changes because of hormonal disturbances. In a few women, ovulatory changes in cervical secretions may be so slight as to not cause any appreciable change in vaginal lubrication.

What is the sympto-thermal method of birth control?

This is a combination of the BBT and vaginal mucus methods. Mastering this method usually requires close supervision by a competent instructor over a period of two to six months.

For those of you interested in any of these natural family planning methods, more information can be obtained by writing to the following organizations:

The Couple to Couple League Int., Inc.
P.O. Box 11084
Cincinnati, Ohio 45211

The Natural Family Planning Association of Connecticut
P.O. Box 250
New Haven, Connecticut 06520

State List of OM Teachers
c/o Integrity
No. 8 Berkshire
St. Louis, Missouri 63117

What about vaginal spermicides?

These include various chemical preparations obtainable without a prescription and marketed as jellies, creams, aerosol foams, suppositories, or foaming tablets. All of them are inserted into the vagina before intercourse by means of an applicator and act by killing sperm on contact as well as by inhibiting their migration through the cervical canal.

How really effective are these preparations?

When used as the sole method of birth control over a twelve-month period, the chances of becoming pregnant range anywhere from 4 to 40 percent.

Of all the vaginal spermicides, aerosol foams are probably the most effective against pregnancy—up to 96 percent according to some clinical studies. Moreover, they are less messy, easy to use, go to work instantly, and can be inserted as long as one hour prior to intercourse.

Vaginal jellies and spermicidal creams are best used in conjunction with either a condom or a diaphragm. When used alone there is a 20–30 percent chance of conceiving within one year.

What about the newer vaginal suppositories?

Although advertised as a revolutionary new era in nonhormonal contraceptives, the new vaginal foaming suppositories are no more or less effective than other vaginal contraceptives. Maximum protection (approaching 96 percent) still depends on proper and consistent use of the product. It is necessary, for example, that the suppository (a waxy ovoid-shaped object) be inserted deep into the vagina and as close to the cervix as possible. Since there is no applicator it may take a little practice before you can place the ovoid with ease and confidence. Following insertion the suppository needs at least ten minutes to effervesce and foam. The foam in turn spreads over the cervix and protects against pregnancy by killing and immobilizing sperm. Failure to delay intercourse the prescribed ten minutes significantly lessens the protection as does having coitus more than one hour after insertion. If intercourse is repeated it is necessary to insert another ovoid. There is only enough spermicide in one ovoid to take care of the sperm in one ejaculation. This of course also applies to other vaginal contraceptives. As an added precaution, if you do want to douche after intercourse, wait at least six hours. Otherwise you'll wash away any protection you might have.

An occasional woman may notice a sensation of vaginal warmth associated with effervescing of the ovoid. There have also been a few reports of vaginal burning and irritation from the spermicide, but other than that, the new vaginal suppositories seem free of side effects. Their growing popularity lies primarily in their compact discreet size, ease of insertion without an applicator, and, of course, their availability without a prescription.

A word of warning: do not confuse vaginal hygienic suppositories with spermicidal suppositories.

What about douching as a contraceptive method?

With a pregnancy risk well over 40 percent, douching as a method of birth control might as well be forgotten. Jumping out of bed right after intercourse to douche has the distinct disadvantage of interrupting what might be for many couples a moment of deep and tender intimacy.

Is there such a thing as the morning-after pill?

The "morning-after" pill is in reality ten 25-mg. tablets of diethylstilbestrol, a synthetic estrogen. Such high doses of estrogen when taken for five days prevent implantation of the fertilized egg by altering the uterine lining. However, because DES has been linked with vaginal and cervical cancer in the offspring, the drug should not be used by women, who may, if pregnant, not consent to abortion. In these situations other estrogens (also not approved by the FDA for morning-after protection) may be substituted: Estinyl (2 mg. twice a day for five days) or Premarin (25 mg. twice a day for five days). To prevent pregnancy effectively, the medication should be started within twenty-four to seventy-two hours of an unprotected act of intercourse presumed to have occurred around the time of ovulation. The woman should also be advised not to have intercourse until after her next menstrual period.

Despite extensive publicity, the use of these pills is not an alternate method of birth control, nor is it without undesirable side effects. High doses of estrogen can cause nausea, vomiting, breast soreness, and headaches. There is also apt to be temporary menstrual irregularity. As of now, the use of the morning-after pill is strictly an emergency measure and largely limited to the prevention of pregnancy in rape victims.

What about birth control in the woman just recently delivered?

Since ovulation can occur by the thirtieth day following a fullterm delivery, pregnancy is possible if unprotected intercourse occurs after the fourth week postpartum. This means that the selection of a birth control method for the recently delivered woman will partly depend on when she resumes intercourse as well as on the type of contraceptive control she prefers.

For women interested in birth control pills, the vast majority of them will begin the pill on day five of the first menstrual cycle following delivery. Where reliable protection against pregnancy is desired before the advent of the first period (which may be delayed as long as twelve weeks), some doctors advise starting the pill the fifth day after delivery.

If the woman wants to use an intrauterine device, the best time for insertion is during the first or second period after delivery.

For women who prefer using a diaphragm, it is advisable to wait at least three months postpartum. This time interval allows the vagina and its supporting tissues to return to normal and thus assures a better diaphragm fit.

Other contraceptive methods such as the condom, vaginal foam, and even coitus interruptus (withdrawal) can be used as temporary stop-gap measures and for some couples may even remain the method of choice on a long-term basis.

What about birth control for the woman who is breast feeding?

With the exception of birth control pills, the use of other contraceptive methods as described in the preceding paragraphs also applies to the lactating mother. Birth control pills, although not contraindicated, may by virtue of their high hormonal content decrease the output of breast milk. Therefore, if you are planning to breast feed for several months, it is preferable to select a contraceptive method other than the birth control pill.

Doesn't breast feeding suppress ovulation?

To a certain extent yes, but breast feeding should not be relied upon as a method of contraception. Some lactating mothers can ovulate within the first three months after delivery, while in others ovulation can be postponed for several months. The fact that a woman ovulates two weeks before an anticipated period makes it possible for her to become pregnant again without ever having had a period following delivery. Therefore, if you are breast feeding and want to avoid another pregnancy, the best advice is to use some form of birth control as soon as you resume intercourse.

Are there any newer contraceptive methods on the horizon?

Researchers are experimenting on a wide variety of contraceptive possibilities ranging from long-term injectable hormone preparations to antisperm antigen shots. For the moment, however, there is no method under investigation that is free of significant shortcomings.

Thus, while we await the ideal contraceptive—something completely acceptable to all women, absolutely safe with no side effects, 100 percent foolproof against pregnancy, inexpensive, readily available, requiring little or no motivation and forethought, and instantly reversible—we must be content with what we have at the moment. This means that for the thoughtful woman, the selection of any one method of birth control over another is still a matter of her knowing and assessing the advantages, disadvantages, and potential risks involved.

19. The Ultimate Choice—
Is Sterilization for You?

Until recently, no woman could be voluntarily sterilized unless she was of a certain age, had a certain number of children, or else suffered from a serious physical condition that could prove fatal if a pregnancy were superimposed. In addition, she was required by law to be married, have the written consent of her husband, and have her request for sterilization unanimously approved by a special hospital committee. Single women, divorced women, or married women whose husbands either could not be found or who refused permission for the procedure were just out of luck.

Today, fortunately, women have a little more to say about their bodies. During the past two years in the United States, well over 800,000 women and 1.5 million men have been voluntarily sterilized. With fewer legal restrictions now imposed, sterilization as a means of permanently avoiding pregnancy is rapidly becoming the right of the individual to decide.

What is the definition of sterilization?

To render incapable of reproducing. In women, although any number of procedures are effective in this regard, voluntary sterilization usually implies surgical interruption of both Fallopian tubes.

Without a functional tubal passageway, there is no way for the sperm to meet the egg.

Sterilization in the male involves an interruption of his tubes, the vas deferens. The procedure is called a vasectomy and consists of blocking the vas deferens, or the two passageways along which sperm travel from the testicles to the penis.

Isn't sterilization the same thing as castration?

Absolutely not. Castration implies either the surgical removal of the gonads (both ovaries or both testicles) or in special circumstances the destruction of these organs by specific X-ray technique (irradiation). Castration, therefore, would not only render the individual permanently sterile but would obviously eliminate the production of sex hormones by these glands.

How is sterilization in the woman accomplished?

At the present time there are four different surgical procedures being used to block the Fallopian tubes: abdominal tubal ligation, ligation of the tubes by minilaparotomy, vaginal tubal ligation, and electrocoagulation of the tubes via laparoscopy.

The procedure used will depend primarily on your doctor's preference and whether the sterilization is done immediately following childbirth or at some other time.

What is an abdominal tubal ligation?

Tubal ligation or, specifically, abdominal tubal ligation is currently the most common procedure used in voluntary sterilization. It entails making an abdominal skin incision just big enough to provide operating space. If the procedure is done immediately following childbirth, the incision will usually be located about one or two inches below the navel, or at the same level where the Fallopian tubes branch off on either side from the top of the uterus. It should be remembered that following delivery the uterus is still quite large, almost as big as a grapefruit. The Fallopian tubes therefore ride fairly high in the abdomen.

In nonpregnant women who have a normal size uterus, the incision will of course be much lower and can even be hidden in the pubic hair line just above the mons.

Does a tubal ligation simply mean tying the tubes shut?

No. The term tubal ligation is a misnomer. Almost without exception, a tubal ligation involves the surgical removal of a portion of each tube. The two cut ends of each tube are then pinched shut and individually tied. The exact technique will vary among gynecologists, but the result is the same: an anatomical disruption in the continuity of the tubes. Thus, the passageway is not only blocked but part of it is missing.

An abdominal tubal ligation is a relatively simple and straightforward procedure requiring no elaborate equipment or unusual instrumentation. As an operation it carries little risk and the results in terms of preventing pregnancy are predictably good—close to 100 percent effective. Since only a small portion of each tube is ultimately destroyed or excised (leaving a good part of the tube undamaged), abdominal tubal ligation is potentially reversible in selected cases. More about this shortly.

When is the best time to have an abdominal tubal ligation?

Almost anytime you decide that sterilization is for you. For most women the ideal time is immediately after childbirth. If the delivery has been done under general or regional block anesthesia, the tubal ligation can frequently be done under the same anesthesia. The surgery takes less than thirty minutes and your total stay in the hospital for both delivery and tubal ligation will still average only three to four days. Tubal ligation at the time of delivery also avoids the inconvenience and expense of another hospitalization.

If you have natural childbirth and request tubal ligation, the procedure will be done as soon as possible following delivery. This, however, will require putting you to sleep with sodium pentothal or else injecting a local anesthetic into the skin area where the incision is to be made.

If you are delivered by Caesarean section and want your tubes tied, the procedure will of course be done at that time and through the same incision.

Should you decide you want a postpartum (after-delivery) tubal ligation, make sure to tell your doctor well in advance of your delivery date. This will give him ample time to discuss the procedure with you and to make the necessary hospital arrangements.

What about ligation of the tubes by minilaparatomy?

A minilaparatomy is essentially a modified abdominal tubal ligation performed through a small (2.5 to 3 cm.) transverse incision just above the pubic hairline. The chief technical difference between this procedure and a conventional ligation is the use of a uterine manipulator, an instrument which allows an assistant to position the uterus and tubes directly in line with the incision. Thus, with a minimal incision the surgeon can ligate the tubes under direct vision.

The operation is simple, fast, and can frequently be done under local anesthesia on an outpatient basis. Consequently, hospitalization expense can be kept to a minimum. A minilaparatomy is an interval procedure and as such is not performed during the postpartum period.

What about a vaginal tubal ligation?

Although a vaginal tubal ligation can be done concurrently with an early therapeutic abortion, this method of sterilization is never performed immediately after a full-term delivery. Following childbirth, the vaginal tissues are too congested, and even more important, the Fallopian tubes are way out of reach.

Vaginal tubal ligations are therefore usually limited to non-pregnant women. Since this procedure is done entirely through the vagina, operating space is more limited. Being a candidate for a vaginal tubal ligation requires normal pelvic organs and a fairly roomy vagina. Only your doctor can really decide.

How can the tubes be tied through the vagina?

By means of a small incision in the upper vagina just behind the cervix, the abdominal cavity is entered through a space between the uterus and the rectum. Once the tubes are located, they can then be grasped and a portion of each tube removed and the cut ends tied shut. Sometimes the gynecologist will elect simply to remove the fimbria (see Chapter 2) from each tube and tie the free end.

A vaginal tubal ligation has certain obvious advantages. There is less discomfort after surgery and, of course, no visible scar or stitches to take out. Most women can be discharged from the hospital within forty-eight to seventy-two hours.

Are there any disadvantages to vaginal tubal ligations?

Yes. The procedure can be technically more rigorous, because of difficulty in properly exposing and visualizing the pelvic structures. Blood loss from a vaginal tubal ligation is therefore apt to be greater than that usually encountered in other forms of sterilization. Another potential complication is pelvic infection. Vaginal bacteria (despite sterile precautions) can be inadvertently introduced into the pelvic cavity during the operation. Considering these various drawbacks, vaginal tubal ligation is probably one of the least popular methods of female sterilization.

What about the laparoscopy method of sterilization?

With few exceptions, this procedure is primarily limited to women not recently pregnant. Hailed by the press as "band-aid" surgery or "belly-button" surgery, electrocoagulation of the tubes by laparoscopy is currently vying for first place as the most common method of sterilization. Prior to 1970, laparoscopic sterilization was a known but little-used technique. As of now, well over 200,000 women per year undergo this procedure and the number keeps rising.

Is electrocoagulation of the tubes a reliable method of sterilization?

The failure rate following such a procedure is approximately 0.2 percent, a figure that compares favorably with other methods of tubal sterilization.

Exactly how is this procedure done?

Under general or, less commonly, local anesthesia, pure carbon dioxide gas is slowly released into the abdominal cavity through a small puncture wound just below the umbilicus. Since the patient's body is also tilted head down, the carbon dioxide gas not only inflates the abdominal cavity but displaces the bowel away from the pelvic organs, thus exposing the uterus and tubes. The puncture wound is then sufficiently enlarged to permit the passage of the laparoscope, a slender tube shaped like a telescope and equipped with a bright heatless light.

Once the tubes are clearly visible through the laparoscope, a second instrument, the operating scope (coagulating instrument) is inserted either through the same puncture wound alongside the laparoscope or, more commonly, through a second puncture wound in the lower abdomen. By carefully manipulating the Fallopian tubes with the operating scope, each tube is gently lifted and seared (coagulated) in two or three places. Some gynecologists also routinely excise the segment of coagulated tube. At the close of the procedure, the carbon dioxide gas is simply allowed to escape and any remaining gas is harmlessly absorbed.

What are the advantages and disadvantages of this tubal technique?

Since tubal coagulation is done primarily on women not recently pregnant, most women can be discharged the day after surgery if all goes well. In a few centers, women are sent home the very same afternoon. Thus, with minimal hospitalization required, the cost of sterilization for the individual patient can be markedly reduced.

But electrocoagulation of the tubes by laparoscopy should never be considered a minor procedure. On occasion there have been serious complications such as intractable abdominal hemorrhage, perforation of an organ, and electrical burns of the bowel necessitating further surgery. Another disadvantage of this technique is its relative irreversibility because of extensive tubal scarring and fibrosis.

As of this writing modifications in instruments and technique are being devised to reduce potential risks further. Some researchers are advocating laparoscopic occlusion of the tubes by means of springs, clips, and bands rather than actual tissue destruction. The advantage of this type of laparoscopic sterilization would, of course, be its potential reversibility.

Is there any other method of tubal sterilization?

Yes, hysteroscopic sterilization. This method involves the passage of a narrow, telescopelike instrument through the cervical canal and into the uterine cavity. Thus, once the minute openings of the two Fallopian tubes are located, a tiny cauterizing instrument is passed through the telescope and the tubal openings are coagulated under direct vision.

The advantages of this method are many: the procedure takes less than five minutes; it requires no incision or elaborate surgical equipment; and ultimately the procedure could probably be done in a doctor's office. Although relatively few women have undergone this procedure, success in terms of complete tubal blockage is running close to 90 percent. Perhaps as this technique is used more extensively, hysteroscopic sterilization may one day prove to be the easiest, fastest, safest, and least expensive way for a woman to be sterilized.

How soon can you resume intercourse after sterilization?

That depends on the procedure used, how comfortable you are, and what your doctor tells you. In general, restrictions against intercourse following a postpartum tubal ligation will, of course, be those imposed because of the delivery rather than the ligation. For the nonpregnant woman who undergoes sterilization via laparoscopy or by abdominal tubal ligation, intercourse can be resumed within one to two weeks (if she is sufficiently comfortable). On the other hand, a vaginal tubal ligation usually requires at least four to six weeks of sexual abstinence to assure proper healing of the upper vaginal incision.

Unlike a vasectomy in the male, there will be no temporary need for any birth control following the tubal procedure. As soon as the

Fallopian tubes are closed, you are protected against a possible pregnancy.

Will having a tubal sterilization affect your sex life?

Absolutely not. In fact, it may even improve relations. With the worry of pregnancy off your mind, you may find intercourse much more pleasurable.

What about your periods and female sex hormones?

Regardless of whether your tubes are cut, pinched, tied, or coagulated, the uterus and ovaries are not affected. You will continue to ovulate, menstruate, and have a perfectly normal output of female hormones. Physiologically, you will be exactly the same as before with only one exception. You won't be able to become pregnant.

What happens to the eggs that are released by the ovaries?

With no place to go and no sperm to meet, they just disintegrate and are harmlessly absorbed.

If you change your mind and want another baby, can the tubes be reopened?

Don't count on it. The results of plastic tubal reconstructive surgery following any one of these sterilization procedures have been very disappointing. It can never be overemphasized that a request for tubal ligation or tubal coagulation is a serious step.

Rushing into voluntary sterilization, especially if you are under thirty, without serious thought and consideration, is foolhardy. At the moment, sterilization may seem the ideal solution to your contraceptive problem, but will you feel that way in another five or ten years? Are you certain that you might not someday want another child? What if something should happen to the children you now have?

Unless you are absolutely convinced that you will never want any more children, better reconsider any decision for sterilization. All of these tubal procedures as described are intended to be permanent and irreversible.

Aren't some of these tubal sterilizations potentially reversible?

To a limited extent—but successful reversal largely depends upon the type of tubal sterilization originally performed as well as the degree and location of the tubal damage. If, for example, you had a vaginal tubal ligation with removal of the fimbria (outermost portion of each tube), the chances for reversibility are just about zero. The fimbria play an indispensable role in the transport of the freshly released egg from the ovary to the tube.

Widespread tissue destruction of the tubes by laparoscopic electrocoagulation also stands a poor chance of reversal. Following such a procedure there may be less than one inch of normal tube remaining —much too short a segment to be functional. If, in contrast, you had a conventional tubal ligation in which only a small portion from the middle of each tube was surgically removed, the chances for successful reversal may be as high as 60 to 70 percent.

Prior to any corrective surgery, however, you would probably have to have an X-ray of the tubes (hysterosalpingogram) and laparoscopic inspection of the pelvic organs. In that manner your doctor could accurately determine the condition of the tubes and the type of reparative surgery necessary to restore function. More recently, the use of microsurgical techniques has improved the outlook for reversibility of tubal sterilization.

What is microsurgery of the tubes?

Tubal reconstructive surgery performed under some form of magnification. The instrument used may be as simple as a magnifying lens or as complicated as a dissecting microscope. Microsurgery also implies meticulous, painstaking surgery performed with delicate instruments, ultrafine suture material, and atraumatic technique. The tissues are handled with utmost gentleness to minimize adhesion formation. The surgeon may in fact be seated and have his forearms cradled in supports to minimize any hand tremor. Since microsurgery is a new technique to gynecology requiring specialized training, the procedure is currently available at only a few medical centers. In the near future the technique is likely to be more widespread as interest and research in tubal surgery repair increases.

Among women whose tubes are hopelessly damaged or in whom reparative surgery has failed, there may still be hope for pregnancy by means of in-vitro fertilization. (See Chapter 17.)

However, for those of you still seeking a solution to your contraceptive problem . . .

Should you talk your partner into a vasectomy?

Other than subtly suggesting that he could solve your birth control problem, the decision to have a vasectomy should be entirely his. If he can't volunteer cheerfully and willingly, forget it.

With more and more men having the procedure done, there may come a time when even your partner might consider it a good idea.

Who should your partner see about a vasectomy?

If his own doctor can't perform the surgery, he should probably consult either a urologist or a general surgeon. Otherwise he might try contacting the local Planned Parenthood Association. They will know what facilities are available in the community.

What exactly is a vasectomy?

The male equivalent of a tubal ligation. Since all sperm are transported from the testicles to the penile urethra (urinary channel) through the two vas deferens, a vasectomy is simply an interruption of these passageways at their most anatomically accessible place— right under the skin on either side of the scrotum. In fact by gently rolling the scrotal skin just above the testicles on either side (if your partner will let you), you can easily feel those two hard cordlike structures.

How is a vasectomy performed?

A vasectomy is a twenty- to thirty-minute surgical procedure done in a doctor's office, clinic, or hospital outpatient department. Under a local anesthetic, a small skin incision is made on either side of the scrotum; a segment of each vas deferens is removed and the free ends are tied shut.

Most men experience little physical discomfort and can usually resume normal activities within one or two days. But after the operation, it will still be necessary to continue using some form of contraception, at least for a while.

Why is birth control still necessary immediately after a vasectomy?

Unlike women who release one egg a month, men will still have millions of sperm swarming above the point where the vas were tied. This means that either you or your partner must continue to use some form of birth control until he gets the all-clear from his doctor. In most men, it takes at least six weeks to two months of regular intercourse to discharge the remaining sperm. Many urologists, however, are now suggesting a careful follow-up period of at least three and sometimes four months just to be absolutely sure that the semen is free of all sperm (zero sperm count).

Will your partner be the same sexually?

Vasectomy will not interfere with the output of male hormones or the ability to perform sexually. Your partner will still be able to have an erection, reach a climax, and ejaculate. If he did it before, he'll do it again.

Is there a change in the amount of semen ejaculated after vasectomy?

No, same as before. Semen or seminal fluid is actually a mixture of secretions from the prostate and seminal vesicles. At the moment of orgasm these secretions will still be discharged through the penis.

Are vasectomies reversible?

Not as reversible as previously thought. Although it is possible to reconnect successfully the vas deferens by microsurgery in 80 to 90 percent of men, not all such men will regain their fertility. And the reason is frequently related to the presence of sperm antibodies. Following vasectomy there may be leakage of sperm protein fragments into the tissues at the site of the original surgery. These protein fragments are then absorbed into the blood stream and thus stimulate the production of sperm antibodies. So although the vas deferens are again anatomically intact and sperm can be discharged from the testes through the penis, the presence of these antibodies can markedly impair fertility.

Nonetheless, if a man is seriously considering having his vasectomy reversed (and this is long, tedious, and expensive surgery), best results are apparently obtained if the repair is performed within ten years of the original vasectomy.

Can a man have his sperm frozen before vasectomy?

Frozen sperm banks are now catering to the man who may be hesitant about having a vasectomy. For a modest fee, these new facilities will carefully label, freeze, and store any man's sperm for possible future insemination should he later decide to have a child.

For the man desiring to store his sperm, there are only two problems: finding a sperm bank (there are currently very few), and the lack of a long-term guarantee against retrieving damaged goods. As yet, nobody really knows how long human sperm can be kept alive and sufficiently vigorous to impregnate an egg. The longevity claims for frozen human sperm run anywhere from a scant sixteen months to ten years and beyond.

Thus, it is obvious from the above that the decision for vasectomy should be as carefully considered as that of any tubal sterilization.

Is there any hope for a more reversible type of male sterilization procedure?

Some work is being done on shunts, plugs, valves, and clips to block the sperm temporarily from ascending through the vas passageways. Here again, the potential problem of the development of sperm antibodies is a real detriment to any of these newer techniques.

In conclusion, voluntary sterilization of either partner should be limited to those individuals emotionally mature enough to know their own minds and who, after careful consideration and forethought, sincerely desire an effective and permanent solution to their contraceptive needs. It goes without saying that if you and your partner are absolutely convinced that you don't want any more children under any circumstances, then sterilization is probably the ideal answer.

20. Population Zero—Abortions, Spontaneous and Induced

There is no doubt that abortion on demand continues to be one of the most emotionally charged issues of this decade. No matter what your personal attitude may be, the woman seeking termination of an unwanted pregnancy needs emotional support and wise counsel.

Currently, more than one million therapeutic abortions are being done each year in the United States. In California alone, for every three babies born alive, one is legally aborted; in New York, the ratio of live births to therapeutic abortions is averaging two to one.

What is an abortion?

The interruption or loss of any pregnancy (regardless of the cause) that occurs before the period of fetal viability. For medical-legal purposes, this period has been arbitrarily established at twenty weeks or less. Any fetus delivered after the twentieth week of pregnancy is therefore considered theoretically capable of surviving and is no longer classified as an abortion.

Are there different kinds of abortions?

All abortions can be lumped under three headings: spontaneous abortions (miscarriages); criminal abortions; and therapeutic abortions, which are sometimes referred to as elective or legal abortions.

How common are spontaneous abortions (miscarriages)?

Very common. About 10 to 15 percent of all pregnancies are spontaneously aborted. In the United States, that adds up to over 1 million miscarriages per year. For the women involved, the majority of spontaneous abortions are really a blessing in disguise. If nature hadn't equipped women with a built-in mechanism to flush away a defective embryo, there would be many more congenitally abnormal babies.

What causes most spontaneous abortions?

Any number of things. Gross chromosomal defects in either the egg or sperm account for about 25 percent of the losses. Aside from these genetic errors, which would be completely incompatible with life, the remaining 75 percent are probably a combination of various factors: faulty implantation of an otherwise normal egg, inadequate hormonal or nutritional support of the growing embryo, or less commonly a maternal infection during the vitally important early weeks.

When are you most apt to abort?

During the first twelve weeks following conception. Once you pass the magic three-month limit, chances are excellent that your pregnancy will remain intact.

This does not mean that you should curtail your normal activities during those first three months. Any good fertilized egg once firmly entrenched within the uterine lining is hard to shake loose. If jogging, bicycling, swimming, or even judo is part of your usual routine, there's no need to stay home and take up basket weaving.

The old myth of avoiding intercourse during those days when you would normally menstruate (if you weren't pregnant) can also be discarded. It stands to reason that if any early pregnancy could be so readily disturbed, there wouldn't be the current line-up of women seeking therapeutic abortions.

How soon can you tell whether you are pregnant?

Unless you happen to be keeping an accurate basal body temperature chart as described in Chapter 7, you will probably be at least two to three weeks pregnant before getting your first real clue—missing a period. Not remembering when your last period was or having somewhat irregular menses can further delay early recognition of pregnancy.

So-called morning sickness or nausea doesn't usually start until the fifth week of pregnancy, but don't depend on that. Half the pregnant women are never bothered with gastrointestinal upsets. Breast tenderness and engorgement as well as having to urinate more frequently are also unreliable signs of early pregnancy.

How else can you tell if you are pregnant?

By a urine pregnancy test. Currently, pregnancy tests are available at little or no cost at most Planned Parenthood centers, family planning clinics, community health centers, and of course through your own doctor. Do-it-yourself pregnancy test kits, although somewhat less reliable, are also available.

Most pregnancy tests depend upon detecting the presence of certain placental hormones excreted in the urine. However, since it normally takes twenty-one days following implantation of the fertilized egg for these hormones to be detectable in the urine (with current laboratory methods), a fairly reliable yes (you are pregnant) or no (not this time) answer from this test depends on your being at least three weeks pregnant or approximately ten days late for a period. In addition to the time factor, the accuracy of any pregnancy test can be adversely affected by the presence of protein in the urine, concentration of the urine, and so on. *Needless to say, you can be pregnant and still have a negative pregnancy test.* For this reason and particularly if you would want an abortion if you were pregnant, check with your doctor for *his* diagnosis as soon as possible.

Isn't there a more sensitive pregnancy test available?

Yes. As mentioned elsewhere, there is a blood test which can detect pregnancy as early as six to seven days following conception. The test itself takes less than two hours to run and requires only a small amount of serum.

Moreover, with its high reliability in detecting very early pregnancies, it will ultimately eliminate unnecessary menstrual extractions. (More about this shortly.) As of now 15 to 30 percent of women who undergo mini-abortions (menstrual extractions) because of a late period are not actually pregnant.

How early can your doctor diagnose pregnancy?

Rarely earlier than four weeks by just examining you. Around this time the only physical finding indicative of a possible early pregnancy will be a somewhat softer uterus and cervix. After four weeks there is a perceptible increase in uterine size. At six weeks the uterus is usually sufficiently enlarged in most women to establish a presumptive diagnosis of pregnancy. Reliance on the bluish discoloration of the vaginal mucosa and cervix as an objective sign of early pregnancy can be misleading. This color change may also precede menstruation or be present whenever there is increased venous congestion of the genital tissues.

However, should your pelvic examination and pregnancy test both be inconclusive and you are still concerned about the possibility of an unwanted pregnancy, you may be a candidate for menstrual extraction, also known as menstrual induction or the "instant period" technique.

What is menstrual extraction?

An alternate method of early abortion. For women who have missed a period but in whom a pregnancy cannot as yet be confirmed, the aspiration of tissue from the uterine cavity by means of a plastic syringe or cannula is meeting with success in a few birth control clinics. The technique, although very similar to that used for first trimester abortions (vacuum aspiration), differs in the type of equipment used. In menstrual extraction the cannula is finer and of smaller caliber, thus frequently eliminating the need for any cervical dilation. Moreover, since there is also relatively little tissue to be aspirated in such an early pregnancy, a small suction machine or even a simple foot pump can be used.

However, most centers that perform menstrual extraction prefer that a woman be at least seven to fourteen days late for a period.

Why isn't the procedure done earlier?

For one thing, many women are just late getting a period. Proceeding too soon with menstrual extraction would therefore subject a disproportionately large number of women who aren't pregnant to an unnecessary procedure. On the other hand, if menstrual extraction is postponed until seven to fourteen days after a missed period, approximately 85 percent of the women who do undergo this procedure will indeed be pregnant.

How can menstrual extraction prove that a pregnancy did exist?

Although there may be less than a tablespoon of tissue and blood removed from the uterine cavity it is possible to identify placental tissue as early as seven days after a missed period. In fact it is mandatory to examine all tissue aspirated from the uterine cavity. In that way a woman who was pregnant can be assured that she was successfully aborted. In contrast, not finding placental tissue would raise three possibilities: (1) the woman was not pregnant; (2) she may still have an intrauterine pregnancy that was somehow missed during the procedure; or (3) she may have an ectopic pregnancy, that is, a pregnancy in one of her Fallopian tubes. For these reasons, not finding placental tissue makes it especially important that such a woman be closely followed with repeat pregnancy tests and pelvic examinations. But regardless of the tissue diagnosis, all women undergoing menstrual extraction should keep their follow-up appointments.

What, then, is the advantage of menstrual extraction over other early abortion methods?

It is relatively safer, faster, less expensive, and does not require general anesthesia. Since the procedure is also performed relatively earlier, there is no obvious sign of a fetus. Moreover, the term menstrual extraction for many women is much easier to accept than the word abortion. Thus, women who would otherwise be reluctant to have an abortion may find menstrual extraction a desirable alternative.

Are there any other uses for menstrual extraction, or the "instant period" technique?

There are some women who are advocating menstrual extraction on a routine monthly basis for purposes of bypassing the inconvenience of menstruation or as a substitute for contraception. A few sobering facts are in order for them: menstrual extraction, even when performed by competent personnel, is not without risk. Among the potential hazards inherent in this procedure are perforation of the uterus, introduction of infection into the uterine cavity, and tissue trauma from the use of suction equipment. Furthermore, repetitive menstrual extraction at four-week intervals would not only substantially increase the likelihood of genital-tract injury and infection, but could also ultimately impair a woman's future fertility. For these reasons, the use of menstrual extraction other than as a very early abortion method demands serious reevaluation. So, for women who are eager advocates of the "instant-period" technique, the question remains, is it really worth it?

Isn't there a pill or shot that can bring on a late period?

Yes, but it will work only if you are *not* pregnant. In these cases, uterine bleeding can usually be induced by the hormone progesterone given by injection or taken by mouth. Within three to ten days after receiving the hormonal medication, the uterine lining will slough and a period will start. No menses (absence of bleeding) will be presumptive evidence of pregnancy.

If you are pregnant, will the shot or pills hurt the baby?

There is recent evidence to suggest that the use of any synthetic progesterone or estrogen-progestin compound during the early weeks of pregnancy may (in a few isolated instances) result in a congenitally malformed infant. Therefore, until further investigations either prove or disprove that these compounds may adversely affect the fetus, the administration of any such hormonal agents in pregnancy testing is being discouraged.

Suppose you are pregnant and want an abortion?

Since ancient times women have sought various means to terminate unwanted pregnancies. All manner of potions, draughts, and intestinal irritants have been ingested. None of these have worked. Drugs such as ergot, pituitary extract, and quinine to stimulate uterine contractions also fail to abort an early pregnancy. The hazardous practice of forcing objects through the cervical canal can be lethal for both mother and fetus. Perforation of the uterus, bladder, or bowel, as well as massive uncontrollable hemorrhage or overwhelming infection with septic shock are just a few common causes of death from this method. The injection under pressure of chemical or soap solutions into the uterine cavity by means of a douche has also been responsible for instantaneous death as the result of a massive embolus to the brain. The fact that the cavity of the pregnant uterus is lined with multiple thin-walled blood vessels allows any material injected under pressure to diffuse rapidly into these vascular channels and thus be carried by the bloodstream to the brain. Sadly enough, the occasional sexual practice during love play of blowing air into the vagina of a pregnant woman has similarly caused her sudden death via a massive air embolism of the brain.

Regardless of your reasons for wanting to have an abortion, don't ever try to do it yourself or have it done illegally. Hospital and morgue records are replete with cases of women who, in desperation, unwittingly and tragically signed their own death certificate. The very nature of the pregnant uterus, with its soft walls, its tremendously increased blood supply, and the presence of large blood vessels within the uterine lining, makes any of these ill-advised abortion attempts little better than outright suicide.

Today, with liberalized abortion laws in many states, no woman need resort to these dangerous practices or seek less than competent medical help. If you are seeking an abortion and have no private physician, the best advice is to contact your local Planned Parenthood Association, public health department, or family planning clinic. Trained and experienced pregnancy counselors are available, usually at no cost, to counsel or assist you in obtaining responsible medical care. You can have a safe abortion, and without jeopardizing your health or your ability to bear children.

When should an elective abortion be done?

For the woman who views abortion as her only "way out," it is medically and psychologically important that she reach this decision as early in pregnancy as possible. Currently, the majority of therapeutic or elective abortions are being done in women less than twelve weeks pregnant. Beyond three months gestation, the increased size of the uterus makes the termination of a pregnancy much more complicated.

How late is too late to be legally aborted?

After twenty weeks. Although in New York state, abortions are legal through the twenty-fourth week, few, if any, are done beyond the twentieth week without a valid medical indication. This implies that the continuation of the pregnancy would be seriously detrimental to the woman's physical health.

How are abortions done?

At the present time there are several medically sanctioned methods for terminating a pregnancy, from simple vacuum aspiration of the uterine contents to major surgery in a few selected women.

For pregnancies of less than twelve weeks duration, vacuum aspiration has become the method of choice.

What is the vacuum aspiration method of abortion?

Removal of the uterine contents by suction. In contrast to the conventional and older D and C (dilatation and curettage) method, termination of an early pregnancy (less than twelve weeks) by vacuum aspiration is faster, easier, safer, and involves less blood loss. Cervical dilatation or stretching of the cervical canal is minimal and frequently not even necessary.

In brief, once the woman is either sufficiently relaxed under a local cervical anesthetic or asleep under light general anesthesia, the procedure in most cases rarely takes longer than five minutes. The technique involves the passage of a slender, flexible plastic tube (cannula) through the cervical canal and into the uterine cavity. A controlled negative pressure is then transmitted to the cannula by means of a special vacuum pump, and within seconds the entire contents of the uterine cavity can literally be sucked out.

Is hospitalization necessary?

Not usually. Many states now have outpatient units especially equipped to handle abortions on a "come in the morning and go home in the afternoon" basis. In certain selected women with a very early pregnancy (less than eight weeks), anesthesia may not even be necessary.

How will you feel physically after this procedure?

Remarkably well. Ninety-five percent of the women have no associated pain following vacuum aspiration, and bleeding, if any, is usually confined to vaginal spotting for a few days. In most cases you can expect your next menstrual period within four to six weeks following the procedure.

Check with your doctor about when you can resume intercourse. Since ovulation can occur as early as day ten following termination of a pregnancy by either therapeutic abortion or miscarriage, your doctor will probably want to discuss birth control with you. If you should have any questions or problems after your abortion, be sure to contact your doctor. And don't forget to keep your follow-up appointment.

What kinds of problems could you have?

In some 5 percent of the women so aborted, there may be temporary heavy vaginal bleeding or lower abdominal tenderness with fever. Although these problems are more apt to occur in late first trimester abortions (ten to twelve weeks), neither condition is usually serious, providing you seek prompt medical attention. Appropriate medication on an outpatient basis can successfully remedy the situation in almost every case.

Can there be any serious complications associated with early abortions?

Despite the excellent safety record of first trimester abortions, there is a slight risk of uterine perforation or the inadvertent passage of the cannula through the soft uterine wall. Many uterine perforations, however, can and do heal spontaneously without causing further problems. Nonetheless, a uterine perforation can be complicated by hemorrhage, necessitating immediate abdominal surgery. For this reason, even outpatient abortion facilities are required to have trained medical personnel as well as major operating facilities readily available in case of an emergency.

What happens if you are more than three months pregnant and want an abortion?

Past the third month of pregnancy, both the uterus and the fetus undergo rapid development. The growing fetus begins to assume a more obvious human form. In addition, the uterine walls become thinner (more stretched) and the uterine cavity becomes correspondingly larger. For these reasons, a different method of abortion now becomes necessary.

How are more advanced pregnancies aborted?

Most commonly by the injection of a hypertonic saline (extra salty) solution into the uterine cavity and specifically into the amniotic sac (bag of waters). However, success with this method (saline amniocentesis) requires a fairly well developed amniotic sac, which usually means waiting at least until the sixteenth week of pregnancy.

For the woman who delays seeking help beyond her third month, the necessity of having to "wait it out" until her sixteenth and sometimes eighteenth week of pregnancy, plus the anticipation of going through a miniature labor, makes late therapeutic abortions much more traumatic for everyone concerned.

How are saline abortions done?

Following completion of necessary laboratory work (blood and urine tests), most women will be admitted directly to a saline induction unit in the hospital. Under a local anesthetic a needle with an attached catheter is passed through the abdominal skin and directed downward through the uterine wall and into the amniotic sac. When the catheter is properly positioned, the doctor then withdraws a certain amount of amniotic fluid and replaces it with a sterile saline solution. The procedure rarely takes longer than fifteen minutes, and the patient is then returned to her assigned hospital bed—to wait.

What does the saline solution do?

It kills the fetus and provokes labor. Since there is normally a delay of several hours between the saline injection and the first uterine contraction, most women will not deliver for at least twenty-four to thirty-six hours. Labor is usually short and pain medication and sedation are given as needed. Most women are allowed to remain in their hospital rooms and deliver spontaneously.

If everything goes as anticipated, the average hospital stay runs two and sometimes three days depending on how long it takes to effect delivery. Following discharge from the hospital, most women will have some vaginal bleeding similar to that seen after a full-term delivery. Menstruation will probably resume within six to ten weeks.

Can there be any problems associated with saline amniocentesis?

Unlike early pregnancies, which can be easily and safely terminated in virtually every case, abortion by saline amniocentesis is not a benign procedure. Complications both minor and major can run as high as 30 percent.

Besides fever and abdominal pain, one of the more common problems is related to delivery of the placenta (afterbirth). In 15 to 25 percent of the women so aborted, the placenta becomes entrapped within the uterine cavity or only partially separates. Although not usually a serious problem, it may necessitate removal of the retained tissue under general anesthesia.

What about serious complications from saline amniocentesis?

Hemorrhage, severe infection, or toxic reaction to the saline solution are not that uncommon. Inadvertent injection of the saline solution into a blood vessel has also taken its toll.

Since the majority of serious complications as well as most fatalities (seven deaths per 100,000 therapeutic abortions) occur in women being aborted by saline amniocentesis, a few doctors prefer an alternate method of terminating second trimester pregnancies in selected women.

How else can a pregnancy over twelve weeks be aborted?

By the combined use of dilatation, curettage, and suction. This involves mechanical dilatation of the cervix, aspiration of amniotic fluid, and piecemeal removal of the fetus and placenta by specially designed long-handled instruments. The chief hazards of the procedure are perforation of the uterus and excessive blood loss necessitating transfusion. However, when performed by doctors experienced in the technique, this method of abortion can be safer than that of saline instillation. It is also more rapid, direct, and can be performed on an outpatient basis under local anesthesia.

Another method occasionally employed for the termination of second trimester pregnancies is hysterotomy—a miniature Caesarean section.

With this procedure, the fetus and attached placenta are removed through a small incision in the uterus. Thus, the fetus, although usually born alive, rapidly succumbs within a few moments because of its gross immaturity.

In younger women requesting sterilization at the time of their abortion, a hysterotomy in combination with a tubal ligation may be the procedure of choice in pregnancies beyond fourteen weeks gestation.

However, if the woman may someday want children, hysterotomy as a method of abortion has definite drawbacks.

What are the disadvantages in being aborted by a hysterotomy?

There is, of course, the longer hospital stay because of major abdominal surgery. Second, the presence of a scar in the uterine wall usually necessitates Caesarean sections for future delivery of full-term infants. Despite good healing following hysterotomy, any incision through the entire thickness of the uterine wall is always a future site of potential weakness during a subsequent pregnancy. For this reason a Caesarean section at term would eliminate possible separation of the old scar (uterine rupture) under the stress of forceful labor contractions.

Needless to say, aborting second trimester pregnancies by hysterotomy, saline amniocentesis, or dilatation and curettage leaves much to be desired. Currently, intensive research is being directed to making late abortions relatively safer and easier. Toward this goal, the use of prostaglandins as abortifacients is being evaluated.

What are prostaglandins?

As you will recall (see Chapter 6), prostaglandins are hormonelike substances which can evoke uterine contractions. Of the fourteen different prostaglandins known to occur in the human, two have proved effective in aborting early, unwanted pregnancies as well as inducing labor at term.

In women sixteen to twenty weeks pregnant, limited studies indicate that the injection of one of these prostaglandins into the amniotic sac may provide a faster means of inducing labor than the use of saline inductions. Prostaglandin instillations have (at least in some series) been associated with a somewhat higher rate of pelvic infection and retained placental tissue. As of now, more clinical studies are needed to provide statistically valid conclusions regarding their efficacy and safety.

Prostaglandins in suppository form, according to clinical researchers, may one day revolutionize family planning and current abortion practices.

How is that?

By providing women with a method that can be self-administered. According to recent reports, early unwanted pregnancies have been aborted by vaginal applications of prostaglandins.

If prostaglandins can eventually be inexpensively synthesized and proved entirely safe as an abortion method, perhaps two or three tablets of this magic substance slipped into the vagina after a missed period may be the ultimate answer to contraception and unwanted pregnancies for many women. Only time and much research will tell.

Is a better contraceptive the current answer to preventing unwanted pregnancies and abortions?

Apparently not, for despite the effectiveness of available birth control methods, the vast majority of women seeking an abortion will readily admit to not having taken any contraceptive precautions. There is no question that among unmarried women a single, unexpected act of coitus does account for many unwanted pregnancies. But other than this group, there are still thousands of sexually active and knowledgeable women who, although they have easy access to a reliable birth control method, consistently fail to protect themselves for a variety of psychosexual reasons.

Pregnancy, although unwanted, may for some be proof that they have been loved and desired. For others, the use of any birth control detracts from the spontaneity of the moment and the feeling of total commitment to their sexual partner. Not uncommonly because of religious reasons, a woman may consider birth control unnatural and therefore sinful. A denial of reality is sometimes seen in young, healthy women who are absolutely convinced that they are immune to pregnancy. And yet, following abortion, they again become pregnant within a few weeks out of fear that the first abortion did indeed leave them infertile. Others delight in sexual roulette, finding coitus more exciting when it carries a real risk of pregnancy.

Among teenagers, however, lack of proper sex information and inability to obtain a reliable contraceptive are important contributing causes to the growing number of unwanted pregnancies. But here again, it seems that psychosexual reasons, both conscious and unconscious, prevent many from using birth control even when freely and confidentially available: in California alone, 40 percent of all younger women currently requesting a therapeutic abortion are "repeaters." Adolescence, with its tremendous awakening of sexual needs in combination with intellectual and emotional immaturity, is a difficult period in which to appeal to rational judgment.

In the final analysis, there will always be women seeking abortions. The wider dissemination of birth control information, easy availability of effective contraceptives, and wise counsel will never eliminate the problem of unwanted pregnancies, but at least it will bring us somewhat closer to the best possible solution.

Part VI

Changes in the Natural Woman

21. Common Happenings Along the Female Tract

The genital tract is the site of many common problems frequently misunderstood by women. Among these are various vulvar lesions, genital warts, cervical cysts and erosions, fibroid tumors of the uterus, and benign ovarian growths. Since these conditions can and do occur independently of one another, let's start at the vulva and proceed to the cervix, uterus, and ovaries.

What are sebaceous cysts doing on the vulva?

When you consider that the labial lips are rich in oil glands (sebaceous glands) it is not surprising that sebaceous cysts also occur on the vulva. A sebaceous cyst is simply a cystic tumor of the skin which results when the duct or outlet to an oil gland becomes blocked. Thus, the oily material produced by the gland accumulates and forms a non-tender yellowish or skin-colored swelling of varying size. Most vulvar sebaceous cysts grow slowly, remain small (5 mm. or less), and usually appear around the clitoris and along the inner margins of the labia majora (outer lips). If one of these cysts is drained or squeezed, a grayish-white somewhat malodorous cheesy material may be extruded.

Can sebaceous cysts ever cause problems?

As a rule they remain asymptomatic and are usually discovered while bathing. On occasion, however, sebaceous cysts can become infected and form a painful abscess. Incision and drainage will provide temporary relief but recurrences are sometimes possible. Permanent cure requires surgical removal of the entire cyst. Sebaceous cysts do not become malignant.

Another kind of cyst occurring in the area of the vulva is the epidermal cyst. These are also cystic skin tumors which closely resemble sebaceous cysts. Since they too are benign and tend to remain small and asymptomatic, treatment is rarely required.

Another common vulvar cyst is the Bartholin's duct cyst.

What is a Bartholin's duct cyst?

As mentioned in Chapter 2, Bartholin's glands are two mucus-producing glands whose sole function is to help lubricate the lower vagina and introitus. The main duct of each gland empties just outside the vaginal opening. Ordinarily, the glands are too small to be seen or felt on routine pelvic examination. Cyst formation occurs when the duct becomes plugged, causing mucus secretions to accumulate and form a non-tender swelling that can vary in size from that of a small marble to that of a hen's egg. In extreme cases a Bartholin's gland duct cyst may be large enough to block the vaginal opening. Typically, the swelling is just to the right or left of the vaginal opening. Although the cause of ductal blockage is frequently unknown, infection, trauma, or even congenital narrowing of the duct have been implicated.

How are these cysts treated?

If the Bartholin's duct cyst remains small and doesn't cause problems, most doctors would advise leaving it alone. A cyst that because of size causes pressure symptoms, interferes with intercourse, or becomes a source of recurrent abscess formation requires surgical treatment. Simple drainage usually results in prompt recurrence. A good-sized cyst is best treated by a procedure called marsupialization. This simply means creating a small but permanent opening in the cyst wall to allow mucus secretions adequate drainage. Marsupialization is a relatively short and simple procedure that can sometimes be done under local anesthetic in a doctor's office. Postoperative pain is minimal and healing is usually complete within three to four weeks. Surgical removal of the entire cyst is another form of treatment, but it is seldom done nowadays.

How does a Bartholin's duct cyst become infected?

Abscess formation in a Bartholin's gland usually starts when bacteria enter by way of the duct. Although gonorrhea was once blamed for many of these infections, other bacteria such as *E. coli* are frequently responsible. Abscess formation invariably produces an acutely hot, tense, and painful swelling. If the bacteria are particularly virulent the abscess can become full-blown within two to three days. Such a rapid-growing abscess can be an emergency as any pressure against the vulva can cause excruciating pain. Simple activities like walking or even sitting can become almost unbearable. At times the application of heat or sitz baths may help localize the infection and precipitate spontaneous drainage. But even then there is little relief as the site of rupture is usually too small to provide adequate drainage and closes over promptly.

The best treatment is surgical incision and complete drainage of the abscess, as soon as possible. This can usually be done under a local anesthetic in the doctor's office. Once the abscess is properly drained, the relief is almost miraculous. In women who have recurrent abscess formation, marsupialization as described for a Bartholin's duct cyst can provide permanent relief.

What about genital warts?

You may know that a virus is responsible for the common skin wart. But did you know that another closely related virus can also cause warts to grow and thrive around the moist vulvar folds and, frequently, inside the vagina?

Genital warts are nothing new. They have been plaguing both men and women for centuries. Until recently they were even called venereal warts because of the prevalent belief that the responsible virus was transmitted exclusively by sexual intercourse. However, the virus on occasion can be acquired without such intimate contact. Be that as it may, genital warts have assumed epidemic proportions during the past two years and especially among sexually active women between fifteen and thirty.

What do genital warts look like?

Genital warts frequently make their debut as tiny, discrete pinkish-tan growths not much bigger than a grain of rice. At first only two or three may be noticed around the vaginal opening or clustered along the labia. However, where conditions are favorable for their growth, genital warts can flourish and spread.

What makes them flourish?

Scratching because of itching or minor irritation can spread the virus to other vulvar areas and thus cause new warts to appear. Moreover, once the warts have gained a foothold, excessive vulvar moisture seems to be the most important factor in their continuing growth. Among women with vaginal infections and abnormal discharges, genital warts can be particularly annoying. Similarly, increased vaginal secretions such as occur during pregnancy or from taking birth control pills can also cause genital warts to thrive and flourish. During pregnancy especially, what might have started out as only two or three small warts can mushroom into several cauli-flowerlike masses.

Can these warts ever be serious?

Other than being unsightly and a source of local irritation and itching, they seldom cause problems. If neglected, however, large warts may become infected as a result of scratching or poor vulvar hygiene. On rare occasion neglected warts have been known to cover the entire vulva and even block the vaginal opening.

What can be done about genital warts?

As long as excessive vaginal secretions or discharge continue to bathe the vulva, genital warts are tough to eradicate. Small warts can disappear spontaneously by simply clearing the vaginal infection or minimizing vaginal secretions. For women taking birth control pills, this may mean interrupting medication temporarily. Clothing which tends to trap moisture such as nylon underwear, pantyhose, or tight pants should also be avoided.

Otherwise, specific treatment varies with the size and extent of the warts. Small warts are usually treated with topical applications of podophyllin, a caustic substance which in two to four days will cause the warts to slough. Since podophyllin can irritate surrounding normal skin, the medicine should be carefully applied and the area washed with soap and water four to six hours after treatment. Furthermore, only a few lesions should be treated at any one time because podophyllin can be absorbed through the skin and mucous membranes with toxic results. During pregnancy in particular, excessive use and absorption of podophyllin has caused abortion and fetal death. In fact, vigorous treatment of warts during pregnancy may have to wait until after delivery. Interestingly enough, genital warts may spontaneously disappear during the postpartum period.

Larger warts are best treated by electrocautery, cryosurgery (freezing), or surgical excision. Although most of these treatments can be done under a local anesthetic in the doctor's office, a woman with extensive warts of the vulva or vagina may require hospitalization. Regardless of the treatment selected, the vulva, because of its rich blood supply, usually heals well with little or no scarring.

What's all this talk about cervical cysts?

Of all the possible happenings along the female tract, cervical cysts, also known as Nabothian cysts, are by far the most common. In fact, cervical cysts are so prevalent that they can almost be considered normal. Nonetheless, the word cyst for many women seems to have an ominous pathological ring. And if something sounds pathological, can major surgery be far behind? For this reason, let's clarify all the confusion and needless worry.

What exactly are cervical cysts?

Nothing more than plugged-up cervical glands filled with mucus secretions. Cervical cysts can occur singly or in groups, depending on how many cervical glands are involved. They rarely get any bigger than a small pea and usually appear as white pimplelike elevations on the surface of the cervix. To put it simply, cervical cysts are to the cervix what pimples are to the face. They are not the least bit serious, but their presence indicates some past or recent cervical infection or irritation.

Is treatment always necessary?

No. But treatment will make your cervix pink and beautiful again. Since cervical cysts are associated with cervical irritation or infection, most doctors will elect to treat such a condition. In addition, any bothersome discharge because of chronic cervicitis should also be eliminated.

Because the surface of the cervix is relatively insensitive to pain, most cysts can be comfortably and readily treated by cauterization right in your doctor's office. Cauterization, by destroying the infected tissue and allowing trapped mucus secretions to drain, permits areas of chronic inflammation to be replaced by new and healthy cervical tissue within four to six weeks. If you should notice a watery discharge or a pink staining for several days following cauterization, don't be alarmed. This is perfectly normal and will rapidly disappear as your cervix heals.

What is meant by a cervical erosion?

Cervical erosion is a term frequently and casually applied when a cervix appears red or irritated. It is also used to describe a cervix with an obvious ulceration due to infection or mechanical irritation (as from wearing a pessary, etc.). In actuality, a cervical erosion is the replacement of normal cervical tissue on the surface of the cervix with tissue from within the cervical canal. Since this endocervical tissue is normally red and granular, it gives the cervix a red, eroded, and inflamed appearance. When this tissue is present in adolescents and young women, it forms a perfect red ring around the cervical opening. In these cases, as it is merely a variant of normal and not associated with any infection, it is known as a congenital cervical erosion.

At other times (and particularly in adult women) a cervical erosion may result from infection and require treatment because of excessive discharge and thick mucus formation. Under these circumstances, light electrocautery or cryosurgery of the cervix can usually clear the problem.

But let's move on and consider more serious gynecological problems—specifically, fibroid tumors of the uterus.

What exactly are uterine fibroids?

Benign (non-malignant) growths made up of muscle and fibrous tissue. Although it is possible to have just one fibroid tumor, multiple tumors are much more common. In most women, fibroid tumors (also known as fibroids, myomas, or leiomyomas) generally begin as several small seedings embedded throughout the thick muscular wall of the uterus. As these seedings progressively enlarge and become more nodular, they can encroach upon the uterine cavity and/or grow outward and distort the normally smooth outer contour of the uterus. (See Fig. 1.)

With regard to size, fibroids can vary tremendously. Some have even weighed as much as twenty pounds.

What causes fibroid tumors?

Nobody knows for sure, but their growth seems to depend on estrogen stimulation. Thus, as long as a woman is still having regular periods, fibroid tumors will usually continue to enlarge. Birth control pills, especially those with a high estrogen content, can also accelerate their growth. As a general rule, however, most fibroids grow slowly even among women using oral contraceptives.

Once the menopausal years begin and estrogen output decreases, fibroid tumors will cease to grow and in many instances shrink in size.

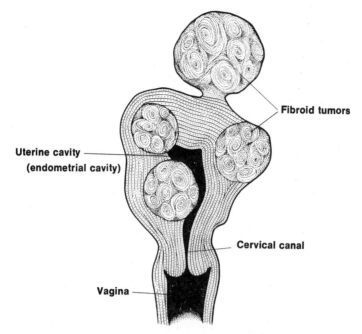

Fig. 1. Uterus with multiple fibroid tumors

How common are fibroids?

With the exception of pregnancy, fibroid tumors are the most common cause of an enlarged uterus. Although infrequent in women under twenty-five, the incidence of fibroid tumors increases sharply thereafter. Approximately 20 to 25 percent of all women over thirty will have uterine fibroids. In fact, more hysterectomies are done because of fibroid tumors than for any other female pelvic problem.

But having fibroids does not necessarily mean surgery, nor do these tumors always cause problems. Symptoms, if any, will depend on the size of the tumors and their location within the uterus.

Do fibroid tumors ever become malignant?

Very rarely. In fact, to perform a hysterectomy on the basis that a fibroid tumor may become malignant is not justified. According to recent statistics, less than 0.4 percent of all fibroids ever become cancerous, and then predominantly in women well past the menopause.

Can a woman with fibroid tumors ever become pregnant?

Yes, indeed. Fibroid tumors as a rule do not interfere with fertility. The one possible exception would be where the tumors actually block the Fallopian tubes, thereby preventing sperm from meeting the egg.

However, once pregnancy is established, previously small and asymptomatic fibroids frequently enlarge because of higher estrogen levels and increasing uterine size. Under these circumstances, other problems may occasionally arise.

How can fibroids interfere with pregnancy?

Although many women have successfully delivered a full-term baby in spite of uterine fibroids, these tumors can create difficulties during pregnancy. If, for example, the fibroids bulge or jut into the uterine cavity, the baby may have insufficient room to grow properly. In these instances, premature labor and delivery, sometimes as early as three to five months before term, are not uncommon.

In women who do carry to term, normal vaginal delivery may not always be possible. Thus, where tumors block the birth canal or even cause the baby to lie in an abnormal position, a Caesarean section may be necessary. Following delivery fibroid tumors usually shrink to the size they were before the pregnancy.

Are fibroid tumors a common cause of abnormal bleeding?

No. Surprising as it may seem, fibroid tumors do not usually cause bleeding or spotting between periods. If the tumor or tumors bulge into the uterine cavity, however, heavy and long periods with the passage of large clots can occur. Any tumors that distort the normal contours of the uterine cavity can cause heavier menstrual blood loss by increasing the bleeding surface of the uterine lining. Such bleeding can come in gushes and be unexpectedly profuse. If untreated, recurrent monthly bleeding of this magnitude could cause a significant anemia.

What about other problems?

Large fibroids can cause a sensation of pelvic fullness or discomfort. At times a fibroid may press against the nearby bladder and thereby limit the amount of urine the bladder can effectively hold. Although this in itself is rarely serious, it can create an annoying problem—having to urinate more frequently. Less commonly, a large fibroid may interfere with normal stool evacuation by impinging against the rectal wall. Even small tumors can create problems if they press against a particularly sensitive area. Nagging backache, for example, can occasionally be caused by a small fibroid impinging against pelvic nerve fibers.

Pain, however, is not normally a symptom of fibroid tumors un-less there is a complication involving the tumor. Tenderness over a fibroid or dull abdominal pain with fever may indicate infection of the fibroid or perhaps degenerative changes. A fibroid that hangs on a stalk may twist or turn in such a way that the blood vessels feeding the tumor may become kinked. In these instances pain can be sud-den and severe requiring hospitalization and even surgery to correct the situation.

Yet, despite these potential problems, the majority of women with fibroid tumors are remarkably free of symptoms.

Can a woman have fibroid tumors and not know it?

Absolutely. In fact, for many women, fibroid tumors are inadver-tently discovered during routine pelvic examination.

Can the presence of fibroid tumors usually be detected?

Most fibroids distort and enlarge the uterus. Nonetheless, it is possible for a uterus to seem perfectly normal on pelvic examination and yet have its cavity distorted by a single small fibroid. Suspicion that such a fibroid exists may be aroused by an unaccountably profuse menstrual flow. Under these circumstances, an X-ray of the uterine cavity (hysterosalpingogram—see Chapter 16) or a D and C (dilatation and curettage) would be necessary to confirm the diagnosis. However, fibroid tumors that jut into the uterine cavity (submucous fibroids) cannot be "scraped away" by curettage, as they are embedded in the muscle wall.

If you have fibroid tumors, is removal of the uterus necessary?

Not always. Treatment will depend on several factors: the size of the tumors, the problems they are causing, and, equally important, your age and whether or not you want children.

Since many fibroids remain relatively small and asymptomatic, your doctor may merely advise "watchful waiting." In these instances regular pelvic examination every six months or so will usually be sufficient to keep track of any change in size and shape. The fact that fibroids regress during the menopausal years makes this conservative approach very practical in a great many women.

Where the tumors are large, however, hysterectomy is frequently the treatment of choice in the older woman. Fibroids that create general pelvic discomfort or consistently cause heavy menstrual bleeding are also best handled by removal of the uterus. But even in such situations, hysterectomy may not always be the best answer.

Why not?

Even among women who have completed their family, removal of the uterus may be regarded as a threat to their femininity, sexuality, or self-image. The fact that fibroid tumors are benign lesions makes it especially important that a woman's reaction to possibly losing her uterus be carefully evaluated before a hysterectomy is advised.

Unfortunately, few women are aware that there is an alternate surgical treatment for symptomatic fibroid tumors.

What is the alternative treatment?

Myomectomy or multiple myomectomy—removal of the fibroid tumors without sacrificing the uterus. Although this procedure is usually reserved for the younger woman with symptomatic tumors or for the woman whose fibroids may possibly interfere with pregnancy, myomectomy can nonetheless be done on any woman, providing that the uterus is not involved too extensively.

Why, then, are so many hysterectomies done for fibroid tumors?

As effective as myomectomy can be, there is a good chance that a new crop of fibroid tumors may develop, particularly in the woman under forty-five. Then too, if fibroids are really causing problems, most women, especially if they are over forty, would just as soon have the problem permanently resolved. Furthermore, myomectomy as a surgical procedure can be technically more difficult and involve greater blood loss than hysterectomy. Apart from these considerations, fibroid tumors are sometimes associated with endometriosis (see Chapter 22) or other pelvic conditions. Under these circumstances, removal of the uterus, particularly in the older woman, may also be indicated on the basis of these coexisting conditions.

What happens if you have a hysterectomy?

Despite the prevalence of this procedure, much confusion still exists as to what a hysterectomy really entails. Whether your doctor chooses to call the operation a simple hysterectomy, a complete hysterectomy, a pan-hysterectomy, or a total hysterectomy, all of these terms mean or should mean exactly the same thing, namely, removal of the body of the uterus plus its cervix. Unfortunately even doctors sometimes become casual in their terminology and may at times use one of these terms to include removal of the tubes and ovaries. Needless to say, the best advice is to check with your own doctor as to what he or she means by a particular term. Regardless of the qualifying adjective preceding the term hysterectomy, the procedure should refer only to removal of the entire uterus.

The two exceptions to the above are the so-called partial hysterectomy and radical hysterectomy. In the partial hysterectomy the cervix is left in place and only the body or upper portion of the uterus is removed. Partial hysterectomies, although popular thirty years ago, are rarely if ever done nowadays, and only under very extraordinary conditions. A radical hysterectomy, on the other hand, implies removal of the uterus plus adjacent pelvic lymph nodes. This extensive surgical procedure is reserved strictly for certain pelvic malignancies.

Having a hysterectomy therefore means no more periods and no more pregnancies. Other than that, a hysterectomy will not interfere with ovarian function or female hormone production. In other words, you will not go through the menopause any sooner than nature intended by simply losing the uterus.

Is there a special term to indicate removal of the tubes and ovaries?

Yes, indeed, a very long, fancy term: bilateral salpingo-oophorectomy. Salpingo refers to the Fallopian tubes; oophor, to the ovaries; ectomy, to removal of; bilateral simply means both sides. Therefore, a bilateral salpingo-oophorectomy means removal of both tubes and ovaries.

But having a hysterectomy, especially for fibroid tumors, does not mean that your ovaries have to be removed as well. There are few pelvic conditions that require sacrificing normal ovaries. Nonetheless, if your doctor has advised a hysterectomy, make it a point to find out exactly what he or she plans to do. And don't sign any operating permit until the procedure has been thoroughly discussed and explained to you. Far too many gynecologists while performing a hysterectomy will also routinely remove perfectly normal ovaries from any woman over forty.

Removal of the ovaries with a sudden and abrupt loss of estrogen can be a shock to any woman's system even if she is close to fifty. After all, the ovaries do continue to produce some estrogen even up to age sixty and beyond. Unlike normal menopausal symptoms that gradually appear as estrogen levels decrease slowly over a period of years, symptoms from a surgically induced menopause can be dramatic and not so easily controlled with estrogen replacement therapy. In short, there is nothing like your own two ovaries producing their own estrogen.

Why, then, do some gynecologists routinely remove normal ovaries in women over forty?

Primarily to prevent the possible later development of ovarian cancer. There is no denying that cancer of the ovaries is a dangerous malignancy, but fortunately it is not that prevalent. According to recent statistics, eight out of every 100,000 women die from this disease each year. In contrast, twenty-nine out of every 100,000 pregnant women die each year from complications directly attributable to either the pregnancy or delivery.

In the final analysis, where there exists no current and valid reason for castration at the time of hysterectomy, the decision of whether or not to remove normal ovaries should belong to the individual woman.

What about ovaries that aren't normal?

When nature blessed women with ovaries, she packed inside those prune-sized organs not only a fantastically complex hormone factory complete with an egg-processing plant, but she also endowed each ovary with the potential to develop all manner of cysts and tumors. When you consider that the ovary, even from infancy, can harbor about twenty different types of growths, both benign and malignant, it is little wonder that the finding of an enlarged ovary on pelvic examination can be a problem in diagnosis. To make the problem of ovarian growths even more complex, some can disappear as readily as they appeared while others can grow to fantastic sizes if left unattended.

How big can an ovarian growth become?

Large enough to fill the entire abdomen. One such ovarian tumor made medical history back in 1809 when a dashing and fearless frontier surgeon, Dr. Ephraim McDowell, performed the world's first removal of an ovarian tumor in Danville, Kentucky. Working under primitive conditions and without a whiff of anesthesia, he skillfully extracted a 22.5-pound ovarian tumor while the intrepid patient, Jane Todd Crawford (tired from a three-day trip on horseback to reach the good doctor), distracted herself by reciting psalms during the surgical ordeal. Happily for all concerned, Mrs. Crawford made a rapid and uneventful recovery and Dr. McDowell joined the select group of medical notables.

In contrast to such a phenomenon, most benign ovarian growths are rarely that spectacular.

What about ovarian cysts?

Each year thousands of women are told, "You have an enlarged ovary." But in spite of all the diagnostic possibilities to account for an enlarged ovary, such a finding in an otherwise healthy woman during the childbearing years is most likely to be a physiological cyst, that is, either a follicle or a corpus luteum cyst.

What exactly are physiological cysts and why are they so common?

As you may recall from Chapter 6, all functioning ovaries normally contain small cystic structures (follicles) in various stages of growth or degeneration. Thus, in order for one ovarian follicle to mature and release its egg (ovulation) during any single menstrual cycle, countless other follicles fail in the attempt and rapidly disintegrate into microscopic specks of scar tissue. As long as these follicles behave properly, none of them will grow any larger than a fraction of an inch in size. Occasionally, however, and for some usually obscure reason, the chosen follicle may fail to release its egg or one of the competing follicles may refuse to disintegrate. In either case, the disturbed follicle may continue to enlarge and fill with clear fluid (follicle cyst).

Similarly, a cyst can develop from the remnants of the follicle that has extruded its egg, thus forming a corpus luteum cyst.

Do these particular cysts ever cause problems?

Since most physiological cysts rarely get bigger than the size of a lemon, dull, aching pelvic pain sometimes associated with larger ovarian growths may be absent. Follicle cysts seldom cause problems. In fact, they frequently disappear spontaneously after one or two menstrual cycles. For this reason many gynecologists will simply advise a repeat pelvic examination within two or three months. If, however, the cyst should remain and increase in size, or start to cause pain, etc., surgery may be indicated.

Corpus luteum cysts, on the other hand, are more likely to cause menstrual irregularities as a result of hormonal disturbances. At times, therefore, intermittent spotting or bleeding and even a delay in menstruation is possible. Corpus luteum cysts can also regress, but on occasion they may rupture and cause internal bleeding sufficiently heavy to necessitate immediate surgical removal of the cyst.

In contrast to these physiological cysts, other ovarian growths (whether they are solid or cystic or a combination of both) will continue to grow and ultimately cause problems. Examples of such ovarian growths are the dermoid cyst and mucinous cystadenoma.

What are dermoid cysts and mucinous cystadenomas?

A dermoid cyst is one of the more common benign tumors. Although it can occur at any age, it is more prevalent among young children and women between twenty and thirty. The cyst itself is unusual in that it frequently contains oily material, hair, teeth, bone, and cartilage. The presence of these radio-opaque substances makes it one of the few ovarian growths that can sometimes be diagnosed by X-ray. Rupture of a dermoid cyst can cause serious chemical peritonitis, as the oily material is highly irritating to the pelvic tissues.

The mucinous cystadenoma is another common ovarian tumor. It is usually filled with gelatinous straw-colored fluid and can attain enormous size. Some mucinous cystadenomas have weighed as much as thirty pounds.

Symptoms from these growths as well as from other benign ovarian tumors are surprisingly few, at least initially. In fact it is truly amazing how large these tumors can sometimes become before their presence is even suspected. But even in the absence of symptoms surgery is advisable.

Why is surgery usually necessary when dealing with such ovarian growths?

Regardless of how competent your gynecologist may be, there is no way of accurately determining by pelvic examination alone whether an ovarian mass is benign or malignant. Shape, size, and consistency of the growth may be helpful in this regard, but these physical findings can be deceptive.

Symptoms, at least initially, are also of little diagnostic value. Menstruation, for example, usually remains normal with either a benign or malignant ovarian growth. Then too, any ovarian tumor or cyst, if sufficiently large, can cause pelvic or lower abdominal discomfort. In certain cases X-rays of the pelvic area may provide additional clues to the nature of the ovarian mass, but here again the findings are frequently unreliable. Thus, only by surgically removing the ovarian growth and examining the tissue under a microscope can an accurate diagnosis be made.

Fortunately, very few ovarian growths prove to be malignant. Even assuming one could be certain that a particular ovarian mass was benign, surgery would still be advisable. Apart from the fact that ovarian tumors and cysts can occasionally rupture, bleed, become infected, twist, or cause pelvic havoc, there is another important reason to favor early surgical intervention.

What reason is that?

In contrast to most physiological cysts, other ovarian growths, whether they be cysts or solid tumors, will usually continue to enlarge and ultimately cause problems. Continuing growth of such an ovarian mass, for example, can gradually constrict and press against the surrounding normal ovarian tissue and reduce its blood supply. Thus, in time, with less blood flow and nourishment reaching the otherwise normal and uninvolved portion of the ovary, it may eventually atrophy, shrink, and cease to function. Therefore, delaying or postponing surgery in these cases may unnecessarily jeopardize the entire ovary. On the other hand, fairly prompt removal of such a tumor or cyst can avoid this potential problem and allow the doctor to spare the remaining portion of ovary.

It is only natural for anyone to want to avoid surgery, particularly if pain and other symptoms are absent. But ovaries are far too precious to be inadvertently compromised by prolonged "watchful waiting" under these circumstances. For when it comes to a "true" ovarian mass in contrast to a physiological cyst, surgical removal of the offending tumor or cyst (ovarian cystectomy), with preservation of normal ovarian tissue whenever possible, is still the best treatment.

22. The Thorn Inside—
Endometriosis

Ever since endometriosis (pronounced endo-me-tree-o-sis) first came to the attention of gynecologists more than a century ago, it has continued to be one of the most puzzling of all pelvic diseases. Not only can it cause a variety of symptoms and mimic other pelvic conditions, but it can take the joy out of any woman's sex life. The fact that endometriosis afflicts thousands of women during their prime years (twenty-five to forty-five) and can be responsible for menstrual misery, infertility, and severe pain during sexual intercourse gives it a well-deserved place in any book on female problems.

What exactly is endometriosis?
A condition where fragments of tissue from the uterine lining (endometrial tissue) are deposited, become embedded, and grow outside the confines of the uterine cavity. Although the exact cause is unknown, endometriosis is most likely the result of tiny shreds of endometrial tissue finding their way through the Fallopian tubes and into the pelvic cavity during menstruation. Thus, as these tissue fragments from the uterine lining spill onto the ovaries and implant themselves along the outer surface of the uterine wall and elsewhere in the pelvic area, various problems can be precipitated.

How do these tissue fragments create problems?

Endometrial tissue in these unusual locations behaves much like the tissue lining the uterine cavity. In other words, these newly deposited tissue fragments also swell, thicken, and bleed every month in response to hormone stimulation from the ovaries. The amount of bleeding is, of course, minute but it does cause the surface of the endometrial implants to become sticky and to adhere to adjacent normal tissue.

Even more peculiar is the tendency for this misplaced tissue, although non-cancerous, to merge and slowly encroach onto neighboring pelvic organs. Tissue fragments, for example, deposited along the outer back wall of the uterus, may gradually invade the nearby bowel wall. Nature, in an attempt to protect the surrounding pelvic organs from further involvement, covers these areas of endometriosis with scar tissue. In women with severe endometriosis of long standing, the scar tissue can literally cement the bowel to the female pelvic organs.

What kind of symptoms does endometriosis provoke?

The symptoms of endometriosis do not necessarily match the extent of the disease. Women with severe endometriosis can be symptom-free. Women with just a few tissue implants along the back wall of the uterus may have the most pain. In general, the onset of increasingly painful periods after perhaps years of relative comfort is probably the earliest and most common complaint. Cyclic bleeding from these abnormally located endometrial tissue fragments causes a steady, dull-to-severe lower abdominal pain which frequently radiates to the back. Initially, the pain may be noticed just before or during a period. Later on, as more and more of the implants accumulate, swell, and press against the confining scar tissue, a nagging soreness in the lower abdomen and back can precede menstruation by two and even three weeks. For some women the pain can begin as early as day fourteen of their cycle and reach a peak at midperiod. The week following menstruation may be the only time of relative comfort.

In isolated instances a condition known as cyclic sciatica has been attributed to endometrial implants along the roots and sheath of the sciatic nerve. Women with this problem have radiating pain from the buttocks to the back of the thigh and along the outside of the leg. The pain occurs during menstruation and is aggravated by sitting or extending the leg.

In some 20 percent of women with endometriosis, heavy periods, more frequent periods, or totally irregular periods can be other symptoms.

Why does endometriosis cause bleeding problems in some women?

Probably because of hormonal imbalance. If the ovaries are extensively involved with endometriosis they may simply fail to function normally. Thus hormone output and even ovulation may be adversely affected. In severe endometriosis, large single or multiple cysts (endometriomas) of both ovaries are not uncommon. Some doctors refer to these cysts as "chocolate cysts" because of their thick brown syruplike fluid content as a result of previous bleeding episodes. The fact that these cysts are very thin-walled makes them more vulnerable to rupture with subsequent spillage of their contents onto the delicate pelvic tissues. In these cases there may be sudden severe abdominal pain. Otherwise, such ovarian endometriomas can grow quite large and still remain asymptomatic.

Dyspareunia or pain during intercourse is another real problem for three out of four women with endometriosis.

What kind of pain on intercourse and why?

Not just any pain, but on deep penile penetration a sharp, shooting pain somewhat like being impaled on a knife. Since endometriosis frequently involves the uterine ligaments, which are richly invested with multiple nerve fibers, even the slightest touch or pressure against these affected ligaments can cause marked discomfort. During sexual intercourse, therefore, each penile thrust against the upper vagina or cervix brings about acute and unbearable pain by stretching the involved uterine ligaments. Under such circumstances intercourse, though previously enjoyable, may now by necessity be avoided or, in some instances, only tolerable for two or three days immediately following menstruation. Partners may attempt different coital positions to limit the depth of penile penetration, but at best endometriosis can be a real sexual turn-off.

Approximately 40 percent of women with endometriosis will also be infertile.

Why are these women infertile?

For pregnancy to occur, the released egg must find its way into one of the Fallopian tubes. In women with endometriosis, scar tissue may impair the normal mobility of the Fallopian tubes. Needless to say, if the tubes are bound down by fibrous adhesions, they can't possibly swing over to the ovary and scoop up the egg at the time of ovulation.

Infrequent intercourse because of severe pain during coitus probably also contributes to a low conception rate. Lack of regular ovulation because of extensive involvement of the ovaries is another likely explanation for infertility. But sometimes there doesn't seem to be any reasonable explanation. All known factors necessary for conception seem normal—including regular periods, normal monthly ovulation, and open and functioning tubes. In these cases some experts theorize that a chemical factor, possibly a prostaglandin, may interfere with the proper transport of the egg down the tube.

Are some women more susceptible to endometriosis?

Yes. Endometriosis occurs predominantly in women who menstruate and ovulate regularly. Therefore, the longer a woman goes without any interruption in normal ovarian function, the greater her chances of eventually developing endometriosis. A woman who ovulates regularly and who postpones pregnancy over a period of several years is more likely to be a candidate. As an aside, the use of tampons during menstruation does not play a role in the development of this condition. At one time it was suspected that tampons were a possible cause of menstrual debris backing out through the Fallopian tubes and spilling onto pelvic structures.

How common is endometriosis and how long can it last?

Endometriosis affects an estimated 10 to 15 percent of women in their prime years. Symptoms usuallly begin in the early twenties and may persist until menopause. Most cases are diagnosed between the ages of twenty-five and thirty-five but the process probably starts shortly after the onset of regular menstruation.

How can your doctor tell if you have endometriosis?

The first real clue is the symptoms themselves. If your history includes increasingly painful periods, dyspareunia (painful intercourse), and the inability to conceive, endometriosis is a likely suspect. When pain on deep penile penetration is a major concern, the uterine ligaments can frequently on pelvic examination be felt as thick, beaded cords. Furthermore, the pain experienced during intercourse can readily be reproduced by manually stretching the affected ligaments.

When the diagnosis is less obvious, visual inspection of the pelvic organs may be necessary. Nowadays this usually means the examination of the pelvic organs by laparoscopy. This is an operating room procedure (under local or general anesthesia) and involves the passage of a telescopelike instrument into the abdomen through a small puncture wound just below the navel. With this technique the presence of endometriosis can be verified and the extent of the disease evaluated. Endometrial implants look somewhat like small blood blisters and are most commonly found on the surface of the ovaries and along the back wall of the uterus. In women with infertility problems, laparoscopy is particularly helpful in allowing the doctor to inspect the tubes under direct vision for adhesions and scar tissue. The findings on laparoscopy also help determine the best possible treatment for the individual woman.

For the women who do ultimately develop endometriosis much can be done. And sometimes endometriosis can even be nipped in the bud before real problems develop.

Can the problems of endometriosis really be avoided?

For the young married woman who already has symptoms of early endometriosis, the best advice is to get pregnant as soon as possible— if at all feasible. It is truly amazing how the absence of ovulation and menstruation during the months of pregnancy will effect an almost miraculous cure. Areas of endometriosis rapidly shrink and frequently disappear. In fact, after delivery, it may never again be a problem. In women who do have recurrences, however, spacing their children closer together rather than waiting three or four years between pregnancies is also helpful in preventing flare-ups.

Avoiding the progression of endometriosis therefore narrows down to interrupting periodically normal ovarian function. For this reason, with the advent of the menopause, the symptoms of endometriosis may spontaneously improve.

Is there any way to avoid endometriosis completely?

Possibly. Although unproved, long-term use of birth control pills with suppression of ovulation for extended periods of time may be a factor in preventing endometriosis from developing in susceptible women. In addition, since most birth control pills also tend to decrease menstrual flow, the chances of significant amounts of menstrual debris backing out through the Fallopian tubes are greatly lessened. Nonetheless, where endometriosis already exists, the use of birth control pills in the doses conventionally prescribed for contraceptive purposes is usually inadequate to control the progression of symptoms.

What, then, is the treatment for endometriosis?

Symptoms from minimal endometriosis may at times spontaneously improve without the benefit of either pregnancy or special medication. In other instances, progressively increasing pelvic pain makes treatment necessary. Ideally, the treatment of endometriosis should halt the progression of the disease, eliminate active areas of endometriosis, alleviate pain, and increase the fertility potential among women desiring pregnancy. Toward this goal, there are two therapeutic approaches depending on the symptoms and physical findings: hormone therapy and/or surgery.

What about hormone therapy for endometriosis?

Unless there are specific reasons for surgery at the time of diagnosis (for example, large ovarian chocolate cysts), most doctors will initially treat endometriosis with hormone therapy. This means preventing ovulation and menstruation by creating a state of false or pseudopregnancy. The fact that pregnancy can cause areas of endometriosis to shrink and atrophy is the basis for this treatment approach. In the past several years, birth control pills taken daily and in doses high enough to prevent menstruation as well as ovulation have been a common form of treatment. Enovid, Norlutin, and Ortho-Novum have been the pills most frequently used. In other cases, injections (usually at two-week intervals) of a long-acting progesteronelike compound such as Depoprovera have been substituted.

Although these hormone treatments may initially aggravate the pain by causing edema of the endometrial implants, relief of symptoms will be noticeable by the third month of treatment. At this time areas of endometriosis will begin to atrophy and literally melt away. Pelvic pain will disappear and sex can once again be enjoyed. Where there is a favorable response most doctors advise continuing treatment for six to twelve months. Once medication is stopped, an estimated 60 percent of women may remain comfortable for as long as three to five years.

As effective as hormone therapy can be, it is not always the solution.

Why not?

Once the medication is stopped there is always the possibility of recurrence. In other words, once ovulation and menstruation resume, areas of pelvic endometriosis may be restimulated or new areas may even form with the subsequent return of all the old problems. Side effects such as nausea, vomiting, or excessive fluid retention may make discontinuation of medication necessary. The potential risk of blood-clotting problems is another consideration in the use of high-dose estrogen preparations. Also, the return of ovulation and menstruation may be delayed after the hormones are discontinued, which is a consideration among women anxious to conceive. Injections of Depopro-vera in particular can delay return of menstruation for many months. In some cases, hormone therapy may fail to provide relief from en-dometriosis or even be contraindicated on the basis of other medical conditions.

Where any or all of the above-mentioned problems exist, Danazol may be the answer, at least for some women.

What is Danazol?

Danazol (danocrine) is a new chemical approach to endometrio-sis. It is a synthetic androgen hormone that creates a menopauselike state. What it does is block pituitary stimulation of the ovaries by preventing the output of LH (Luteinizing Hormone) and FSH (Folli-cle Stimulating Hormone). When this drug is taken on a daily basis, ovulation and menstruation cease and estrogen levels are corre-spondingly low. In contrast to the results of conventional hormone therapy, areas of endometriosis begin to shrink and atrophy almost immediately once the drug is started. Although therapy is usually continued for six months, Danazol frequently relieves symptoms within the first month or two of treatment. When medication is stopped there is a prompt return of ovulation and regular menstrual cycles. This rapid restoration of normal function makes Danazol par-ticularly helpful to women anxious to conceive following treatment for their endometriosis.

Because Danazol does not have any estrogen or progesterone effects it is frequently better tolerated than the conventional hormone preparations. In addition, Danazol does not increase the risk of blood-clotting problems.

What about side effects with Danazol?

Side effects are primarily related to its being a weak androgen (masculinizing hormone). In some women increased oiliness of the skin, acne, and perhaps even deepening of the voice may require discontinuation. Weight gain can occur but it is usually limited to ten pounds in most women. For others on Danazol therapy, the presence of low estrogen levels may cause hot flashes, sweats, and other menopausal symptoms. Some women may be particularly bothered by vaginal dryness because of atrophic changes while on medication. Fortunately, symptoms do clear following discontinuation of the drug. Expense is another consideration. At current pharmacy prices the cost of a one-month supply of Danazol can exceed one hundred dollars depending upon the dosage used.

Danazol is not a panacea or a cure, however. Recurrences can and do happen. In these cases, as well as in women with severe endometriosis, conservative surgery may be the best treatment.

Conservative surgery—what's that?

A sometimes long and meticulous surgical procedure performed through a lower abdominal incision. Since endometriosis is usually first diagnosed in women between the ages of twenty-five and thirty-five, conservative surgery further implies the preservation of the reproductive organs while ideally preventing recurrences of the disease by eliminating all areas of endometriosis. For example, endometrial implants on the ovaries (endometrial cysts) can be removed, leaving normal ovarian tissue intact. Similarly, endometrial implants along the uterus and pelvic ligaments can be excised or cauterized and thereby permanently destroyed. If the uterus is tied down by scar tissue, it can be freed and resuspended in a more normal position. As a further precaution against the recurrence of pelvic pain, some gynecologists may strip away the tiny nerve fibers that carry pain impulses from the uterus (presacral neurectomy).

Last but not least, scar tissue around the Fallopian tubes can be removed and the normal mobility of the tubes restored.

How successful is conservative surgery in endometriosis?

Where endometriosis is the only cause of infertility, approximately one third to one half of all women who undergo conservative surgery may happily conceive within three to six months following the operation. When the surgery is performed primarily to relieve pain, results will vary from woman to woman. Successful eradication of all areas of endometriosis can at times be difficult. For this reason temporary hormone therapy following surgery is frequently necessary to prevent recurrent minor flareups. Nonetheless, in 40 percent of the women so treated, the subsequent recurrence of intractable pelvic pain will ultimately necessitate more radical surgery to effect permanent relief.

Regardless of the outcome, conservative surgery is definitely worth a try whenever possible in the woman under forty.

What kind of radical surgery is sometimes necessary?

In a minority of women with long-standing and extensive pelvic endometriosis, removal of the uterus and at times even the ovaries may be the only effective way to eliminate all pain. As radical as this procedure may seem, would it be less radical to allow such a woman

to remain a pelvic cripple, as well as unable to tolerate sexual intercourse?

Should removal of the ovaries be necessary, however, estrogen
replacement therapy can be given without running the risk of reac-
tivating the condition. Today, fortunately, with better techniques for
early diagnosis and more effective hormone therapy, extensive surgery for this disease is becoming increasingly less necessary.

In summary, endometriosis remains a baffling problem, potentially capable of creating pelvic havoc and sexual disharmony. As in all
problems to which women are heir, early treatment still offers the best
chance for complete recovery.

23. The Menopausal Years— A Time for Reevaluation

At no other time in a woman's life is there such a complex interplay between physical and psychological factors as during the menopausal years. Along with the physical stresses brought about by hormonal imbalances, the psychological and emotional reactions of each woman to this normal transition will vary depending upon her previous life style, attitudes, and self-image.

For centuries women have been programmed to accept their ability to reproduce and raise children as their prime function in life. Even today, any woman who persists in asserting her identity to the detriment of her conventional role runs the risk of being ridiculed or labeled either neurotic or blatantly unfeminine. Because of these deeply ingrained sexist attitudes together with our society's preoccupation with youth, is it any wonder that many women regard the menopause as the beginning of the end?

It is all too easy to equate aging with the chronological passage of time and to compartmentalize our lives and attitudes on the basis of years lived. Thus, at thirteen we become teenagers, at eighteen are magically transformed into adults, between forty and sixty are relegated to being middle-aged, and at sixty-five are arbitrarily tossed onto the nonrecyclable heap by mandatory retirement.

But is aging solely a function of time, as our culture would have us believe? Surely all of us have known women whose vitality and appearance surprisingly belied the date on their birth certificate. In addition to the passage of time, the rate of physiological aging among all individuals also depends on the dynamic interplay of genetic, environmental, and psychological factors. If you believe that being forty, fifty, or sixty constitutes being old, then regardless of anything else, you will assuredly feel and act accordingly. For how we think and what we truly believe profoundly affect our bodily functions and influence our ability to handle change.

In 1900 the life expectancy of the average American woman was forty-nine years. Today, most women in this country have a reasonably good chance of reaching the age of seventy-five. This means that a forty-five-year-old woman has probably another thirty years, or more than half of her adult life, yet to live. From these figures it is evident that the menopause, rather than being the beginning of the end, should be viewed in its true perspective, as a normal transition and a new beginning in the middle of adult life—a time to pause and evaluate what we have done with our lives, but more important, what we hope, plan, and expect to accomplish during the many potentially rewarding years that lie ahead.

Is the menopause the same thing as the "change of life"?

Not exactly. Although these terms are frequently interchanged, the word menopause simply means the permanent cessation of all menstruation as ovarian function declines. The so-called change of life represents the sum total of all normal hormonal readjustments, from the gradual decline in estrogen production through the body's adaptation when it reaches a new and different state of hormonal balance. In most women the change of life (menopausal years or climacteric) usually spans a four- to six-year period, whereas the actual menopause is only an isolated event in this normal physiological transition.

What actually brings on the menopause?

Ovarian failure because of a gradual depletion of ovarian follicles. As you will recall from Chapter 6, each woman is born with only so many follicles. Once these follicles are "gone" (and by age fifty there are relatively few left) the main source of ovarian estrogen is also gone. For it is the follicles which produce estrogen and which ultimately ripen into ova. Without maturing and functioning follicles there can be no ovulation, no formation of a corpus luteum, no production of the hormone progesterone, and thus no cyclic ovarian function. At the same time, the ovaries become less and less responsive to pituitary hormone stimulation. This in turn causes a marked compensatory rise in the production of the pituitary hormones (FSH and LH), which persists throughout the remainder of a woman's life.

What about the woman who stops having periods at age thirty-five; could this be considered an early menopause?

Although it is true that women as young as thirty-five and even younger can be menopausal, it is important to distinguish between a truly early physiological menopause and lack of menstruation stemming from some other cause. There is only one reason for a bona fide early menopause and that is premature ovarian failure. But why the ovaries fail or become unresponsive to pituitary stimulation or simply "run out" of follicles and ova before normally anticipated are questions that frequently remain unanswered. Women who do stop menstruating before the age of forty, however, should have the reason for their lack of periods investigated.

Are there any laboratory tests which can diagnose menopause?

Yes. The diagnosis can be established by finding persistently high blood levels of the pituitary hormones FSH and LH. As mentioned earlier, ovarian failure and absence of estrogen output cause these hormones to be secreted in large amounts. In fact, a sustained elevation of these pituitary hormones occurs only in the presence of ovarian failure (menopause), surgical removal of the ovaries, or congenital absence of the ovaries.

When your periods finally do stop, does this mean that your body no longer produces estrogen?

Not entirely. A few follicles can persist for five to ten years and continue to produce some estrogen. It all depends on your biological timetable. For example, a woman may stop menstruating at age fifty and yet at age sixty, her vaginal and vulvar tissues may be comparable to those of a much younger woman because of small but continuous estrogen stimulation. In contrast, a woman whose ovaries completely retire at an earlier age may already show thinning and atrophy of the genital tissues within three years after her last period.

There is, however, another source of estrogen and one which becomes increasingly important to postmenopausal women.

Another source of estrogen in the postmenopausal woman?

Yes. Not all estrogen comes directly from the ovaries or even from the adrenals. It has now been shown that the primary source of estrogen in postmenopausal women comes from the conversion of an androgen into estrogen. This androgen (known as androstenedione) is produced by both the ovaries and adrenals and released into the blood stream. A percentage of this hormone is then picked up and converted into estrogen in the fat deposits of the body, most probably the fat deposits of the abdomen and breasts. Although the total amount of this androgen produced in postmenopausal women is considerably less than that produced by young women, the percentage conversion of this androgen to estrogen is substantially increased in the older woman. In other words, this source of estrogen, although of very secondary importance in the young woman with functioning ovaries, now becomes a primary (albeit small) source of estrogen to the older woman. Moreover, aging, obesity, and certain metabolic diseases such as diabetes and liver disease can substantially increase the percentage of androgen hormone converted into estrogen. The amount of estrogen derived from this conversion varies, of course, from woman to woman, but in simple terms—the fatter postmenopausal woman may enjoy a smoother menopausal transition period than her thinner friends because of her greater supply of endogenous (self-made) estrogen. As you will shortly see, this endogenous supply of estrogen may make the very same woman an increased risk for developing endometrial cancer.

How can you know when you are beginning the menopausal years?

Trying to pinpoint the beginning of the menopausal years is as difficult as deciding at what moment a girl becomes a woman. Since it takes years for the ovaries to withdraw all hormonal support, early symptoms referable to decreasing estrogen levels may initially be very subtle. Women who fully expect to "fall apart" as soon as they hit forty naturally blame every mood swing, feeling of depression, or vague ache and pain previously taken in stride on the "change."

Actually, the first real indication that the ovaries are beginning to slow down is usually a change in menstrual pattern. For most women these menstrual irregularities commonly start between forty-five and fifty, but in a few instances, they can begin as early as thirty-five or as late as fifty-five.

In what way are your periods likely to change?

They frequently become increasingly unpredictable. A few women will experience an abrupt cessation of all menstruation. Others will tend to have lighter periods that gradually become further apart until they cease altogether.

Some women, however, do experience more distressing irregularity. In these instances, length of flow, amount of bleeding, as well as intervals between periods can be extremely variable. Thus it is not too unusual to have one heavy period, whereas the following period may be relatively light. Length of menstrual cycle can also fluctuate, with periods coming as frequently as twenty-one to twenty-four days alternating with a delay of six to eight weeks or longer.

How can you be sure whether that irregular bleeding is really normal?

Other than checking with your gynecologist, there is no way to be absolutely certain. Nonetheless, there are certain types of bleeding that should be considered abnormal until proved otherwise: bleeding or spotting recurring at intervals of less than twenty-one days, persistently heavy, flooding periods, or bleeding lasting longer than eight days. In addition, any spotting after intercourse or douching or the sudden reappearance of bleeding after having seen nothing for six months or longer should also be evaluated.

How long do these menstrual irregularities usually last?

Anywhere from a few months up to one, two, and even three years. If it has been twelve months or more since your last menstrual flow, you can now consider your periods to be permanently over. Any recurrence of bleeding or spotting after twelve months should not be considered normal.

When is it safe to stop using birth control?

If you are not on birth control pills and are still menstruating (no matter how irregular your periods may be), ovulation and pregnancy are still possible. Your ovaries may be slowing down, but they haven't given up yet. Using contraceptive protection will also relieve you of unnecessary anxiety when periods are skipped or delayed.

As a general rule, if you are forty-eight or over and have had no periods for at least six months, you are probably safe from pregnancy. If you are younger than forty-eight, it is best to continue using some form of birth control unless it has been twelve months or more since your last period.

For the older woman taking birth control pills, periods will probably continue to be regular as long as the uterine lining can still respond to hormonal stimulation. It is thus possible for a woman to have artificially induced periods beyond the advent of the menopause.

What about other menopausal symptoms?

For 20 percent of women the cessation of menstruation may be the only apparent sign of having been through the menopause. Another 65 percent of women, although occasionally bothered with menopausal symptoms, will be able to cope with them effectively with minimal help. For the remaining 15 percent, however, true menopausal symptoms such as hot flashes, sweats, insomnia, tingling of the hands and feet, headaches, occasional heart palpitations, and fatigue may be sufficiently distressing to warrant appropriate treatment and counsel.

Are hot flashes really common?

Next to menstrual irregularities, hot flashes head the list of menopausal complaints in four out of five women. Although not the least bit serious, hot flashes can be disconcerting. One moment you can be cool and comfortable and in the next overwhelmed with a spreading sensation of fiery heat from the waist up, accompanied by drenching perspiration and a marked flushing of the face and neck. Hot flashes can be infrequent and disappear altogether within a few weeks. In other women, they can occur ten to fifteen times a day, last up to a full minute, and persist for months.

For some perverse reason, hot flashes also take great delight in striking after hours. A woman who has hot flashes during the day may still spend most of her sleep time throwing off the covers and rushing to the nearest window. Fortunately for all concerned (including bed mates who also lose sleep), frequent and bothersome hot flashes are among the most easily controlled of all menopausal symptoms. (More about this later.)

Does anyone really know what causes hot flashes?

Not really, but the most probable explanation is an upset in the hormonal balance between the ovary and computer headquarters (pituitary and hypothalamus) in the base of the brain. (See Chapter 6.) Try imagining for a moment a giant seesaw. On one side are the pituitary hormones (FSH and LH); on the other are the ovarian hormones (estrogen and progesterone). For thirty-five years or so, regular menstrual cycles have depended upon the pituitary and ovarian hormones seesawing back and forth in perfect harmony. Thus, each time the ovaries produced more estrogen, down went the level of pituitary hormones; when the ovaries put out less estrogen, up went the level of pituitary hormones.

But now as the ovaries begin slowing down during the menopausal years, this beautifully balanced seesaw is thrown off kilter. With less and less estrogen being produced by the ovaries, the pituitary responds by pouring out five, ten, or even a hundred times more FSH than ever before in a desperate attempt to stir up the sluggish ovaries. In short order, the hypothalamus also becomes affected.

What does the hypothalamus have to do with hot flashes and other menopausal symptoms?

Since the hypothalamus, or master gland, is ultimately responsible for the smooth functioning of the pituitary, it too becomes irritated by lack of sufficient estrogen to balance the hormonal seesaw. As the hypothalamus also controls such bodily functions as sleep, heat regulation, energy levels, and the vast network of special nerves that feed into every organ and blood vessel (autonomic nervous system), it is little wonder that temporary disturbances in this important control center can precipitate such a variety of symptoms.

Thus, hot flashes, tingling sensations, insomnia, heart palpitations, and occasional migrainelike headaches can frequently be traced to temperamental outbursts of an estrogen-hungry hypothalamus. In addition, intermittent fatigue after relatively minor physical exertion may also be the result of sporadic malfunction of this master gland.

Do the 15 percent who are severely bothered with menopausal symptoms experience all of these problems?

Heavens, no. No woman will ever have all of these problems or even most of them. Moreover, menopausal symptoms are not constant sources of irritation. Even in the absence of any specific hormonal treatment or estrogen replacement, there will be intervals of complete comfort followed eventually by permanent relief, usually within three to five years, as the body readjusts to a different hormonal tempo.

Why, then, do some women become tense and irritable?

Physical stress as such is certainly one factor. If, for example, you are intermittently seized with devastating hot flashes, have trouble sleeping at night, and suffer from recurrent migrainelike headaches, is it any wonder that at times you may be tense and irritable?

Headaches, especially the ones described as "sick headaches," which seem to radiate all the way down to the toes and last forever, are occasionally sources of real apprehension. A woman so afflicted may well believe that she is losing her mind.

The fact remains that symptoms truly related to an estrogen deficiency will respond to estrogen therapy. Not so for other problems.

What other problems?

The menopause unfortunately coincides with "middle age," which in itself can be a trying period especially for the biologically oriented woman. For example, the woman who has attached too much importance to being youthful and sexually attractive may regard the menopausal years as a prologue to old age, with its attendant loss of everything she considers worthwhile. If, in addition, her life interest has revolved around being a wife and homemaker, her apprehension can be further aggravated by a husband frequently too busy with work to give her the reassurance and attention she needs. Children, if any, are likely to be approaching maturity and anxious to set out on their own. Seemingly no longer needed by either children or husband and lacking any real appreciation of her individual worth, she may view her situation with dread and anxiety. Thus, emotional, psychological, and sexual maladjustments hitherto submerged in a sea of activity may now bubble to the surface and erroneously be blamed on the "change."

What about sexuality in the woman over fifty?

Assuming that you have a compatible partner, your enjoyment of the sex act during or after the menopausal years will depend upon your previous coital experiences, your mental and emotional attitude toward love making, and your self-image. If, for example, you believe that advancing age or perhaps the surgical removal of some female organ makes you less sexually desirable, then your capacity to enjoy coitus will be adversely affected. Interestingly enough, sexual drive or libido in women is only partially dependent on functioning ovaries or the presence of estrogen. Psychological factors play a far greater role.

In brief, feeling sexy and being able to perform sexually are not limited by age or lack of female hormones. Women can enjoy sexual intercourse and remain orgasmic all the days of their life. In fact, for some women, sex is even better after the menopause.

In what way can sex be better after the menopause?

With pregnancy no longer possible, many women experience a renewed interest in sex. Furthermore, by the time most women reach their middle fifties, major family responsibilities are frequently over. Thus, with less worry, more spare time, and perhaps financial security at last realized, many women can enjoy sex on a more mature and emotionally gratifying plane.

Why, then, do some women withdraw from sex as they grow older?

There are any number of reasons. Even in this supposedly enlightened age, sex is still popularly regarded as the sole prerogative of the "young." For the older couple who perhaps grew up with this misconception, feelings of guilt or shame because of wanting or needing sex may gradually suppress all overt sexuality.

For other women, the marital bed may never have been a source of joy and delight. After years of personal sexual maladjustment or consistent lack of gratification because of a clumsy and inept husband, advancing age may now serve as an attractive and legitimate excuse to shy away from further contact.

One must also remember that as a woman becomes older, her partner is also aging. In men over fifty-five especially, psychological impotence or repeated difficulty in obtaining or sustaining an erection invariably leads to complete abandonment of coitus. This is indeed unfortunate for the woman desiring physical intimacy. Then too, in this age category many women are widowed or divorced. Frequently considered too old by society's double standards to find a suitable mate, the older divorcee or widow desiring sexual activity must either suppress her feelings or find an alternate outlet. The fact that many women resort to automanipulation under these circumstances is certainly understandable.

However, in women who have the opportunity for a satisfying sexual relationship, local genital changes as a result of estrogen deficiency can create problems during intercourse.

How does a lack of estrogen affect the vulva, vagina, and uterus?

It is important to realize that changes such as thinning and loss of elasticity in the vulvar, vaginal, and uterine tissues occur only after a long and significant lack of estrogen. Therefore, unlike other menopausal symptoms (hot flashes, etc.) genital organ changes occur much later. It may be as long as five to fifteen years after the menopause before any of the genital changes become apparent. Much depends upon how well the ovaries continue to function and whether or not supplemental estrogen is taken.

With regard to the external genitalia (vulva), pubic hair becomes sparse and there is a gradual loss of fatty tissue. The lips (labia) become thin, flat, and lose some of their elasticity. The clitoris, which previously was partially covered and protected by the labia, subsequently becomes more exposed. Although this now makes the clitoris appear relatively larger and more prominent, it too actually decreases in size.

Lack of estrogen also causes the uterus to shrink in size and the vagina to undergo atrophic changes in the postmenopausal woman. In time, therefore, with thinning of the vaginal walls, loss of elasticity, and a decrease in blood supply to the area, the vagina becomes shorter, narrower, and less capable of producing adequate lubrication during sexual excitement.

In what way can these local genital changes interfere with sexual enjoyment?

If the vaginal opening becomes relatively smaller and in some cases insufficiently lubricated, penile entry may be uncomfortable. Decreased elasticity of the vaginal walls also prevents the proper dilatation and expansion of the vagina. This in itself can make attempts at deeper penile penetration a potential source of discomfort.

When there is also marked thinning of the vaginal tissues, repeated penile thrusts can irritate the nearby urethra and bladder. Under these circumstances and particularly in elderly women, burning on urination and bladder spasms may be noticed immediately after intercourse. (See Chapter 14.)

During extended intercourse, a few women may even complain of clitoral irritation. In the postmenopausal woman whose clitoris is relatively more exposed because of labial atrophy, this exquisitely sensitive organ now becomes vulnerable to more direct stimulation during coitus. Needless to say, too intense, too prolonged, and too direct stimulation, rather than being exciting, can actually be distressing and unpleasant.

Less commonly, acutely painful uterine cramping during orgasm, and particularly in women past sixty, can be another reason for avoiding coital contact. Although the exact cause of this phenomenon is not completely understood, it can be corrected by appropriate hormonal therapy.

Interestingly enough, the maintenance of a fairly active sex life in the postmenopausal woman will definitely help avoid some of these problems during intercourse.

How can having sex avoid sex problems?

Even when there are vaginal atrophic changes, there is nothing like regular intercourse to help keep the vagina dilated and flexible. Vaginal lubrication, although decreased in amount, may still be sufficient to permit easy penile penetration. If, however, lubrication is insufficient, K-Y lubricating jelly (non-prescription) applied around the vaginal opening as well as on the penis prior to coitus can be helpful.

Can lack of estrogen cause other physical problems?

Yes indeed. And one of the most serious and potentially disabling diseases that can affect postmenopausal women is osteoporosis.

What is osteoporosis?

An abnormal softening and demineralization of bone so that it becomes weaker, lighter, more porous, and vulnerable to fractures. These fractures can occur following little or no provocation. Sometimes simply bending over to tie a shoe lace or trying to open a window will create sufficient mechanical stress to cause a fracture. The bones most commonly involved are the spinal vertebrae, the hip, and the wrist.

How serious is osteoporosis in women?

In this country alone, over 750,000 fractures per year occur in women over forty-five on the basis of osteoporosis. Among women over sixty, 25 percent have spinal compression fractures with wedging and collapse of the vertebrae. By age sixty-five, almost 80 percent of women have already lost one to two inches in height because of such bony changes in the spinal column. Osteoporosis also accounts for 80 percent of all hip fractures, and postmenopausal women sustain ten times as many hip fractures as men in the same age group. A hip fracture in an aging female can cause not only pain and permanent disability but it can be potentially fatal. It is currently estimated that as many as 58,000 postmenopausal women in this country die every year as a direct or indirect result of a hip fracture.

Isn't advancing age also a factor in the development of osteoporosis?

Not so much as one might think. Women who are over fifty and still menstruating have the same bone density as young women in their late teens and twenties. Men rarely have appreciable osteoporosis until well after eighty, and even then it is considerably less severe than that experienced by women. On the other hand, once a woman stops menstruating there is a rapid and precipitous loss of bone mass, amounting to 1 to 3 percent every year. Since this loss is initially painless and subtle, symptoms do not usually occur until a critical amount of bone loss has been sustained. If untreated, some women may ultimately lose as much as one half of their entire skeletal bone mass. This does not mean that they will invariably have fractures, but it does imply that they are very vulnerable. Women who are castrated, that is, have their ovaries removed prior to natural menopause, and who are not given estrogen, sustain comparable bone loss regardless of age. On an average, one out of four women will have significant osteoporosis within ten years of castration or natural menopause if untreated. For reasons unknown, black women tend to have relatively little osteoporosis regardless of age or hormonal status.

Is bone loss largely due to lack of estrogen?

Although it is true that regular physical exercise, good nutrition with vitamin supplements, and adequate amounts of calcium can help retard bone loss, the lack of estrogen in the postmenopausal woman is probably the most important factor in the development of osteoporosis. Bone resorption along with changes in calcium and phosphate metabolism correlate with loss of ovarian function and specifically with loss of estrogen. Unfortunately, women seldom notice bone loss until it is too late.

Can estrogen really prevent osteoporosis?

Yes. Not only can small amounts of estrogen prevent osteoporosis but estrogen can halt further progress of the disease in advanced stages. In so doing, estrogen can thus prevent the associated pain, deformity, and disability and significantly decrease the incidence of fractures in the aging woman. The fact that one out of four women will have clinically significant osteoporosis within ten years of the menopause is perhaps one of the most compelling reasons for estrogen replacement therapy.

What can be done about menopausal and postmenopausal problems?

Regardless of whether a woman is just beginning the menopausal years or is several years past menopause, symptoms and distress referable to an estrogen deficiency can be immeasurably helped by estrogen replacement therapy.

What can a woman expect from estrogen therapy?

Contrary to what many women believe, taking estrogen will neither delay the onset of the menopause nor prolong this normal period
of transition. The primary purpose of estrogen replacement during
the menopausal years is to help women go through this temporary
phase more smoothly and to retard and perhaps even prevent the
later development of other estrogen-related deficiency problems.
With or without supplemental estrogen, the body will still follow its
own biological timetable and adapt normally and naturally to waning
ovarian function.

Women who expect estrogen to stop the clock, or prevent hair
from turning gray, or skin from wrinkling, will be sorely disappointed.
As wonderful as estrogen is, the secret of perpetual youth has yet to
be discovered. Nevertheless, if a true estrogen deficiency does exist,
estrogen can help keep the skin, hair, and blood vessels in better
health. Breast tissue will also keep its firmness and elasticity longer
than it would otherwise. Taking estrogen will also help avoid the
redistribution of fat, or that "middle-age spread," provided, of course,
that you watch your diet and exercise regularly.

Other complaints during the menopausal years, such as excessive
weight gain, lapses of memory, emotional instability, and loss of sexual
interest, are rarely the result of hormonal deficiency per se.

How can estrogen help in the early menopausal years?

Hot flashes and sweats in particular can frequently be eliminated
or markedly reduced in frequency and intensity. Less common complaints, such as tingling sensations, headaches, insomnia, and heart
palpitations, can also be controlled if they are truly related to an
estrogen deficiency. Thus, in many instances, nervousness, irritation,
and even depression stemming from these physical stresses can be
relieved by estrogen.

In cases where various psychosomatic complaints masquerade as
hormonal deficiencies, estrogen therapy may prove disappointing. In
women who manifest extreme anxiety or nervousness (not related to
estrogen deficiency), the temporary use of tranquilizers or mild sedatives can afford needed relief.

Can estrogen therapy ever increase a woman's sex drive?

Only indirectly. If there are times when your sexual desire is low
because of hot flashes and such, estrogen can help by making you more
comfortable physically. Even the most sensuous woman can be an
unenthusiastic lover when she feels out of sorts. Other than that,

estrogen is no panacea for a sagging libido, nor will it transform a previously unresponsive woman into an orgasmic nymphomaniac.

For the older woman, however, who is involuntarily celibate because of genital atrophic changes, estrogen therapy can really improve her sex life.

How can estrogen help postmenopausal sexual problems?

It is truly amazing how estrogen replacement therapy can revitalize atrophic vaginal and vulvar tissues in the older woman. Within a remarkably short time the vaginal walls become thicker, more pliant, and distensible. Fatty tissue previously lost from the labial folds can be partially regained. Thus, with better vulvar padding the clitoris can once again be protected from too direct and oftentimes irritating stimulation. In addition, with more blood now coursing through these tissues, effective vaginal lubrication during sexual excitement occurs more rapidly and lasts longer. A better blood supply to the entire genital area also intensifies and prolongs a woman's sexual response.

Are birth control pills ever used in controlling menopausal symptoms?

Where there is still a possibility of pregnancy, the use of birth control pills in the premenopausal woman can be helpful not only in regulating periods, but also in controlling symptoms such as hot flashes. However, by the time most women reach fifty, the chances of impregnation are so remote that most doctors favor using less potent estrogen therapy to control menopausal symptoms. More recently, the high incidence of myocardial infarction among women over forty who smoke and use the pill has persuaded many doctors to avoid prescribing oral contraceptives to any woman over forty on general principle.

How do birth control pills differ from other types of estrogen therapy?

Birth control pills are synthetic preparations which contain relatively large doses of estrogen in order to prevent ovulation. The fact that high doses of synthetic estrogen can be associated with unpleasant side effects—including the potential for blood-clotting problems and cardiovascular disorders—makes their use and attendant risks unadvisable to women no longer concerned about the possibility of pregnancy.

For the older woman who needs only to supplement her waning estrogen in order to control distressing menopausal symptoms, small doses of natural or biologic estrogens found in nature are far safer and better tolerated than birth control pills. The natural estrogens include estrone, estrone sulfate (Ogen, Evex), conjugated estrogen (Premarin), estradiol, and estriol. Examples of synthetic estrogens are mestranol and ethinyl estradiol (the estrogens in birth control pills), diethylstilbestrol (DES), and chlorotrianisene (Tace).

How is estrogen therapy usually given?

When it comes to menopausal symptoms, most doctors prefer giving some form of natural estrogen by mouth on a cyclic basis, usually three weeks on medication and one week off. How much you need will depend upon the severity of your symptoms. Dosages can always be increased or decreased according to your response after a three- to four-month trial. During the week off medication you should not have any appreciable return of menopausal symptoms. If you are no longer having periods, taking estrogen cyclically rather than continuously will also help prevent excessive stimulation of the uterine lining, which could bring about the reappearance of some bleeding.

Estrogen by injection is less commonly used, for several reasons: it requires frequent visits to your doctor, the medication is more expensive, and most important, the effects are less predictable than with estrogen taken orally. For the most part, estrogen by injection is usually reserved for the rare woman who cannot tolerate or properly absorb oral medication.

What about estrogen in the form of creams or suppositories?

Although estrogen in cream or suppository form can be locally absorbed, oral estrogen is far more effective in rejuvenating vaginal and vulvar tissues. Nonetheless, these topical applications are helpful in treating relatively minor vaginal or vulvar problems in estrogen-deficient women. Not infrequently their only complaint may be occasional vaginal dryness and itching (not necessarily associated with intercourse). In these cases, intermittent applications when necessary of an estrogenic vaginal cream may be sufficient to provide prompt and complete relief.

Medicinal estrogen products, however, are available only by prescription and should not be confused with cosmetic creams containing estrogen. By comparison, these so-called hormone creams sold for beautifying purposes contain only minimal amounts of estrogen.

Can a vaginal smear test identify the woman in need of estrogen?

To some extent. The best-known vaginal smear test and probably the most accurate is the Maturation Index. This is a measure of estrogenic effect on the vagina. In brief, the vaginal mucosa is made up of three cell types: superficial, intermediate, and parabasal. These cell types are named according to their maturity and differentiation. Superficial cells are the most mature; parabasal cells are the least mature. A vaginal smear with many superficial cells indicates the presence of estrogen. No other hormone can give this cellular picture. A smear with mostly parabasal cells would indicate no estrogen stimulation. Such a smear might be found in an elderly woman or a child under seven. Most cellular patterns actually fall somewhere between these two extremes.

The Maturation Index (MI) is a way of tabulating the relative proportions of these cell types in each 100 vaginal mucosal cells counted under the microscope. It is expressed in percentages and written as P/I/S (Parabasal, Intermediate, Superficial). For example, a Maturation Index at the time of ovulation in a young woman might read 0/30/70 or 0 parabasal, 30 intermediate, and 70 superficial cells. Such a good proportion of superficial cells would indicate an adequate amount of estrogen for that phase of the menstrual cycle.

As helpful as this test can sometimes be, it has serious limitations. Interpretation is sometimes difficult and may not always reflect the true hormonal picture. At best the MI must be evaluated in relationship to the age of the woman, her physical findings, and clinical history, including symptoms.

Can there be any problems associated with estrogen replacement therapy?

Overstimulation of the uterine lining by estrogen can cause irregular bleeding. Although this is no cause for alarm, it may raise the question in a postmenopausal woman as to whether the unexpected bleeding is the direct result of hormone therapy or unsuspected uterine pathology. The fact that endometrial cancer (that is, cancer of the uterine lining) is more prevalent among older women makes any unexpected bleeding or spotting a matter that deserves prompt evaluation. At times, simply lowering the estrogen dose or temporarily stopping the medication will resolve the bleeding problem. More commonly, your doctor will probably suggest other tests or even a D and C just to make certain that all is well. In any event, don't increase your estrogen on the mistaken belief that if a little estrogen makes you feel good, more estrogen will make you feel great.

Since 1975, various articles in magazines and newspapers have focused public attention on another potential problem—a possible link between estrogen replacement therapy and the development of uterine cancer.

Is there a risk of developing uterine cancer by being on estrogen?

One of estrogen's normal physiological functions is to stimulate growth of the uterine lining in anticipation of receiving the fertilized egg. Without this effect of estrogen on the uterine lining, no woman could ever bear a child. But it is also true that continuous and unopposed estrogen stimulation (that is, not balanced with progesterone) can cause cystic hyperplasia of the endometrium, a benign overgrowth of the uterine lining. (See Chapter 25.) Recent reports now suggest that in "predisposed women," the use of continuous and unopposed estrogen over a long period of time can also lead to premalignant tissue changes and ultimately even to cancer of the uterine lining. According to some studies, the risk of developing endometrial cancer appears to increase with the dosage and duration of estrogen therapy. In one particular survey, women who had taken estrogen for two to four years or longer had a four- to eightfold increased risk of developing endometrial cancer. In contrast, the risk of endometrial cancer was negligible in women who had taken estrogen for less than two years.

Other studies suggest that a fifty-year-old woman with an intact uterus and on estrogen therapy has approximately a 1 percent chance of developing endometrial cancer by age fifty-five; after ten years of estrogen therapy her cumulative risk for endometrial cancer increases to 3.6 percent, and after fifteen years of estrogen the risk is assessed at 7 percent. A fifty-year-old woman with an intact uterus and not on estrogen therapy has about a 0.3 percent chance of developing endometrial cancer by age fifty-five. By age sixty her risk has increased to 0.8 percent and by age sixty-five to about a 1 percent chance.

So although there appears to be an association between estrogen therapy and the development of endometrial cancer (at least in some women), a cause-and-effect relationship has not been established. Perhaps as more solid information is gathered from long-term and comprehensive studies, some of the unresolved issues will be clarified.

In the meantime there are ways of minimizing the risk of developing endometrial cancer while still enjoying the benefits of estrogen.

If you are taking estrogen, how can you protect yourself against endometrial cancer?

There are basically five steps: (1) First and foremost it is important that you use the lowest estrogen dose possible to alleviate your symptoms. You may feel wonderful on a daily dose of 1.25 mg. of Premarin, for example, but are you sure you won't feel just as comfortable on half that dose or 0.625 mg.? Should you still have hot flashes on 0.625 mg., you might try taking (with your doctor's approval) 1.25 mg. one day and then switching down to 0.625 mg. on alternate days. For those of you who can be comfortable on 0.3 mg. of Premarin, so much the better. Experts report that as little as 0.3 mg. to 0.625 mg. of Premarin (or a comparable estrogen) may be sufficient to prevent osteoporotic changes. (2) The estrogen should be taken cyclically. This means that there should be a regular interruption in therapy. Most doctors suggest taking estrogen three out of four weeks or for the first twenty-five days of each month. Interrupting estrogen therapy for at least a week helps prevent overstimulation and overgrowth of the tissues lining the uterine cavity. (3) In addition, some experts advise a five- to seven-day course of Provera (or comparable progestational agent) on a monthly basis. The use of Provera (when combined with estrogen during the third week of therapy) would mimic the "normal cycle" and result in withdrawal bleeding. This regular shedding of the uterine lining by preventing excessive tissue build-up would be further protection against the development of endometrial cancer. Although this approach has not been commonly used by many physicians, it is gaining support. (4) If you are on estrogen, you should definitely plan to have a physical check-up including a pelvic and Pap smear every six to twelve months. It would also be ideal to have a biopsy of the uterine lining at least every eighteen months. (See Chapter 25.) This would be especially important among women who are known to be at high risk for endometrial cancer. As an aside, endometrial cancers diagnosed among women on estrogen therapy tend to be more localized and biologically less invasive than cancers diagnosed among women not on estrogen. (5) And lastly, make sure to report promptly any unexpected bleeding or staining regardless of how minimal. This is of particular importance for women who have gone at least six months without any bleeding or spotting whatsoever.

What about estrogen therapy in a woman who has had a hysterectomy?

If you have had a hysterectomy, you will never develop uterine or endometrial cancer. If, however, your uterus was removed because of a uterine malignancy, estrogen replacement therapy could conceivably stimulate the growth of any remaining cancer cells in the pelvis.

In these cases the use of estrogen most likely would be contraindicated. (See Chapter 25.)

Does taking estrogen increase the risk of breast cancer?

Innumerable studies have failed to show any connection between estrogen replacement therapy and breast cancer. In other words, taking estrogen during the menopausal and postmenopausal years does not increase a woman's risk of breast cancer. Interestingly enough, estrogen in high doses is sometimes the treatment of choice for recurrent breast cancer in postmenopausal women.

Are natural estrogens associated with an increased risk of cardiovascular problems?

Natural estrogens (unlike the synthetic estrogens used in birth control pills) have not been linked to an increased risk of stroke, myocardial infarction, and thromboembolic problems. On the contrary, some recent reports indicate that the risk of non-fatal myocardial infarction was definitely decreased in postmenopausal women on estrogen replacement therapy. Other limited studies indicate that estrogen-treated postmenopausal women may also have a lower incidence of stroke. Although these reports are encouraging, further well-controlled studies are needed before any definite conclusions can be reached.

How long can a woman stay on estrogen?

Until more information is gleaned regarding the long-term effects of estrogen replacement therapy, there are no absolute rules as to length of time. If estrogen makes a woman feel and look better and there are no contraindications to its use, estrogen can be taken for years. Apart from softening the effects of aging by controlling menopausal symptoms, keeping the genital tissues in good condition, and preventing osteoporosis, natural estrogens in judicious doses may also be a factor in protecting women against other degenerative diseases such as hardening of the arteries, heart attacks, and strokes.

Needless to say, not all doctors are in agreement about how long estrogen replacement therapy should be given. Regardless of their individual philosophies, each woman should be evaluated and treated on the basis of her own specific needs. Moreover, each woman should be fully informed by her physician of the risks and benefits of estrogen therapy. Only in that way can she partake intelligently in any decision regarding estrogen replacement therapy.

What about the woman who doesn't take estrogen? Is there any help for her menopausal symptoms?

Certainly. There are various "aids" which can mollify some of the more disturbing symptoms. Hot flashes for many years have been treated with the prescription drug Bellergal. This is a combination of phenobarbital and autonomic nervous-system depressant drugs. This drug sedates and helps inhibit some of the vasomotor disturbances. Some women find it helpful; others are less enthusiastic. Fortunately, hot flashes will ultimately taper off and disappear with no treatment.

Vaginal atrophic changes, as previously mentioned, are a later development and tend to occur five or more years after cessation of menstruation. Where vaginal dryness is a source of irritation and dyspareunia (painful coitus), the use of lubricating jellies can alleviate symptoms. An active sex life is another important factor in maintaining the genital tissues in optimal condition.

More recently, the influence of diet, regular exercise, and vitamin and mineral supplements in the prevention of osteoporosis has gained attention. According to some experts, osteoporosis can be prevented by the daily ingestion of 2.6 grams of calcium carbonate. It would be advisable, however, to check with your doctor before taking such large doses of calcium, as there can be unpleasant side effects.

In the final analysis, the menopause need not be a time of dread or apprehension for any woman. Much can be and is being done. Estrogen replacement therapy as well as other medication can handle the temporary physical stresses. Equally important, rapidly changing and more realistic attitudes regarding the role of women and expanding options for creative living are also going to temper the psychological and emotional stresses of this period. It is already an undeniable fact that career women or those having interests in addition to their roles as homemakers are the ones most likely to breeze through the menopausal years.

Perhaps when all women realize that their ability to live fully rewarding and sexually gratifying lives does not depend upon the reproductive function, the myths surrounding the menopausal years will at long last be laid to rest.

24. Breast Problems, Benign and Malignant

Unlike the mammary glands of other species, whose sole function is lactation, the breast of the human female is also an erogenous area and to some a symbol of sexuality. Thus, any disease process which threatens the female breast can assume prime psychological importance aside from any potential impact on general health.

Within the next twelve months approximately 250,000 women in the United States will undergo minor surgery for benign breast lesions, and an additional 108,000 women will be told that they have breast cancer. And yet, among the women who will ultimately die of breast cancer, how many of them could remain alive and well had their malignancy been discovered earlier? Going to your doctor for an annual or semiannual checkup is not enough. You as a woman should also become an expert in this most important of examinations.

How often should you examine your breasts?

Regardless of your age, make it a point to examine your breasts at least once a month. If you are still menstruating regularly, the best time to check your breasts is during the week following your period. Examinations done premenstrually or during your period can be less reliable because of breast engorgement or tenderness. You should also pick a time and place when you can be undisturbed and unhurried.

What is the technique for thorough breast self-examination?

Under good lighting, strip to the waist and either sit or stand in front of a mirror. With your arms resting naturally at your sides, observe both breasts for any differences in size, shape, and contour. As some of you may have noticed, one breast might be somewhat fuller. This may be perfectly normal. Needless to say, what we are concerned with is the detection of differences that were not previously observable. Pay particular attention to the nipples. Do they look the same? Are they symmetrical and at the same level, or does one nipple seem to be pulled to the side? Unless you have always had an inverted nipple or nipples, the retraction or turning in of one nipple is not normal. Similarly, any dimpling of the breast skin should also be noted. Now raise both arms overhead and repeat the same observations. Elevating the arms exposes the undersurface of the breasts and further helps detect any changes in contour or symmetry.

Following this simple mirror inspection, the next and most important step is feeling or palpating the breasts.

How should you palpate your breasts?

Since any breast irregularity can be detected more easily by allowing the breast tissue to flatten against the chest wall, this part of the examination is best done lying down. If your breasts are heavy or pendulous, place a small pillow beneath the shoulder on the side to be examined. This will help distribute the weight of the breast more evenly along the chest wall.

To examine the left breast, lie on your back with your left hand beneath your head and your elbow resting comfortably out to the side. With the right hand, using only the flat surface of the four fingers, palpate the breast tissue between your fingers and the chest wall with a gentle rotary motion. Although there are various ways to ensure a thorough examination, if you think of your breast as representing the face of a clock with each hour equal to one segment of breast, you are less likely to overlook any irregularity. For example, begin at twelve o'clock and work your way from the outside of the breast to and including the nipple. Then move on to one o'clock and through the remaining ten segments, always starting from the outer edge of the breast and moving toward the nipple. To examine the right breast, repeat the process using the left hand.

In addition, check each nipple for any discharge by gently squeezing it between the thumb and index finger.

There is another method of breast self-examination which you can perform while bathing or taking a shower. Lather your hands and breasts with a bar of soap. Then raise your left arm well above your head and firmly run your right hand (flat of the fingers) over the entire left breast including the nipple and areola. Do the same for the opposite side. The soap film allows your fingers to glide effortlessly. Most of you will be impressed by how much more you can feel as compared to examining yourself by the conventional "dry" method. In fact, direct skin-to-skin contact (without the soap film) tends to dull certain sensory receptors located along the palmar surface of the fingers. In contrast, the soap film enhances tactile sensitivity. Since this is such a simple and easy way to examine your breasts you should try to do it on a weekly basis.

If you are not bathing and want to increase your tactile sensitivity, you can apply the same principle as the soap film by simply palpating your breasts through a piece of fine nylon, polyester, or other thin fabric.

What do normal breasts feel like?

Since breasts vary in texture and consistency depending on your age, hormone levels, and amount of adipose tissue, don't be discouraged if initially you can't tell for sure what you are feeling. Small breasts, for example, may feel more glandular, whereas large breasts may feel soft and doughy. Other women may even notice tiny gritty areas scattered throughout both breasts. In any event, regular self-examinations will allow you to become familiar with what your breasts feel like normally. This is especially true if you check yourself more than once a month. Thus, with practice you will be able to detect any change such as a lump, thickening, or irregularity that may subsequently appear.

Do breast lumps occur more frequently in certain breast areas?

Although a breast tumor or cyst, whether benign or malignant, can occur in any area of either breast, many breast cancers first appear in the upper outer quadrant. In other words, this would correspond to the area between twelve and three o'clock on the left breast and between nine and twelve o'clock on the right breast. For this reason, it is especially important that these areas be meticulously examined.

Can a doctor determine the nature of a breast lump by palpation alone?

Most doctors can make a fairly accurate presumptive clinical diagnosis by palpation alone. But it is not always possible by simply feeling a lump or an irregularity to be certain of whether it is benign or malignant. No doctor, regardless of how competent, can always be certain of the diagnosis by physical examination alone. Nevertheless, there are various methods that can be helpful in arriving at an accurate diagnosis. (More about this shortly.)

The fact that breast problems are so prevalent also makes it important to know something about the most common breast conditions: fibrocystic disease (cystic mastitis), fibroadenomas, breast cancer, and another symptom which can cause considerable concern, nipple discharge.

What is the significance of a nipple discharge?

It all depends on whether the discharge is physiological or pathological. The best-known examples of a normal or physiological nipple discharge are the secretion of colostrum during pregnancy and lactation following delivery. In these instances the discharge involves both nipples, arises from multiple ducts, and is generally produced by manual expression or suction.

On the other hand, a true non-physiological nipple discharge is spontaneous, non-lactational (non-milky), and tends to persist or recur. The first sign is usually the appearance of a stain on the bra or nightclothes. Although such a discharge can involve both nipples, it most commonly affects only one nipple and arises from a single duct opening on the surface of the nipple. In typical cases the discharge will always appear at the very same point on the nipple. Sometimes pressure along the corresponding portion of the areola overlying the involved duct will similarly produce a drop of discharge from the same duct opening. The type and color of the discharge may give valuable clues as to its cause.

Of particular concern are bloody discharges, serous-type discharges (yellowish or blood-tinged), and thin watery discharges. These types of discharge can be associated with benign as well as with malignant lesions. The fact that a nipple discharge may be the very first sign of an underlying cancer makes the prompt evaluation of a nipple discharge a matter of importance.

What types of breast lesions give rise to nipple discharge?

The most common breast lesion associated with a nipple discharge is an intraductal papilloma. This is a tiny nodular growth which arises from the lining of a nipple duct. The discharge is usually bloody or blood-tinged but can be yellowish or watery. Intraductal papillomas can occur in any woman over twenty, and the vast majority of them are located in the central third of the breast, fairly close to the nipple. Surprisingly enough, even tiny papillomas that can neither be felt nor detected by mammography can cause significant nipple bleeding. At times the discharge can vary in appearance depending upon the concentration of red blood cells. It can be bright red, pink, or sometimes even dark brownish-black. If there is any question, the presence of blood can easily be verified by examining the discharge under a microscope. Intraductal papillomas are strictly benign lesions and never undergo malignant transformations.

Less common causes of bloody discharge include certain types of fibrocystic disease, local duct irritation, and the presence of an intraductal carcinoma (cancer). Should there also be a mass or lump palpable beneath the areola, the likelihood of an intraductal cancer is further increased, particularly in a postmenopausal woman. Depending on whose statistics are quoted, anywhere from 3 to 47 percent of all bloody nipple discharges will be caused by an intraductal cancer. When diagnosed and treated early, intraductal cancers have an extremely good prognosis.

What about other types of nipple discharge?

A somewhat thick yellowish-green discharge or one that obviously contains pus is usually caused by a low-grade infection involving the areola or a major duct system. This type of discharge is seen more commonly in women of childbearing age. Conditions such as acute mastitis following childbirth or even a central breast abscess can cause purulent drainage through one or more duct openings on the nipple. Antibiotic treatment is usually effective in most cases, but abscess formation requires incision and drainage.

Another fairly common type of nipple discharge frequently involves both nipples as well as several ducts. The discharge is usually sticky and greenish or grayish-brown in color and is invariably caused by a benign process, most typically duct ectasia. This is a condition wherein there is distention and dilatation of the ducts with a low-grade inflammation. Women with this problem may complain of a drawing, pulling, and burning sensation with occasional swelling of the areola and nipple area. In these cases surgery is rarely indicated.

The problem can usually be cleared by local medical measures including the use of daily Phisohex washings.

Are Pap smears and breast X-rays ever helpful in diagnosing nipple discharge?

The microscopic examination of a nipple discharge for the presence of malignant cells is not always reliable. This is particularly true in the diagnosis of very small and early cancers of the ductal tissue. As many as 20 percent of small, early intraductal cancers can go undetected by this method. Similarly, mammograms can also miss a small, occult cancer, especially in the absence of a clinically palpable lump. In these cases the use of contrast mammography can be helpful. This involves identifying and probing the affected duct and then injecting it with a water-soluble dye. Although time-consuming, this technique can sometimes successfully outline on close-up mammography intraductal lesions such as papillomas and small occult ductal cancers. Should both the Pap smear of the discharge and the mammograms be negative, further evaluation of the nipple discharge is still necessary.

What then is the treatment for nipple discharge?

Since discharges which are bloody, serosanguinous, or thin and watery can be associated with a malignancy, the treatment of choice is surgical exploration and local excision of the involved duct. In this manner not only is the diagnosis established but if the lesion proves to be benign, treatment would be definitive. Should the lesion be malignant, further treatment would be required.

Are there other types of nipple problems?

Yes. Occasionally there can be infection of the Montgomery glands in the areola and nipple base. These are sebaceous or oil-producing glands which help keep the nipple and areola soft and lubricated. During pregnancy these glands become particularly prominent. When infected they can produce a purulent type of discharge. Closer inspection, however, will reveal that the drainage is not coming from the nipple proper. Local measures usually clear the problem.

Another lesion which requires special attention is Paget's disease of the breast. This is a form of cancer and should be promptly reported. The initial symptoms are burning, itching, and soreness of the nipple. This is gradually followed by repeated fissuring, weeping, oozing, and crust formation of both the nipple and areola. Since the early stages of this disease somewhat resemble eczema, diagnosis is sometimes delayed. Paget's disease of the breast occurs most commonly in postmenopausal women.

In the past few years medical attention has focused on yet another breast condition, galactorrhea, also known as inappropriate lactation. This is the presence of a milky discharge from both nipples in women not recently pregnant. Although this condition is not associated with any disease process directly affecting the breast or nipple, it may represent disturbances in other body systems.

What sorts of disturbances?

All of us are of course familiar with the normal physiological milky discharge following pregnancy. Sometimes, however, the very same milky discharge (termed galactorrhea) can persist for months and years even in the absence of breast feeding or a recent pregnancy. There have been reported cases of such nipple discharge in women who are taking oral contraceptives and on rare occasions even in men.

Among the many conditions associated with this milky discharge are pituitary tumors, endocrine conditions such as hypothyroidism, and the long-term use of certain drugs. The more common drugs linked with galactorrhea are antihypertensives (Reserpine, Aldomet), tricyclic antidepressants (Triavil, Tofranil), and tranquilizers, particularly the phenothiazine derivatives (Thorazine, Compazine, Stelazine, Mellaril, Prolixin, Temaril). In general, discontinuation of these drugs will usually result in resolution of the galactorrhea. Less commonly, galactorrhea has occurred following trauma to the chest wall and also as the result of persistent oral or manual manipulation of the nipples. Sometimes there is simply no known explanation for the milky nipple discharge.

Oftentimes the basic cause of galactorrhea in many of these conditions can be traced to an elevated blood level of the pituitary hormone prolactin. This hormone in turn directly stimulates the mammary glands to produce milk. All of the drugs mentioned above, for example, do cause a moderate increase in the output of the hormone prolactin. When there is an exceptionally high level of this hormone in the blood stream, the secretion of the other pituitary hormones necessary to maintain normal ovarian function, FSH and LH, may be inhibited. So what happens? Women with this problem not only have a persistent milky discharge from the nipples but frequently stop menstruating.

The important issue is not the presence of a milky nipple discharge nor even the absence of periods, but rather what these symptoms may represent. Most seriously, a woman with galactorrhea and amenorrhea (no periods) is at a high risk of having a pituitary tumor (adenoma). This is especially true if there is a very high blood level of the hormone prolactin and a negative history with regard to the use of oral contraceptives and the other aforementioned drugs. Women with galactorrhea but no menstrual difficulties should also be evaluated for the possible presence of a pituitary tumor. Although pituitary adenomas grow slowly and are relatively uncommon, they can, if undiagnosed, ultimately encroach on and destroy the remaining portion of the pituitary gland and cause irreversible loss of vision. In the past, diagnosis of pituitary tumors was rarely made until the individual had been symptomatic for years. Nowadays it is possible by means of new X-ray techniques (polytomography) to identify microadenomas, tumors less than 10 mm. in diameter.

Among women with galactorrhea (with or without amenorrhea), treatment will vary depending upon whether a pituitary adenoma is identified.

What is the treatment for women with galactorrhea and amenorrhea?

In the majority of women with no evidence of pituitary tumor, limited studies have shown that the new drug bromergocryptine will decrease the prolactin levels, correct galactorrhea, and restore ovulatory menses within eight weeks. From all reports this drug is proving to be a safe and effective treatment for this previously difficult and sometimes insoluble problem.

Among women with galactorrhea and amenorrhea as a direct result of a pituitary tumor, treatment must of necessity be individualized. If the pituitary adenoma is very small and there are no other symptoms present, patients may simply be followed. Some tumors can apparently remain small and asymptomatic for twenty to thirty years or even a lifetime. Since it is not possible at the moment to determine which tumors will progress and which tumors will remain relatively stable, many experts feel that long-term follow-up with periodic checks on prolactin levels and other measures of pituitary activity may be adequate in selected patients. However, if there is obvious progression of the tumor with increasing severity of symptoms or if the woman is intensely anxious to have a baby, surgery may be the procedure of choice. Although the operation is not without risk, new microsurgical techniques as well as the transsphenoidal approach to the pituitary (that is, through the sphenoid sinus via an incision between the upper gum line and nasal passageway) now makes it possible to resect these tumors without damaging or destroying normal adjacent pituitary tissue. Removal of the tumor is usually followed by prompt correction of the galactorrhea and restoration of ovulatory menses.

Let us now return to the discussion of breast problems per se and specifically fibrocystic disease.

What is fibrocystic disease of the breast?

A common benign (non-cancerous) condition characterized by the presence of multiple small cysts interspersed with mild fibrous thickening of the breast tissue. The cause of these cysts is not completely understood, but their development does seem to depend upon cyclic estrogen stimulation of the breast tissue. Fibrocystic disease affects well over 30 percent of all women during the reproductive years. However, with decreasing estrogen levels after the menopause, the incidence of this condition drops rapidly.

What kinds of problems does fibrocystic disease cause?

Sometimes none at all. It all depends on the size and number of cysts and how much breast tissue is involved. In many women the cysts may be so small as to go completely unnoticed. However, where several small cysts are clustered together they may become more prominent and quite tender premenstrually because of fluid retention. A larger single cyst in particular may cause more local discomfort because of a rapid distention of its capsule with fluid. In these instances, such a cyst may enlarge noticeably prior to menstruation and shrink with the onset of the period. The fact that these cysts can cause breast tenderness, as well as fluctuate in size depending upon the phase of the menstrual cycle, is an important distinguishing feature of the condition.

Can these cysts ever disappear spontaneously?

Tiny cysts may disappear, but larger ones will frequently persist.

Can anything be done for breast discomfort caused by fibrocystic disease?

When fibrocystic areas become sore, tender, and sensitive to the touch because of premenstrual fluid accumulation, restriction of one's salt intake and sleeping in a good uplift bra during the week before menstruation will definitely help. If symptoms are more severe, ice packs applied to the breasts two or three times a day for five to ten minutes or even diuretics (water pills) when necessary can give additional relief. More recently, the use of the drug Danazol (see Chapter

22) has proved remarkably effective in relieving the distress associated with severe fibrocystic disease in a few selected cases.

If, however, there is one dominant lump or cyst, more definitive treatment is usually necessary.

Why is that?

Needless to say, the presence of any persistent lump or mass, especially if it is solitary, should never be ignored. The lump may feel and act like a benign cyst, but a definite diagnosis cannot be made by palpation alone.

Then too, breast cancer can coexist in the same breast with fibrocystic disease. On occasion a large, single, benign cyst may even overlie a beginning breast cancer, thus obscuring its presence and preventing early detection by palpation. For these reasons it is important to establish a definite diagnosis when dealing with any breast lesion.

How are these benign cysts sometimes treated?

Until recently, surgeons routinely excised any breast lump, cyst, or irregularity to establish a diagnosis. Today the use of needle aspiration (that is, draining the cyst through a small puncture) frequently establishes the diagnosis without the need of resorting to surgery. If the cyst disappears completely following withdrawal of its contained fluid, it was obviously not cancerous and a biopsy is unnecessary. The fact that some women may develop several such cysts during their lifetime makes needle aspiration under these circumstances preferable to repeated excisional biopsies. If, however, the aspirated fluid is cloudy or blood-tinged, or if the cyst remains palpable, further studies including a biopsy are necessary.

Can needle aspiration of breast cysts ever be harmful?

Even if the supposed cyst should prove to be a solid tumor and is diagnosed on subsequent biopsy as breast cancer, an unsuccessful attempt at needle aspiration will not cause malignant cells to spread. Needle aspiration of breast cysts (whether or not totally successful) is a safe office procedure that is being utilized by more and more surgeons.

Suppose the breast lump is solid and not cystic, what then?

Here again, much useful information can be gleaned by physical examination of the breast mass in question. If the lump is firm, well circumscribed, and *freely movable* within the breast tissue somewhat like a marble, chances are excellent that it is probably a fibroadenoma or at least a benign lesion.

What is a fibroadenoma?

A common benign breast tumor usually found in women under thirty-five and not infrequently in teenagers. Most fibroadenomas occur singly and vary in size from one to two inches in diameter. On occasion, however, they can grow larger and even be multiple, but this is rare. Since they are not tender and do not cause symptoms, they are often discovered inadvertently by the woman or else detected on a routine physical examination.

What can be done about a fibroadenoma?

If the nodule is discovered in an adolescent girl, local excision may be postponed until later. Premature removal of such a lump in a teenager could conceivably interfere with the proper development of the breast. If, however, the lump progressively enlarges or is discovered in a teenager with fully developed breasts or in an older woman, most doctors will recommend an excisional biopsy (removal of the entire nodule through a small incision).

Why is removal usually advisable?

Despite the fact that fibroadenomas never become cancerous, there is no way of being 100 percent sure that the lump in question is indeed a fibroadenoma short of actually examining the tissue under a microscope. Deferring surgery or "watchful waiting" could in these instances (and especially if the woman is over twenty-five) be detrimental. More than one cancer has physically masqueraded as a clinically benign lesion.

Nevertheless, there are certain diagnostic techniques that can be extremely helpful in distinguishing between benign and cancerous tumors.

What diagnostic techniques?

Recent refinements in breast X-ray techniques (mammography) and thermography are making the detection of early breast cancers both feasible and practical.

Thermography—what's that?

A simple and rapid method that detects temperature differences within the breast tissue. Malignant tumors, because of accelerated cellular activity, will emit more heat than normal breast tissue. Thus, by means of an infrared scanning apparatus, any subtle changes in heat production within the breast can be localized and visualized on a special screen. Thermography requires no exposure to radiation, is effective regardless of breast size, and is about 80 to 85 percent accurate in detecting cancerous tumors. Its big disadvantage, however, is the fact that hot spots or false positive readings have been reported in 35 percent of the women with benign breast lesions and in 15 percent of the women with normal breasts. Because of this unreliability, thermography as a diagnostic tool has lost favor.

What about the new breast X-ray techniques?

Low-dose mammography is currently the best ancillary method for detecting very early breast cancer. In contrast to older breast X-ray techniques, this new method can pinpoint minute malignant changes with far greater accuracy, speed, and reliability than ever previously imagined. In many instances low-dose mammography has detected cancers prior to their being physically evident. In one particular study in which 132 breast cancers were discovered, forty-four would have been completely missed if mammograms had been omitted. Even more startling is the growing evidence that breast cancers may actually exist for as long as two to eight years before being palpable as a tiny (less than one-half inch) discrete lump or thickening.

How safe are today's mammograms?

There has been a great deal of concern regarding the possible risk of inducing breast cancer by radiation exposure. There is no question that high levels of ionizing radiation can be carcinogenic. But these high degrees of exposure cannot in any way compare to the low levels of radiation employed in breast screening examinations by low-dose mammography. Risk is directly proportional to radiation dose. In the past several years the technique of mammography has undergone many substantial changes and improvements. Only a few years ago a skin exposure dose of 8 to 15 rads was commonplace for mammography. Nowadays it is possible to get a clearer and more detailed X-ray picture with a skin dose of only 0.5 to 0.9 rads per exposure. To translate this into more meaningful terms, this means that if a fifty-year-old woman had a mammogram every year for twenty consecutive years, her risk of breast cancer over those twenty years would be increased from a natural risk of 7.6 percent to perhaps 7.9 percent. In comparison to this almost negligible increase in potential risk for breast cancer, the benefits are considerable. Screening programs have shown that as many as one third of all breast cancers are initially detected by X-ray alone. Moreover, the five-year survival rates in these early minimal cancers exceeds 96 percent.

But as accurate as low-dose mammography can be (close to 90 percent), breast tumors that are palpable on physical examination may on rare occasion go undetected radiographically. Needless to say, if breast cancer is to be diagnosed in its curable stage, reliance must still be placed on regular, meticulous breast examinations, ancillary diagnostic methods (low-dose mammography), plus immediate biopsy of any suspicious area, whether detected by physical examination and/or by mammography.

How common is breast cancer?

Within the next twelve months approximately 35,500 women in this country will die of breast cancer and an estimated 108,000 new cases will be diagnosed. Not only is it the most common malignancy affecting women between the ages of twenty-five and seventy-four, but ultimately one out of every fifteen women in this country will develop breast cancer. From these figures it is obvious that the disease represents a potential threat to every woman.

Yet despite extensive surgical procedures, superrefined radiation therapy, and new wonder drugs, the mortality rate from breast cancer has remained almost unchanged during the past thirty-five years.

Why have all these procedures failed to improve survival rates?

For the simple reason that many cancers when first diagnosed have already spread (metastasized) beyond the confines of local lymph nodes. Although new and sophisticated diagnostic methods can detect distant tumor spread, small metastatic lesions may occasionally be missed. Thus, at the time of initial treatment for the primary breast tumor, clinically unsuspected cancer may already exist elsewhere in the body. Under these circumstances no amount of breast surgery or radiation therapy, regardless of how effective in eradicating the original (primary) tumor, can effect a cure.

How long can a breast cancer remain localized?

Unfortunately there is no way of determining this with any degree of accuracy. Generally speaking—but there are always exceptions—the smaller the tumor the greater the likelihood that the cancer is still confined to the breast proper.

If untreated, however, malignant cells will invariably spread to other parts of the body in time.

Where and how does cancer of the breast spread?

Most breast cancers will initially spread to adjacent lymph nodes, which act as temporary filters or traps for the malignant cells. Exactly where the tumor seeds (spreads) depends in part on its location. Thus, for example, a cancer in the upper outer quadrant of the breast will usually spread to the nearby axillary (underarm) nodes. Tumors situated closer to the nipple or along the inner aspect of the breast tend to involve the nodes lying behind the breast bone (internal mammary lymph nodes). However, owing to the fact that the lymphatic drainage of the breast is such an intricate, interconnecting system of tiny capillarylike channels, tumor cells can seed almost anywhere and at times even spread to the opposite breast and axillary area.

In more advanced cases, malignant tumor cells can spread to the lungs, bone, liver, and other organs.

What, then, is considered an early breast cancer?

A cancer that is potentially curable—that is strictly localized in the breast or else involves only the local lymph nodes of that breast. In other words, all other studies such as chest X-rays, bone surveys (simple X-rays of the bony skeleton), and other available diagnostic methods to detect distant spread should be unequivocally negative.

Theoretically, therefore, with no objective evidence of distant tumor spread (metastasis), surgical removal of the cancerous tissue and/or radiation therapy to destroy the local cancer should be "curative." Needless to say, before any potentially curative treatment is undertaken, tests should be made to determine that the cancer is indeed early and has not spread beyond the confines of the area to be treated.

Are these diagnostic studies to determine distant tumor spread commonly done prior to treatment?

Not always. At times little effort is made to detect distant tumor spread before subjecting a woman to major and extensive breast surgery. That these diagnostic studies should be undertaken whenever radical surgery is contemplated goes without saying. Mastectomy (breast removal) and particularly radical mastectomy is an emotionally and physically devastating experience for any woman. Therefore, if radical surgery in particular is to be done, a woman should be reasonably assured that she has a good chance for potential cure. Prior knowledge that there is distant tumor spread would certainly argue against any extensive radical procedure.

In the past five years, bone scanning techniques (radionuclide imaging) have proved enormously helpful in pinpointing minute tumor invasion of bony structures. Far more accurate than conventional X-ray pictures (bone surveys), these new scanning techniques can detect cancerous changes months before they ever become obvious by ordinary X-ray methods. In fact, as a result of these screening techniques, it is becoming increasingly apparent that metastatic spread to bone in women with a supposed "early cancer" is more common than previously believed.

Perhaps as these newer diagnostic procedures become more generally available in all hospitals and are utilized prior to surgery in any patient when a strong clinical suspicion of cancer exists, the old operating room routine, "If it's cancer, we'll just go ahead and do a radical," will come to an end.

Is there a treatment of choice for early breast cancer?

Until recently the vast majority of early or minimal breast cancers were treated by radical mastectomy. How the individual woman felt about losing her breast, or the possibility of being physically incapacitated because of a swollen arm or weak shoulder, was immaterial. Radical mastectomy as originally devised by Dr. William Halsted in 1882 was for many years universally considered the only medically acceptable and legitimate treatment for early breast cancer.

It was logical to assume that if breast cancers first spread to the adjacent axillary area, then radical mastectomy—that is, the removal of the entire breast, chest wall muscles (pectoralis major and minor muscles), and all axillary lymph nodes—would give a woman the best chance for cure.

In the 1930's, however, with the discovery that a portion of the breast's lymphatic system drains into lymph nodes situated beneath the breast bone (internal mammary nodes), it became apparent that radical mastectomy would fail to cure women surgically if their breast cancer had already spread to these particular nodes. Consequently a few surgeons reasoned that by extending the operation to include removal of the internal mammary lymph nodes, more women would be "cured." But follow-up results from the extended radical mastectomy failed to show any significant improvement in survival rates. With few exceptions this extended and traumatic procedure is rarely done nowadays.

Today, a real controversy exists among surgeons both here and abroad regarding what constitutes the best treatment for early breast cancer. From statistics on survival and recurrence rates among women with supposedly early breast cancer, it is apparent that the conventional radical mastectomy as routinely performed on thousands of women each year leaves much to be desired. Even when one quotes the most favorable statistics for radical mastectomy as performed in the United States, 85 percent of the women with *no* axillary involvement will survive five years, and in ten years, only 70 percent will still be living. Among women with positive axillary nodes at the time of radical mastectomy, the figures drop precipitously to a 60 percent overall five-year survival rate and a 41 percent ten-year survival rate.

It is also important to note that among many women who have had no recurrence of the disease ten years or more following radical mastectomy, the microscopic examination of all tissues removed at the time of surgery failed to show any extension of the malignancy beyond the confines of the primary breast tumor. In other words, all adjacent tissues that were sacrificed during the radical mastectomy in these instances were found to be healthy and free of any cancer cells. For this reason many cancer specialists believe that equally good results in terms of survival rates can be effected by less radical surgery in selected women with a clinically early breast cancer.

What other surgical procedures are some doctors doing for early breast cancer?

Modified radical mastectomy, for one thing. In many centers this lesser procedure is replacing the classical radical mastectomy as the preferred treatment of early breast cancer. The breast, axillary nodes, and pectoralis minor muscle are removed, but the pectoralis major is preserved. By sparing this large chest muscle, shoulder and arm strength remain normal and cosmetic deformity is minimized. In other cases the operation is limited to simple mastectomy (removal of the breast only) or partial mastectomy. With regard to women undergoing partial mastectomy or removal of a portion of one breast including the overlying skin, reconstructive surgery at the time of the operation can minimize the deformity to a certain extent. In a few selected women who are emotionally unprepared to accept any of these procedures, a lumpectomy—that is, an excisional biopsy (removal of the entire breast tumor along with a margin of normal tissue) with follow-up radiation therapy—is being done.

What about survival rates with these lesser procedures?

Reports have been interesting. Among women undergoing a modified radical mastectomy, five- and ten-year survival rates are as good and in some series superior to those achieved by radical mastectomy.

In women with no clinical evidence of axillary node involvement, simple mastectomy (removal of the breast only) and partial mastectomy have effected an 85 percent five-year survival rate.

Simple excision of the breast lump (lumpectomy) followed by radiation therapy has also brought forth startling statistics. In one series conducted in Finland in 1954, the five-year survival rate in 127 patients so treated was 85 percent. Studies reported by the University of Texas M. D. Anderson Hospital and Tumor Institute of Houston showed that in women undergoing local excision and radiation, five-year survival rates ranged from 70 to 50 percent depending upon the absence or presence of clinically evident axillary node involvement. In a more recent report involving 176 women treated with lumpectomy and radiation between 1969 and 1977, results were even more encouraging. Among patients with Stage I breast cancer (negative nodes), there was a 96 percent five-year survival rate. Women with axillary nodal involvement had a 68 percent five-year survival rate. Statistics on ten-year survival rates should soon be forthcoming. According to many experts, radiation therapy with local tumor excision is the most promising alternative to mastectomy in the management of women with early breast cancer. In fact, results in terms of long-term survival may be as good if not better among women treated with lumpectomy and radiation than among those managed with mastectomy or modified radical mastectomy.

And so the controversy of how best to treat early breast cancer continues. Nonetheless, almost all cancer specialists agree that success in terms of curing early breast cancer depends primarily on the extent of the disease at the time of the initial treatment. Some experts even state that once the tumor has extended beyond the breast and local lymph nodes, survival rates are not affected regardless of the local surgical and/or radiation treatment undertaken. In other words, once the cancer has seeded to distant areas in the body, a woman's chance of survival will be essentially the same whether she undergoes a radical mastectomy or a lumpectomy.

How common are recurrences following initial treatment?

Approximately two thirds of all women who are treated for breast cancer will ultimately suffer a recurrence within months to years regardless of initial treatment. The recurrence can be localized to the breast area originally treated or it can involve metastatic tumor in distant organs and tissues. A local chest wall recurrence does not adversely affect survival rates nor does it necessarily mean that there will ultimately be distant spread of the disease. In an effort to control these tumor recurrences as well as to decrease their incidence, other therapies and treatment modalities are being studied. In recent years the use of the estrogen receptor assay test has become increasingly important in helping select treatment programs for women with recurrent disease.

What is the estrogen receptor assay test?

Almost half of all breast cancers are hormone dependent and as such are affected by the *presence or absence* of certain hormones. The estrogen receptor assay test for breast cancer is a method of identifying those cancers which are specifically influenced by estrogen.

The test basically involves exposing a small sample of the cancerous tissue to radioactive estrogen. If the tissue is estrogen dependent, a specific receptor protein located within the cancer cells will bind the radioactive estrogen. A negative test implies the absence of this specific receptor protein. Although an estrogen receptor protein test (ERP) can sometimes be performed on tissue removed from metastatic or recurrent tumor, the vast majority of ERP tests are done on the primary cancer at the time of the initial tissue diagnosis. If a hospital is not equipped to run this elaborate test, the operating surgeon usually makes arrangements to have a tissue sample promptly shipped to a testing center. Test results are then recorded, filed, and kept as a part of the patient's permanent medical record. In the event of recurrent disease appropriate therapy can then be selected on the basis of the ERP results. As of now, other hormones, including progesterone, are being studied for similar receptor protein tests.

The primary value of this test is its usefulness in selecting patients who should benefit most from hormone manipulation in the event of recurrent disease. Of the women with recurrent breast cancer and a positive ERP test, approximately 55 to 65 percent will benefit from hormone manipulation.

What is meant by hormone manipulation?

There are primarily two forms of hormone manipulation in the treatment of recurrent breast cancer: (1) surgical ablation and (2) additive hormone therapy. Surgical ablation is the operative removal of endocrine glands and specifically the ovaries. In some cases this may even involve removal of the adrenal and pituitary gland. Additive hormone therapy is the administration of hormones, usually androgen or estrogens, in very high doses. According to most experts, women who are ERP positive should be offered one of these methods of hormone manipulation at the time of tumor recurrence. The specific therapy selected would largely depend on the hormonal status of the woman. Premenopausal women or women within two years of the menopause who are ERP positive would probably undergo oophorectomy, removal of the ovaries. A favorable response to this procedure would be the objective regression of the tumor with subjective improvement of symptoms lasting a minimum of six months. Women who have had a favorable response to oophorectomy may subsequently also do well with antiestrogen medication such as Tamoxifen. If a woman is five or more years past the menopause and ERP positive, the treatment of choice would most likely be either androgen or an oral estrogen. As contradictory as this may seem, high doses of estrogen in older postmenopausal women can cause regression of their breast cancer. Subsequent therapy if any would of course depend on the length and degree of response.

Among women with recurrent breast cancer and a negative ERP test, hormonal therapy would probably be bypassed in favor of chemotherapy or other treatment.

What is chemotherapy?

By strict definition, chemotherapy is the treatment of any medical condition by means of drugs. In practice, it is the treatment of malignant disease by anti-cancer drugs. These drugs are given either to achieve cure or to control the spread of the tumor. All of these drugs are cytotoxic agents or cellular poisons. They destroy cells by interfering with their metabolism and reproduction. Since cancer cells have increased metabolic rates and multiply more rapidly than normal cells, they are more susceptible to these toxic agents. But none of these drugs is selectively lethal to cancer cells. They can also destroy and injure normal cells. In addition, the therapeutic range of these drugs is very close to the toxic range. This means that the margin of safety between just the right amount of drug and a little bit too much drug is very narrow.

Particularly susceptible to injury from cytotoxic drugs are such tissues as bone marrow, blood-forming elements, the gastrointestinal tract, and the oral mucosa. Thus, the development of profound anemia and the suppression of platelets and white blood cell production sometimes make it necessary to discontinue a drug. Other common side effects associated with some of the cytotoxic agents are nausea, vomiting, loss of appetite, hair loss, skin eruptions, and ulceration of the oral mucosa. Although most of these side effects are predictable and to a certain extent controllable, all patients on chemotherapy must be closely monitored, have frequent blood counts, and physical examinations with strict regulation of dosage and timing of drug therapy.

There is no question that chemotherapy can be extremely difficult for the individual patient, but in many instances it can offer long-term disease control and perhaps even cure. Combination drug therapy, that is, the use of two or more drugs, rather than single drug therapy seems to be consistently more effective in this regard.

Is chemotherapy ever used in the early treatment of breast cancer?

In some cases combination drug chemotherapy is also given immediately following mastectomy to women who have positive lymph nodes or are otherwise considered at high risk for recurrence. The rationale for this therapy (termed adjuvant chemotherapy) is that minimal residual disease remaining after surgery may later account for the subsequent development of metastasis. Thus, if chemotherapy can eliminate or destroy tiny nests of malignant cells before they spread and develop elsewhere, the chances for a longer recurrence-free period or perhaps even an ultimate cure are improved. To date such therapy has proven beneficial among selected premenopausal women. Postmenopausal women so treated, however, have not shown any significant lengthening of recurrent-free intervals as compared to postmenopausal women in the control group not given chemotherapy.

Can other factors affect survival rates in breast cancer?

It can never be stressed too strongly that the earlier a breast cancer is detected and treated, the better the chance for cure. And yet, there are so many variables in breast cancer that regardless of the local extent of the disease at the time of diagnosis, no one can predict with any accuracy the eventual outcome for the individual woman. Factors such as size and location of the tumor as well as axillary node involvement have, of course, important prognostic implications. Then too, breast cancers also differ in type and degree of malignancy. A large bulky tumor, for example, may have a very low potential for early spread, whereas a lump that is barely palpable may on rare occasions have already seeded beyond the confines of the local lymph nodes. Moreover, in some women the breast cancer may be multicentric. This means that in addition to the obvious tumor, there may be small nests of malignant cells elsewhere in the breast which can neither be felt nor seen by X-ray. In such a case, simple excision of the dominant lump would obviously fail to effect a surgical cure.

Perhaps of even greater significance in terms of patient survival is the body's immune system, that is, its inherent ability to fight malignant disease and foreign invaders. Although this is one of the most difficult variables to assess clinically, a functioning immune system may well make the difference between cure or failure in women undergoing identical treatment for identical tumors. Furthermore, certain breast cancers because of hormonal stimulation (estrogen in particular) may grow more rapidly. Other breast malignancies exposed to the same hormonal influence may be totally unaffected or even tend to remain in check. Age as well as general health of the woman will also affect the ultimate survival rate.

Aside from these physical and biological variables (of which only a few have been mentioned), there is growing awareness that a woman's psychological and mental attitude toward her illness plays a significant role in the eventual outcome. In ways as yet unknown, attitudes of despair and hopelessness do lessen the body's resistance to malignant disease. On the other hand, there are many documented instances where a positive and optimistic mental outlook and a strong will to live have worked seeming miracles in women who by all objective medical findings had little or no hope left.

Does anyone know what actually causes breast cancer?

Unfortunately no—at least not yet. Nonetheless, there is increasing evidence to indicate that breast cancer may be caused by a particular virus particle. How this virus is acquired or transmitted or if, indeed, a virus is responsible for the various types of breast cancers— these are all matters currently under intensive clinical and research investigation. Much of this evidence is, of course, based on animal studies. Interestingly enough, the same virus particles capable of inducing mammary cancer in mice have been recovered in the breast tissue of some women with proved breast cancer. Moreover, these very same virus particles in a few instances have also been recovered in the milk of lactating women with no evidence of breast cancer. The question is therefore being raised—could transmission of these virus particles during breast feeding account for the subsequent development of breast cancer among female offspring as in the case of laboratory mice? This fact has led some investigators to caution women who have these particular virus particles in their milk against breast feeding female offspring. As of now, however, so few facilities are available for testing human breast milk in this regard that some doctors are simply advising against the breast feeding of any female offspring where there is a family history on either side of breast cancer.

With regard to genetic and hormonal factors that may conceivably play a role in the development of breast cancer, much has yet to be learned. Currently there is no way of accurately pinpointing the woman destined to develop breast cancer. Nonetheless, breast cancer does seem somewhat more prevalent among certain women as compared to others.

Which woman is statistically most likely to develop breast cancer?

The woman most likely to develop breast cancer is Caucasian, between thirty-five and sixty-five, with few or no children, or has postponed pregnancy until after the age of twenty-eight. In addition she probably began menstruating at a relatively early age and possibly had previous breast problems such as fibrocystic disease. With regard to family history, having a mother or sister with breast cancer increases a woman's risk of this disease two or three times over that observed in the general female population.

It should be emphasized, however, that the above profile is at best only a general guide. No woman is immune to breast cancer. But by the same token, fulfilling all of the aforementioned criteria does not imply that a woman is destined to develop this malignancy. Suffice it to say, if survival rates for breast cancer are going to improve, all women should be aware of how best to protect themselves.

How can you as a woman protect yourself against breast cancer?

You must take an active role in your own well-being and not rely entirely on periodic examinations by your doctor. Specifically this means at the very least monthly examinations. With rare exceptions, almost all early breast cancers are completely painless. Therefore, unless you conscientiously examine yourself regularly, the presence of a breast malignancy may go undetected. Equally important, you should promptly report any lump, thickening, or irregularity regardless of how vague or indefinite it may seem to you. Do not wait to see if it enlarges.

Furthermore, any discharge from the nipple other than milk in a woman who has recently delivered is not normal, particularly if only one nipple is involved. Any persistent burning and itching of the nipple or local skin changes involving the nipple area, such as redness, flaking, weeping eruptions, and crust or scab formation, can also be warning signs of an early breast cancer. With regard to other skin changes, any dimpling, puckering, or reddening over any portion of either breast also demands prompt professional attention.

As of now, breast cancer is not only the leading cause of death from cancer among women, but also the most common cause of death among American women between the ages of forty and forty-four.

Considering this fact, it would be ideal if every woman between the ages of thirty-five and forty had at least a base-line low-dose mammogram. For women over forty a low-dose mammogram every three to four years or more frequently if indicated would undoubtedly also save many lives by detecting minimal breast cancers prior to their being physically palpable.

However, short of such mass screening which in itself would require a prodigious expansion of existing facilities, periodic mammography is definitely advisable in certain women.

Are you a candidate for periodic screening by mammography?

Regardless of how normal your breasts may feel on physical examination any one of the following is a valid indication for your doctor to recommend mammography.

1. A family history of breast cancer, particularly if it involves a close relative such as a mother or sister.

2. Previous problems with fibrocystic disease of the breast. Although opinion is still divided about whether or not women with this condition run a higher risk of developing breast cancer, fibrocystic disease is frequently responsible for vague nodularities throughout both breasts. At best these kind of "lumpy-bumpy" breasts are difficult to evaluate properly. Then too, as previously mentioned, benign cystic areas can occasionally overlie and thus obscure an early breast cancer.

3. In women whose breasts are unusually large or heavy, screening by mammography would give further assurance that all is well. Despite a meticulous physical examination, a tiny breast lump that would otherwise be detected on a smaller-breasted woman may be inadvertently missed.

4. For women who just worry about breast cancer on general principles. Sometimes a negative breast X-ray report can be more comforting than a negative physical examination by the most competent of doctors.

If, however, there is any vague or questionable breast irregularity, mammography in many instances can be helpful in determining whether a biopsy is necessary.

Suppose you have an obvious breast lump; is mammography still worthwhile?

Absolutely. Even if your breast lump feels benign on palpation, presumptive confirmation of its non-cancerous nature by mammography prior to definitive diagnosis by biopsy would certainly be advantageous. When you consider that three out of every four breast lumps are benign, it means that approximately 250,000 women admitted to the hospital for breast surgery each year must endure the mental torments of uncertainty while awaiting the final tissue report. Surely, preoperative breast X-rays could minimize this unnecessary anxiety in many women. And in some women, preoperative mammography has also proved invaluable by alerting the surgeon to a previously unsuspected but suspicious-looking lesion elsewhere in the breast.

Should your doctor clinically suspect a breast cancer, all the more reason for mammography. Under these circumstances, presumptive X-ray evidence of a probable malignancy would afford him the opportunity to order other screening tests he deems necessary to evaluate the situation thoroughly as well as to determine the possible extent of the disease. Thus, by having this information beforehand, all the facts could be presented to you. In this manner you could discuss alternate treatment possibilities more rationally with your doctor if the biopsy should prove confirmatory.

If you have early breast cancer, can you have a choice of treatment?

There is little doubt that if the five- and ten-year survival rates for radical mastectomy were invariably superior to those obtained by lesser surgical procedures, there would be no present controversy over treatment of early breast cancer. As it is, no surgical procedure and/or radiation therapy can guarantee any woman a 100 percent cure regardless of how minimal her disease. At best, all therapy currently available for early breast cancer carries with it some risk of ultimately being ineffective. Thus, for all practical purposes, nobody really knows, nor can anyone predict which treatment (whether it be radical mastectomy or a procedure as minimal as excisional biopsy) will or will not prove "curative" for the individual woman with early breast cancer.

There are some surgeons who still insist that radical mastectomy is the preferred treatment. Other surgeons, and they are becoming increasingly more numerous, favor modified radical mastectomy and in some women simple or even partial mastectomy. Excisional biopsy followed by radiation therapy is also proving to be a medically valid option. But regardless of what your own doctor believes would be the best treatment for your particular situation, you and only you have the final say. No surgeon can perform any procedure without your express, written consent. If you are mentally and emotionally unprepared to undergo extensive breast surgery and are willing to accept the greater risk that some experts believe these less radical procedures may carry, then that is your right as an individual to decide.

In recent years, women with early breast cancer have also been given another option—reconstructive breast surgery.

What is reconstructive breast surgery?

It is the rebuilding of a new breast following mastectomy. The rationale for this surgery is to minimize disfigurement and restore a more natural physical appearance to the chest wall. Perhaps even more important, reconstructive surgery helps the individual woman achieve a better psychological and emotional adjustment to her disease. Although to date relatively few women have undergone such surgery following mastectomy, the trend is growing, particularly among younger women.

How extensive is reconstructive surgery and which women are eligible?

Ideally, reconstructive breast surgery should be reserved for the woman whose disease has the most favorable prognosis. This would include women who are considered disease-free following treatment or women with no evidence of axillary node involvement or distant tumor spread. In some cases it could also include women with positive axillary nodes but in these instances most doctors would prefer a five-year waiting period to determine the success of the original treatment.

Currently the most common type of breast reconstructive surgery is a one-stage operation involving the insertion of a silastic implant (silicone prosthesis). Women who have had a simple mastectomy or a modified radical mastectomy make the best candidates for this particular procedure. Both operations spare the pectoralis major muscle and thus provide an adequate soft tissue covering for the implant. In fact most surgeons do prefer to insert the prosthesis beneath the pectoralis muscle whenever possible. This achieves a better breast contour and also reduces the risk of postoperative complications.

Acceptable cosmetic results can be further enhanced if preparations for reconstruction are done at the time of the original cancer surgery. One example of such prior preparation could be the preservation of the nipple and areola from the involved breast. If, for example, the location of the cancerous breast tumor was fairly remote from the nipple and areola area, the surgeon could spare these structures and temporarily graft them onto the abdominal wall. Then, at the time of breast reconstruction, the nipple and areola could be regrafted onto the dome of the new breast. In cases where the nipple and areola could not be salvaged the surgeon could elect to take a piece of areola from the normal breast and construct a new nipple. It is also possible to fashion a new nipple and areola by taking a graft of pigmented skin from the vulva, most commonly the labia minora. Needless to say, nipple sensation following any of these grafting procedures would be impaired. During the original cancer surgery the surgeon could also facilitate future reconstruction by preparing the tissue bed for the later reception of the silastic prosthesis. The insertion of such a prosthesis does not stimulate dormant cancer cells should they be present, nor does it prevent the prompt identification of any local tumor recurrence.

Is reconstructive surgery possible in women who have had a classical radical mastectomy?

Yes, but in these cases the procedure is somewhat more complicated. The basic problem is lack of sufficient tissue to cover adequately a breast prosthesis. Following a classical radical mastectomy there is usually only a thin, taut layer of skin overlying the ribs. It is therefore necessary to add tissue to the chest wall and this means grafting. In the not-too-distant past tissue grafts were obtained from the upper thigh or abdomen. Sometimes as many as two and even three different surgical procedures were required to complete the breast reconstruction. Nowadays the procedure of choice is a one-step operation in which a combination muscle-and-skin flap is taken from the latissimus dorsi area of the back. The latissimus dorsi is the large triangular muscle which covers the lumbar and flank areas on either side. This flap, which is composed of an island of skin on a muscle pedicle (stalk), is then tunneled under the armpit to the front and used to replace the missing skin and underlying tissues removed at the time of the original cancer surgery. Since it is a pedicle graft and not a free graft (no attachment) the blood circulation to the tissue is not impaired and good healing results. The only evidence on the back is the incision (which can be hidden by a bra) and a slight depression of the area. During the same operation a breast implant can be inserted beneath the muscle-skin flap and a new nipple (if so desired) electively reconstructed. Complete nipple reconstruction, however, usually requires a second operation. Among women who have had such reconstructive surgery, cosmetic results have been gratifying.

How soon after mastectomy can reconstructive surgery be performed?

Most surgeons prefer to wait at least three and usually six months following mastectomy. This allows ample time for complete wound healing and softening of the surrounding tissues. Women who may have had a mastectomy several years before are also eligible. Among women receiving radiation therapy, surgery is usually postponed for at least six weeks to three months following the last treatment.

Should the normal and uninvolved breast be considerably larger than the newly formed breast, as it may, some surgeons advise altering the normal side using either a reduction mammoplasty or even a subcutaneous mastectomy with insertion of a silastic implant. A subcutaneous mastectomy is the removal of all the glandular breast tissue while preserving the skin, nipple, and areola. Here too, nipple sensation may be reduced. The fact that there is an increased risk for cancer in the opposite breast makes subcutaneous mastectomy a reasonable approach when there is considerable discrepancy in sizes between the breasts.

In summary, the last few years have seen not only a great improvement in screening methods for the early detection of breast cancer, but also changing attitudes with emphasis on more conservative surgical procedures. In the past, far too many women delayed seeking medical attention for a potentially early and curable breast cancer out of fear and dread that their only option was radical mastectomy. Today, there are more viable treatment options available to both the doctor and patient. Moreover, breast reconstructive surgery following mastectomy has added another dimension to the treatment of this disease. It must be kept in mind that in the final analysis, the ideal treatment of breast cancer for the individual woman is both the eradication of the physical disease and the preservation of a life that she deems worth living.

25. Biological Breakdown— Cancer of the Female Pelvic Organs

No organ in the human body is immune to malignant changes. Each year approximately 75,000 women in the United States develop a cancer of the female pelvic organs. But whether that malignancy involves the cervix, uterus, ovary, tube, vagina, or vulva, cancer is curable and there are thousands of women who can personally testify to that fact.

With the fantastic strides being made in cancer research, more has been learned about the cause, treatment, and prevention of cancer since 1970 than in the previous five decades. Experts now predict that within our lifetime the mystery of how and why perfectly normal cells become cancerous will be uncovered. Already there is mounting evidence that viruses are implicated in many of the one hundred different types of cancers known to afflict humans, and the same may be true for cancer of the cervix, the most common pelvic malignancy.

Within the next twelve months approximately 7,400 American women will die of cervical cancer and an estimated 16,000 new cases of invasive cervical cancer will be diagnosed. Since the cervix is so accessible to examination and the Pap smear such a simple and effective method of detecting cervical cancer, it is indeed tragic that any woman need die of this disease. All too often, reluctance to be examined and the mistaken notion that lack of symptoms means being free from cancer are common stumbling blocks to early detection. Today, only five women out of every ten in this country have routine Pap smears. Ironically enough, the woman most likely to develop cervical cancer is also the one most apt to avoid periodic examinations even when freely offered.

Which women are most likely to develop cervical cancer?

Cancer of the cervix may one day be considered a venereal disease. As shocking as this statement may be, it is an undeniable fact that sexual intercourse is somehow involved in the development of cervical cancer. Although proof is still lacking, cancer of the cervix may be caused by a sexually transmitted virus (herpes simplex virus type II). The fact that women with high blood antibody levels to type II herpesvirus do have a greater incidence of cervical cancer as compared to other women lends support to this current theory. (See Chapter 12.) Whether or not a virus is ultimately proved responsible, studies have repeatedly shown that the younger a woman is at the time of her first intercourse and the more active her sex life, the greater her chances of developing cancer of the cervix—and of developing it at an early age. The teenager, for example, who begins having frequent intercourse at the age of fifteen or sixteen and especially with multiple partners runs a significantly higher risk of developing cancer within twenty to twenty-five years. On the other hand, a woman who delays her first coitus until after age twenty and limits herself to one partner considerably lessens her risks of ever acquiring the disease. Although no woman is immune, cervical cancer is virtually never seen in nuns or other celibate or homosexual women.

How common is cancer of the cervix?

Currently only 2 to 3 percent of all women develop cancer of the cervix, and most cases are diagnosed between the ages of twenty-five and fifty-five. But despite the fact that improved techniques for detection and treatment are saving more lives, the overall incidence of cervical cancer is steadily increasing. In 1979 there were approximately 45,000 cases of preinvasive cervical cancer diagnosed. It is also predicted that within the next few years, early cervical cancer will be seen more frequently among younger women.

Why the predicted increase in younger women?

For several reasons. Since an early and active sex life significantly adds to a woman's chances of ultimately developing cervical cancer, increasing numbers of young women are unwittingly placing themselves in this high-risk category. There's no denying that sexual activity among teenagers and young women is definitely on the upswing. In addition, the use of the pill, while allowing even greater sexual freedom, is also eliminating the use of the condom and diaphragm as contraceptive methods. Although difficult to prove conclusively, if the cervix is protected from direct contact during sexual intercourse by either a condom or diaphragm, the risk of cervical cancer may be lessened.

Then too, as more doctors are routinely taking Pap smears on younger women, more early cancers are being detected. Perhaps even more significant are the large numbers of premalignant or pre-cancerous cervical lesions (cervical dysplasia) being diagnosed among women in their teens and twenties.

What is cervical dysplasia?

A condition of abnormal cellular differentiation involving the surface cells of the cervix. Cervical dysplasia is further subdivided into mild, moderate, and severe depending upon the extent of the cellular changes. Although the condition is benign, it can (if untreated) gradually progress to become an early cancer of the cervix. A woman with severe cervical dysplasia will frequently have a Class III Pap smear. (See Chapter 5.)

What exactly is an early cervical cancer?

A malignancy involving only the most superficial cells of the cervix without any invasion of the deeper tissues. The malignant changes in early (preinvasive) cervical cancer (also known as Stage 0, or carcinoma-in-situ) are so discrete and localized as to be invisible to the naked eye. Consequently the cervix can appear perfectly normal. Equally important, early cervical cancer does not give any warning signs or symptoms. Detection therefore depends upon the microscopic examination of cervical cells by means of a Pap smear. With proper treatment, cure rates in early cervical cancer can be virtually 100 percent.

If the cancer remains undiagnosed during this early phase, the malignant cells will gradually invade the deeper layers of the cervix (Stage I). In some women this may be a fairly slow process perhaps taking as long as two to ten years or even longer. Less commonly, an early cancer can become invasive within twenty-four months.

What are the symptoms of a more advanced cervical cancer?

Although cervical cancer does not have any characteristic symptoms, irregular bleeding as well as spotting after intercourse or douching are among the most common complaints. Not infrequently, infection of the growing cervical tumor can also produce an intermittent foul-smelling, blood-tinged vaginal discharge. Proper treatment at this stage can still save four out of five women.

If the cancer remains undiagnosed, it eventually spreads beyond the confines of the cervix to other pelvic organs. Ultimately the vagina, the body of the uterus, the bladder, and even the rectum can be invaded. As you can well imagine, the cure rate for these late stages drops precipitously, with the mortality rate well over 50 percent.

Unlike the early stages of the disease, advanced cervical cancer usually progresses fairly rapidly. Thus the time between the onset of symptoms (irregular bleeding, etc.) and the terminal stage of the disease is frequently not longer than two or three years if left untreated.

How is cancer of the cervix diagnosed?

Where symptoms are absent and the cervix appears normal, a Pap smear will alert your doctor to a possible early cervical cancer. Nonetheless, whenever a Pap smear is reported as abnormal or even positive for malignant cells, other studies are necessary to confirm the existence of cancer. As discussed in Chapter 5, a Pap smear of and by itself does not prove or disprove the presence of cancer. Final confirmation depends entirely on a biopsy.

What is a biopsy?

The surgical removal of tissue for microscopic examination and diagnosis. If there is an obvious ulcer, sore, or other suspicious area on the cervix, a portion of tissue (biopsy) from that area is removed for microscopic examination. In cases where the cervix looks perfectly normal, staining it with an iodine solution can help outline areas of abnormal cells. Normal cells because of their glycogen content will stain a dark mahogany brown whereas abnormal cells, which lack this carbohydrate substance, will not pick up the stain. Non-staining areas can then be biopsied.

The colposcope has also been helpful in outlining abnormal areas for biopsy in an otherwise normal-appearing cervix. The colposcope is essentially a low-power microscope that stereoscopically magnifies the surface of the cervix. With this instrument, abnormal areas previously undetected can frequently be pinpointed and selectively biopsied without damaging surrounding normal tissue. Such tissue or "punch" biopsies can sometimes be performed in the doctor's office. Among young women with premalignant conditions of the cervix (dysplasia) as well as preinvasive cancer of the cervix, the use of the colposcope has sometimes eliminated the need for more extensive tissue biopsies.

At other times, however, hospitalization for a cone biopsy of the cervix is still necessary to establish a definite diagnosis.

What is a cone biopsy of the cervix?

A cone biopsy of the cervix is the removal of a cone-shaped section of cervix for microscopic examination. It includes tissues from the surface of the cervix and from the inside of the endocervical canal. It is a hospital procedure and requires anesthesia. Because the amount of tissue removed is relatively large compared to that removed by "punch" biopsies, healing time may take up to six weeks. In selected cases a cone biopsy may constitute treatment for an early cancer of the cervix.

What happens if the biopsy is positive for cervical cancer?

Definitive treatment depends on several factors: the extent of the disease, the age of the woman, her general health, and her desire for pregnancy. If the cancer is Stage 0 or still limited to the surface of the cervix, the treatment of choice in most cases is complete hysterectomy, that is, removal of the cervix and uterus only. Cancer of the cervix does not spread to the ovaries nor does estrogen exert any adverse effect upon cervical cancer. For this reason the ovaries need not be removed. It also means that in later years estrogen therapy for menopausal symptoms can be given if necessary to women previously treated for cervical cancer. Hysterectomy when performed for Stage 0 cancer has a cure rate of almost 100 percent.

Is hysterectomy always necessary when dealing with an early cervical cancer?

No, not always. Not too long ago preinvasive cervical cancer was usually diagnosed in relatively older women (over thirty-seven). Nowadays the majority of women with preinvasive cancer and dysplasia of the cervix are under thirty. These abnormal cervical changes are also being seen among teenagers with greater frequency. Since these women are young and deeply concerned about preserving their childbearing function, alternate treatments are becoming more commonplace. Cone biopsy of the cervix (as previously discussed) can be definitive treatment for preinvasive cancer provided, of course, that the edges of the tissue specimen removed are cancer-free. This would imply that the excised segment of tissue had been ample enough not only to remove all the malignant cells but a margin of normal tissue as well.

More recently, cryosurgery has emerged as a promising new treatment for preinvasive cancer. Since cryosurgery is also being used with increasing frequency in the treatment of benign cervical conditions as well as dysplasia, a few more details are in order.

What is cryosurgery?

Cryosurgery is the destruction of abnormal tissue by the application of extreme cold. It is an office procedure and does not require anesthesia. The equipment looks somewhat like a ray gun fitted with a probe and a small metal tip through which a coolant flows. The metal tip is placed firmly against the abnormal tissue and the coolant (usually carbon dioxide or nitrous oxide) is allowed to circulate through the apparatus. Within a matter of seconds the temperature of the metal tip drops to sub-zero readings and literally freezes the tissue in contact with and immediately adjacent to it. Such rapid freezing of the cellular protein destroys the abnormal cells and tissue. The process is then repeated until all the abnormal areas have been treated. An entire cervix (if need be) can be covered within a few minutes. Cramping may sometimes be noticed but otherwise the procedure is relatively painless. Cold in itself is a good anesthetic agent. For two to three weeks following cryosurgery there will be a profuse watery vaginal discharge caused by the sloughing of the devitalized cervical tissue. Afterwards, normal cervical tissue rapidly regenerates and within six to eight weeks healing is usually complete. Post-freeze complications are minimal with little or no bleeding and scarring. Among women so treated, fertility has not been affected. Cryosurgery, however, does have its limitations. Its use is primarily reserved for those cases where the lesion (as proven by biopsy) does not involve the cervical canal but rather is confined to the exterior surface of the cervix. Under these conditions the entire lesion can then be treated under direct vision.

As an aside, investigative work is now being directed toward the use of the CO_2 laser as a possible alternative to cryosurgery.

What kind of follow-up is necessary after treatment for early cervical cancer?

Regardless of treatment, there is always the possibility of recurrence. Although this risk is minimal among women treated by hysterectomy, regular pelvic examinations and Pap smears of the upper vagina are still necessary. Women who have been treated with a cone biopsy or cryosurgery have an estimated 5 to 10 percent chance of recurrence. Repeat Pap smears and pelvic examinations should be conducted every three months during the first year and at least every four to six months thereafter. Not uncommonly, women who have had these lesser procedures will later elect to have a hysterectomy after their family is completed.

How are more advanced cancers of the cervix treated?

If the cancer is still limited to the cervix but has invaded the deeper cervical tissues (Stage 1), there is always the possibility that some tumor cells may have already spread to adjacent pelvic lymph nodes. Treatment of the disease in this stage is usually by radiation therapy or, less commonly, by extensive surgery, including removal of pelvic lymph nodes. Although there are advantages and disadvantages to both treatments, therapy must always be individualized. Whichever the treatment, the chances for cure run 75 to 85 percent.

With rare exception, more advanced cancers that extend beyond the limits of the cervix are always treated by radiation therapy.

What about cancer of the uterus (endometrial cancer)?

Despite the fact that the uterus can be the site of various rare malignant tumors, cancer of the uterus commonly means a malignancy involving the lining of the uterine cavity; hence the name, endometrial cancer.

After cervical cancer endometrial cancer, although very different, is the second most common pelvic malignancy, accounting for approximately 38,000 new cancer cases per year and 3,200 deaths annually.

How does uterine cancer differ from cervical cancer?

In many ways. Symptoms appear early. Growth and spread of the cancer is somewhat slower in advanced stages, and for this reason five-year survival rates are appreciably better than in cervical cancer. All in all, uterine cancer is less treacherous than cervical cancer. As favorable as these facts may be, however, early detection of endometrial cancer by a Pap smear is notoriously unreliable. Furthermore, the fact that this malignancy arises within the uterine cavity also makes it impossible either to see or feel on routine pelvic examination. For these reasons more sophisticated detection methods are necessary.

In addition, endometrial, unlike cervical, cancer does not seem related to previous sexual activity. Although the cause of endometrial cancer is still elusive, certain women seem more predisposed to its ultimate development.

Which women are more susceptible to endometrial cancer?

The women most apt to develop endometrial cancer are usually over fifty, are more likely to have had previously irregular periods, sporadic ovulation, difficulty in becoming pregnant, and infertility problems as a result of the Stein Levinthal syndrome. (See Chapter 10.) Equally interesting is the finding that obesity, high blood pressure, and diabetes are also more common in women with endometrial cancer. Exactly why this should be is not known. Nevertheless, this particular combination of medical problems coupled with a history of menstrual irregularities and infertility has led experts to believe that endometrial cancer may be linked to some basic genetic and metabolic disturbance. Increasing evidence also indicates that the uterine lining in such women may be hypersensitive to the effects of estrogen. For example, women who develop endometrial hyperplasia, endometrial polyps, or other benign growths of the uterine lining also run a higher risk of ultimately developing cancer of the endometrium. More recently the long-term use of estrogen in the treatment of menopausal symptoms has been linked with endometrial cancer.

It should be stressed, however, that endometrial cancer does not develop overnight from a normal endometrium. There are premalignant tissue changes which in themselves usually cause early symptoms. These tissue changes range from cystic endometrial hyperplasia to more severe degrees of hyperplasia.

What is meant by hyperplasia?

Hyperplasia is a general term which simply means overgrowth and overactivity of a tissue or organ. Although such activity is never normal there are stages or degrees of hyperplasia. With regard to the tissue lining the uterine cavity (endometrial tissue), the most benign degree of hyperplasia is cystic hyperplasia. Cystic hyperplasia is least likely to progress to endometrial cancer. More serious degrees of overactivity include adenomatous hyperplasia and, in particular, atypical adenomatous hyperplasia. Most doctors consider atypical adenomatous hyperplasia to be a form of very early endometrial cancer. Among women with adenomatous hyperplasia (without atypia), approximately 10 to 30 percent will subsequently develop endometrial cancer unless treated.

Since the most common symptom of endometrial hyperplasia is abnormal bleeding, the diagnosis is usually made at the time of a D and C (dilatation and curettage). In many women, treatment with a progestogen such as Provera for three to six months can reverse most degrees of hyperplasia to normal endometrium. Following treatment, however, another D and C or at the very least an endometrial biopsy would be necessary to make certain that the hyperplasia was no longer present. Persistence of the hyperplasia after treatment would signify a more ominous type of tissue activity. In these cases, hysterectomy might be advisable.

Can hyperplasia and endometrial cancer cause the same symptoms?

Yes, and in older women the most common symptom is spotting or bleeding after the menopause. Approximately 40 percent of women who bleed or spot after cessation of all menstruation will be found to have an early uterine cancer. The bleeding need not be heavy. It may be nothing more than an occasional pink or tan stain on the toilet paper noticed after voiding. In any event, no postmenopausal bleeding regardless of how minimal or how infrequent should ever be ignored. This is particularly true if the bleeding appears more than twelve months after the last period.

In women who are still menstruating, grossly irregular periods and/or bleeding or spotting between periods may be the first indication that all is not well. Particularly among women in their forties, excessively long, heavy, or frequent bleeding episodes can represent premalignant changes (such as adenomatous hyperplasia). Since 25 percent of all endometrial cancers occur in *pre*menopausal women it would be foolish to assume that all menstrual irregularities are the result of benign or hormonal problems.

How can your doctor diagnose endometrial cancer?

Since virtually all early endometrial cancers will cause abnormal uterine bleeding in some form, it is imperative to report any unusual bleeding promptly. Armed with this information, your doctor can proceed accordingly. As previously mentioned, Pap smears are not reliable in detecting an early uterine cancer. More often than not, malignant cells from the uterine lining may not be shed into the upper vagina. Detection of both endometrial cancer and premalignant tissue changes depends on sampling tissue from the uterine lining.

Your doctor will probably use one of three office procedures for this purpose: endometrial biopsy, endometrial aspiration, or mini-suction curettage. In taking an endometrial biopsy a small curette is inserted through the cervical canal and a strip of endometrial tissue is removed for microscopic examination. Endometrial aspiration involves flushing out the uterine cavity with a sterile solution and then aspirating the fluid and discarded cells into a special container. The material collected is then examined for malignant cells. Mini-suction curettage removes tissue from the uterine lining by gentle suction. All these procedures, however, are merely screening techniques. It is still possible to miss an early endometrial cancer with any of these methods. For this reason, and especially if there is a strong suspicion that endometrial cancer may exist, a D and C is necessary. Only by removing tissue from the entire uterine lining can an accurate diagnosis be established.

How is cancer of the uterus treated?

Here again, definitive treatment depends upon the extent of the disease and the woman's general physical condition. Usually the treatment is primarily surgical with various combinations of radiation therapy given either before or after surgery, depending upon the circumstances. Surgery for endometrial cancer means removal of the uterus and cervix (complete hysterectomy) as well as both tubes and ovaries (salpingo-oophorectomy). The possibility of hidden tumor cells around the ovaries and the fact that estrogen can stimulate dormant endometrial cancer cells make removal of the ovaries necessary. Estrogen replacement therapy in women previously treated for endometrial cancer is therefore not recommended. Nevertheless, if the cancer was very early, well confined, and believed to have been completely removed, estrogen in judicious doses has occasionally been prescribed by some doctors to control severe menopausal symptoms in younger women.

Interestingly enough, some advanced cancers of the uterus have shown remarkable regression as a result of large doses of a synthetic progesteronelike hormone.

Are there other types of uterine malignancy besides endometrial cancer?

Yes. There are various rare uterine cancers including sarcoma of the wall of the uterus and sarcoma of the uterine lining. A malignancy (leiomyosarcoma) can also arise within a fibroid tumor of the uterus.

Unlike cancers which tend to spread by lymphatic channels, these sarcomas usually invade blood vessels at an early stage with rapid spread to the lungs and other distant organs. For this reason prognosis in these cases is generally poor.

Choriocarcinoma is another rare and highly malignant tumor which may develop following a molar pregnancy (hydatidiform mole). This is an abnormal pregnancy wherein the embryo dies but the placental tissue (synctial trophoblast) undergoes malignant changes. Less commonly, a choriocarcinoma can occur following an abortion or even a normal pregnancy. The tumor usually begins within the muscular wall of the uterus and rapidly metastasizes to other organs. In the past 85 percent of women who had this disease died within one year in spite of treatment. Nowadays, various combinations of drugs (chemotherapy) can completely cure this malignancy in the majority of cases.

What about cancer of the ovary?

Despite the fact that ovarian cancer is far less prevalent than either cervical or endometrial cancer, it is responsible for more deaths than any other pelvic malignancy. In the past year, approximately 17,000 cases were diagnosed and 11,200 women lost their lives to ovarian cancer. It is currently the fourth most common cause of cancer death among American women, being surpassed only by cancer of the breast, lung (now in second place), and large bowel. Overall five-year survival rates are 25 to 30 percent with over 50 percent of women having advanced disease at the time of diagnosis. Yet, when detected early, five-year survival rates in ovarian cancer can be as high as 85 percent.

Are some women at greater risk for ovarian cancer?

In addition to being more prevalent in women between fifty and sixty, ovarian cancer may be linked to other factors. Women who've never had children, for example, or who have had an infertility problem or perhaps endometriosis seem at slightly greater risk for developing cancer of the ovary. Otherwise, ovarian cancer shows no particular predilection for any group of women. Malignant tumors of the ovary have even been reported in children under five and in women over eighty.

Why is ovarian cancer more dangerous than uterine or cervical cancer?

Part of the explanation for the bleak statistics in ovarian cancer is the nature of the disease. Malignant tumors of the ovary develop rapidly and may involve both ovaries simultaneously. Ovarian cancer also tends to seed malignant cells early. A cancer of the uterine lining, for example, can be held partially in check by the thick muscular walls of the uterus. An ovarian cancer, on the other hand, is not bound or confined. This means that tumor cells can be shed and deposited directly onto the surface of nearby organs such as bowel, bladder, and uterus. Thus, in fairly short order these newly deposited tumor cells can grow and form more tumor masses.

Furthermore, lack of definite symptoms (at least initially) makes diagnosis of early ovarian cancer difficult.

How, then, can a woman tell if something is wrong?

The first indication may be little more than a vague discomfort in the lower abdomen or a sense of pelvic heaviness. Persistent indigestion or a feeling of fullness after eating small amounts of food may be another warning sign of early ovarian cancer. In these instances women may unsuccessfully resort to self-medication with antacids or other over-the-counter remedies. Among women who are still menstruating, periods frequently remain deceptively normal, thereby lulling them into neglecting routine pelvic examinations. Bleeding or spotting in postmenopausal women is also uncommon as a sign of ovarian cancer. Many ovarian cancers ultimately produce large amounts of free fluid within the abdominal cavity. Thus, all too frequently a rapidly enlarging abdomen and the sudden inability to fit into one's clothes are the first real indication of ovarian cancer. Less commonly, an abdominal mass or lump may be noticed but ignored until it too suddenly enlarges. More often than not, though, by this time the tumor has usually spread beyond the confines of the ovaries.

How is ovarian cancer diagnosed?

Diagnosing ovarian cancer after it has spread to other pelvic organs is not difficult. The real test lies in detecting the cancer while it is still limited and contained within an ovary. This is not an easy task. To begin with, the ovaries are relatively small, prune-sized organs that lie deep within the pelvis. They are therefore much less accessible to thorough examination than the cervix or uterus. Moreover, if a woman is overweight or fails to relax her abdominal muscles adequately during a pelvic examination it is possible to miss a slightly enlarged ovary. There are no screening tests for ovarian cancer and Pap smears are completely useless in this regard. Even X-rays and ultrasound of the pelvis are rarely of value unless these examinations are prompted by "suspicious" physical findings.

Diagnosis of early ovarian cancer therefore depends on the fortuitous finding of a suspiciously enlarged ovary on pelvic examination. Although the ovary can be the site of many different growths, both benign and malignant, any mass that is suspect because of its consistency, shape, or size demands prompt surgical exploration. In postmenopausal women, for example, the finding of an enlarged ovary is never normal.

What is the treatment for ovarian cancer?

Treatment is primarily surgical with removal of the uterus, tubes, ovaries, and all obvious tumors whenever possible. If the cancer cannot be completely eliminated by surgery, postoperative chemotherapy and radiation therapy are frequently advised. Some experts are now giving antitumor drugs prophylactically even in early cases. Outlook for the individual woman depends upon the type of ovarian cancer, stage of disease, and success of surgery in terms of removing the entire tumor. Age is another factor. Younger women as a group seem to have consistently better five-year survival rates.

At times a slow-growing early cancer of one ovary in an adolescent girl or young woman can be adequately treated by removing only the involved ovary. Certain malignant tumors of the ovary can also be treated by similar conservative surgery, but these cases are indeed rare.

What about the association between DES and pelvic cancers?

There is no longer any doubt that certain rare vaginal and cervical cancers can occur in the offspring of women who took the synthetic estrogen diethylstilbesterol (DES) during pregnancy.

In the 1940's and early 1950's it was believed that estrogen and specifically DES could help maintain pregnancies considered at high risk because of previous miscarriage or bleeding problems. As a result an estimated one to two million women in this country were given DES during pregnancy. In 1954 the effectiveness of estrogen in reducing the risk of miscarriage was discredited, but some doctors continued to prescribe DES on the misguided hope that perhaps it could help. Unfortunately, at that time no one was aware of the possible consequences.

In the late sixties, the first indication of a possible connection between intrauterine exposure to DES and cancer shocked the medical community. Between 1966 and 1969 eight young women, ages fifteen to twenty-two, were diagnosed as having vaginal cancer (clear-cell adenocarcinoma), a particularly rare tumor. Even more startling was the finding that the mothers of seven of them had taken DES during that particular pregnancy.

As of this writing there have now been 333 reported cases of vaginal and cervical adenocarcinoma since 1966 with 68 percent of these cases associated with DES during pregnancy. An estimated 70 to 90 percent of women exposed to DES in utero have also been found to have abnormal tissue changes including adenosis of the vagina and cervix. Vaginal adenosis is the replacement of vaginal mucosal tissue by glandular tissue. The extent and distribution of these cell changes vary considerably from woman to woman. Sometimes only a small portion of the vaginal wall is involved. In other instances, adenosis may be present in several areas, including the cervix. Adenosis is not considered a premalignant condition by most experts, but it does represent an area of cellular transformation which does have the potential of becoming premalignant. For this reason young women with vaginal adenosis should be closely observed, with gynecological examinations at regular intervals. On the more optimistic side, recent studies indicate that vaginal adenosis may spontaneously regress in the majority of women. Even more comforting is the finding that up to now, not a single woman being followed for proven vaginal adenosis has ultimately developed a vaginal cancer. The actual risk of a DES-exposed woman developing adenocarcinoma of the vagina or cervix has been assessed at about one chance in a thousand. If diagnosed early, therapy can preserve the ability to have intercourse and bear children.

How are DES daughters being followed?

Currently most doctors are advising that DES daughters be examined at least once or twice yearly, depending on the results of the initial examination. Since most cases of DES cancer seem to develop after the menarche (onset of menstruation) with a peak incidence at nineteen, the first examination should be performed by the age of fourteen. This would imply a complete physical and careful pelvic examination with close attention paid to the vagina and cervix. Pap smears as well as special iodine stains to outline suspicious tissue areas for biopsy purposes would be included. Where practical, the use of a colposcope (an instrument that magnifies) could also help pinpoint abnormal tissue changes. Among younger DES-exposed girls, the presence of any vaginal discharge or abnormal bleeding should be promptly reported and evaluated.

In addition to the potential cancer risk, DES-daughters may also run an increased risk of complications during pregnancy such as spontaneous abortion and premature labor. Some of these pregnancy losses and problems may be related to DES-induced malformations of the cervix and uterus, notably marked narrowing and elongation of the cervix in conjunction with a small, misshapen uterine cavity. In other DES-daughters the cervical canal may be unusually wide, which in itself can cause early rupture of the membranes and premature labor. Since these uterine and cervical malformations can be detected and better evaluated by a special X-ray (hysterosalpingogram) some doctors are advising that this test be performed prior to any planned pregnancy.

As an aside, male offspring of women who took DES during pregnancy should be examined by a urologist. Although there have been no cases of DES-induced cancer among male offspring, there have been scattered reports of testicular abnormalities, epididymal cysts, undersized penises, and low sperm counts.

For the woman who wants more information about DES and cancer, there are free pamphlets available. Write to DESAD project, National Cancer Institute, Office of Cancer Communications, Bethesda, Maryland, 20014.

What about other pelvic cancers?

Vaginal cancers not related to DES are primarily found in women over fifty and represent approximately 1 percent of all pelvic cancers. Symptoms are usually spotting or bleeding after the menopause. Treatment, either radiation therapy or surgery, depends on the extent of the disease at the time of diagnosis.

Cancer of the Fallopian tubes is very rare but when it occurs does so more frequently in older women. Although it is difficult to diagnose early, abnormal bleeding is present in over half of the cases. Treatment is a combination of surgery and radiation. Five-year survival rates are apt to be poor because of late diagnosis.

Is there such a thing as cancer of the vulva?

Absolutely. In the female the term vulva refers to the entire area between the legs with the exception of the anus. Thus, the vulva includes the inner and outer lips (labia), the vaginal opening, urethral opening, and the clitoris. Cancer of the vulva can begin in any one of these areas and accounts for about 3 percent of all pelvic malignancies.

Itching is by far the most frequent early symptom of vulvar cancer. Among women over fifty, in particular, any persistent itching, irritation, or inflammation of the vulva should be investigated. Other pertinent signs and symptoms include a mole or freckle that becomes darker, more prominent, irregular in outline or otherwise enlarges or changes. Any lump, bump, ulcer, or other growth of more than two weeks duration should also be brought to the attention of your doctor.

Treatment is surgical. Five-year survival rates can be excellent depending on how early the cancer is diagnosed. Needless to say, procrastination by women accounts for many vulvar cancers being relatively advanced before diagnosis is made.

In summary, cancer of the female pelvic organs accounts for approximately 22,800 deaths each year. And yet it is estimated that if every woman in this country had an annual pelvic examination, a Pap smear at least every two years, and if she promptly reported any abnormal bleeding during her menopausal and postmenopausal years, almost 100,000 lives could be saved within the next five years. Death from cervical and endometrial cancer could be virtually eliminated and three out of four women with other pelvic malignancies similarly spared.

There is no doubt that we are now on the threshold of a major breakthrough in cancer prevention and treatment. Until that glorious day when no one need die of this disease, we must still rely on early detection by regular examinations. After all, don't we owe it to ourselves and to those who love us to live our lives in the best possible health?

PART VII

What's in Store for Tomorrow's Woman?

26. A Projection into the Twenty-first Century

With each succeeding decade, the amount of scientific and technical knowledge accumulates at such a staggering rate that thirty years from today what we now know will comprise only a small fraction of what will then be known. So, just to see how a few of the fantastically rapid and mind-boggling changes now occurring in the field of genetics and medicine may ultimately affect women, let's project ourselves into the twenty-first century and envision what the next fifty years may have in store.

Most of these predictions may seem like farfetched fantasies, products of any overly active imagination. In reality, they are based on ideas and research currently well under way. Some of these advances may actually be realized within the next five to twenty years. Others may not be achieved until well into the twenty-first century, but sooner or later everything will come to pass.

Would you like to be fit and sexually active at 110 or even 130?

Apart from the possibility that the average life span of all human beings will be extended some 50 percent by the twenty-first century, the quality of life at that age will also be immeasurably improved. Anti-aging pills, new diet concepts, as well as mental biofeedback techniques for overcoming adverse psychological, emotional, and environmental stresses, will allow many individuals to be as vigorous at 110 as they now are at fifty or sixty.

With regard to women specifically, this physiological youthfulness will be reflected in an increased span of reproductive years. Menstruation will begin earlier and the menopause will correspondingly occur later. Thus, a woman born in the year 2000 will be reasonably assured of remaining fertile well into her late fifties or early sixties. And in women so desiring, the menopause could be completely avoided.

How could the menopause ever be avoided?

By the simple expedient of transplanting a young vigorous ovary. To date, few such procedures have been done and only under very special circumstances, but the time is coming when ovarian transplants to ward off the menopausal years will be just as popular as cosmetic surgery is now.

Could an ovarian transplant make pregnancy possible after sixty or seventy?

In addition to having a new internal source of estrogen and other ovarian hormones (far better than any pill yet available), pregnancy, if so desired, would certainly be possible. Considering the fact that a sixty- or seventy-year-old woman would look and feel thirty years younger, the idea of having a baby even if the egg weren't hers might be appealing. Under these circumstances the selection of the donor ovary would be a matter of paramount importance.

Where would the donor ovary be obtained?

From a biological organ replacement center (BORC). Even assuming that human beings will live longer and healthier lives, suicides, fatal accidents, and other traumatic causes of death will still invariably take their toll. Then too, various organ transplants will be commonplace within the next fifty years, making it also conceivable that many individuals will routinely leave their organs to their own family frozen fund foundation. In fact, with an anticipated life span of some 120 years, a younger woman may even elect to have one ovary removed, frozen, and stored in suspended animation for later reimplantation at age seventy. However, the less farsighted woman desiring a donor ovary will have to rely on her local BORC chapter.

Every major medical center will have its own special unit housing organ replacements—hearts, kidneys, stomachs, lungs, livers, ovaries, uteri, and so on. In addition these special units, fully operative twenty-four hours a day, will be specifically designed to receive, process, preserve, and store human organs, skin, and other body parts for transplantation purposes. Organs such as ovaries and testicles, as well as sperm specimens and human embryos exclusively reserved for purposes of reproduction, will not only be genetically typed according to race, blood group, and hereditary traits, but will also be meticulously classified in regard to intelligence, talent, and other special attributes of the donor. Since each organ replacement center will be intimately linked via giant computers with all other transplant centers, tracking down a donor ovary that meets specific requirements could be done within a matter of minutes. Thus, a woman requesting an ovarian transplant for purposes of pregnancy would be assured of receiving an ovary most likely to produce an egg genetically similar to what her own ovaries might have produced.

Would a woman be able to predetermine the sex of her child?

Absolutely. Artificial insemination with sex-typed sperm is already close at hand. As of now, scientists can identify and differentiate between sperm carrying the X chromosome for female and ones carrying the Y chromosome for male. Furthermore, they are currently perfecting a technique whereby these two types can be separated from each other in any given semen specimen. Therefore, if the couple desired a female offspring, it would be a simple matter to artificially inseminate the woman with only X sperm; if a male child were wanted, only the Y sperm would be used.

Medical advances in the twenty-first century will also make it possible for any woman to become pregnant. The surgical removal of a uterus or the presence of nonfunctioning or blocked Fallopian tubes will no longer be an obstacle to procreation.

How could pregnancy be possible without a uterus or functioning tubes?

By means of a uterine and Fallopian tube transplant. Even more exciting is the possibility that a woman without a uterus could still have a baby. All she would need is one functioning ovary.

Today, it is possible to capture an egg at the time of ovulation, fertilize it outside the body, and then place it back into the mother's uterus. But scientists are also able (at least in lower animals) to take fertilized eggs at various stages of development and to implant them into the uteri of *foster* mothers. That these experiments have resulted in perfectly normal offspring, even from embryos previously frozen, stored, and then thawed prior to implantation, makes it more than likely that such a procedure, if so desired, could ultimately be feasible in the human. Aside from the moral and ethical issues involved, one obvious problem would be the finding of a suitable and willing foster mother.

To circumvent this potential problem, the development of an artificial uterus or womb is currently on the drawing board.

An artificial uterus?

Precisely—in essence a highly sophisticated "biomechanism" capable of assuming all the functions of a real uterus during pregnancy. Such an artificial uterus would be able to sustain the growth and development of a human embryo until full maturity at nine months. Moreover, its ability to simulate a normal intrauterine environment would revolutionize present-day medical care of the premature infant. Babies born two or more months ahead of schedule, for example, would be delivered directly into an artificial uterus and thus reincubated until sufficiently mature to function on their own.

By now you may well wonder how the planet earth will support this ever-increasing population, with all the innovations to preserve and prolong life. Rest assured that new contraceptive methods will be appearing in the not too distant future.

What about birth control in the twenty-first century?

For all practical purposes, long-term contraceptive control by means of the pill, IUD, diaphragm, condom, and all other present-day methods of birth control will be as obsolete as the whale-bone corset. With an impending breakthrough in the application of the body's own defense mechanisms against bacteria, viruses, and other foreign protein material, the ultimate answer to effective, safe birth control may prove to be along immunological lines. Today we know that some women, as well as men, are infertile because of sperm antibody formation. (See Chapter 16.) Furthermore, the fact that sperm are protein substances capable of eliciting antibody formation raises the provocative possibility that one day an antisperm vaccine will be a reality. In men, such an antisperm vaccine would immobilize the sperm. In women, an antisperm vaccine by incapacitating the sperm would thereby prevent fertilization of an ovum. Thus, hormonal function would be undisturbed, ovulation would proceed normally, and undesirable side effects currently associated with the pill and the IUD, as well as the inconvenience of less effective contraceptive methods, would subsequently be eliminated. To go one step further, booster shots of antisperm vaccine every four or five years would also do away with the need for vasectomies, tubal ligations, or other sterilization procedures.

There is also no doubt that further research would also overcome the obvious stumbling block of how to reverse the process if so desired. It is therefore possible that antisperm vaccine good for X number of months or years and capable of being reversed in four to six weeks by an anti-antisperm vaccine may be available for both men and women.

Advances in immunological techniques are also going to play an increasingly important role in the control of many major diseases.

What major diseases?

In the realm of venereal disease, for example, the chances look promising for immunological control of gonorrhea and perhaps even syphilis within the next ten to fifteen years. With a vaccine against gonorrhea currently being developed and tested, routine vaccination in the year 1990 may virtually eradicate this disease within our own lifetime.

Even more exciting is the increasing optimism among researchers that immunological control of breast and cervical cancer is almost within reach.

Vaccines to prevent breast and cervical cancer?

If the mounting evidence linking viruses with breast and cervical cancer is substantiated, effective vaccines against these malignancies may be developed within the next few years. The fact that each year approximately 115,000 women in this country develop either breast or cervical cancer emphasizes the fantastic implications that such a breakthrough would provide for the generation of women now being born. Moreover, the next thirty years are going to revolutionize the diagnosis and treatment of all cancers.

What other advances in cancer diagnosis and treatment are anticipated?

Today, cancer therapy is still primarily limited to removing the tumor surgically or destroying it with radiation therapy or anti-cancer drugs. Methods to detect various malignancies in their early stages are available. But such is not the case for all cancers. Ovarian cancer, for example, all too often eludes early diagnosis, as do certain rare cancers involving the wall of the uterus. In addition, cancer of the colon, the third most common cause of cancer death among women, is frequently unsuspected until obvious bowel symptoms develop.

New screening methods, however, are going to make early detection of cancer feasible long before there is any clinical suspicion of its presence. At the present time, research is being directed toward perfecting a blood test that would signal the possible presence of a beginning malignancy somewhere in the body.

Refinements in other screening techniques will also be forthcoming. The fact that certain malignant cells can be tagged with radioactive tracer materials injected intravenously suggests that one day all minimal (very early) cancers will be detected and accurately pinpointed by briefly suspending the patient in a rotating stereoscopic nuclear scanning chamber.

Moreover, the treatment of cancer as we know it today will be supplanted by immunological and nuclear techniques in which malignant cells will be selectively destroyed without sacrificing adjacent normal tissue or causing systemic damage. Even beyond these advances, the ultimate in cancer treatment, short of prevention, will be the biological and physical transformation of cells from malignant back to normal. As we learn more about the body's amazing ability to protect and repair itself, the most significant breakthrough in the twenty-first century will be the verification that the human mind is intimately linked to the body's immunological defense mechanism. This revelation in itself will shatter many current concepts regarding health, aging, senility, and disease processes.

What does the mind have to do with physical disease?

More than we realize or can even begin to comprehend. Many physical problems are already known to be directly attributable to emotional or psychological stress. For example, individuals who undergo emotional trauma resulting from the death of a loved one are statistically more likely to develop a physical illness within the following year. And the greater their inability to cope with that loss or change in their life, the greater the likelihood that the disease will be serious. That the subsequent illness can in some cases be a malignancy raises several provocative questions. If, for example, viruses are responsible for cancer and we further assume that such a virus was already present prior to the stress, is it possible that negative mental programming actually triggered certain biochemical changes? Is it conceivable that the individual's adverse reaction to stress removed certain blocking agents or immune factors that had previously kept the virus in check? Even assuming that viruses are not a cause of cancer, is it possible that adverse mental mechanisms could, of themselves, grossly disturb cellular function and precipitate abnormal and rampant multiplication of cells?

The answers are very elusive. Yet, from accumulating studies and clinical observations, there is a growing belief that thoughts and attitudes on a conscious and subconscious level actually produce physiological changes in cells for either health or disease.

"Mind power" has and is being successfully used in the treatment and control of such conditions as ulcers, migraine headaches, high blood pressure, arthritis, asthma, and even the common cold. But what is really astounding is that the application of certain simple mental techniques employing altered states of consciousness to program the subconscious for health are resulting in the regression and disappearance of cancerous tumors. That this approach is being used in certain select cases in this country in reputable medical centers and by reputable physicians has not been publicized, perhaps for obvious reasons. Nonetheless, as more evidence accumulates to substantiate the ability of the mind to influence even malignant processes through mechanisms not as yet understood, one of the most elusive pieces in the jigsaw puzzle of what triggers the onset of serious disease may finally slip into place.

The twenty-first century will also witness the use of mental techniques in the realm of sexuality, and specifically in facilitating orgasm at will.

Can orgasm really be mentally programmed?

Yes. The nervous system does not differentiate between what is real and what is imagined. Think back to the last time you went to sleep and dreamed about flying—without an airplane, that is. Didn't you actually feel yourself soaring high above the clouds or perhaps effortlessly skimming two or three feet above the ground? For many people, sexual dreams can evoke orgasmic response. That this phenomenon occurs without actual genital contact and is sufficiently intense to awaken the dreamer is proof that the mind can trigger orgasm. And, if the mind can evoke a real physical orgasm during sleep, there is no doubt that further research into the intracacies of the human mind and brain will one day result in techniques whereby orgasmic dream experiences can be reproduced in the conscious waking state.

What else is in store for tomorrow's woman?

Once researchers zero in on the neural pathways and pleasure centers of the brain that are responsible for eliciting orgasmic response, sex clinics will offer training sessions guaranteed to make any woman orgasmic and even multiorgasmic at will. Moreover, by the year 2050, routine immunizations against most major diseases, transplants of organs both real and artificial, and mental biofeedback techniques to program the body for health will form the basis of modern medicine.

Now, if those researchers would only hurry up and perfect the anti-aging pill they keep talking about, you and I might just be around to see it all come true.

27. Putting It All Together

From the time this book was first conceived to the writing of the final draft, dramatic social changes have taken place. Along with the spirited women's liberation movement, which has shaken a lot of old traditions, women are taking a more active interest in knowing about their bodies and their unique physical problems as women. There are now hundreds of self-help gynecology clinics flourishing in this country and undoubtedly the number will continue to rise. In addition, organized lectures, weekly meetings, and rap sessions to discuss various aspects of female health problems are becoming commonplace in many large cities. That these groups are being enthusiastically supported should give the medical profession reason to pause and reflect, for despite the fact that the vast majority of physicians are providing excellent care for their female patients, could it be that what is needed and often lacking is genuine rapport and communication between doctor and patient?

But doesn't real communication imply more than just having the doctor talk to you? How can you as a woman expect to participate in making decisions concerning your health care unless you yourself are better informed? Without some basic understanding of how your body functions, can you even begin to ask pertinent questions regarding your particular condition, let alone discuss the possibilities of alternative treatments?

More and more doctors are making a conscientious effort to impart needed information. In many cases they are taking the time to explain the reasons for a particular procedure or the need for a specific medication. This is as it should be, for if therapy is to be successful, the close cooperation of an informed patient is essential. But can women reasonably expect their frequently overworked doctors also to assume the sole responsibility for educating them in the complexities of anatomy and physiology?

The time has come for all women to take the initiative in becoming better informed regarding their physical selves. This book, after much painstaking effort, is my contribution toward the realization of this goal. It is also my hope that it will serve to supplement the knowledge you may already have, as well as being a useful reference source.

As of now, other books along similar lines are appearing in print and others will undoubtedly be forthcoming. This is all to the good. For as women become more knowledgeable about their own biological complexities, better doctor-patient communication will hopefully ensue. And perhaps in the long run this meeting on a more common ground will bring about a new era of mutual trust and understanding —a time when, together with the help and guidance of your physician, you can take a more active role in the safeguarding of your most priceless possession, your health and well-being.

Glossary

The following glossary is intended to facilitate the comprehension of this book and this book only. Definitions are therefore intentionally limited and do not necessarily include all possible interpretations for a given term. When a more detailed definition is desired, the reader should consult either a standard general or a medical dictionary.

ABDOMEN   That portion of the body lying between the lower ribs and the groin.

ABDOMINAL CAVITY   The body cavity which contains most of the organs of digestion (intestines, liver, etc.) and the spleen. It is bounded by the diaphragm above and continuous with the pelvic cavity below.

ABORTION   Termination, loss, or interruption of a pregnancy of less than twenty weeks. Types of abortion: criminal—an illegal termination of a pregnancy; therapeutic—a legally sanctioned interruption of a pregnancy for physical and/or psychological reasons; spontaneous or natural abortion—see MISCARRIAGE.

ABSCESS   An accumulation or collection of pus contained within a well-circumscribed area.

ACUTE   Sharp—brief and/or severe; of sudden onset.

ADENOMATOUS HYPERPLASIA   An abnormal overgrowth and proliferation of the tissue lining the uterine cavity, potentially premalignant.

ADENOMYOSIS   Condition in which displaced fragments of endometrial (uterine lining) tissue are abnormally embedded in the muscular walls of the uterus.

ADHESION   Fibrous band of tissue that abnormally binds or interconnects organs or other body parts.

ADNEXAE   Pertaining to the tubes and ovaries. General term used to define the tubes and ovaries.

ADRENALS   Important endocrine glands located atop each kidney; the suprarenal glands.

AMENORRHEA   Prolonged absence of menstruation.

AMNIOCENTESIS   Removal of a sample of amniotic fluid for diagnostic purposes; sometimes used to detect certain congenital defects or to determine the sex of the unborn child. Saline amniocentesis specifically refers to the introduction of a saline (salt) solution into the bag of waters (amniotic sac) for purposes of abortion.

AMNIOTIC FLUID   Fluid contained within the bag of waters (amniotic sac) that surrounds the fetus during its intrauterine existence.

ANAL FISSURE   A deep crack or split in the mucous membrane of the anal canal.

ANALGESIC   Pain-relieving drug or substance.

ANDROGEN   General term applied to any hormone that has a masculinizing effect on either sex.

ANOMALIES   Abnormalities in structure or form.

ANOVULATION   Absence of ovulation.

ANOVULATORY CYCLE   Menstrual cycle wherein ovulation, or release of an egg (ovum), does not occur.

ANTEFLEXED   A normal forward bend of the uterus at the junction of its body and the cervix.

ANTEVERTED UTERUS   A forward tilt of the entire uterus.

ANTIBIOTICS   Large group of chemical substances (e.g., penicillin) that have the ability to destroy or inhibit the growth of bacteria or other disease-producing organisms.

ANTIBODY   Part of the body's natural defense mechanism; a substance found in the blood, other body fluids, or tissues that is manufactured by the body in response to noxious or harmful bacteria, viruses, or other foreign invaders.

ANTI-CANCER DRUGS   Group of chemical substances that can destroy or inhibit the growth of cancerous or malignant cells.

ANTIGEN   Any substance which, when introduced into the body, stimulates the production of antibodies.

ANTIPROSTAGLANDINS   Various drugs which either prevent the synthesis of prostaglandins by the body or block their action on uterine muscles. Useful in relieving painful menstrual cramps.

ANUS   The lower portion of the rectum; the body orifice through which fecal material is expelled.

APHRODISIAC   An agent or drug capable of arousing sexual desire.

APOCRINE GLAND   A skin gland that exudes a milky secretion having a characteristic but inoffensive odor; a scent gland.

AREOLA   The circular pigmented area surrounding the nipple.

ARTIFICIAL INSEMINATION   The deposit of semen into the vagina by means other than sexual intercourse for the purpose of procreation.

ASEXUAL   Not sexual; with no overt sexual interest in either sex.

ASPIRATION   The withdrawal of air, fluid, or other material from a body cavity or space by suction.

ASYMPTOMATIC   Absence of symptoms; no subjective sign of any disease.

ATROPHY   A wasting away or a diminution of size involving an organ or body part.

ATYPICAL   Somewhat unusual, not quite normal.

AU NATUREL   Naked.

AUTOMANIPULATION   See MASTURBATION.

AXILLARY   Pertaining to the underarm or armpit area (axilla).

AZOOSPERMIA   Total absence of sperm in the semen; zero sperm production.

BACTERIA   Broad term that includes microscopic organisms which, when abnormally present, may cause infection and disease.

BARR BODY   A minute particle of the female X chromosome which appears under the microscope as a small dark-staining mass within the nucleus of a cell. Also known as the sex chromatin body. It is normally present in 20 to 90 percent of all somatic or body cells of a female.

BARTHOLIN'S CYST   A swelling or collection of fluid, mucus, or other material within one of the Bartholin's glands.

BARTHOLIN'S GLANDS   Mucus-secreting glands located on either side of the vaginal opening.

BASAL BODY TEMPERATURE (BBT)   The lowest normal body temperature recorded under conditions of absolute rest. For example, the body temperature during sleep or immediately upon awakening.

BENIGN   Mild in character; of a non-cancerous condition.

BILATERAL   Involving both sides.

BIMANUAL EXAMINATION   Examination wherein both hands are used to palpate, or feel, the internal female pelvic organs.

BIOPSY   The surgical removal of tissue for purposes of diagnosis. Types of biopsy: cone—removal of a cone-shaped piece of tissue from the cervix, most commonly done for the diagnosis of a possible early cervical cancer; excisional—surgical removal of an entire lesion or growth; incisional—surgical removal of only a portion of a lesion or growth; needle—removal of only a very small segment of tissue by means of a special large-bore needle; punch—removal of a small wedge of tissue by means of a special (punch) instrument.

BISEXUAL   An individual who is sexually attracted to or who engages in sexual activity with members of both sexes.

BLADDER   The elastic, saclike organ that serves as a receptacle for urine.

BONE SCAN   Sophisticated diagnostic technique utilizing nuclear tracer elements injected by vein to pinpoint cancerous tumor or other abnormal changes in bony tissue.

BONE SURVEY   Routine X-rays of the spine, pelvis, and other skeletal parts to detect the presence of any abnormal or cancerous bony changes.

BREAST PROSTHESIS   Silastic implant; a plastic bag filled with silicone gel or saline. Used to fashion a new breast following mastectomy or to augment the size of a small breast.

BROMIDROSIS   A particularly offensive and fetid perspiration odor; sometimes also used to describe "smelly" feet.

CAESAREAN SECTION   Delivery of a baby by means of an incision through the abdominal wall and uterus.

CANCER   A malignancy; broad term applied to any tumor, growth, or lesion characterized by the rapid multiplication of abnormal cells that have the ability to invade and spread to distant organs or other body parts.

CANDIDA ALBICANS   A fungus frequently responsible for vaginal infection; see MONILIA.

CARCINOMA   A cancer, specifically one which arises from epithelial tissues such as skin, mucous membrane, glandular tissue.

CARCINOMA-IN-SITU   A very early and localized cancer.

CASTRATION   Surgical removal of the ovaries or testicles, or else their destruction by irradiation therapy.

CATHETER   Any tubelike instrument used to inject or withdraw fluid from any body cavity or space.

CATHETERIZATION   Most commonly refers to the passage of a small rubber tube or other instrument through the urethra for the purpose of draining the bladder of urine.

CAUTERIZATION   The destruction of infected or abnormal tissue by heat, cold, or chemicals.

CELIBATE   One who does not engage in sexual activity.

CERVICAL CANAL   Passageway within the cervix proper connecting the vagina and the uterine cavity.

CERVICAL CYST   An abnormal retention of mucus secretions within one of the cervical glands.

CERVICAL DYSPLASIA   Abnormal changes in the superficial cells of the cervix. A benign condition but when severe can be considered premalignant.

CERVICAL EROSION   The term "erosion" is actually a misnomer. Cervical erosion is the replacement of normal cervical tissue on the surface of the cervix by endocervical tissue, which is red and granular in appearance. This condition is usually the result of infection. Sometimes the term is loosely and incorrectly applied to any red or irritated cervix.

CERVICAL OS   The opening leading into the cervical canal.

CERVICAL POLYP   An abnormal but usually benign tear-drop-shaped growth of the cervix that commonly protrudes from the cervical os.

CERVICAL STENOSIS   A narrowing or stricture of the cervical canal.

CERVICITIS   An inflammation and/or infection involving the cervix.

CERVIX   The lower portion of the uterus (womb) that projects into the vagina, sometimes referred to as the mouth of the womb, or neck of the uterus. See also RIPE CERVIX.

CHANCRE   Painless ulcerating sore seen specifically in early syphilis.

CHEMOTHERAPEUTIC AGENTS   A large group of synthetic chemical substances used in the treatment of bacterial or other infections; includes the various anti-cancer drugs.

CHEMOTHERAPY   Treatment of any medical condition by drugs. The treatment of a malignancy by anti-cancer drugs.

CHLOASMA   The appearance of light brown patches on the skin of the face and elsewhere. Increased skin pigmentation occasionally seen in pregnant women and in women taking oral contraceptives.

CHROMOSOMAL SEX   Refers to the sex chromosomes; XX represents a female and XY a male.

CHROMOSOME   Microscopic, threadlike particles of genetic material contained within the nucleus of cells.

CIRCUMCISION   The surgical removal of the foreskin (prepuce) from the penis.

CLIMACTERIC   The menopausal years, the period of time during which menstruation ceases and the body gradually adjusts to waning ovarian function and decreasing estrogen production.

CLIMAX   See ORGASM.

CLITORIS   A small cylindrical erectile structure, extremely sensitive to stimulation and located just above the urethral opening in the female.

COITUS   Sexual intercourse.

COITUS INTERRUPTUS   The practice of withdrawing the penis from the vagina just prior to ejaculation (release of semen).

COLPOSCOPE   Telescopelike instrument used to magnify the surface of the cervix.

CONCEIVE   To become pregnant, to procreate.

CONDOM   A sheath for the penis used to prevent pregnancy or infection; a rubber, a prophylactic.

CONDYLOMA ACCUMINATA   Common genital warts, also known as venereal warts.

CONGENITAL   Existing or present from birth. Can refer to any physical or mental trait, peculiarities, or diseases either inherited or caused by any adverse prenatal influence.

CONGESTION   Engorgement of blood vessels resulting from an increased blood flow to the particular area or an obstruction of the return flow; poor venous drainage or circulation.

CONNECTIVE TISSUE   Fibrous sheets of tissue that support and connect muscles or other body parts.

CONTRACEPTION   Birth control.

CONTRACEPTIVE   Any drug, device, or method used to prevent pregnancy.

CONTRAINDICATED   Against medical advice and judgment.

CORPUS LUTEUM   The yellow-colored ovarian tissue structure formed from the remains of the ruptured ovarian follicle after release of its contained ovum (egg). Important because of its production of the hormone progesterone, which prepares the uterine lining to receive the fertilized egg.

CORPUS LUTEUM CYST   A cyst of the corpus luteum; any abnormal accumulation of blood or other material within the corpus luteum.

CORRUGATED   Having alternating ridges and grooves—not smooth. Frequently used to describe the surface of the vaginal walls in a woman during the reproductive years.

CRABS   *Pediculosis pubis;* pubic hair lice.

CRYOSURGERY   The destruction of abnormal cells or tissue by the application of extreme cold.

CULDOSCOPY   Surgical procedure in which a slender, telescopelike instrument is passed through the upper vagina and into the pelvic cavity to view the internal female organs.

CULTURE   A laboratory method to identify the causative agent or bacteria responsible for a particular infection or disease. In effect, the material to be examined (urine, blood, discharge, etc.) is incubated in special nutrients that allow any organisms or bacteria originally present in the sample material to multiply, thrive, and thus be identified.

CUNNILINGUS   Oral stimulation of the female genitalia.

CURETTAGE   Scraping of any body cavity; for example, scraping the uterine cavity for the purpose of removing tissue or new growths. A common gynecological diagnostic procedure. See DILATATION AND CURETTAGE.

CYCLIC   Occurring periodically or at regular intervals.

CYST   Any saclike structure containing fluid or semisolid material.

CYSTITIS   Inflammation and/or infection of the urinary bladder.

CYTOLOGY   The study of cells both normal and abnormal.

CYTOTOXIC DRUG   A drug which destroys cells by interfering with their metabolism and/or reproduction.

DERMATITIS   Inflammation of the skin from any cause. Contact dermatitis is an inflammation of the skin from contact with an irritant. Allergic dermatitis is an inflammation of the skin as the result of individual sensitivity to a certain substance or material.

DERMOID CYST   A common benign tumor of the ovary.

DIAGNOSIS   The determination of the cause of a specific infection, disease, or other condition.

DIAGNOSTIC STUDIES   Tests to determine the cause of an abnormal condition; also done to eliminate or rule out the presence of an abnormal condition.

DIAPHRAGM   A rubber, dome-shaped device worn over the cervix for the prevention of pregnancy.

DILATATION   The enlargement of any passageway; for example, the dilatation of the cervical os and canal during childbirth.

DILATATION AND CURETTAGE (D AND C)   Minor surgical procedure in which the cervical os and canal are temporarily enlarged to permit the passage of an instrument (curette) for purposes of removing tissue from the uterine cavity.

DILATE   To make wider or larger, to expand.

DISCHARGE   Any abnormal or unusual drainage or secretion.

DISCRETE   Well-outlined, distinct, separate; usually used to describe certain tumors or lesions.

DISEASE   Any abnormal or pathological state that interferes with the proper functioning of the mind and/or body.

DISSEMINATED   Widespread; for example, a disseminated disease is one involving many organs or body parts.

DISTENSIBLE   Capable of being stretched or distended.

DISTENTION   The state of being distended; for example, abdominal distention is a swollen or expanded abdomen usually resulting from the accumulation of gas or fluid.

DOUCHING   Flushing and cleansing of the vagina with a liquid solution, usually medicated.

DUCT ECTASIA   Dilatation and distention of the nipple ducts, frequently responsible for a greenish-gray, sticky nipple discharge.

DYSFUNCTION   Malfunction of an organ or body part.

DYSMENORRHEA   Painful menstruation or menstrual cramps. Primary dysmenorrhea implies painful menstruation without organic cause. Secondary dysmenorrhea implies painful menstruation as the result of a specific pelvic problem or disease.

DYSPAREUNIA   Intercourse that is painful or difficult for a woman.

DYSURIA   Pain and/or burning on urination.

ECCRINE GLAND   A sweat gland.

ECTOPIC PREGNANCY   Any pregnancy that grows outside the uterine cavity. Most commonly used to describe a tubal pregnancy, that is, the implantation of a fertilized egg with subsequent growth of the embryo within one of the Fallopian tubes.

EDEMA   Abnormal accumulation of fluid within the body tissues that produces swelling of a part or an organ.

EJACULATION   Discharge of semen from the penis at the time of orgasm.

EMBOLISM   Obstruction or occlusion of a blood vessel by a transported blood clot or embolus; for example, pulmonary embolism is the obstruction of a blood vessel in the lung.

EMBOLUS   Any undissolved material (for example, air, fat, blood clot) that travels in the bloodstream and subsequently blocks a blood vessel.

EMBRYO   The offspring (product of conception) from the third to the end of the fifth week of intrauterine existence. During the first two weeks of pregnancy the product of conception is known as the ovum; from the sixth week until birth, the fetus.

ENDOCERVICAL   Within the cervical canal.

ENDOCERVICAL GLANDS   Mucus-producing glands of the cervix.

ENDOCRINE   The ductless glands (ovaries, testicles, thyroid, adrenals, pituitary, etc.) that secrete hormones directly into the bloodstream and which profoundly affect other parts of the body.

ENDOMETRIAL   Pertaining to the endometrium, the mucous membrane tissue lining the uterine cavity.

ENDOMETRIAL ASPIRATION   The withdrawal of a sterile solution introduced into the uterine cavity for purposes of collecting endometrial cells for diagnostic purposes.

ENDOMETRIAL BIOPSY   The sampling of endometrial tissue for diagnostic purposes.

ENDOMETRIAL CARCINOMA   Cancer of the tissue lining the uterine cavity.

ENDOMETRIAL CAVITY   The uterine cavity.

ENDOMETRIAL CYST   An ovarian cyst made up of endometrial tissue implants and commonly seen in endometriosis. Sometimes also known as a "chocolate cyst" of the ovary because of the presence of old blood within the cyst.

ENDOMETRIAL HYPERPLASIA   Benign overgrowth of the tissue lining the uterine cavity, usually the result of long, uninterrupted estrogen stimulation.

ENDOMETRIAL POLYP   A tear-drop-shaped growth, usually benign, within the uterine cavity.

ENDOMETRIOMA   An ovarian cyst, usually filled with old blood, and caused by endometriosis.

ENDOMETRIOSIS   A pelvic condition in which fragments of endometrial tissue are found outside the confines of the uterine cavity; for example, on the ovaries, the back wall of the uterus, or in the pelvic space between the uterus and rectum.

ENGORGEMENT   Distention with blood or other fluid, congestion; for example, an engorged blood vessel.

EPISIOTOMY   An incision that enlarges the vaginal introitus so as to facilitate delivery of a baby.

ERECTILE TISSUE   Tissue which, when engorged with blood, becomes swollen and more or less rigid; for example, the penis and clitoris during sexual excitation.

ERECTION   The condition of erectile tissue when engorged with blood. Commonly used to describe the penis when distended and rigid.

ESTROGEN   Hormone produced by the ovaries and responsible for female sexual characteristics.

EXCISE   To cut out, to remove surgically.

EXCISIONAL BIOPSY   See BIOPSY.

EXTERNAL GENITALIA   The vulva, or external sexual organs of the female. Can also apply to the external sexual organs of the male (penis and scrotum).

FALLOPIAN TUBES   Oviducts. The two small passageways or tubes that branch from either side of the uterus and connect with the uterine cavity; the passageway where the egg and the sperm meet.

FECAL IMPACTION   Accumulation of hardened stool in the lower rectum.

FELLATIO   Oral stimulation of the penis.

FERTILE DAYS   The days during which ovulation is most likely to occur.

FERTILITY DRUGS   A group of natural and synthetic drugs capable of inducing ovulation in selected women.

FERTILIZATION   Impregnation; specifically, the fusion of a sperm with an ovum.

FERTILIZED EGG   An ovum that has been impregnated by a sperm.

FETUS   The product of conception from the sixth week to the end of pregnancy.

FIBROADENOMA   A common benign breast tumor.

FIBROCYSTIC DISEASE OF THE BREASTS   A benign breast condition characterized by the presence of multiple small cysts and fibrous thickening of the breast tissue.

FIBROIDS   Benign tumors involving the wall of the uterus; also known as leiomyomas, myomas, or fibromyomas.

FIMBRIA   Small fingerlike projections located at the free end of each Fallopian tube and important for ensuring that a released ovum finds its way into the tube.

FISTULA   An abnormal connection or communication between two organs or structures.

FOLLICLE   A small ovarian saclike structure containing an ovum.

FOLLICLE CYST   An abnormal accumulation of fluid within an ovarian follicle.

FOLLICLE STIMULATING HORMONE (FSH)   Pituitary hormone that stimulates the growth and development of ovarian follicles.

FORESKIN   See PREPUCE.

FORNIX   The upper vagina near the cervix.

FRATERNAL TWINS   Nonidentical twins resulting from the fertilization of two separate eggs by two separate sperm.

FROZEN SECTION   A rapid method of preparing biopsied tissue for the microscopic detection of abnormal and/or malignant cells. Frozen sections are usually done while the operation or surgical procedure is still in progress.

FUNCTIONAL DISEASE   A condition in which an organ or body part is not functioning properly, but in which no lesion, tumor, or change in structure can be determined.

FUNDUS   The top of the uterus; that portion of the uterus lying above the level of where the Fallopian tubes branch off.

FUNGUS   A disease-producing organism that feeds on organic matter; for example, *Candida albicans,* a fungus commonly responsible for causing vaginal infection.

GALACTORRHEA   White milky discharge from both nipples.

GENERIC   General or chemical name of a drug as opposed to its trade name.

GENITAL HERPES   A genital infection caused by the herpesvirus.

GENITALIA   Sexual organs; the organs of reproduction.

GENITAL WARTS   Wartlike lesions along the vulva and/or inner vagina

caused by a virus; can also affect the male external genitalia. See CON-
DYLOMA ACCUMINATA.

GESTATION   Pregnancy; can refer to either a normal (intrauterine) or an
ectopic (extrauterine) pregnancy.

GONAD   Sex gland; ovary or testicle.

GONADOTROPIN   Specifically refers to pituitary hormones directly affecting
or stimulating the gonads; for example, FSH and LH are gonadotropins.

GONOCOCCUS   *Neisseria gonorrhoeae,* the bacteria responsible for gonorrhea.

GONORRHEA   A highly contagious venereal disease.

GRAM-NEGATIVE   Refers to a differential stain used in the laboratory identification of bacteria. For example, a Gram-negative bacteria such as gonococcus (*E. coli,* etc.) will stain pink when subjected to a certain dye; a
Gram-positive bacteria will stain a deep purple when exposed to the
same dye.

GRAVIDA   A pregnant woman.

GYNECOLOGIST   A medical doctor who specializes in the treatment and management of problems affecting the female reproductive system.

HEMATURIA   Blood in the urine.

HEMORRHAGE   Excessively heavy bleeding, either internal or external.

HERPESVIRUSES   Group of viruses responsible for various benign afflictions
(cold sore, fever blister, shingles, etc.). Currently being implicated in the
development of some human cancers.

HETEROSEXUAL   An individual who is sexually attracted to or who engages
in sexual activity with a member of the opposite sex.

HIRSUTISM   Abnormal presence of excessive facial and/or body hair, especially in women.

HOMOSEXUAL   An individual who is sexually attracted to or who engages in
sexual activity with a member of the same sex.

HORMONE   A chemical substance produced by an endocrine gland which
stimulates or affects other organs or body parts.

HOT FLASH   A sudden flushing of the skin accompanied by perspiration and
a feeling of intense heat usually involving the upper portion of the body.

HUMAN CHORIONIC GONADOTROPINS   Group of hormones produced by the
placenta during pregnancy and having properties similar to certain pituitary hormones such as LH and FSH (gonadotropins). The detection of
these substances in the urine (chorionic gonadotropins) forms the basis of
most pregnancy tests.

HYMEN   A thin, semicircular strip of mucous membrane stretched across the
lower edge of the vaginal entrance.

HYMENECTOMY   Surgical removal of the hymen.

HYMENOTOMY   Surgical incision of the hymen to enlarge the vaginal opening.

HYPERPLASIA   An abnormal but benign multiplication of cells. Types of
hyperplasia: cystic endometrial hyperplasia—the most benign form of

endometrial hyperplasia; adenomatous hyperplasia—an extreme degree of glandular and cellular overactivity. A typical adenomatous hyperplasia, an ominous type of endometrial overactivity, considered by many to represent a very early endometrial cancer.

HYPOTHALAMUS   A major control center for various bodily functions, situated at the base of the brain and intimately connected with the pituitary.

HYSTERECTOMY   Surgical removal of the uterus and its cervix either by an abdominal incision or through the vagina (vaginal hysterectomy).

HYSTEROSALPINGOGRAM   Special X-ray procedure used to outline the uterine cavity and the Fallopian tube passageways.

HYSTEROTOMY   An incision into the uterus, usually for the removal of an intrauterine pregnancy; a method of late abortion.

IDENTICAL TWINS   Genetically identical individuals resulting from the splitting of a single ovum fertilized by a single sperm.

IMMUNE   Protected against a disease or other condition.

IMMUNOLOGY   The study of the body's defense mechanisms against various diseases or disease-producing agents such as bacteria, viruses, etc.

IMPERFORATE HYMEN   A hymen that completely occludes or blocks the vaginal opening.

IMPOTENT   Weak; describing a male's inability to obtain or sustain an erection for effective sexual intercourse.

IMPREGNATION   Fertilization.

INCONTINENCE   Lack of urinary control.

INCUBATION PERIOD   The interval of time between the moment of infection and the appearance of symptoms and signs indicative of an infection.

INFANTILE UTERUS   An underdeveloped uterus; specifically, a disproportionately small uterine body as compared to the size of its cervix.

INFECTION   The contamination of any tissue with harmful bacteria or other organisms that adversely affects that tissue.

INFERTILITY   Temporary or permanent inability to conceive or reproduce.

INFLAMMATION   A condition characterized by redness, swelling, heat, and pain of any tissue as the result of trauma, irritation, or infection.

INGUINAL NODE   Lymph node located in the groin.

INSUFFLATION   The injection of air or other gaseous material into a body cavity or passageway. See RUBIN TEST.

INTERCOURSE   Sexual relations, coitus.

INTRADUCTAL PAPILLOMA   Tiny nodular benign growth arising from the lining of a nipple duct, frequently responsible for a bloody nipple discharge.

INTRAUTERINE   Within the uterine cavity.

INTRAUTERINE DEVICE (IUD)   Any device worn within the uterine cavity for the purpose of avoiding pregnancy; for example, a loop, coil, or shield.

INTROITUS   The entrance to the vagina.

INTROMISSION   The insertion of the penis into the vagina.

IN-VITRO FERTILIZATION   Fertilization of a human ovum outside of the body, that is, in an artificial environment.

IRRADIATION   The use of X-rays, radium, cobalt, or other radioactive substances for either diagnosis or treatment.

KEGEL'S EXERCISES   Exercises to strengthen the pubococcygeus muscle.

LABIA   Lips, part of the female external genitalia. Labia majora, the outer lips; labia minora, the inner lips.

LACTATION   The production of breast milk.

LAPAROSCOPY   A surgical procedure wherein a slender telescopelike instrument (laparoscope) is inserted through a small abdominal puncture for the inspection of abdominal and pelvic organs.

LEIOMYOMA   Fibroid tumor of the uterus.

LESION   Any unusual or abnormal localized tissue change; for example, any sore, tumor, growth, wound, injury, etc.

LEUCORRHEA   Nonspecific term to describe any white vaginal discharge.

LIBIDO   Sex drive.

LUTEINIZING HORMONE (LH)   One of the pituitary hormones necessary for ovulation; pituitary gonadotropin.

LYMPHATIC SYSTEM   A complex, interconnecting network of tiny capillarylike channels that drain and filter all body tissue fluid through the lymph nodes and back into the bloodstream.

LYMPH NODE   Part of the lymphatic system. Specifically, a gland which by acting as a trap or filter for bacteria, pus cells, and even malignant cells helps to localize any infection or malignancy to the area being drained.

MACROPHAGES   Large white blood cells that function as scavengers and thus protect the body against harmful bacteria and other foreign invaders.

MALIGNANT   Cancerous. See CANCER.

MAMMARY GLAND   The breast.

MAMMOGRAPHY   X-ray of the breasts for the detection of abnormal tissue changes.

MASTECTOMY   Surgical removal of a breast. Types of mastectomy: radical—removal of the entire breast, chest wall muscles (pectoralis major and minor), and axillary nodes; modified radical—removal of the entire breast and axillary nodes without sacrificing the chest wall muscles; simple—removal of the breast only; partial—removal of only a portion of the breast; subcutaneous—removal of the glandular tissue of the breast without sacrificing the overlying breast skin or nipple (primarily limited to certain benign conditions).

MASTURBATION   The stimulation or manipulation of one's own or another's genitals for sexual gratification.

MATURATION INDEX   A vaginal smear test which gauges the effect of estrogen on the vaginal mucosa. A method of hormone evaluation in the female, sometimes called the Femininity Index.

MENARCHE   The age at which menstruation first begins.

MENOPAUSAL YEARS   See CLIMACTERIC.

MENOPAUSE   Permanent cessation of menstruation.

MENORRHAGIA   Excessively heavy bleeding during menstruation.

MENSES   Menstrual flow.

MENSTRUAL CYCLE   The time interval from the beginning of one menstrual period to the beginning of the next. Also implies the sequence of events necessary to prepare the uterine lining for reception of a fertilized egg.

MENSTRUATION   Periodic bloody discharge from the uterine cavity as the result of specific hormonal changes.

METASTASIS   The spread of cancer cells from one part of the body to another organ or body part usually by way of the lymphatic system or bloodstream.

METASTATIC LESION   A cancerous or malignant tumor that has already spread to a distant body part or organ.

METRORRHAGIA   Bleeding between periods.

MICROSURGERY   Meticulous surgery performed with the aid of a magnifying instrument, such as a dissecting microscope or magnifying lens.

MIDCYCLE   The time in a woman's menstrual cycle during which ovulation usually occurs.

MINI-LAPAROTOMY   A method of female sterilization in which the operation is performed through a very small incision.

MINIPILL   Birth control pill containing a small dose of progestin only.

MISCARRIAGE   Loss of an early pregnancy without outside interference— that is, a spontaneous abortion as opposed to an induced or therapeutic abortion. Types of miscarriages or spontaneous abortions: complete—an abortion in which all the products of conception (embryo and placental tissue) are expelled; habitual—three or more successive spontaneous abortions; incomplete—an abortion in which there is still retained tissue, that is, some products of conception remain within the uterine cavity; missed—intrauterine death of an embryo or fetus, but with retention of all the products of conception for several weeks afterward; threatened— potential loss of an early pregnancy as evidenced by bleeding and uterine cramps.

MITTELSCHMERZ   Midcycle ovulatory pain. Pain and/or bleeding occurring at the time of ovulation.

MOLAR PREGNANCY   An abnormal pregnancy in which the embryo dies but the placental tissue (trophoblast) continues to grow and proliferate. Also called a hydatidiform mole or grape mole.

MONILIA   The fungus *Candida albicans.*

MONILIASIS   Vaginal infection caused by the fungus *Candida albicans.*

MONS VENERIS   Mound of fatty tissue over the pubic bone in women, normally covered with hair.

MONTGOMERY'S GLANDS   The sebaceous (oil) glands in the areola of the nipple.

MOTILITY   The power of spontaneous movement; one of the characteristics of normal sperm.

MUCOSA   See MUCOUS MEMBRANE.

MUCOUS MEMBRANE   Moist, glistening tissue lining the body cavities and passageways that lead to the outside; for example, the mouth, digestive tract, uterine cavity, cervical canal, vagina, etc.

MUCUS   A clear, sticky secretion from a mucous membrane.

MÜLLERIAN DUCT SYSTEM   An embryonic structure which in the female fetus ultimately develops into the uterus, Fallopian tubes, and upper vagina.

MULTIPARA   A woman parturient for the second time, or else a woman who has borne two or more children.

MYOCARDIAL INFARCTION   Heart attack, coronary occlusion.

MYOMA   Fibroid tumor of the uterus.

MYOMECTOMY   Surgical removal of a myoma.

NABOTHIAN CYST   Another name for the common cervical cyst. See CERVICAL CYST.

NEEDLE ASPIRATION   The removal of fluid or other liquid material from a cyst or body cavity by means of a needle and syringe.

NEEDLE BIOPSY   See BIOPSY.

NEOPLASM   Any new growth or tumor, either benign or malignant.

NIT   The egg of a crab louse.

NODE   See LYMPH NODE.

NODULE   A small rounded lump or mass, either benign or malignant.

NULLIPARA   A woman who has never been pregnant.

NYMPHOMANIAC   A woman with an insatiable and uncontrollable desire for sex.

OOPHORECTOMY   Surgical removal of an ovary.

ORAL   Pertaining to the mouth.

ORAL CONTRACEPTIVES   Birth control pills; hormone medication taken by mouth for the prevention of pregnancy.

ORAL GENITAL SEX   Sexual stimulation of the genitals by the mouth, lips, or tongue. See FELLATIO and CUNNILINGUS.

ORGANIC LESION   See LESION.

ORGASM   Climax; the physical sensation of sexual release experienced at the culmination of coitus, masturbation, or other sexual play.

OSTEOPOROSIS   Loss of calcium and other substances from the bone, leading to its generalized softening and weakening.

OUTPATIENT   Not requiring hospitalization; patient whose treatment can be rendered in a doctor's office or a clinic.

OVARIAN CYSTECTOMY   Surgical removal of an ovarian cyst without sacrificing the entire ovary.

OVARIAN RESECTION   Removal of a portion of an ovary.

OVARY   The female sex gland or gonad.

OVERT   Obvious or apparent, not hidden.

OVULATION   The release of an ovum from the ovary.

OVULATORY CYCLE   A menstrual cycle during which ovulation occurs.

OVUM   An egg. The female sexual cell produced by the ovaries.

PALPATE   To discern by touching; to feel with the hands and fingers.

PAP SMEAR   Common name for Papanicolaou smear. A method whereby cells are collected on a glass slide, stained, and then examined microscopically for any abnormal changes. Most commonly used as a screening method for early cervical cancer.

PATHOLOGY   The study of abnormal tissue changes and disease states.

PECTORALIS MAJOR   The large chest wall muscle over which the breast lies.

PEDICULOSIS PUBIS   Pubic hair lice; crabs.

PELVIC CAVITY   The lowermost portion of the abdominal cavity bound by the bony pelvis and containing the internal genital organs (uterus, tubes, and ovaries), bladder, and rectum.

PELVIC INFLAMMATORY DISEASE (PID)   Any inflammation and/or infection involving the internal female genital organs. Commonly used to describe any acute, recurrent, or chronic infection of the Fallopian tubes and/or ovaries.

PENILE   Pertaining to the penis.

PENIS   The male organ of copulation; the phallus.

PERFORATED UTERUS   A uterus in which the wall has been pierced through its entire thickness, usually inadvertently.

PERINEAL BODY   The wedge of fibrous tissue, muscle, and fat between the lower vagina and rectum in the female.

PERINEUM   The area between the vagina and the anus; part of the external genitalia.

PESSARY   Rubber or plastic appliance worn in the vagina to support the uterus and/or vaginal walls.

PHLEBITIS   Inflammation of any vein.

PITUITARY   A major endocrine gland located at the base of the brain.

PLACENTA   The afterbirth; the organ that nourishes the growing fetus during its intrauterine existence.

PLATELETS   Specialized blood cells (also known as thrombocytes) that are necessary for normal blood clotting.

POLYCYSTIC OVARIAN SYNDROME   A hormonal derangement characterized by lack of ovulation, infertility, menstrual irregularities, and enlarged ovaries.

POLYCYSTIC OVARIES   Condition in which both ovaries are studded with multiple small cysts.

POLYP   A small, usually benign mucous membrane growth that dangles on a stalk. See CERVICAL POLYP and ENDOMETRIAL POLYP.

POSITIVE LYMPH NODE   A lymph node or gland which has been invaded by cancer cells.

POSTCOITAL TEST   (SIMS-HUHNER TEST) Examination of the cervical mucus shortly after intercourse to determine its receptivity to sperm.

POSTMENOPAUSAL   Occurring after the menopause.

POSTPARTUM   Occurring after the delivery of a baby.

PRECOCIOUS   Prematurely developed; for example, precocious puberty is sexual maturity before the age at which it normally occurs.

PRECURSOR   Forerunner; any condition that precedes another condition.

PREMENOPAUSAL   Occurring prior to the menopause.

PREMENSTRUAL   Occurring prior to menstruation.

PREPUCE   The foreskin or the skin covering the glans or head of the penis; also, the foreskin of the clitoris.

PRIMIPARA   A woman pregnant for the first time.

PROCREATE   To reproduce, to bear children.

PROGESTERONE   The ovarian hormone produced by the corpus luteum as a result of ovulation.

PROGESTIN   A synthetic progesteronelike hormone preparation.

PROGNOSIS   A forecast or prediction regarding the probable outcome of a disease or injury.

PROLACTIN   A hormone produced by the pituitary. High blood levels of this hormone stimulate the mammary glands to produce milk.

PROLAPSE   A falling down of an organ because of poor or inadequate muscular and fibrous tissue support; for example, a dropped (prolapsed) uterus.

PROLIFERATIVE ENDOMETRIUM   Normal endometrial tissue lining the uterine cavity prior to ovulation as the result of estrogen stimulation.

PROPHYLAXIS   Any measure or method that prevents or protects from a disease or other unwanted condition.

PROSTAGLANDINS   Naturally occurring compounds capable of stimulating uterine contractions. These compounds are currently undergoing clinical trials as an abortion method and for the induction of normal labor at term.

PROTOZOA   One-celled animal organisms.

PSYCHOSOMATIC   Denoting a physical illness or disease that is caused, aggravated, or influenced by an individual's emotional and mental state.

PUBERTY   The age at which an individual becomes sexually mature and thus able to reproduce.

PUBOCOCCYGEUS   A broad band of muscle stretching between the pubic bone in front to the coccyx or tail bone behind that helps to support the female pelvic organs in their proper anatomical position.

PURULENT   Full of pus or containing pus.

PUS   A creamy yellow fluid, the result of an infection, containing bacteria, dead cells, and white blood cells.

PUS CELLS   White blood cells; one of the body's first defense mechanisms against infection.

RAD   A measure of radiation dose. One rad corresponds to the absorption of 100 ergs of energy per gram of tissue.

RADIATION THERAPY   Various irradiation techniques—X-ray, cobalt, radium, etc.—primarily used in the treatment of abnormal and cancerous tissue.

RADIONUCLIDE IMAGING   Diagnostic technique in which malignant cells are tagged with radioactive material for purposes of identification; can also be used in the diagnosis of benign conditions. See BONE SCAN.

RADIOPAQUE   Capable of being seen on X-ray; for example, dyes used in diagnostic studies.

RECTOCELE   A pouching or bulging of the rectal wall into the vaginal canal; prolapse or herniation of rectal wall into the vagina.

RECURRENCE   A condition or disease that reappears.

REDUCTION MAMMOPLASTY   Plastic surgery to reduce the size of the breast.

RESECTION   Surgical term meaning to remove or excise.

RETROFLEXED UTERUS   A backward bend in the uterus at its junction with the cervix; a tipped uterus.

RETROVERTED UTERUS   A backward tilt of the entire uterus toward the rectum; also known as a tipped uterus.

RHYTHM   A method of birth control in which sexual intercourse is avoided during the fertile days.

RIPE CERVIX   The cervix of a pregnant woman that has already thinned and partially dilated prior to the actual onset of labor.

RUBIN TEST   A test to determine whether the Fallopian tubes are open or blocked. This is detected by the injection of carbon dioxide through the cervical canal and thus through the uterine cavity and tubes. See INSUF-FLATION.

SAFE PERIOD   According to the rhythm method, the time during which ovulation is presumed not to occur, thus allowing sexual intercourse without risk of pregnancy.

SALPINGECTOMY   Surgical removal of a Fallopian tube.

SALPINGITIS   Inflammation and/or infection of the Fallopian tubes.

SALPINGO-OOPHORECTOMY   Surgical removal of a Fallopian tube and an ovary.

SALPINX   Another name for Fallopian tube.

SARCOMA   A malignancy, specifically a form of cancer which arises from mesenchymal tissue such as muscle, bone, cartilage, and connective tissue.

SCROTUM   Part of the male external genitalia; the saclike structure containing the testicles.

SEBACEOUS CYST   Abnormal retention of sebaceous or oily material within a sebaceous gland.

SEBACEOUS GLAND   A skin gland that opens into a hair follicle and excretes an oily substance; an oil gland.

SEBUM   The oily substance excreted by sebaceous glands.

SECRETORY ENDOMETRIUM   Normal endometrial tissue lining the uterine cavity following ovulation as a result of both estrogen and progesterone stimulation.

SEMEN   Thick, viscid, grayish fluid discharged by the male at the time of orgasm which contains sperm and secretions from the prostate and seminal vesicles; seminal fluid.

SEROLOGICAL STUDIES   Blood studies that check for the presence of antibodies as the result of recent or past exposure to a specific virus, infectious agent, or foreign invader.

SEROLOGY   Term frequently used to mean specific serological studies to detect past or current infection with syphilis.

SERUM   The liquid portion of blood as distinguished from its formed elements, such as blood cells; that liquid portion of blood that remains after the blood elements have clotted.

SEX CHROMATIN BODY   See BARR BODY.

SIGN   Objective evidence indicating the presence of a disease or an abnormal condition.

SILASTIC IMPLANT   A breast prosthesis, a plastic bag filled with silicone gel or saline. See BREAST PROSTHESIS.

SMEAR   Used to describe the smearing of cells, infected material, or discharge onto a glass slide for rapid microscopic identification of bacteria and/or abnormal cells.

SMEGMA   An accumulation of cellular debris and glandular secretions usually found under a skin fold.

SPECULUM   An instrument that enlarges a passageway for the purpose of inspecting the interior. Vaginal speculum—specifically used to see the interior of the vagina and cervix.

SPERM   The male germ seed produced by the testicles.

SPERMICIDAL   Destructive to sperm on contact.

SPERMICIDES   Vaginal creams, foams, jellies, or suppositories that can immobilize or destroy sperm on contact.

STEIN LEVINTHAL SYNDROME   See POLYCYSTIC OVARIAN SYNDROME.

STERILITY   Inability to conceive, usually on a permanent basis; infertility.

STERILIZATION   A procedure to render an individual permanently sterile or unable to reproduce.

SUCCULENT   Moist, juicy.

SUPPOSITORY   Medication, usually cone- or bullet-shaped, which is inserted into a body cavity such as the vagina, urethra, or rectum.

SYMPHYSIS PUBIS   That portion of the pubic bone that directly underlies the mons veneris in women.

SYMPTOM   A sign or indication of an infection, disease, or other abnormal process which is experienced by the individual.

SYNDROME   A collection of signs and symptoms occurring together with sufficient frequency so as to constitute a specific medical condition.

SYNTHETIC DRUG   A man-made medication as opposed to a naturally occurring compound.

SYPHILIS   Veneral disease transmitted by the spirochete *Treponema pallidum;* lues.

SYSTEMIC   Involving the entire body; not localized.

TAMPON   A plug of cotton or other material worn in the vagina for the purpose of absorbing blood and cellular debris during menstruation.

TESTICLES (TESTES)   Male gonads which produce sperm and testosterone.

TESTOSTERONE   The male sex hormone responsible for male sexual characteristics.

THERAPEUTIC ABORTION   A legally sanctioned medical interruption of an early pregnancy. See ABORTION.

THERMOGRAPHY   A diagnostic procedure to detect cancerous breast tumors by measuring temperature differences within the breast tissue.

UMBILICUS   The navel, the belly button.

URETERS   The two tubes that drain urine from the kidneys to the bladder.

URETHRA   The passageway leading from the urinary bladder to the outside.

URETHRAL MEATUS   The opening into the urethra; the opening through which one urinates.

URETHROCELE   A prolapse of the urethra into the vagina; a bulging of the urethral wall into the vaginal canal.

URINALYSIS   A laboratory examination of urine including a microscopic study of the urine for the presence of cells, bacteria, or other debris.

URINARY RETENTION   Inability to void or urinate.

UTERUS   The womb; the hollow muscular organ of reproduction in which the fertilized egg implants and subsequently develops into a baby.

VACCINE   Any substance which, when injected into the body, will immunize or protect an individual against a specific disease or infection.

VAGINA   The birth canal; the genital canal in the female extending from the uterus to the outside.

VAGINAL AGENESIS   A developmental defect in which a female infant is born without a vagina.

VAGINAL HYSTERECTOMY   Removal of the uterus through the vagina. Sometimes done in conjunction with vaginal plastic surgery.

VAGINAL PLASTIC SURGERY   Any operation done in the vagina for the purpose of resuspending or resupporting dropped or prolapsed organs such as the urethra, bladder, and rectum. Plastic surgery to improve the size and shape of the vagina itself.

VAGINISMUS   Strong involuntary and frequently painful contractions or spasms of the muscles surrounding the lower vagina whenever intercourse is attempted.

VAGINITIS   Any inflammation and/or infection of the vagina.

VAS DEFERENS   The male passageways (from the testicles to the prostatic portion of the urethra) through which sperm travel.

VASECTOMY   Surgical interruption of the vas deferens. Most commonly done as a method of sterilization in the male.

VASO   Refers to blood vessels.

VASOCONGESTION   An engorgement of blood vessels with blood.

VASODILATATION   A widening or dilatation of blood vessels to permit more blood to flow through an area or body part.

VASOMOTOR SYMPTOM   A phenomenon occurring as the result of dilatation and constriction of tiny blood vessels in response to certain nervous impulses; for example, a hot flash is a vasomotor symptom.

VDRL A blood test for the detection of syphilis.

VENEREAL DISEASE (VD) Any infection that is transmitted predominantly by sexual intercourse.

VENEREAL WARTS See GENITAL WARTS.

VENOUS STASIS Poor venous circulation through a body part; inadequate or improper emptying of veins resulting in stagnation or pooling of the blood in that area or body part.

VESICLE A small skin blister usually filled with clear fluid.

VESTIBULE Portion of the vulva bounded by the labia minora (inner lips) that contains the vaginal and urethral openings.

VIABLE Capable of surviving.

VIRGIN A woman who has never had sexual intercourse. Can also apply to a man who has never had sexual intercourse.

VIRILIZATION Masculinization, the appearance of male secondary sexual characteristics in a female.

VIRUS An infectious agent capable of causing infection, disease, or other pathological conditions.

VOLUNTARY MUSCLE A muscle under conscious control, as opposed to an involuntary muscle, which functions below the level of conscious awareness (such as the heart muscle).

VULVA The female external genitalia; that portion of the anatomy that lies between the legs.

VULVITIS Inflammation of the vulva.

VULVOVAGINAL Referring to the vulva and vagina.

WANING Slowing, decreasing in amount or size.

WASSERMANN TEST A blood test formerly used for the detection of syphilis.

WEDGE RESECTION OF THE OVARIES Removal of a wedge-shaped piece of tissue from both ovaries usually for the purpose of inducing ovulation.

WOLFFIAN DUCT SYSTEM An embryonic structure which in the male fetus develops into the epididymus, vas deferens, and seminal vesicles.

WORKUP Medical slang referring to various diagnostic studies made to determine the nature or cause of a specific condition or disease.

XEROMAMMOGRAM Xeroradiography of the breast. A special breast examination, similar to an X-ray, for the detection of abnormal tissue changes or tumors.

YEAST Funguslike organism. Sometimes used to describe an infection by the fungus *Candida albicans*.

ZYGOTE A fertilized ovum.

Index

Abdomen
  definition and examination of, 48
  enlargement of, in ovarian cancer, 387
  premenstrual bloating of, 94
Abnormal bleeding, *see* Bleeding prob-
    lems; Menstruation: irregular
Abortion, 290–302
  assistance in procuring, 295–6
  complications associated with, 294–5,
    297–300
  definition of, 290
  physical evidence of previous, 49
  resumption of menses after, 75, 297,
    299
  spontaneous, 73, 89, 123, 290–1
    associated with fertility drugs, 240
    associated with IUD, 263, 266
    associated with rhythm method, 273
    causes of, 39–40, 291
    in gonorrhea, 151
    incidence of, 291
  therapeutic, 290–1, 293–302
    by dilatation and curettage, 214, 296,
      299
    by hysterotomy, 300
    legal time limitation on, 296

  mortality rate in, 259, 299
  optimal time for, 296
  prostaglandins in, 300–1
  in rape victims, 214
  saline amniocentesis in, 298–9
  in teenagers, 301–2
  vacuum aspiration in, 293, 296–7
  types of, 290–1
Abscess
  of Bartholin's gland, 51
  tubo-ovarian, 150
Adenomatous hyperplasia, 383–4
Adenomyosis, 123, 127; *see also* Endomet-
    riosis
Adrenal glands, 70, 95, 119, 332
Adrenal hypoplasia, congenital, 25–7
Alcohol, 99
  as home remedy for menstrual cramps,
    107, 109
Amenorrhea, 29–35, 118–19, 121; *see also*
    Menstruation: irregular
  and galactorrhea, treatment of, 356–7
Amniocentesis
  as pregnancy test, 248–9
  saline, 298–9
Anal eroticism, 221

A NOTE ABOUT THE AUTHOR

Currently on active duty with the Army Medical Corps, Lucienne Lanson did her premedical work at the University of California in Berkeley. Shortly after receiving her Bachelor of Arts degree, she joined the United States Army for two years, where she was trained and served as a physical therapist in the Women's Medical Specialist Corps. Dr. Lanson received her M.D. magna cum laude from the Medical College of Pennsylvania, did a one-year internship in Denver, Colorado, and then returned to the Medical College of Pennsylvania to complete a four-year residency in Obstetrics and Gynecology. While a resident, she was awarded a fellowship by the American Cancer Society and helped in the establishment of a female pelvic cancer-screening clinic at the medical school. Before returning to the West Coast and entering private practice, she was a clinical instructor in Ob-Gyn for two years at the medical school from which she graduated. She also served as a rotating specialist in gynecology aboard the S.S. *Hope* in Ceylon in 1968 and later volunteered as an attending obstetrician and gynecologist at the Princess Tsahai hospital in Addis Ababa, Ethiopia. Dr. Lanson is a diplomate of the American Board of Obstetrics and Gynecology as well as a Fellow of the American College of Obstetricians and Gynecologists.

A NOTE ON THE TYPE

This book was set in GAEL, the computor version of Caledonia designed by W.A. Dwiggins. It belongs to the family of printing types called "modern face" by printers—a term used to mark the change in style of type letters that occurred about 1800. It borders on the general design of Scotch Modern, but is more freely drawn than that letter.

Composed by The Haddon Craftsmen, Inc. ComCom Division, Allentown, Pennsylvania.
Printed and bound by the Haddon Craftsmen, Inc., Scranton, Pennsylvania.
Text and binding design by Christine Aulicino.